SAGE was founded in 1965 by Sara Miller McCune to support the dissemination of usable knowledge by publishing innovative and high-quality research and teaching content. Today, we publish over 900 journals, including those of more than 400 learned societies, more than 800 new books per year, and a growing range of library products including archives, data, case studies, reports, and video. SAGE remains majority-owned by our founder, and after Sara's lifetime will become owned by a charitable trust that secures our continued independence.

Los Angeles | London | New Delhi | Singapore | Washington DC | Melbourne

A History of Adivasi Women in Post-Independence Eastern India

A History of Adivasi Women in Post-Independence Eastern India

The Margins of the Marginals

DEBASREE DE

Los Angeles | London | New Delhi
Singapore | Washington DC | Melbourne

Copyright © Debasree De, 2018

All rights reserved. No part of this book may be reproduced or utilised in any form or by any means, electronic or mechanical, including photocopying, recording, or by any information storage or retrieval system, without permission in writing from the publisher.

First published in 2018 by

SAGE Publications India Pvt Ltd
B1/I-1 Mohan Cooperative Industrial Area
Mathura Road, New Delhi 110 044, India
www.sagepub.in

STREE
16 Southern Avenue
Kolkata 700 026
www.stree-samyabooks.com

SAGE Publications Inc
2455 Teller Road
Thousand Oaks, California 91320, USA

SAGE Publications Ltd
1 Oliver's Yard, 55 City Road
London EC1Y 1SP, United Kingdom

SAGE Publications Asia-Pacific Pte Ltd
3 Church Street
#10-04 Samsung Hub
Singapore 049483

Published by Vivek Mehra for SAGE Publications India Pvt Ltd, typeset in 11/13 pts PalmSprings by Zaza Eunice, Hosur, Tamil Nadu, India and printed at Chaman Enterprises, New Delhi.

Library of Congress Cataloging-in-Publication Data

Name: De, Debasree, author.
Title: A history of Adivasi women in post-independence Eastern India: the margins of the marginals/Debasree De.
Description: New Delhi, India; Thousand Oaks, California: SAGE, 2018. | Includes bibliographical references and index.
Identifiers: LCCN 2018002756 | ISBN 9789381345382 (pbk.: alk. paper) | ISBN 9789381345405 (epub 2.0) | ISBN 9789381345399 (ebook)
Subjects: LCSH: Women, Adivasi—India—Social conditions. | Marginality, Social—India.
Classification: LCC HQ1742 .D397 2018 | DDC 305.40954—dc23 LC record available at https://lccn.loc.gov/2018002756

ISBN: 978-93-81345-38-2 (HB)

SAGE Stree Team: Aritra Paul, Amrita Dutta and Guneet Kaur

*To my father, the late Asim Kumar De,
and my mother, Sonali De,
with love and respect.*

Thank you for choosing a SAGE product!
If you have any comment, observation or feedback,
I would like to personally hear from you.

Please write to me at **contactceo@sagepub.in**

Vivek Mehra, Managing Director and CEO, SAGE India.

Bulk Sales

SAGE India offers special discounts
for purchase of books in bulk.
We also make available special imprints
and excerpts from our books on demand.

For orders and enquiries, write to us at

Marketing Department
SAGE Publications India Pvt Ltd
B1/I-1, Mohan Cooperative Industrial Area
Mathura Road, Post Bag 7
New Delhi 110044, India

E-mail us at **marketing@sagepub.in**

Get to know more about SAGE
Be invited to SAGE events, get on our mailing list.
Write today to **marketing@sagepub.in**

This book is also available as an e-book.

Contents

Acknowledgements	ix
Introduction	xi
1 Demystifying Adivasi Women: Some Epistemological Issues	1
2 Changing Livelihood Pattern of Adivasi Women in West Bengal	49
3 Adivasi *Rejas* in Bihar	88
4 Adivasi Women and Land Rights in Jharkhand	113
5 Adivasi Women and Destructive Development in Odisha	156
6 Increasing Marginalization of Adivasi Women: The Process of Cultural Silencing	201
Epilogue	252
Bibliography	267
Index	286
About the Author	294

Acknowledgements

I EXPRESS MY deep sense of gratitude to Professor Amit Bhattacharyya, Department of History, Jadavpur University, for his expert guidance and uplifting inspiration. He always offered complete support, without which the present work could not have come to light. I am immensely grateful to Professor Himadri Shankar Bandyopadhyay, Professor Suchibrata Sen, Professor Chittabrata Palit and Professor Anuradha Roy for their invaluable suggestions and assistance.

I am especially thankful to the villagers of different adivasi villages, sarpanch, ward members, teachers of village schools and Anganwari workers for their kind cooperation during data collection. The book would not have come to a successful completion without the help I received from my guides, namely, Gopinath Mishra, Madhusudan Rao, Pravin Toto, Ranjit Hansda, Bikash Singh Sardar, Ananda Paramanik, Milan Singh Sardar, Birendranath Sarkar, Mahadeb Patihar, Arjun Baske, Sukumar Giri and Sanjoy Das.

This book draws upon my PhD dissertation, and a UGC Junior Research Fellowship at the Department of History, Jadavpur University, supported my research, for which I am thankful. I am also indebted to the anonymous reviewers and experts who provided critical and constructive comments and to Stree and SAGE for their support.

Above all, I express my indebtedness to my beloved father, the late Asim Kumar De, whose blessings have always been with me. I am beholden to my mother, Sonali De, for her motivation and encouragement, which inspired me to carry out this work despite all the hardships of life. I remain indebted to her for teaching me the value of perseverance. I thank the contribution of my uncle and aunt, Dipak Dutta and Minati Dutta and all my friends, Sweta, Amitava, Mangalda, Raju, Suvajit and Kamrul, for their invaluable support and timely help. Many thanks are due to my sister, Rajasree Dalal, brother-in-law, Dibyendu Dalal and little Shubhangi (Mishti) for their willing support without which I would have been alone in this long journey.

Introduction

> Bhanmati had on a short plum coloured sari that she wore above her knees, a green and red necklace of hinglaj, and she had a spider lily tucked into her hair. She looked more healthy and comely than when we had last met—her slender body brimmed over with a sweet youthfulness, though the expression in her eyes spoke of the same innocent girl I knew.

THIS MESMERISING DESCRIPTION of Bibhutibhushan's Bhanmati creates a perfect picture of a tribal woman.[1] But this portrayal of Bhanmati gives us a partial notion about a tribal woman. This is no doubt one among the many shades of her life. The rest is unspoken and extremely under-researched.

I

Seventy years after independence and about the same span of planned development, women's position in India is still grim. Their position has worsened considerably in almost every sphere of life with the exception of some gains for middle-class women in terms of education and employment. The available literature on women in India has brought to light many negative social practices like rape, wife-battering, domestic violence, dowry deaths, prostitution, and working long hours within and outside the home without recognition. All this indicates that women are still perishing at the periphery of the mainstream (read male-stream) society.

This study focuses on the nature and dimensions of changes in the life and status of tribal women, rural and urban, in eastern India. It deals with the changing livelihood pattern of the adivasi women in four states: West Bengal, Bihar, Jharkhand and Odisha of eastern India. Gender issues are manifested differently in different locations and hence one should not ignore the sociology of space while discussing such issues. The impact of modern forces and institutions on tribal women are more conspicuous in the urban spaces relative to the rural areas. These changes have exacerbated some new gender and class issues unprecedented in the purportedly egalitarian society of the tribals. Within this context, the struggles of Indian tribal women against class and gender inequality acquire particular significance. The notion of 'indigenous' is especially germane here, for tribals are considered India's earliest inhabitants. Moreover, tribal women's resistance has generally occurred quite autonomously from urban feminist movements.

Previously, gender studies was regarded as an addendum and women's movements as a concomitant movement. It is the indigenous women who are leading grassroot democracy. Women have always been doubly colonized. Their stories have always remained at the periphery. Realization of this is evident in the establishment attached to various universities in India. An objective and scientific interpretation of culture from the women's point of view is, however, still lacking. Women scholars have not yet been able to carve out a niche for themselves where their position is secure. There is still a voice in the wilderness; a voice seldom heard even by women themselves. And it is not surprising that not a single woman scholar has ever tried to deal with the status of tribal women. What Begum Rokeya Sakhawat Hossain did on Muslim women, M. Borthswick did on Bengali upper caste *bhadramahila* and Devaki Jain on working class women; we do not find that extensive research on tribal women by any woman historian. Among those who are striving hard to represent women are anthropologists. As Mahale has rightly stated:

> By providing a new perspective for women's studies, anthropologists have encouraged a good deal of re-examination of existing theories, critical questioning and research and have contributed towards extending the frontiers of Anthropology.[2]

But women and anthropologists have a long way to go, and this is even truer for tribal women. Thus it automatically creates the vacuum. There are a large number of studies on tribal communities but only a few are focussed on tribal women. There is hardly any substantial work undertaken in order to understand the concept of tribal women. Interests seem to revolve around the social status of tribal women and not on conceptual clarifications and on the problems they are facing today. Reviewing the studies of tribal women, K.S. Singh has concluded that there is 'need for generating studies which can fill the information gap about variations that exist and about the role and status of tribal women from one region to another and one community to another'.[3] Singh has also reiterated that there are materials on tribals in general but the existing literature specifically on tribal women is limited.[4] Health statistics also give an overall picture and data on gender differentiation of longevity, level of health, extent of mortality, infant mortality, nutrition are not available. There is a dearth of base-line data on certain basic parameters relating to tribal women, their status, that data on various tribes at least are needed as they differ from one another.[5] Generally speaking the parameters used to define tribal women, their roles and status are different from those used for men. This is unfortunate. They are, for instance, depicted as the preservers of culture and social life whereas men are glorified as hunters and killers. The general tendency to define men in tribal society in terms of role categories like warriors, hunters, statesman and elder has little to do with their relationship with women. Women by contrast tend to be defined almost entirely in relational terms, in terms of kin roles as wife, mother, sister. In other words, while men can be defined independent of women, the latter cannot be defined independent of men.

I see tribal woman as a category or as an interest group which is considered as a 'labour force', a 'victim', a 'protester' by the policy makers and planners or is increasingly being looked down upon as a 'witch' or as a mere 'sexual object' by the tribal and non-tribal men respectively. The work studies, the production of tribal women as invisible and oppressed, 'backward' continue in the written history of India. My focus is on understanding the discursive and material contexts that have historically produced tribal women as victimized, invisible and mute. The specific disappearance of the tribal women in Bengali literature and the ways in which they have been marginalized and made to disappear within both the conventional (colonial and nationalist) and critical historiography of India is a matter of concern. As entrenched realities of adivasi women's life—lived and thought—the problematic of gender and ethnicity have constantly questioned my bourgeois/educated standpoint. I have always tried to be a part of their journey of identity, making, unmaking and remaking it through gendered lenses.

Tribal women of eastern India are not a homogeneous group, although they are known by the generic category 'tribal women'. They are a socially excluded category which has not appeared suddenly but is created through a historical process. It is true that there are a lot of differences and discrepancies among the different tribal groups. These are essentially cultural differences. We find varieties of culture in tribal communities of India. It is important to remember that 'tribal women' are also diverse ethnically, linguistically, geographically and also historically. The social factors sometimes contradict as well because the nature of patriarchy differs from one tribe to another. The main cultural areas where different tribal groups differ are—language, script, festivals, customs, folk traditions (songs, lore, tales, proverbs, and so on), art and crafts, ornaments, dress, marriage ceremonies, sexual behaviour, social taboos and the like. But does culture mean only these things? I think culture denotes a way of life. These are, in fact, the colourful side of the tribal life, but there is also a dark side as the women in tribal societies are often considered doubly disadvantaged, in the first instance as tribal and in the second, as a woman. The discrimination, humiliation, torture, harassment that a caste woman faces, is also faced by her. If she is beaten by her drunk husband she feels pain, if she works hard the whole day she gets tired, if she gets displaced she laments for her hut, if she loses her job in the course of deforestation for mining she starves, if she gets raped her entire personality shatters. She takes up arms to save the forests (in the Chipko movement by Bhutia women); the hills (movement against Vedanta by Dongria Kondh women of Niyamgiri hills); the lands (Bhil women in Dhulia land struggle of Maharashtra; movement in Kalinganagar against TISCO); the rivers (Dongria Kondh women against damming the Indravati River, Odisha. Tribal women are also active in the Narmada Bachao Andolan, Gujarat, Madhya Pradesh and Maharashtra); the dignity and the future of her children that have been destroyed by the gargantuan consumptive greed of the global market.

According to Bina Agarwal,

> Tribal women are the second major category facing substantial disabilities in inheritance. Given the non-codification of their laws, tribal communities are governed by customs which (except under matriliny) discriminate against women. And even the limited customary land rights many tribal women enjoyed historically have been eroding.[6]

So, we should attempt to link land resource rights for tribal women as the central point of all the gender inequity making its entry in the tribal community, and we should not forget patriarchy can take various shapes and forms: from globalization 'thrusted' to feminization of poverty to violence against women in the name of customs. Simon de Beauvoir has suggested in *The Second Sex* that *'one is not born a woman, but, rather, becomes* one'.[7]

For de Beauvoir, women are designated as the Other, women are the negative of men, the lack against which masculine identity differentiates itself. There are hundreds of attempts being tried to create a better world for tribal women: from the tribal identity protection perspective, from women's right perspective, from the perspective of community control over natural resources, from labour rights perspective in this globalized economy. But still there is concern for a society based on justice and this includes gender-justice issues in tribal community.

II

Coming to the question of patriarchy in tribal society it is pertinent to say that a tribal woman generally bears a double burden of patriarchal inscription on her body within the dominant-subaltern power contestation. On the one hand, her own subaltern group 'others' her for her gender, on the other, the dominant ideology 'others' her twice over, both as an embodiment of femaleness and as an embodiment of her class, caste or racial location. Patriarchy is perhaps one of the oldest and most resilient forms of exploitative division of socio-cultural geography. Though the patriarchal manifestation and operations are apparently distinct in public and private spheres, yet their agenda overlaps. Through its interrelated structures and strategies, it works towards the same hegemonic ends, that is, the legitimization and naturalization of gender enclosures and hierarchies in both spheres—inner and outer, within and without—of sociopsychological interaction.[8] As a flesh and blood entity, an adivasi woman negotiates her place in a given gender order by the way she conducts herself, that is, how she responds to, opposes or claims the place she is supposedly given in everyday life.

Patriarchy makes and remakes the female body for its own consumption. It comes under intense pressure especially during the period of transition from feudalism/tradition to capitalism/modernity and leaves its traumatic repercussions on tribal women. It is a well-known fact that tribal forest economy is primarily a women's economy, and it is women who are most directly affected by the corporate exploitation of their traditional lands. All available laws—those relating to lands, forests, minor forest produce, water resources, and so on—restrain people from using forests. Communities who live near or inside forests are evicted from the land they have lived on for centuries and reduced to a floating population. On the other hand, private interests have started a process of decimating forests.[9] Thus primary resources such as fuel, fodder and minor forest produce which were available free to villagers are today either non-existent or have to be brought commercially. Tribal women have to walk several kilometres to fetch potable water in order to avoid polluted rivers and rapidly dying wells, or spending four to six hours hunting for firewood in deforested terrains. Disappearing grazing lands make their animal husbandry tasks even more difficult. Governmental 'development' programmes have played havoc on poor people's lives. The construction of dams such as the Srisailam Dam on the Krishna River near Hyderabad; the Sardar Sarovar Dam on the Narmada River in Gujarat, threatens to displace thousands of (mainly tribal people) who were not compensated in any way. The mining companies are not only subverting India's laws, they are also changing them, through Acts such as the SEZ Act (2005) and the new National Mineral Policy (NMP drafts 2006–2008), which are heavily influenced by foreign companies' interest in getting hold of key mineral deposits in India.

Tribal people are losing control over their land and forest by the onslaught of globalization and the early communitarian systems of control, management and output sharing are disintegrating. The worst hit are women, whose status seems to decline in direct proportion to shifts from forest to land and the increasing influence of caste values in everyday life. Thus the participation of women in the local community in terms of politics and resource management declines as we move from the foraging tribes (Birhor) to mainly agriculturist tribes (Santhal, Ho, Munda and Oraon). In this way, the feudal-capitalistic gaze reduces the already hierarchized and inferiorized body of the female other into a pliable commodity that could be easily exchanged for land and money. Within these exploitative patriarchal locations—economic, social or political—the body of the tribal woman becomes a lust-quenching commodity for upper-caste gratification. The exigencies of survival force her to rationalize that very socio-economic order whose sensual gaze encroaches upon the autonomy of her body and superimposes its desires on her sexuality. In other words, the dominant gaze not only frames subaltern sexuality but also appropriates it as a tag to vindicate its status.[10]

Post-independence mainstream intervention into the margins turns out to be disastrous for the adivasi woman. Through the mechanism of constant surveillance and community policing (like Salwa Judum), the patriarchal state in the name of 'protection' demarcates the spatial in such a manner that whatever she does, she does within the threshold of the patriarchal norms. The modern state can be defined as a patronizing and hegemonic space that through its various welfare measures actually appropriates the adivasi woman and her body, thus divesting her of her agency.

Therefore, the struggle of the tribal women has been about human rights to live in dignity and freedom to pursue a way of life and livelihood that is centred on a complex relationship fostered over generations with the entire forest landscape. The ancestral plural relationships that women hold with the forest space are depicted by how this space is used in multiple ways: shifting cultivation, grazing, food production, foraging for wild fruits, vegetables, tubers and medicines, saving seeds and breeds, collecting fuelwood, forest produce and materials to build homes, worshipping their ancestors and gods and a space to celebrate and mourn. It is these 'productive' and other 'non-economic' interactions and relationship with the forest that have been constantly contested, challenged and have come into direct conflict with the interests of the state since before independence and have intensified in independent India.

III

When I started writing on tribal women of post-independence eastern India, I encountered some serious problems, one of which is regarding the terminology. I have used both the terms 'adivasi' and 'tribal' deliberately, because these two terms are identical. These groups do not correspond to the conventional anthropological formulation of the 'tribe', and this term in any case now carries derogatory and politically incorrect connotations in western academic circles. Myron Weiner describes a sense of negative identity among tribals in 'Sons of the Soil',[11] and other studies have had similar findings,[12] suggesting that this is fairly common amongst tribals across India. Crispin Bates advocates the use of adivasi (original settler), noting that this appellation may itself rest on the same prejudices as tribal, but arguing that it is preferable as the name employed by members of Indian indigenous peoples' movements themselves.[13] Adivasi is indeed the term best known internationally, but many others are in use. In the southern states, the word 'adivasi' is not used; they prefer 'girijana' (hill people), 'vanabasi' (forest people) are also in use in some parts of the country. However, much of this book concerns the pan-Indian classification, including non-hill and non-forest dwellers, making girijana and vanabasi inadequate. The global indigenous people's movement turns this characterization to political use, providing strength in numbers to populations on the edge of each country's borders and marginal to each country's citizenship by integrating them into a larger community with greater political clout. This political unity is to a large extent concentrated on the matter of land rights. Hence the choice of names such as adivasi and vanabasi, which highlight settlement and forest rights respectively. The word 'tribe', at least as frequently as any other, is widely used in Indian popular and academic English-language writing, and is in pan-Indian usage. Although controversial in the West, it should be remembered that the legal term for these groups is the scheduled tribes. In order to free tribal from the negative associations carried in many quarters, I have treated it as an indigenous (Indian-English) term. However, since I am not dealing with the tribals of south India and, more importantly, the term 'adivasi' is widely used in eastern India, I have made no distinction between the two. This represents an idea of what it means to be 'adivasi', 'tribal', or 'indigenous', in a more globally acceptable language, similar to the romantic western model. Both see adivasi people as spiritually linked with 'nature' and their environment.

Second, it is believed that research has been a process that exploits adivasi people, their culture, their knowledge and their resources. Linda Tuhiwai Smith wrote,

> From the vantage point of the colonized, a position from which I write, and choose to privilege, the term 'research' is inextricably linked to European imperialism and colonialism. The word itself, 'research', is probably one of the dirtiest words in the indigenous world's vocabulary ... The ways in which scientific research is implicated in the worst excesses of colonialism remains a powerful remembered history for many of the world's colonized peoples. It is a history that still offends the deepest sense of our humanity.[14]

This book deals with the history of their everyday sufferings and reveals the nuances of their values and practices that can make their story a profoundly rich one. To tell their stories is the most powerful form of resistance and it was a pretty difficult task to write a 'good history'.

My conscious attempt has always been to write a 'history of the historyless'. However, so-called societies without histories cannot be thought of as societies without memories. They remember their pasts differently. Nothing more fully expressed my feelings than Sherna Gluck's rousing declaration of independence in the 1977 special issue of, *Frontiers*, a new feminist journal:

> Refusing to be rendered historically voiceless any longer, women are creating a new history—using our own voices and experiences. We are challenging the traditional concepts of history, of what is 'historically important', and we are affirming that our everyday lives are history. Using an oral tradition, as old as human memory, we are reconstructing our own past.[15]

Recent debates around the inclusion of the histories of the previously excluded groups have often fuelled the discussion of minority histories. Minority histories are still fighting for their proper recognition in the mainstream (or male-stream) history writing. Begun in an oppositional mode, minority histories can end up being additional instances of 'good history'. One can ask legitimate Foucauldian questions about who has the authority to define what 'good' history is or what relationships between power and knowledge are invested in such definitions, but let me put them aside for the time being. The expressions 'majority' and 'minority' are no natural entities, but constructions. To explain 'minority histories' in other way, it is the history of the marginalized (read non-modern) or simply of the small voices. The history of the tribal women thus always has been 'inferiorized' by considering it 'of lesser importance' as if in order to even engage with the modern they must remain exclusively dependent on their reproduction as the modern subject of history as non-present yet re-presentable. When we talk to a tribal woman, her statements are regarded as the evidence for anthropology. In fact, the aboriginal women use 'dirty' words and their voices cannot be found in archives, many of which are still buried and not yet separately catalogued. We treat their beliefs as just that 'their beliefs', and do not write history from within those beliefs in order to produce a 'good' history. There are also some limitations that we cannot completely envisage: the lack of information and an irreducible plurality in our own experiences of historicity that precludes authenticity. As Shahid Amin has rightly said,

> Testimony to the incompleteness of the existing record, familial memories are, however, themselves witness to another history, namely, the recent nationalization of the event.[16]

Tribal culture has been described as unique and exotic to legitimize the theory of 'unity in diversity' that occupies the very first chapter of a school history textbook. One thing that we forget here is the contradictions of their society, the inner conflict between the tribal way of life as a whole (as a general 'other') and that of their non-tribal counterparts. The non-tribals prefer to describe the tribals as 'primitive', 'backward', 'savage', 'wild and cruel cannibals', 'survivors of another time', a 'child' (who doesn't understand what is good for him or her) as if they have been entrusted with the duty to 'civilize' these tribal people with the wand of 'development'. Simultaneously, they have maintained a safe distance with them socially, culturally and psychologically. Colonial officials had always exercised some kind of benevolently paternal rule over the tribes. British administrators assumed that the changes they imposed on tribal people formed part of a necessary process of civilizing them, and that Indian administrators have inherited this tendency. The theory of the 'white man's burden' was the colonizers' self-regarding defence of their actions as bringing a beneficent order to backward peoples, and now in 'post-colonial' India this idea that 'we' know better than the poor about what 'they' need has yet not been discarded.[17] It seems like we are the 'white men' and the poor tribals are our 'burden'. And when the non-tribals need to display ostentatiously the so called 'unity' to the outside world, they start imposing the obligations of Hinduization and Sanskritization and give them an inferior status in the caste society to maintain a complete avulsion or separation. This tendency emanated as an opposition of the attempt of the Christian missionaries, who wanted to 'reform' or 'purify' tribal religion. Thus the internal disunity brewing by the non-tribals and their abhorrent attitude towards the tribals never let the distinction to be blurred. Then the question may arise that what is there about 'primitiveness' in a post-colony that makes the adivasis to proximate and yet so discomfiting to the self-conscious middle-class intelligentsia (read Bengali bhadralok), fighting his own 'backwardness' and seeking to make history? One thing that we, the non-tribal intelligentsia, forget is that, once we also were considered as 'backward', 'lacking history', 'lacking agency' by the colonial masters who claimed that they forced us into modernity and therefore into history as if history is best written by an outsider. And for tribals we constitute that 'outsider'.

The colonial practice of viewing tribal societies through various ethno-centric parameters and mainstream perspectives has resulted in many stereotypes. In this context, it is essential to understand the 'tribal psyche' in more objective terms, identifying the primal characteristics of such societies in relation to nature, resources, the collectivity (of people around), and the ultimate values in life representing the universality of their traditional ways of thinking. The distinct self-conceptualization of tribals in the context of natural, social and historical processes is referred as 'tribal consciousnesses'—mutual knowledge in distinguishing groups, *self* from the *other*. They carry a strong sense of distinct identity. It generally is expressed by attributing an 'ingroup' label to their members and the mother tongue spoken by them. They call themselves by words which literally mean 'us, men, people'. For example, in the Chotanagpur region of Jharkhand, a tribe called Ho means 'people'; Santhals are known as *hor* 'people'; in Munda language *horo* signifies 'people', they are often referred as *horoko*; the tribe Korku means 'men' (*kor* 'man', *ku* 'plural suffix'). The tribe Birhor comprises of *bir* 'jungle' and *hor* 'people', 'the jungle people'. This consciousness brings into focus 'tribal corporate personality' which pervades the tribal ethos throughout the country. Essential characteristics of such 'primal' groups at one end of the *civilization continuum* radically contrast with the 'modernized' groups on the other extreme who claim to be 'developed' societies on the scale of progress.

IV

Where do women stand in this analysis? I believe that by creating a romantic picture of tribal 'culture' we are actually trying to dilute the real problems regarding gender from it. It is said that tribal women enjoy a greater autonomy than their non-tribal counterparts. There is bride price instead of dowry, the right to have premarital sex, right to divorce, right to remarry. But will it be correct to say that tribal women hold a superior position in their society on the basis of bride price? Or, should sexual freedom be considered as an important yardstick to describe women's higher status in tribal society?

Tribal women have an intense sexuality with their demure and innocent nature. But the increasing in-migration of the non-tribal *dikus* into the tribal areas in the course of large-scale industrialization debars them from exercising their sexual freedom. The non-tribal dikus envisage the sexual behaviour of the tribal women as promiscuous and with 'free sex'. They loathe their sexual explicitness as raw and lurid and thus rupture their image completely. This is the reason why the *ghotul* (youth dormitory) is gradually becoming extinct from tribals' life. Here the question can be raised why are the adivasi women accused of sexual extravagance even today? Whenever they went to the police station to report a case of sexual exploitation, the patent answer they got from the police officers is that they should take it lightly as they were reputed to be lax about sexual mores.[18] In general, men and women of caste society are not expected to have sex before marriage. While there is some laxity with regard to men's sexual behaviour, women's chastity is still greatly valued. However, studies show that there is premarital sexual activity in the country.[19] In the popular media, there is now a sense that sex before marriage is on the rise among caste women with the social and economic changes brought about by globalization. The increasing exposure of youth to western culture is thought to have effected a change in moral attitudes towards sex before marriage. Further, certain trends such as the increase in urbanization, financial independence among young women through employment, and the age at marriage support this argument, as do studies gauging the attitudes of youth to premarital sexuality. There is a strong relationship between education and household wealth and the levels of premarital sex among higher- and middle-class women. At the same time, when it comes to sex and women, gender operates within the context of a complete and enduring silence. As such, the inter-linkages between class and sexual choices are complex in a culture with strong unwritten rules and regulations on women's bodies. In tribal society these rules are more flexible and premarital sexual intercourse has been socially sanctioned by the youth dormitories which are rapidly disappearing.

On the issue of bride price, it was once widely practised, but the increasing infiltration of mainstream Hindu patriarchal ideology and practices have vitiated tribal societies in which a marriage traditionally had meant neither dowry payments nor the bride's lifelong subservience to a hierarchical household. It is astonishing that patriarchal hierarchy or domination, preference for son, and associated gender biases in contemporary India have hardly declined even amongst the materially and educationally better-off. Similarly, gender bias has over time become noticeable across the country. With the steady influx of plains Hindu ideas in the tribal region, however, the tribal traditions are changing quite quickly. Indeed, the practice of giving bride price is declining amongst the Oraon tribe in the southwestern part of the Jharkhand, although it is still common amongst the Munda, Ho and Santhal tribes in the south and southeast.

T. Scarlett Epstein, in her landmark research on South India reveals how tribal villagers in a bid to improve social ranking in the 1970s had started adopting brahmanical names and rituals, including dowry (*varmana*) in replacement of bride-wealth (*tara*). Epstein has attributed the changeover to a system of dowry to the interaction between four important variables. First, is the increased wealth that enables the Mandya peasants of south India to spend more lavishly on weddings in their struggle for social recognition. Second, it has become a matter of prestige for wealthier peasants that their womenfolk do not work on the land; young girls, no longer trained to do field work, become capricious and demand more and costlier items of jewellery. Where formerly a peasant wife was an economic asset, she has now become a liability. Accordingly, the groom's family now want to be paid for taking over the responsibility of keeping her where previously they had been prepared to compensate her father for the loss of her productive contribution. Third, there are now a small but growing number of young educated male peasants whose parents feel justified in claiming compensation from their son's in-laws. Lastly, brahmins, who provide the reference group for village peasants, practise a dowry system; imitating brahmin customs means sanskritizing one's style of life in the hope of raising one's social status.[20] This is true in the other tribal areas as well, specifically those who live near to the cities.

Another possible reason of the gradual weakening of the tribal socio-cultural features, such as bride price, can be traced into the aggression of corporate imperialism that has thrown it out into oblivion by putting restrictions on their traditional right to collect forest products. The multinational corporations bulldozed their huts for land acquisition. It has created a grim situation of wanton deficiency of wealth. They were poor, true, but not destitute. Everything is being snatched away from them on account of living in a 'national sacrifice area'.

V

There is the need to focus on some crucial issues so that they can never be diluted from the history of adivasi women: the issues of migration, trafficking, forceful displacement and resistance. Here again question will arise what form of resistance is acceptable or 'valid' (in legal sense) for us? Do we need a bio-diversity of resistance? Grassroot resistance or protests, though in different forms like violent (movement in West Midnapur), or non-violent (movement in Jagatsinghpur), reflect the common wrath and grievances of adivasi people in general and adivasi women in particular against the enemies who possess a common aim, that is, to wipe out these indigenous people and to marginalize their womenfolk in every possible way. Here one pertinent question can be asked: What is actually meant by a 'non-violent movement'? Is there really any movement that has shunned violence completely, that is not related to any sort of violence in any way? According to Partha Chatterjee, a fast also cannot be called a 'non-violent movement' because it means the application of violence on the very person who has launched the movement.[21] Hence, a violent movement is not necessarily related to the use of arms. In fact, the naked protest launched by the Manipuri women against the Armed Forces Special Powers Act (AFSPA) was both violent (morally) and 'non-violent' (unarmed) simultaneously, which showed that woman's body can also become the site of protest. And if the state does not listen to the demands of the adivasis through a peaceful movement then what exactly remains to them as an alternative? Varavara Rao has answered to these questions in his prison diary. He said,

> It is expected that, since man possesses the power of discrimination, he should continue, as far as possible, to abjure the violence which is unavoidable in nature. While inequality, oppression and exploitation are the expressions of violence on the part of the exploiters, hatred, rancour and revenge are expressions of counter-violence by the exploited. The consciousness of the people alone can result in revolutionary violence that will unveil non-violence. Only that can assure us of a future in which agitation has no place.[22]

In this process three factors are highly important: one, the development programmes; two, the nature of compensation; and three, the nature of state violence. The government (both centre and state) has initiated a uniform model of development for all the tribal communities. To quote Arundhati Roy,

> If the well-being of adivasi people is what is uppermost in the Planners' minds, why is it that for fifty years there have been no roads, no schools, no clinics, no wells, no hospitals in the areas they live in? Why is it for all these years they didn't take any steps to equip the people they care so deeply about, for the world they were going to be dumped in? Why is it that the first sign of 'development'—a road—brought only terror, police, beatings, rape, murder? Why must the offer of Development be conditional, that is, *You give up your homes, your lands, your field, your language, your gods, and we'll give you 'development'*?[23]

Recent tribal unrest is not only an outcome of underdevelopment or lack of development, or in the language of economics 'aspiration failure', but the police administration and governmental policies are more responsible for their resentment. As a result, these destructive developments have failed to understand the predicament of ethnic identity and culture in the face of unrestrained globalizing forces and promote over-consumption. It denies the fact that the tribals should be allowed to develop according to their own genius. Adivasis traditional skills and knowledge are not recognized.

Introduction

The state policies have been proved as hazards for them and caused their impoverishment.

Not only that, the compensation for displacement follows the same path. The R & R Policy (Resettlement and Rehabilitation) is designed in a similar pattern. It never acknowledges or rather avoids the different requirements of different tribal communities. Vedantanagar, the R & R Colony, can be a good example where the tribal people became a captive labour pool, living without land between refinery and mountain. Let me quote a few lines from Felix Padel and Samarendra Das to throw light on this issue,

> Villagers had not expected this sudden removal and destruction, and bitterly regretted saying yes. This is when a woman in the colony [Vedantanagar] said to us, 'They even destroyed our gods', for the main Kondh deities, Darni Penu and Jakeri Penu, exist in the stones and posts embedded in the centre of each village. These had been bulldozed into oblivion ... they had nothing ... just alien concrete shells to live in, no land, no gods, and little self-respect or community. The houses and fields they and their parents made and worked at for so many years—all gone.[24]

The displaced villagers are even labelled 'encroachers on government land' simply because their land was never registered by the survey commissioners. The victims are themselves identified as perpetrators, the guilty! The same mechanism of 'blaming the victim' is being applied everywhere. These policies have also created a breach between the receivers and the non-receivers of the compensation as well. Most Corporate Social Responsibility is mere eyewash intended to fend off the claims of campaigners and hoodwink the public.

The third factor is, of course, the nature of state violence. If we look at colonial history we find that the colonial government perpetrated brutal repression towards all contemporary tribal movements starting from Santhal *Hul* to Munda *Ulghulan*. Colonial interpretations largely proclaimed these repressive measures as the 'policy of pacification', and the tribal movements were termed as 'insurrection' to demean their cause. The concept of 'pacification' implies a contrast between 'state of war' and 'state of peace', as well as between 'state of war' and 'war to impose a state of peace'. And now we are experiencing the same repressive strategy of the Indian state in the name of 'Peace March' that is decimating the tribals considering their movements as an 'insurgency' (a rising in opposition to a lawful authority) or an 'internal security threat' and justifies its act of violence as for maintaining law and order situation. It is nothing but a manufactured civil war. Is there any difference between these two ages? Perhaps yes because the tribal people of today are the citizens of an independent state that has mercilessly exposed them to unprecedented levels of exploitation and penury. Perhaps yes because the forms of state violence towards these tribal people have acquired improved technology, shrewd tactics, lethal weaponry and a new 'divide and rule policy' specifically for tribals by which a section of tribals is being instigated and armed against another section. The present policy has superseded the previous one in brutality, inhumanity and barbarity, be it in Kalinganagar, Bastar, Gadchiroli or more recently Narayanpatna.

Indian history, by contrast, shows a pattern of coexistence between adivasis and mainstream cultures. Is this culture of coexistence under threat now? A local manifestation of global 'War on Terror'—the war against extremism—is causing mass displacement of adivasis, and its underlying cause is almost certainly the internal colonialism exacerbating through land grab and privatization of resources. The womenfolk are the most innocent victim of this insatiable hunger for land, sacrificing for the 'greater good'. It caused a massive drop in their standard of living when their land is taken away. Tribal women are still facing the same kind of atrocities in the course of 'resource wars' or let's replace the word 'war' with 'creating a good investment climate',[25] as said by Arundhati Roy. They are still regarded as the 'soft corner' and are being attacked as a means of providing the masculinity of the non-tribal men. This is, of course, a well-known, if heinous, tactic of dishonouring an entire tribal community. The question of women's dignity was one of the main issues of Santhal Rebellion (1855–1856) as well as of the Santhal movement in West Midnapur (2008–2010). A new dimension that the tribal women have added to these movements is, indeed, a matter of discussion: they are now appearing as the leading protesters of all these movements. As Maria Mies and Vandana Shiva said,

> What are the links between global militarism and the destruction of nature? As feminists actively seeking women's liberation from male domination, we could not, however, ignore the fact that 'modernization' and 'development' processes and 'progress' were responsible for the degradation of the natural world. We saw that the impact on women of ecological disasters and deterioration was harder than on men, and also, that everywhere, women were the first to protest against environmental destruction.[26]

Adivasi women have started to indoctrinate themselves in the armed revolutionary ideology. This is no doubt a recent phenomenon. But here again I am stereotyping their role. I do not think that there is any necessity to dig out their separate group identity; what is more important here is their commitment to a cause. I have seen them as a community of interest that does not necessarily occupy the same geographical space. The community has its own borders, priorities and particularities. She may be a Kondh or a Gond or a Oraon or a Santhal, but more important are her sacrifices that she makes to fight against the gigantic forces of global market economy and its indomitable hunger for natural resources, that have been unleashed. She knows that she will not be able to defeat it but yet she is unperturbed and firm in conviction. Moreover, the nomenclature used by various tribes in India to address themselves bears different meanings. Contrary to the self-identification of the Oraons, for example, as Kurukhs, groups and people other than Oraons had identified the Oraon tribe by different names until their identity was stabilized as 'Oraons'. According to Joseph Marianus Kujur, the identity of the Oraons as 'Oraon' had been an imposition from outside. It did not resonate with the self-identification of the group itself. Ironically, it has been the identity-tag 'given' that has been internalized by the Oraons, and has persisted even to this day.[27] S.B. Mullick argues, 'present names of most of the tribes in India have been given to them by the invading societies.'[28] This is the case, for example, in the nomenclature 'Naga'. The latter is used to refer to mean 'the naked people' for a group of people in the northeast. Such is also the case of the nomenclature 'suar' (swine) for the Sabar or Saora in Odisha, 'panias' (slaves) for a group in South India, Dhangar identity of the Oraons was linked with impurity (the term 'dhangar' is used only for the female Oraon migrants).

The 'resource curse' has eaten up colourful, joyful, simple tribal culture. The world outside once saw it in timber, and now in the wealth of minerals that lies buried in its earth. The poverty comes from an old history of colonial extraction, to which independent India has now added seventy years of exploitation, and a continuing disdain for adivasi people. It is meeting with growing resistance and there are the sounds of war from across India. In writing the history of eastern India, it does not mean that the tribal women are active participants of these movements only within this boundary. In fact they are no less active in Dantewada, Chhattisgarh. The artificial boundaries are somewhat brittle today, for the adivasis of all the states of eastern and central India have been pushed into what is described as an emerging 'commodity frontier'. The extraction of mineral resources is not new nor the resistance movements, but the women's participation in these movements is perhaps more recent because they are actually paying the 'price of progress'. Notwithstanding, why does the figure of the dancing and singing adivasi woman appear so frequently in Bengali literature and films?

VI

Considerable research has been done on the 'tribal problem' till today. But the problem is not the tribals. We are the problem; our way of looking at the tribal people constitutes the biggest problem because we, the representatives of dominant caste society, are not ready to consider them even as human beings. It is said that 'the aboriginals are the real "swadeshi" products or the oldest "inhabitants" of India, in whose presence everyone is a foreigner'.[29] Problematizing the adivasis is a colonial obsession. The discourse has shifted away from cultural deficit views to cultural diversity views that create the illusion of 'India Shining' (the development slogan of the Bharatiya Janata Party or BJP government of 2000–2004) alive.

I have already talked about the physical genocide that is the indiscriminate killing and raping of the tribals by tribal people militia. The other form of genocide is cultural genocide. It would be more relevant to focus on this 'cultural genocide' in this present context, instead of on the cultural distinctiveness of the tribals, since cultural genocide means psychic death for the adivasis. In the contemporary climate of 'development', the configurations of traditional and modernizing milieus are bound to affect one another. How are these dynamics influencing the socio-cultural profile of tribal communities? When the norms and values of one culture dominate the other through subjugation, colonization, or in the name of development, these can generate dissonance between the two or result in the assimilation of one culture, weaker in demographic and economic terms, with the other. Feelings of resentment against outsiders and virtual rejection of the outsiders among a section of tribals indicate their uncertainty, a sense of helplessness, about their future. 'A Bhil may brave a tiger in forest, but is afraid to face even an insignificant outsider.'[30]

Another crucial aspect is the 'linguistic genocide' or 'rape of language', that is, the gradual obliteration of tribal languages. This is one of the most important instruments of the infamous 'assimilation policy' borrowed from America. Nineteenth-century Europeans treated the absence or presence of literacy, and of a written script, as indicative of how advanced a society was, or what its relationship with the time of modernity was. When the ethnologist Campbell inveighed against the suggestion of his predecessor that the Khondhs were civilized, their lack of a script accounted for one of his fusillades: 'The author of this report represented the Khondhs as a refined people, overflowing with the most ingenious ideas. This was very much at variance with the notorious fact that they were without a written language'.[31] Like the Khondhs, most of the other communities eventually classified as primitives did not possess written scripts.

The tribals are unlettered in the conventional academic sense and have often been trapped by written documents starting from the debentures of moneylenders to the MoUs.[32] Their tradition transmits orally from generation to generation. Some of them have script (like the Santhals have Ol Chiki) but that it is their own indigenous script. Their languages and scripts are gradually going into oblivion for want of proper preservation, so that later generations can automatically be assimilated into caste society. Thus, all the elements that constitute their culture, their way of life, will be darkened and it is not a mere assumption since they have already started facing the crisis of their individual identities.

The diagnosis probes into the question such as how have the issues related to forest management and community rights been tackled in the post-1947 years? How are the modernizing pursuits (notably industrialization) affecting the tribal women's 'mindset'? Do these pursuits accentuate the awareness of belonging to a distinct culture or of integrating into the mainstream? Is there any violence being perpetrated to integrate them that can be termed as 'cultural genocide'? How is this awareness reflected through various processes of acculturation, for example, claiming one's mother tongue identity through the 'ancestral' language or switching over to the language dominant in the region? Is there any force being applied to extinguish tribal languages that can be called as 'linguistic genocide'? The study provides a comprehensive understanding of the ways in which the tribal women in eastern India have responded to the thrust of 'development' during the post-independence era.

One thing is certain that 'tribal consciousness' has been acquiring a sharp edge over the past few decades. It, therefore, becomes imperative to utilize this consciousness by extending and creating the avenues of participating among the tribals through which all that is best in the tribal society, culture, language and art could be preserved, strengthened, and developed. Tribal consciousness in relation to its own tradition and history and in relation to outsiders is taking shape as an important part of the subaltern consciousness of the nation. Tribals during the past three centuries have gone through the trauma of various domineering forces in the name of progress and development. First, they were the targets of the 'missionary solution' which detribalized their rituals, customs and morals; it was followed by a vigorous reaction of the forces promoting Hindu institutions, disturbing their segregation under the garb of 'protectionism' of Excluded and Partially Excluded areas; tribals were linked with primitiveness, and the task of defining their direction of change was delegated to colonial administrators, guided by the theory of 'isolation'.[33] Third, the Indian government after independence charged with the sentiments of 'national integration', enshrined guarantees in the Constitution of the economic, socio-cultural and educational upliftment of scheduled tribes.

Predictably, instead of addressing the outcome of exploitative socio-economic structures that produced the conditions of endemic starvation, what began to pour in from above was a whole slew of so-called poverty alleviation schemes engendering only the familiar corruption that has come to be associated with this model of development. Developmental projects are based on a false notion of the 'national interest', and every local interest felt morally compelled to make sacrifices for what seemed the larger interest. It was only during the 1980s when the different 'local' interests met each other nationwide, they realized that what was being projected as the 'national interest' were the electoral and economic interests of a handful of politicians financed by a handful of contractors and industrialists who benefit from the construction of all dams.

Another crucial aspect of today's tribal life is the forced migration and the trafficking of tribal women. The third space (after nature and land) for which modern men yearn is woman, more precisely the woman's body. Women's bodies are the projection screen for most of men's desires and constitute the 'third colony'.[34] It is through this practice of forced transportation, that tribal women are to be materially constituted as nothing but body-commodity. In nineteenth and twentieth centuries, the Bengali *arkattis* became so insidious that adivasis feared every other Bengali to be a labour agent. Harilal Bandopadhyay, in a play called *Arkati Natak* (1901) comprehensively indicated the arkatti system. This practice is still in force in rural Bihar and arkattis now belong to the Bihari community which has been dealt with in the case of brick kiln adivasi women workers of Bihar (see Chapter 3). The capture of adivasi women as coolies could not always be punished, because recruitment is not a legal offence like sexual abuse. In fact, as Kaushik Ghosh shows, the 'primitive' was perhaps created out of this process of its circulation as pure labouring bodies, much before it was produced through techniques of anthropologization.[35] Middle-class intelligentsia still shares the colonial 'modern' understanding of tribal people in general and women in particular as primarily bodies, lacking culture, history, and location. We have discussed the outlook of Bengali middle-class intelligentsia towards the adivasi women in Chapter 6. With such a worldview, the tribals are often looked upon as 'museum specimens' to be cherished for their exoticness and to be clinically observed and analysed before their extinction—a sort of pre-mortem (instead of post-mortem). Satnam has thrown light on this issue in case of Bastar,

> No media crew has come here to record interviews. Discussions, propaganda and advertising are all carried out by the rich and the powerful, who promote or demote as they wish. They are now pushing to bring the 'robbers' of Bastar into the mainstream. They want to gain control over the natural resources and beauty of Bastar, to put its tribal culture and life into museums and capitalize on it, turn it into a tourist haven. Tourism entails crime and creation of profit centres for the rich who plan to bring ancient tribes like the Araaon and the Pahari Korva into the fold of 'civilization'. This unwarranted intrusion into the peaceful life of the tribals is termed development and an employment opportunity ... Now, a new development project has been suggested for converting the tribal areas of Jashpur in Chhattisgarh into golf courses for the entertainment of the super rich of the country ... Will the ancient tribes of Jashpur permit the conversion of their vast jungles into golf courses? Or will they take up the bow and arrow like the tribals of southern Bastar and Bihar and of the Koyal-Kaimur range spread over Jharkhand? The days to come will tell.[36]

These museums actually form an intrinsic part of the process of cultural genocide. As Felix Padel has rightly observed,

> Yet the greater tendency is still to try and 'save' tribal societies symbolically or at an abstract level, by preserving information, photographs, recordings, or artifacts of their traditional culture. This makes tribal culture into a commodity, as if its 'social facts' could survive in the abstract, without the human beings to whom the culture belongs. There is an aspect of this 'preserving' that is as detached and impersonal as scientists who preserves animal specimens in jars, or administrators who try to preserve forests by evicting their adivasi inhabitants.[37]

All these roles thus have a tendency to dehumanize, to alienate tribal women from their humanness and to sacrifice their quality of life. Needless to say, corporate and business interests now dominate the country's media, as Satnam has justly pointed out, both through direct ownership and through advertisements. Mainstream media primarily reflect the interests of certain sections of the society and promote a model of development that favours corporate dominance and accumulation through dispossession. Though alternative media are gradually emerging in the vernacular and on the web they face significant challenges.[38]

The tribal 'festivals' and 'exhibitions' organized by the government in the name of promoting tribal culture, be it the annual 'Dongar Festival' of Koraput or the 'Adivasi Mela' of Bhubaneswar, have merely perpetuated the ideology of the colonial museum, separating the adivasis from their lived reality and exhibiting their culture as curiosities and specimens from the past for the entertainment of non-adivasi society. For the government, such exhibitions are 'institutionalized steps towards mainstreaming the tribal people'. Ironically, the theme of Adivasi Mela of 2012 was 'Sustainable Development of Tribes' while it was sponsored by Tata, Essar Mining and Odisha Mining Corporation Ltd.[39] The adivasis of Odisha are fighting a life and death battle against the incursions of these very corporations which are threatening to jeopardize their communitarian existence, leave alone culture. And yet, the government of Odisha deems it fit to collaborate with these corporations for the 'promotion' of tribal culture.[40]

How many of these adivasi women have been able to tell their stories? And how many have disappeared into the womb of history without telling their stories? How do we write the history of those uncounted and unnamed 'grey' faces that were denied expression? How do we reconstruct their past? Any account of the past can be absorbed into, and thus made to enrich, mainstream historical discourse if two questions can be answered positively. First, can the story be told or can we write the history of suppressed groups? Second, does it allow for a rationally defensible point of view or position from which to tell the story? Or to put it more specifically, do we qualify to write the history of the marginalized? Who is representing whom, and how and why? Who and what are left out? Could we have enough potential to extract the history from their memories, the memories which have suffered from acute marginalization and silencing? Truly speaking, these memories are not easy to revisit. The investment in a certain kind of rationality and in a particular understanding of the 'real' means that history's exclusions are ultimately epistemological. But we need a certain minimum agreement about what constitutes fact and evidence and their rational understanding. Iggers suggests,

> Objectivity is unattainable in history; the historian can hope for nothing more than plausibility. But plausibility obviously rests not on the arbitrary invention of an historical account but involves rational strategies of determining what in fact is plausible.[41]

Dipesh Chakrabarty has optimistically stated,

> Successfully incorporated 'minority histories' are like yesterday's revolutionaries become today's gentlemen. Their success helps routinize innovation.[42]

Tribal women's empowerment is thought to be one of the main issues when talking about gender equality, economic growth and poverty in the academic world today. It is argued that women need to be 'empowered' in the realm of decision making so as to facilitate their 'real' empowerment. When India was under colonial rule it was only the restricted (upper caste and wealthy) male members who could vote and contest elections while a very few women were found in doing active politics. It was Gandhi who, without challenging their traditional role in society, could make women an important social base for the nationalist movement. But he remained unsuccessful in breaking out of the middle-class ideological moorings on women which can only posit their role within the household.[43] Gandhi wanted women to act as moral guardians of society, as social workers and do-gooders without competing with men in the sphere of power and politics because that would be a 'reversion to barbarity'.[44] Violations of tribal rights take place at regular intervals. In December 2001 in the state of Madhya Pradesh, tribals who were relying on fishing for their livelihood in a reservoir as their sole means of subsistence were up in arms against the state government as they feared that steps were being taken to deny them the right to market their produce.[45] In Gujarat, more blatant violations have taken place recently when the government denied reservation to tribals just 48 hours before the village council elections were announced. Scheduled tribe men and women who get elected to office are not allowed to function in the decentralized institutions of self-government. Just like the scheduled caste, the tribals also are not treated with dignity by the panchayat bureaucracy. Elected tribal women members face violence and rape if they dare to challenge the authority of the officials or the powerful. A tribal woman sarpanch was stripped naked while unfurling the national flag on 15 August 1998 in a district of Rajasthan. In another case a tribal woman sarpanch in Madhya Pradesh was stripped naked in a gram sabha meeting because she was not consulting the leader of the dominant caste. Such violations of human rights are everyday occurrence in the tribal areas of India, in spite of powerful legislations for decentralized governance.[46]

There is, however, a big difference between representation and participation. It is relatively easy to legislate representation, but it is rather a complex and difficult task to create conditions for participation. Proper representation does not automatically lead to proper participation. It is important that women are in a position to influence decision making and prepare and implement schemes for economic development and social justice. Unfortunately at the grassroot levels of Panchayati Raj institutions, there have been strong roadblocks and obstacles to women's entry into politics and a backlash of violence to keep them away from electoral politics.[47]

Introduction

Thus, adivasi women have remained largely marginalized in history writing in India as well as the emerging research on gender. Adivasi women gained their first visibility in history through descriptions on anti-colonial movements. Yet even in the available research on adivasi revolts, the gender component is largely misplaced. Occasional, incidental or fragmented references pose great problems for researchers seeking to understand and analyse the contours, trends and dynamics of women's role in adivasi life ways. This book seeks to discuss qualitative aspects of their participation in economic activities, development and local self-government, and situate them in the larger context of women's agency and dominant ideology of our society. It underlines the linkages between women and various adivasi movements of today as well, such as movements against POSCO, Vedanta Alumina Ltd.; movements in Kalinga Nagar, Narayanpatna, Koel Karo; movements in tea gardens of North Bengal, stone crushers of Birbhum, and so on. It tries to reconstruct contours of women's participation in various development initiatives, locating women's participation in the larger context of patriarchy and social hegemony. It shows how women's issues still remain peripheral to the 'mainstream' adivasi history writing. There is a need to move away from visible movements to more mundane 'everyday forms of resistance' in trying to provide some entry points into alternative understandings of women's agency. Finally, it attempts to discuss the emergent trends in women's negotiation of the socio-political space.

In fine, it can be said that studies on tribal women have not been many nor in depth. Most of the works have explicitly discussed the social status of women in tribal society and that also far from uniformly. The concern shown towards women in tribal studies is no doubt very recent. This work attempts to locate and contextualize the changing nature of women's role both social and political in tribal societies. There is a need to study adivasi women, not only in relation to 'politics of presence', but in their day-to-day struggles as well, where power relationships operate in subtle yet entrenched ways.

Hopefully, this study will contribute at least to some extent to fulfil the vacuum.

NOTES

1. Bibhutibhusan Bandyopadhyaya, *Aranyak—Of the Forest*: 181.
2. P. Mahale, 1991. 'Towards an Anthropology of Women', in *Relevance of Anthropology: The Indian Scenario*, edited by B.G. Halbar and C.G. Hussain Khan (Jaipur: Rawat): 103.
3. K.S. Singh, 'Tribal Women: Anthropological Perspective', in Singh, Vyas and Mann, eds, *Tribal Women and Development*.
4. K.S. Singh, 'Tribal Perspectives—1969–1990', in Miri, ed., *Continuity and Change in Tribal Society*: 5–10; and also see Singh, 1993. 'Status of Scheduled Tribes Some Reflections on the Debate on the Indigenous Peoples', *Social Change* 23, 2&3.
5. B. Singh, 1993. 'An Outline of Work to Be Taken Up on Tribal Women', Working Papers: NCW.
6. Bina Agarwal, 2005, 'Women's Inheritance: Next Steps: A Look at the Disabilities Non-Hindu Women Face'; column, *The Indian Express*, Monday, Oct. 17.
7. De Beauvoir, *The Second Sex*: 301.
8. Rekha, 2015. *Gender, Space and Creative Imagination: The Poetics and Politics of Women's Writing in India* (New Delhi: Primus Books): 29.
9. Estimates of annual loss of forests vary from 5.6 millions hectares to 20 million hectares, *Times of India*, 17 October 1986.
10. Rekha, *Gender, Space and Creative Imagination*: 69.
11. Weiner, *Sons of the Soil*.
12. A.K. Singh, 1995. 'Tribal Attitudes to the Tribals and Non-Tribals in South Bihar', in Singh and Jabbi, eds, *Tribals in India*.
13. Crispin Bates, 1995. 'Lost Innocents and the Loss of Innocence: Interpreting *Adivasi* Movements in South Asia', in *Indigenous Peoples of Asia* edited by R.H. Barnes, Andrew Gray and Benedict Kingsbury (Ann Arbor: Mi: Association for Asian Studies): 109–19.
14. Smith, Tuhiwai, 2012. *Decolonizing Methodologies*: 1.
15. Sherna Berger Gluck, 'What's So Special about Women? Women's Oral History', *Frontiers* 2, 2 (Summer 1977).
16. Amin, *Event, Metaphor, Memory*: 194.
17. The analysis of imperialism has been referred to more recently in terms such as 'postcolonial discourse'. Just because the word 'globalization' is substituted for the word 'imperialism', or the prefix 'post' is attached to colonial, it does not mean that we have been free from their challenges. Colonialism is not an over, finished business. Colonizers have left but the institutions and legacy of it have remained.

Introduction

18. Vinay Kumar Srivastava, 2010. 'On Tribal Economy and Society', in *Tribal Economy Crossroads* edited by S.N. Chaudhary (New Delhi: Rawat): 15–16.
19. At the national level, reported premarital sex is still fairly low among women (1.8%) and somewhat higher among men (12%). For more details see Lekha Subaiya, 'Premarital Sex in India: Issues of Class and Gender', *EPW* (29 November 2008): 54–59.
20. Scarlett Epstein, 1973. *South India*: 194–200.
21. *Anandabazar Patrika*, 5 July 2011.
22. Varavara Rao, 2010. *Captive Imagination: Letters from Prison* (New Delhi: Penguin Viking): 116–17.
23. Arundhati Roy, 2000. 'The Cost of Living', *Frontline*, 17, 3 (5–8 February).
24. Felix Padel and Samarendra Das, 2010. *Out of this Earth: East India Adivasis and the Aluminium Cartel* (New Delhi: Orient Blackswan): 154.
25. Arundhati Roy, 2012. 'Capitalism: A Ghost Story', *Outlook*, 26 March.
26. See introduction, Maria Mies and Vandana Shiva, 2010. *Ecofeminism* (Jaipur: Rawat).
27. Joseph Marianus Kujur, 2009. 'The Hinduisation of Tribals: A Special Reference to the Oraons in Chhotonagpur', in *Proselytisation in India: The Process of Hinduisation in Tribal Societies*, edited by Dharmendra Kumar and Yemuna Sunny (New Delhi: Aakar Books): 262.
28. Bosu Mullick, Jayadas, Akkara, and Jaydas, eds, *Indigenous Identity*: 6.
29. Mamoria, *Tribal Demography in India*: 35–46.
30. Doshi, *Bhils*.
31. John Campbell, 1864. *A Personal Narrative of Thirteen Years Service among the Wild Tribes of Khondistan, for the Suppression of Human Sacrifice* (London: Hurst and Blackett).
32. Currently, over 60 Memorandum of Understanding have been signed in eastern India between mining multinationals and state governments to promote large-scale, open-cast mining of bauxite and iron ore as well as that of other less important minerals, and to build processing plants and port export facilities (Ministry of Coal and Mines, Department of Mines, Annual Report 2003–2004, Government of India), available at http://www.mines.nic.in accessed on 11 July 2011.
33. C. von Furer Haimendorf, 1939. *The Naked Nagas* (London: Methuen).
34. Mies, Bennholdt-Thomsen, Werlhof, 1988. *Women—The Last Colony* (London: Zed Books).
35. Kaushik Ghosh, 1999. 'A Market for Aboriginality: Primitivism and Race Classification in the Indentured Labour Market of Colonial India', in *Subaltern Studies*, X, edited by Gautam Bhadra, Gyan Prakash and Susie Tharu (New Delhi: Oxford University Press): 8–48.
36. Satnam, *Jangalnama*: 120–22.
37. Felix Padel, 2009. *Sacrificing People: Invasions of a Tribal Landscape* (New Delhi: Orient Blackswan): 273.

38. Sudhir Pattnaik, 2014. 'Who Does the Media Serve in Odisha?' *EPW* 59, 14 (April 5): 74–81.
39. See http://odishaadivasimela.com/Updated_Events.htm accessed 11 July 2011.
40. A fact finding team of DSU (Democratic Student Union) of students of Delhi University, Jawaharlal University and IGNOU published a report in a booklet after visiting the area from 11 April to 16 April 2011: *The Flames of Narayanpatna: Two Reports on the Narayanpatna Struggle in Koraput, Odisha*, 2012 (Chandigarh: Charvaka Publications): 109.
41. Iggers, *Historiography in the Twentieth Century*: 145.
42. Dipesh Chakrabarty, 1997.'Minority Histories, Subaltern Past', from 'Viewpoints' column in the November, *Perspectives*, available at http://www.historians.prg/perspectives/issues/1997/9711/index.cfm accessed 11 July 2011.
43. Sujata Patel, 1988. 'Construction and Reconstruction of Women in Gandhi', *EPW* (Feb. 20): 377–87.
44. For details see Madhu Kishwar, 2010. 'Gandhi and Women's Role in the Struggle for Swaraj', in Sekhar Bandyopadhyay, ed., *Nationalist Movement in India: A Reader* (New Delhi: Oxford University Press): 239–56.
45. *The Hindu*, 14 December 2001.
46. George Mathew, 2003. 'Panchayati Raj Institutions and Human Rights in India', *EPW* (Jan. 11–17): 155–62.
47. Praveen Rai, 2011. 'Electoral Participation of Women in India: Key Determinants and Barriers', *EPW* (Jan. 15): 54.

CHAPTER 1

Demystifying Adivasi Women: Some Epistemological Issues

ENGELS HAD IDENTIFIED the 'world historic defeat' of women with the rise of private property and the consequent overthrow of women's autonomy in the domestic sphere: 'The man seized the reins in the house; also, the woman was degraded, enslaved, the slave of the man's lust, a mere instrument for breeding children.'[1] Private property, it should be noted, is not just a matter of the private ownership or possession of the instruments and means of production; it is the ability of the owners of land, tools, and so on, to appropriate the labour of other individuals. Thus the formation of private property is synonymous with the splitting up of society into classes, which, in turn, requires the institution of the state, to maintain the class rule of the owners of private property. Engels, following Marx's hints in his notebooks, and based on the anthropological work of Lewis Morgan, analysed the effects of the formation of private property and the state on the position of women and the nature of the family.

In India, society before the advent of class or pre-class society is called tribal society[2] and thus it is necessary to analyse the changes in women's position at this stage. Engels had identified the domestic sphere as being the province of the woman, and identified her defeat with man taking command of the house too. Since Engels, we have come to know that even in gathering societies and in early agriculture, women do a major part of the work of non-domestic production. Engels was thus wrong in identifying the domestic sphere alone as women's province. But what he pointed to was the autonomy of men and women in their own spheres, the loss of which autonomy for women resulted in their subordination.

The origins of sexual stratification lie in women's role in production and not in the powers of reproduction. There is a stage of social development, which has been named the 'lineage' mode of production, which is the period of the transition from communal property to private property. At the level of the family, women's labour is the major part of social labour, but any accumulation from this labour takes place in the male line, and is thus outside the control of the women. The subordination of women took place in this period of kinship-based or lineage societies because of the formation of group property (a form of property held by the corporate kin group) and the patrilocal rules of residence. In the development of surplus production, women's labour provided, in a sense, the base, while men's labour was the variable element. Women in gatherer-hunter appropriation and in extensive systems of agriculture (slash and burn) do the major portion of the labour and provide a major part of the sustenance for the family. The rise of lineages means that there is a differential access to production resources. Women's labour is crucial in realizing the possibilities of differential accumulation. But this accumulation takes place in the family of the husband.

DEFINING THE WORD 'TRIBE'

Can the above analysis be of any help in understanding the position of women in Indian tribes? Of course, the word 'tribe' covers a wide range of societies ranging from food gatherers, to slash-and-burn agriculturists, to light plough to settled agriculture. Some order needs to be brought into the vast amount of anthropological material on these tribes. The reason for clubbing these disparate societies into one category of 'tribes' is that they are all, in a sense, pre-class societies or at best very rudimentary forms of class society. But pre-class societies themselves cover a considerable variety of social organization. So it is necessary to identify the nature of these tribes more clearly. This identification will both depend on and in turn help illuminate the changing position of women as we move from food gatherers up to settled agriculturists.

The term 'tribe' is derived from the Latin word 'tribus'. The term 'tribal' is nowhere defined in the constitution and in fact there is no satisfactory definition. To the ordinary person it suggests simple folk living in hills and forests; to people who are a little better informed, it signifies colourful folk famous for their dance and song; to an administrator it means a group of citizens who are the special responsibility of the President of India; and to an anthropologist it indicates a special field for study of a social phenomenon. The current popular meaning of a tribe in India is a category of people included in the list of scheduled tribes. As these groups are presumed to form the oldest ethnological sector of the population, the term 'adivasi' (adi= original, and vasi= inhabitant) has become current among certain people, otherwise there is no indigenous word for tribe in any of the Indian languages. In Sanskrit, there is a word *atavika jana* (forest dwellers) which was used to denote agglomeration of individuals with specific territorial, kinship and cultural patterns. Words like 'vanyajati', 'vanavasi', 'pahari', 'adimjati', 'anusuchitjati', have been coined to designate these people. The names of tribes like Kurumba, Irulu, Paniya in south India; Asura, Saora, Oraon, Gond, Santhal, Bhil in central India; Bodo in northeast India; occur in classical Indian literature. But we should remember that the word 'adivasi' has a Sanskrit origin which has been popularized by the Hindus amongst the tribals of India.

It is interesting to examine the changing notions of this term over this period. Rising adivasi consciousness was given an impetus by the activities of Christian missionaries and by colonial writings which categorized people into essentialized tribal identities with fixed boundaries. The romanticization of tribes also started becoming a part of the stereotype. According to Vinita Damodaran, the embracing of the identity of indigenous or adivasi must be seen in political terms. Given the effects of economic exploitation, political disenfranchisement, social manipulation and ideological domination on the cultural formation of minority subjects and discourses, a redefinition of the subject position of tribes and an exploration of its strengths and weaknesses, and of the affirmations and negations of the term adivasi itself was inevitable.[3] It is also necessary to deconstruct some established notions regarding tribe and gender, so that the tribal issues can come more to the centre of our discussions in contemporary India than remaining at the margins, as is the case today. The challenge always is to demystify, to decolonize. The following questions have thus become an integral part of the analysis which will help demystification or demythicization of adivasi women: *(i)* How far the romanticization of tribal life is true? *(ii)* Are Adivasis Hindus? *(iii)* What were the colonial perceptions regarding Adivasi people?

The Validity of the Romanticization of Tribal Life

Verrier Elwin was the most influential personality in the debate on the tribal question between 1930s and mid-1940s. He was in against of the application of the modernist view in the tribal development. Since he himself experienced the negative impact of the imperialistic policies of the West and modern capitalism in the tribal society, he criticized civilization and celebrated cultural primitivism. Ramchandra Guha has stated in this regard, 'With the long shadow of Nazism cast over the warring nations of Europe, the primitivist view could effectively challenge a view of human progress in which savages of the forest were placed at the bottom of the hierarchy and modern civilised society was at its apex.'[4]

Elwin's celebration of tribal culture was based on ecological romanticism, the way in which the English Romantics (William Wordsworth, John Ruskin, Edward Carpenter) described the harmful impact of the industrial revolution on the environment of England. But there is an important difference in that Elwin wanted to protect tribal culture, customs, and traditions, so that it could be a good alternative of the modern way of life. His efforts laid the foundation of the environmental ideology and became one of the most crucial factors of the Gandhian Environmentalist movement of the twentieth century. Thus, the ecological romantics rose up in protest against modern capitalistic development and upheld the traditional way of life as viable alternatives.

Those who are against the introduction of modern industrial mode of production in tribal society, said that from the ancient times tribal people have been living harmoniously with the nature. They were the indigenous inhabitants and their institutions and habits gave them a certain social coherence and stability within their own society. This belief has paved the path of modern ecological romanticism.[5]

On the other hand Elwin's philosophy indirectly supported the imperialist clause of the protectionist policy enshrined in the Government of India Act of 1935, because he advocated the policy of 'partial isolation' of the tribal people in order to prevent their exploitation of the non-tribal societies. For this reason, G.S. Ghurye, a critic of Verrier Elwin, called him as 'revivalist' and 'no changer'.[6]

At present the environmentalists are fighting against neo-liberalism and communalism. But their notion about the alternative and about the means of resistance is still influenced by ecological romanticism.[7] In the age of globalization when agriculture is continuously being threatened and local livelihood pattern devastated, they are forced to negotiate with the current paradigm of modern development. It is correctly said that tribes are now confronting two forms of opposing relations: one with the state and another with international capital.[8] The evidence of such an effect on the tribes is further reflected in terms of decline of their working population during the years of globalization and economic reforms. Falling of forests and land resources are some of the most important factors of decelerating employment opportunities.⁹

What type of development is accepted and for whom? Theoreticians of ecological romanticism have failed to answer this question. All the secular and democratic forces consider the expropriation of natural resources under capitalism is harmful for the marginal people. There is a great discrepancy between theory and practice. They have failed to find out an appropriate alternative of modernity.

Archana Prasad has attempted to argue that the theory and practice of ecological romanticism prevent these movements from opening up the discourse to an alternative notion of modernity. She has shown that romantic ideas of 'the first inhabitant', 'eco-friendly customary practices' and the community are ahistorical as they do not take the problems of feudal and capitalist exploitation into account. There is thus a need to develop a sustainable modernity that is outside the framework of this system, and which helps to rejuvenate and upgrade local practices. As the historian D. D. Kosambi aptly stated, 'Golden Age lies not in the past, but in the future'. Archana Prasad has shown that an attempt to revive the past will not redeem our future.¹⁰

Are Tribals Hindus?

The transition from tribe to caste is one such change. The outstanding exponent of the Marxist interpretation of Indian history in all its complexity and the one who ushered in a paradigm shift in the study of ancient Indian history was D.D. Kosambi. The transition from tribe to caste was for him a basic historical process in India. His focus was on the two ends of the social spectrum: the organization of the brahmana 'varna' and the creation of the 'shudra varna'. The former was that of the highest ritual status and in later periods included the substantial number of recipients of grants of land.[11] The shudra varna, within which he included the 'dasas', provided the labour force and was essential to the definition of class. He compared this category to the Greek helots. They were a category outside caste and a pre-class formation. Tribe and caste were contrasting conditions.

The relationship between tribe and caste society is sometimes reformulated today as that between a clan-based society and the state. The change from tribe to caste is a complex historical process. In the juxtaposition of tribe and caste or of clan and state, the encroachment on the tribe by caste society frequently resulted in its incorporation into the state. Kosambi very perceptively observed, '[For the] disruption of the tribal people and their merger into general agrarian society ... would not have been possible merely by winning over the chief and new leading members ... The tribe as a whole turned into a new peasant "jati" caste-group, generally ranked as shudras, with as many as possible of the previous institutions (including endogamy) brought over.'[12] The result of this process of transition was the formation of institutions like private property, the caste system, the state and the patriarchal family. While this change took place over a long period of time and included a number of intermediate stages, it was not just uniformitarian, in the sense of gradual and constant cultural growth and modification, a kind of accretion as it were. There were periods of accretion of small changes (say, the Vedic period, or within tribal systems), and there were also subsequent periods when these small changes gave way to major changes, qualitative changes in ways of living, relating to each other and even in ways of making sense of things.

The denial of such a major break in South Asian history has varied manifestations. In sociology and anthropology it is seen in G.S. Ghurye's refusal to allow any separation between the tribes and castes. For him, the tribes were only 'backward Hindus'.[13] Of course, this stand itself is part of a 'nation-building' project, one which requires the amalgamation of all peoples into a Hindu nation. The denial of distinct forms of living and being, of making sense of things, is a form of ethnocentrism.[14]

In India ethnocentrism consists in seeing the history of all communities as being merely the striving to become Hindu, to become a caste. There is no distinction between tribe and caste. All communities are castes, only the degree of being castes is different. Baidyanath Saraswati has insisted on the 'cultural oneness' of tribe and caste. He asked for 'tribe' to be treated as 'caste', and 'caste' to be understood as a cultural unit. Powerful support for these ideas of castification[15] comes from the analysis of inequality in society. According to André Béteille, if social inequality is a common condition of all human societies, then can we draw a valid distinction between tribal equality and caste inequality? Is there a contrast in the ethical foundations of these two purportedly different forms of society? In an essay on 'Tribe and Peasantry', he states that the country's tribal populations are like peasants anywhere in India.[16] In this essay Béteille takes each of the four criteria that are usually used to differentiate tribes from castes—size, isolation, religion, and means of livelihood—and argues that in each, there is no distinction between tribe and peasantry in India. But later he shows how the words 'native' and 'tribe' have been replaced by the term 'indigenous', pointing out that in India no given population can claim indigeneity because there are no other populations that can reasonably be described as settlers or aliens.[17] In some ways, his argument mirrors that of Crispin Bates, who proposes that the term 'adivasi' is a colonial invention and argues that we need to admit that in one sense all Indians are adivasis.[18] Well, whether the word 'tribe' is a colonial construction or not that will be debated in the next section.

When Elwin's pro-exclusion stances were being criticized, Elwin had himself begun to review the relationship between tribals and Hinduism. By the mid-1940s one essential element of Elwin's romanticism had undergone a significant change. In the wake of Christian missionary activities in the Central Provinces, Elwin's argument that the tribes were culturally different from caste Hindus and outside the fold of the varna system underwent a change. His call for mobilization of Hindu organizations was accompanied by a demand that the Christian missionary activity be banned in the tribal areas. Elwin began to look towards right-wing nationalists to push out Christian missions from tribal areas. But in the process he facilitated the penetration of right-wing Hindu nationalists in tribal areas, which was enabled by the setting up of the Niyogi Committee that recommended the expulsion of all Christian missions from the Fifth Scheduled areas.

In the 1951 Census the religion of the tribes was termed as tribal religion. The Census enumerators being high-caste Hindus invariably mentioned the tribal religion as Hindu religion. With the coming of the conservative political parties in power the debate came into existence by the statement that the tribals are Hindus. But we do not have empirical evidence which suggest that the tribals are Hindus—ethnically, racially and bio-anthropologically. An analysis of trends in tribal religion from 1961 onwards shows that there are three trends: first, there has been a remarkable spread of Christianity among the tribes in north-east India, including Arunachal Pradesh.[19]

According to K.S. Singh, tribal religion is seen in relation to the local forms of Hinduism as far as shamanistic practices, rituals and propitiation of local deities are concerned. It has also been seen in the regional context.[20]

Colonial Perception of the Adivasis

One of the major issues in tribal studies today pertains to the 'definition' of 'tribe'. Many of us think that the term 'tribe' is a colonial construct. The Lokur Committee declared some criteria for identifying a particular community as Scheduled Tribe. These are: *(i)* the tribals are an ensemble of primitive traits; *(ii)* distinctive culture; *(iii)* geographical isolation; *(iv)* shyness of contact with the outside world; and *(v)* backwardness. Which of the above criteria are relevant today for defining a tribal community, and which of them have become defunct? Second, what is meant by 'primitive traits'? Many of the traits found in the so-called primitive societies like polygyny may also be found among the contemporary affluent and patriarchal societies. Ironically, when these characteristics are found among the latter, they are not called primitive.

The 'community way of living' has also broken down. Tribal families are moving out of their areas in search of jobs, and sometimes they have to travel thousands of kilometres to reach a suitable location where their never-ending struggle for survival begins. Tribal culture today cannot be described as unique. In the name of theory, then as Sumit Sarkar points out, there has appeared in the present approach of the Subalterns, a tendency 'towards essentialising the categories of 'subaltern' and 'autonomy', in the sense of assigning to them more or less absolute, fixed, decontextualised meanings and qualities',[21] because conflicts must also be located within the internal hierarchy of the tribal communities. Similar views have been expressed by Sanjukta Das Gupta that recent studies have highlighted conflicts within the internal hierarchy of the adivasi communities, on the one hand, and, on the other, have challenged the Subalternist contention of tribal autonomy by emphasizing linkages between the tribal communities and the supra-village power structure.[22]

We may site here an example of an adivasi village-structure in Koraput district of south Odisha where every tribal group is internally segmented into hierarchical parts. This hierarchy is expressed through different idioms, such as *boro/sano* and essentially denote 'elder/younger' dichotomy. But one has to remember that this hierarchical system in no way connotes a rigid status distinction that the caste society upholds. In an interior adivasi village of Koraput three levels may be distinguished within a general hierarchy, including the lower castes and sub-tribes. At the top there are categories of Rona, Kamar, Goudo, Mali and Sundi. As a sign of their higher status all members of these categories (men and women) wear the sacred thread and worship the tulsi plant. They do not consume beef or pork. On the middle level we find the different adivasi categories: Gadaba, Parenga, Paraja, Jhoria, Didayi, Bonda and Kondh. All the adivasi categories are internally divided into two segments, the senior or *boro* (like Boro Paraja, Boro Bonda) and the junior or *sano* (like Sano Gadaba). The *boro* and *sano* Gadaba men and women often interdine and intermarry. The Gadaba think of the Bonda as their elder and of the Parenga and Kondh as their younger brothers/sisters. They consider the Jhoria as to be still junior and the Didayi to be of lowest status. Ghasia, Dombo lies at the bottom of this hierarchy.[23] This intermingling with the lower castes sometimes leads the adivasi groups to take on a different shape. They sometimes incline to adopt some of the practices of the castes people and remould their hierarchical structure accordingly.

Some anthropologists still depict the same stereotypical mould from the colonial times in which they want to situate the 'tribes'. B.K. Roy Burman had proposed that because of the pejorative connotation, the term 'primitive tribes' should be changed to 'vulnerable tribes'.[24] Bhupinder Singh has made the analogical distinction between two types of tribal communities: first, those that demand the 'first-aid treatment' (which means little help); and second, those which require 'hospitalization' (or proper intensive care). The primitive tribe groups (PTGs) fall in the second category. Incidentally he also proposed that they may be called the 'primary tribes'.[25] D.D. Kosambi's notion of tribe is also not beyond criticism. Kosambi said the agrarian village economy came to replace the 'tribal' way of life. He tends to mistake Stone-Age hunter-gatherers for tribes.[26] Kosambi went so far as to state that among tribes the way of life has remained 'largely unchanged' since prehistoric times.[27] But according to Shereen Ratnagar, hunting-gathering-fishing constitutes the pre-tribe stage of cultural development. The tribe as a social formation came into existence only with the coming of agriculture. She has also criticized Kosambi for using the term 'largely unchanged' for the tribal way of life because it amounts to denying marginalized groups a history and it was an assumption handed down in the Orientalist tradition.[28] According to Partha Chatterjee, the adivasis of India are largely forest-dependent or pastoralists. He said,

> In every region of India, there exist marginal groups of people who are unable to gain access to the mechanisms of political society. They are often marked by their exclusion from peasant society, such as low-caste groups ... or tribal peoples who depend more on forest products or pastoral occupations than on agriculture. Political society and electoral democracy have not given these groups the means to make effective claims on governmentality.[29]

Mihir Shah has criticized Partha Chatterjee's notion of tribes. He has mentioned the Sivaraman Committee Report of 1981 on the Development of Tribal Areas that was concluded by saying, 'settled agriculture is the primary source of livelihood for the overwhelming majority of the tribal population in the country'.[30] Data from the 1981 Census already showed that over 93 per cent of tribal 'workers' in India are engaged in agriculture and allied activities, more than two-thirds of these being cultivators.[31] Mihir Shah has further stated that,

> Even more surprising is Chatterjee's notion that adivasis are somehow beyond the pale of political society. He appears to forget that adivasis played a decisive role in the change of regimes in Madhya Pradesh, Chhattisgarh and Jharkhand in the 2003 assembly elections, earlier having been part of the struggle for the creation of Chhattisgarh and Jharkhand. Adivasis are at the heart of some of the most significant political movements of our time.[32]

Those anthropologists who have worked with South African stateless tribes argue that in political anthropology the concept of 'tribe' is used as 'holders'. But the concept has been criticized on ideological grounds. According to Morris

Godelier there are two societies—the tribal society and the state society. Godelier brings out the dispute and the crisis of concept of tribe, saying anthropologists and politicians 'see in the contradiction attributing to tribalism not so much a relic of pre-colonial status, but which flower again even violently as a legacy of the colonial period and the new relations involved in new colonial domination.'[33]

Susan B.C. Devalle sees the tribe as essentially a construct, a colonial category.[34] Jagannath Pathy has argued that the concept of tribe originated in India with colonial rule. He avers that in the pre-colonial period people were either unconscious of their ethno-national identities or called themselves 'people' versus outsiders.[35] He further stated that in ancient Indian literature there was no equivalent for the English term 'tribe', an argument to which historian Niharranjan Ray subscribed as well.[36] In 1935, the British began calling them as 'backward tribes'. Both the words, 'caste' and 'tribe', are non-indigenous terms and were used by the foreign writers while describing Indian social structure as they understood it. It has been further argued that Indian elites appropriated the European racial ethnography both to justify an Indian hierarchy and to assert parity with the European upper classes.[37] According to Sanjukta Das Gupta, such an emphasis on the 'imagined' nature of caste, tribe and other identities and their 'invention' through deliberate collaboration of European officers and their Indian informants have developed almost into a 'post-colonial essentialising', countering the 'orientalist essentialising' of earlier indologists and anthropologists.[38] The colonial discourse on tribe in India had been largely informed by prevailing concepts among the dominant caste groups and in this sense, tribe may be considered to be a brahmanical construct rather than merely a colonial one.[39]

Asoka Kumar Sen has denied the notion of tribe as a 'colonial creation'. According to him, it smacks of European ethnocentrism which does not as if accept the beingness of any people prior to colonial rule. This contention posits colonial ethnography within the famous subject-objects dichotomy.

Just as the subjective idealists' contention that no material substratum exists in the mind of a subject, because to be is to be perceived, in the same fashion the British committed the 'fallacy of initial predication' when they thought that they constructed the tribe, as if it were non-existent before their intervention. He said that tribalism was a pre-colonial notion, which the British were reconstructing instead of constructing it.[40]

According to Crispin Bates, as mentioned in the Introduction, 'The Indian term 'adivasi' derives from the Hindi words 'adi', meaning 'beginning' or 'of earliest times', and the word 'vasi' meaning 'resident of'. The epithet was in fact invented by political activists in the area of Chotanagpur in the 1930s, an invention motivated not so much by the idea of abolishing the concept of the 'tribal' altogether (as was later attempted by nationalists in Africa), but rather with the aim of forging a new sense of identity among differing 'tribal' peoples—a tactic which has enjoyed considerable success, with the term subsequently becoming widely popularized. Thus, there is nothing at all 'indigenous' about the term, nor the people which it purports to describe. Indeed, it could be argued that the concept of the adivasi is a product of Orientalism. Orientalism has not just been a problem in the western understanding of non-western societies, but a phenomenon that has deeply affected Indians themselves as they have incorporated into their own understanding of Indian society the statistical, canonical, materialistic and self-justificatory interpretations purveyed by colonial administrations. As a result India, over the generations, has in many aspects been re-made in the image invented for it by European colonialists ... the adivasi shares ... a vital debt to colonial prejudice.'[41]

Moreover, the tribal identity claims of different communities has loosened the idea of tribe from its classical anthropological moorings and pushed it towards being a politically productive 'notion'. More recently, it has actually been to their advantage to call themselves 'adivasis'. A consequence has been that since the introduction of the policy of reservation, the number of adivasis in India as a proportion of the total population has actually increased. The question that arises is: do we take the view that once a tribe is always a tribe? It is significant that the tribal policy acknowledged the need for a process of 'de-scheduling' so as to exclude the people of the creamy layer who are conspiring to retain their status as ST in order to have the facilities of reservation. The most recent instance is that of the Gujars of Rajasthan seeking the status of ST. This hints at the emergence of a reverse process of Sanskritization.[42] It is noteworthy that the Rajbansis were previously tribals but later they were detribalized and incorporated into caste society. It is a process of Kshatriyazation where the group acquired the status of Kshatriya into the Hindu fold. But Kshatriyazation process has greatly affected the status of Rajbansi women. The old system of bride price has been given up and so have been companionate marriage, connubial union, divorce and remarriage, widow remarriage, levirate, polygamy; their freedom has been curtailed and their status has been lowered.[43]

The contemporary ethnicization of tribal identity in the Darjeeling hills is certainly a new development. The concept of a tribe has been strategically posed along the continuum of politics-community-power. Tamangs, along with Limbus, did mobilize themselves for tribal status and were accorded the scheduled tribe (ST) status in 2002. This energized the other Mongoloid groups (like Rais, Magars, Gurungs, Sunwars, Yakhas, Thamis, to name a few) to clamour for the ST status. In the case of the Gorkhas, the Gorkhaland movement also demanded tribal status for them to gain the advantages of ST quota provided by the Indian constitution. The GTA Act, by March 2012, incorporates in it a provision stipulating that the state government facilitate the demand of ST status for all the Gorkhas except the scheduled castes, because the Gorkhas were originally the martial castes in the colonial period. In a situation like this—where the state approval meant almost every community could become a tribe—answers to vexed questions like 'who is a tribe?' or 'what is a tribe?' were to be sought not in ethnographic literature or in welfare imperatives, but in the discourses of power.[44]

Colonial rulers had several, often contradictory, policies. For example, in the 1941 Census, population of tribal and aborigines were defined linguistically as Bhotiya, Cakama, Damai, Gurum, Hadi, Kami, Khasa, Kuki, Lepaca, Limbu, Mamgara, Meca, Mru, Munda, Neoyara, Saotala, Saraki, Toto, Shabara, Kora, Garo, Khand, Bhumija, Tharu, Malapahadiya, Ho, Mahali.[45] Thus, while identities were certainly not fixed, given or unchanging, their construction cannot be reduced to colonial policies alone. Tribal identity formation, being part and parcel of the history of Indian society, cannot be seen in isolation from wider socio-economic and cultural dimensions. That is why in recent years terms like 'indigenous' and 'indigenes' are widely being used to avoid the controversies related to the word 'tribe'. Keeping in mind the fact of ceaseless demoralization of tribes, Levi-Strauss said that the concept of *indigene* (indigenous, native) was giving place to that of *indigent* (poor, needy, destitute). The former was presented romantically, depicting the bounteous beauty and charming aesthetics of the tribal persons; the latter was its opposite. It was an account of how the tribes were losing control over their habitat, its land and resources, dehumanized and displaced.[46]

But, the question remains of which criteria would determine who is indigenous and who is not. David Hardiman rejects the use of the term 'tribe' because the term is still carries a racist content and used in an evolutionist manner. He, therefore, prefers to use the term 'adivasi' in the Indian context. He has speculated that the term 'adivasi' appeared to have originated in the Chotanagpur region of Bihar in the 1930s. According to Gail Omvedt, the tribals of western India do not like words like 'girijana' or 'vanavasi', rather they prefer the term 'adivasi'. She prefers the term 'tribal' instead of 'adivasi'. Her argument is that tribal has both a scientific and a common sense meaning. Simultaneously, she has expressed her doubts about the use of the word 'tribe' in the

Indian context.[47] Morris Godelier has very rightly observed that the concept 'tribe' is 'in crisis'; and needs to be redefined to evaluate its real significance.[48]

The term 'tribe' is also unfavourable to the people themselves. They are called with various names such as adivasi, girijana, vanavasi, janajati. I would say the image and meaning underlying the category was far from being a colonial construction. We must not forget about the pre-colonial depiction of the tribal people of India as 'dasyus', 'daityas', 'rakshakas' and 'nishadas', while juxtaposed with the mid-nineteenth century western racial concept. The term 'adivasi' with its implication of 'original settlement' is debatable and appears to be unacceptable in a wider South Asian context. Nevertheless, in the final analysis, 'adivasi', with all its inherent problems is an acceptable solution. Therefore, in this book I have adopted both the terms and have used them interchangeably at times to indicate social structure distinct from caste hierarchies in India even while not subscribing to evolutionary or racist theories.

DEFINING GENDER

Like 'tribe' or 'adivasi', the word 'gender' also involves constructions. Arthur Mawick says that originating primarily as a grammatical term, it was picked up by the feminists and introduced in intellectual and then everyday discourse as an alternative to 'sex' to signify what they maintained was culturally constructed as distinct from what was biologically given. A distinction was thus sought to be made between the physiological 'sex' and social 'gender', between 'female' and 'feminine'; 'female' being the biological category to which women belong, while 'feminine' behaviours and roles were a product of social construction. It was argued by the feminists that whereas sex was a natural difference, the roles and behaviours associated with gender were created historically by different societies.[49] Therefore, femininity is not biologically based but socially constructed. The secondary place of women in relation to men was because of the imposition of strong environmental forces of education, social tradition, legal and political restrictions under the purposeful control of men. Proponents of gender have argued that it serves as one of the primary ways of signifying power relationships and that the changes in the organization of social relationships always correspond to changes in representation of power.

Women and tribals have long been marginalized sections in Indian history writing. Tremendous hopes were aroused, however, in the 1970s and early 1980s, when history writing was modified in two more or less parallel, but largely unconnected developments: the cataclysmic advent of 'history from below', mainly the early Subaltern School, and a quantum leap in women's studies, increasingly informed by feminist approaches. The first wave of women's history in India, very powerful and original, questioned the triumphal narrative of 'unilinear advance' in the 'status' of women through male initiated nineteenth-century social reform, later women's participation in Gandhian, revolutionary terrorist or Left-led movements. The 1990s saw promising results for women's history writing with some limitations. The subject again largely continued to be middle class-women or dominant Hindu castes. It is only with the maturing of 'total history' and the adoption of an interdisciplinary approach that tribes began to be situated in works on history. In such attempts at expanding the domains of history, the accent was more on ethnographical details or the colonial experiences with only incidental references to tribal women.

Comparative Understanding of the Struggling Character of Adivasi Women

The first or the earliest reference to women in history writing could be seen in the occasional passages in descriptions on anti-colonial tribal revolts. During the colonial period adivasi women did take part in different tribal movements: Santhal Rebellion (1855), Kondh Revolt (1869), Koya Movement

(1879), Sardari Agitation (1887), Rampa Rebellion (1911), Bastar Uprising (1911), Gond and Kolam Movement (1941–62), and so on. In all these movements, women invariably stood firmly behind their menfolk. Whatever 'perks' the colonial state offered to the tribals later have not been in any way beneficial to them. According to Manoshi Mitra, women participated in large numbers in the Kol Rebellion:

> In many instances women organised the defence of their villages and withstood pressure for a period of time before being forced to surrender. Many women were arrested by the British authorities.[50]

In Ranajit Guha's description of Santhal Hul, 'the entire female population of the Santhal districts in 1855 could have been accused of acting as the providers and as the eyes and the ears of the rebel forces.'[51] To S.C. Roy, women played an important part in the Munda Uprising.'[52] Speaking of the same movement, K.S. Singh noted, 'A large number of the tribals were killed which also included three women fighters, namely, the wives of Bankan Munda, Manjhia Munda and Dungdung Munda.'[53] Besides, during 1930s Rani Gaidinliu was the well-known leader of the Naga Uprising in northeast India. Rajmohini Devi led the freedom struggle in Surguja of Madhya Pradesh. She was the leader of Manjhi community of Gond tribals.

Today tribal women are amongst the poorest, most marginalized and backward people. Even today they have no rights over the forest and cultivating forest lands is considered an offence. In spite of their important contribution in various types of labour, within the tribal community too, women are oppressed by various traditional male chauvinistic practices. Tribal women are also victims of incessant sexual violence and abuse by contractors, government officials and the police. By luring tribal women to cities with the promise of providing jobs, criminal gangs are engaged in illegal trafficking and ruining their lives. The economic policies of the central and state governments, in keeping with liberalization, privatization and globalization, have opened the gates for imperialist plunder. Since the last few years, various Indian and foreign, or multinational corporate houses have been expanding their activities or entered into agreements with the state governments of Odisha, Jharkhand, Chhattisgarh and Maharashtra. These are companies like Jindal, Essar, Mittal, POSCO, Tata, Reliance. Hindutwa communal organizations are making an all out effort to saffronize the adivasi community.

In the post-independence era, like the colonial era, adivasi women have risen up in struggle against their exploitation and oppression. The state itself is directly targeted other than the landlord moneylenders. Though the movements are still regional, they are gradually crossing the boundaries and defusing in broader areas successfully. Second, adivasi women, though away from the cities and the mainstream women's movements, have continuously waged militant struggles along with their menfolk. Recent tribal movements have set the example of the formation of separate women's organizations. These adivasi women's wings, women cadres, women troops are organized and conducted by the decisions of its women members. Today, they are more united, organized and self-conscious. They are negotiating with full competency and this is the greatest achievement.

Third, tribal women have been portrayed in rather aggressive modes in some of the communist led movements. In the Tebhaga (1946–1947), Peter Custers argues that it was 'the doubly oppressed rural poor women who manifested themselves as most courageous and capable of leading the combined anti-feudal and anti-colonial movement'.[54] Vasanth Kannabiran and K. Lalitha write that women's contribution in the Telangana movement (1946–1951) ranged from transporting guns, arranging and running shelters, travelling through forests to address meetings, as also cooking and providing food to party comrades. There were some high, visible points in the movements: 'two hundred peasant women stood together in Penukonda and chased the police out of the village. In Appaijipet, women encircled a police van, attacked the police with pestles and chilli powder and secured the release of the Sangham activists.'[55] Tribal women had also added the militant character to the movements of 1970s. They were in the forefront of the Naxalbari and Srikakulam movements.[56] In the contemporary revolutionary movements in Bihar, Jharkhand, Andhra Pradesh, Chhattisgarh, Odisha and Maharashtra, they have built up a huge women's movement. In the movement of West Midnapur (2008–2010) their role was more constructive. In northeast India, where nationality movements are going on, tribal women in places like Manipur and Nagaland have active women's organizations. In the Narmada Valley, Kashipur and Kalinganagar, they have agitated against imperialist backed 'development' projects.

Fourth, by trying to crush these movements with intense and brutal repression, the state has made clear its anti-tribal stand. In spite of arrests, beatings and torture by the police, in spite of false cases being foisted on them, whether it is TADA (Terrorist and Disruptive Activities [Prevention] Act) or POTA (Prevention of Terrorism Act), which have been used against struggling tribal women, they have carried on fighting courageously. The state continues to try and crush their movements through campaigns like Salwa Judum and Sendra where mass rapes and murders of tribal women are taking place in the name of a state sponsored 'peace campaign'.

Fifth, another important feature is the synchronization between the women's movement and environmentalist movements in the post-1947 era. Thus a new chapter has been added to the history of the movement of the adivasi women: the Ecofeminist movement. Ecofeminism is an activist and academic movement that sees critical connections between the domination of nature and the exploitation of women. Growing protest against environmental destruction and struggles for survival and subsistence point to the fact that caste, class and gender issues are deeply interlinked. Ecofeminism emerged as a product of the peace, feminist and ecology movements of the late 1970s and early 1980s. Wherever women protested against ecological destruction, threat of atomic destruction of life on earth, new developments in biotechnology, genetic engineering and reproductive technology, they discovered the connections between patriarchal domination and violence against women, the colonized non-western, non-white peoples and nature. It has led to the realization that the marginalization of women by patriarchal domination and the destruction of biodiversity go hand in hand and liberation of women cannot be achieved in isolation from the larger struggle for preserving nature and life on this earth. Ecofeminist theory has brought into sharp focus the links between development and gender. It has highlighted the fact that the violence against nature and against women is built into the dominant development model. We have seen, for example, the women in the Chipko movement of the 1970s in the Garhwal-Himalaya—where women struggled for the protection and regeneration of the forests.

Some of the major debates that engaged the women's movement were issues of women's oppression, violence against women, the campaign for women's rights that challenged the dichotomy between public and private sphere and the social, cultural, economic and political manifestations of 'gender'. The debate over growth, development and equity issues from a woman's perspective have thrown new light on the dimensions and causes of gender inequality. Issues of peripheral groups of tribals, poor, landless women also gained recognition.

Aspiration Failure and Tribal Women

It is generally believed that lack of development or underdevelopment is the core issue of tribal discontent and tribal movements. A most crucial issue is what does mainstream society mean by 'development'? In spite of dying of starvation the tribals of Amlasole[57] or Kalahandi did not raise arms. And those who raised arms in Lalgarh[58] were not hit by chronic poverty. In the fact-finding reports it has been categorically mentioned that the main demand of the adivasi protesters of Lalgarh was to end police terror, not to initiate development while according to the National Family Health Survey 2, half of the children in the state of West Bengal are anaemic; among the adivasis the rate is 95 per cent. Paschimanchal Development Board has failed completely to initiate development of the tribals.[59] Development undoubtedly was there in their charter of demands, but the movement was launched precisely for the sake of dignity and not for food.[60] Similarly, the grievances in Amlasole were not regarding development, but about the gradual shrinking of the forest resources and being prevented by police from collecting forest resources. The first condition of development is to dream for development or to aspire for development. Aspiration relates to how people want to be in the future, for which reason people use their existing capabilities differently from a situation where they do not have this aspiration. For various reasons this aspiration has not been created or rather has been deterred by the government; it is called 'aspiration failure'.

The hunting-gathering tribes have a traditional way of production; they produce or work only when they need to acquire food or other necessities. This is because they do not have any surplus to store or exchange. Shifting cultivators too have a subsistence-oriented production system. What, however, can be observed today is that these tribals have changed their production orientation to a more surplus and accumulation-oriented production.[61] What is common to all parts of the developing world is the development of new needs, for example, medical services and education; also of entertainment, radio or television, good clothing. The creation of new needs together with the dependence on the market leads to a shift in the production objective.

Nowadays parents want something different for their children. Most of the tribal women of West Bengal, Jharkhand and Odisha told me that they want their daughters to be educated. With communication and growth of markets, collection of Non-Timber Forest Products (NTFPs) has allowed the tribals to acquire income beyond immediate needs. Agriculture and other labour markets have also opened up new possibilities for earning income through wage employment. The majority of tribal women of my study area said that they work whenever work is available.

What is the connection between aspiration and tribal unrest? Here comes the question of capacity or what Arjun Appadurai calls 'the capacity to aspire',[62] which is not evenly distributed among different tribal communities of different regions, causing complete failure of fulfilling those aspirations. There is an uneven distribution of the capacity to aspire between women and men as well. According to Dev Nathan, this uneven distribution is related to a number of factors: the gender division of responsibilities, their economic roles and everyday practice of economic relations with others, the changes in various types of economic and cultural practices, and so on.[63] The uneven distribution of the capacity to aspire is based to a high extent on the uneven distribution of what Bourdieu calls 'cultural capital',[64] using the term to explain class differences in performance in the so-called merit-based examinations; here, cultural capital is a factor that influences the capacity to aspire.

Perpetually living on the brink of starvation, the aspirations of the tribal women of Amlasole for themselves were for developing capabilities of an elementary kind, like having two meals a day or a permanent source of income. Their other aspirations too were quite modest—to look clean, in short, the capacity to appear in public without shame. But if we look at the comparatively better-off tribal areas, we will find some more ambitious aspirations, like to educate their children so that they can work as a teacher or barefoot doctor, to construct a cement-brick house, buy a TV or a mobile phone, and so on. Amlasole women have established Amlasole Birsa Munda Village Development Committee in July 2004. The Committee made a micro plan giving priority to the source of income and safety, health facilities, education and houses for Sabars. In August 2004 Amlasole Primary Health Centre was founded by the Committee. In the same year Berabhenge school with a mid-day meal programme was started as well.

But all these are local initiatives called the community-led structural intervention theory based on community mobilization, creating enabling environment and ownership over the process and product of intervention.[65] These elements are neither easy to find and sustain for long, especially when there is a severe dearth of food. So, the fundamental needs of life are more important for them than anything else. It limits their capacity to aspire.

Subalterns aspire for having an equal status, honour and human rights. For example, the Sabar children of Amlasole are not allowed to join the 'mainstream' school in their own village being dishonoured as 'criminals, untouchables and suspected as drug addicts'. Amlasole therefore remains Amlasole, year after year. A Lalgarh is created whenever there are violations of human rights. Lalgarh asked for something more than the basic needs.[66] Following the Sonamukhi rape incidents,[67] Nari Ijjat Bachao Committee (Committee to Save Women's Honour) was formed with ordinary adivasi women, hitherto unknown, to save their own dignity, pride and democratic rights.[68] Even, in the course of Lalgarh movement the People's Committee Against Police Atrocities (PCAPA) initiated an alternative model of development in the area. The Committee members distributed lands, built a small check dam in Bohardanga village, collected money for tractor and the *morrum* for the construction of roads, installed mini tube-wells and submergible pumps, a People's Health Centre at Kantapahari village.[69]

When acts are enacted for land acquisition followed by displacement, the adivasis resist, not only because land is their source of income but also, more painful than the poverty itself, is the erosion of people's sense of community and cultural identity, values, and traditions, which invariably accompanies their separation from the land. For them land is the symbol of dignity. Adivasi identity is closely bound to the earth, evoked in a dance-song of women from Kucheipadar, a village that has led the people's movement against mining in Kashipur: *'Matiro poko, mati bina aame bonchiba kahee?'*

(Earthworms we are—without earth how to survive?)[70] Displacement does not only mean being uprooted but also a permanent detachment from their culture. Displacement dislocates them into a social structure of broken relationships and fragmented space.

Communications have had a big impact on aspiration. Migration too has created new forms of aspirations. Exposure to the outside world and spread of literacy can help develop the capacity to aspire. Lack of education, health facilities and employment are the most important barriers before discarding the traditional subsistence economy. Due to the want of governmental initiatives, the tribals are not gaining expertise in using newer technological equipment and methods. During the colonial period the tribals struggled to save their economy from the greed of the zamindars–moneylenders nexus with the colonial masters. But now another cause has got attached to it and that is aspiration. The poor implementation of national tribal policies and the ignorance of these aspirations on the part of the government are basically responsible for its failure which belied the hope of protection, welfare and development of the tribal people that came with India's independence.

Adivasi and Non-Adivasi Women's Socio-Economic Roles

What are the differences between the tribal and the non-tribal women regarding their socio-economic roles. There are two diametrically opposite views on this subject: *(i)* tribal women enjoy a relatively low status in comparison to the caste Hindu women. Except in the case of matriarchal, matrilineal and polyandrous tribal communities, the status of women in most of the tribes is inferior to men; *(ii)* tribal women enjoy a relatively high status to their non-tribal counterparts.

Both the views are correct because an inferior status of women has been reported from a number of Indian tribes. For example, Todas do not touch their women during certain periods and they are entirely excluded in a number of ceremonies.[71] Similarly the Kharia woman is not allowed to cook for her husband or any stranger.[72] Grigson has reported low status of women of the Maria Gonds where they are tabooed when menstruating and are debarred from attending festivals in spite of premarital sexual freedom and freedom in the choice of her husband.[73] According to Verrier Elwin, 'Tribal woman has a wide freedom, which she seldom abuses. She can go to a bazar, even by herself. She can visit her friends. She can dance and sing, especially before marriage, as she pleases. She can laugh and joke with men without reproach. Her freedom becomes naturally somewhat restricted after marriage, but even then she can be herself.'[74]

Among the Tharus of the Nainital Tarai (Uttar Pradesh), women's status is proverbially high. They are dominant over their husbands, have property rights, keep poultry, own it, they fish, make baskets and sell the products of their labour.[75] Writing about Nagas, Elwin said that Naga women hold a high and honourable position. They work on equal terms with the men in the fields and make their influence felt in the tribal council.[76] He makes a similar observation with regard to the Baigas; there is no clear division of labour between men and women.[77] Furer-Haimendorf referring to the Nagas writes, 'many women in most civilised parts of India may well envy the women of the Naga Hills, their high status and their free happy life . . . you will think twice before looking down on the Nagas as savages.'[78] In a similar vein, Hutton attributes a higher social status to Sema Naga women on the ground that marriages among the Sema Naga are choice-based and a girl is never married against her will. The Sema Naga woman occupies a high position in her husband's house and is treated well.[79]

In his statistical account of Assam, Hunter has reported very high status of women among the Garos and the important position the women occupy among them.[80] Garo society is matrilineal. Property, among the Garos, is inherited only by the female, and she owns the fields, house and other valuables of the household.[81] Similarly in the Andaman Islanders, women are equal to men. They are eligible to speak out and form opinion.

At the end of the debate it can be said that in tribal society, while women's labour has an important role in accumulation, control of which is in male hands, still women have not completely lost their limited autonomy. The autonomy, it must be stressed, is limited, not only because it does not cover all or most of women's activities, but also because the requirements of accumulation very much determines the uses to which women's income is put. Such limited autonomy too, it would seem, does have a role in maintaining some dignity for women, a dignity that the further development of private property is bound to erode. Therefore, tribal women are indeed in many ways the equal, if not the rival, of the tribal man.[82]

Changing Patterns of Livelihood and Tribal Women

It is now a well-accepted theory that there was less inequality between the sexes in tribal communities. With the intervention of external economic, social and cultural forces, the status of tribal women has deteriorated more than that of men. This is attributed mainly to the delinking of their life from the natural resources on which women depended more than men did. Such delinking is done through three main modes: denial of access to forests and land, displacement by development projects, and outmigration either of men alone or of the whole family. Under colonial rule the informal tribal economy for the first time started transforming into formal sector. The changeover has been intensified during the four decades of planned development.

Because of the important role played by women, tribal economy has often been called by Ester Boserup as 'female economy'.[83] The tribals accordingly developed a culture geared to keeping a balance between human needs and environmental imperatives, because this conservation-orientation of their culture was crucial for women's workload. Walter Fernandes says it is not merely that the conservation-orientation of the tribal culture conferred a higher status on her, but also that the predominant role she played in the forest economy was a major factor in the conservation-orientation of their culture. She had a bigger vested interest than the men did, in a balanced use of the resource according to human needs and its conservation for posterity. That is why tribal women are more aware of their ethnic identity than men.[84]

Traditional tribal informal society was community-based, and was oral tradition-based as against the written word of the present system. In this system, oral undertaking of the individual was accepted in trust by the community, not evidential as in the litigation-based formal system that was imposed on such a society in which literacy is low. Moreover, the informal economy did not have the concept of property as it is understood today: something that can be used or destroyed by the individual owner or the corporate sector according to its will. The concept of property ownership or control over resources brings out the major difference between the two systems more than any other aspect. Land and forests were a community resource, not merely an object of agriculture or construction as is the case in the formal system in the property owner has an absolute right over it. Consequently, when the formal system entered their area with the support of the state apparatus, the tribals were not prepared to meet it.

Tribals were integrated into the mainstream formal economy as subordinates; as suppliers of cheap labour and raw material, to the benefit of the small minority controlling the formal system. Tribal women were affected by these developments in various ways, such as: *(a)* those women who continue to live in their village were impoverished by deforestation and other forms of environmental deterioration; *(b)* the women who were displaced by development projects did not get proper rehabilitation and compensation since the Common Property Resources (CPRs) are not their property according to the present law.[85] Finally, *(c)* women were affected by outmigration. This vicious circle ensures the transition of the tribals from constructive to destructive dependence on what was once a renewable resource. While all the tribals are thus alienated from these resources and impoverished, women are the worst hit since their role was crucial in the traditional economy. At the social level one witnesses the transition from shifting to settled agriculture, with the implications for ownership. At the same time, competition begins for the scarce resources and the community as such breaks down and class formation follows. It leads to the emergence of a class of tribal elite. Finally, at the cultural level there is Sanskritization in the strictest sense as enunciated by M.N. Srinivas.

Deforestation definitely increases the burden of work for the tribal women, but at the same time with displacement their contribution to the family economy declines, because then men become the only or main income earners since most jobs go to them. According to Walter Fernandes, loneliness, drunkenness (both for men and women) and wife-beating then become their response to the trauma of displacement. Women also accept status symbols like expensive clothes and other trinkets to cope with the tension of displacement.[86] With an increased exposure to urban and industrial set-up, the attitude of women has undergone a change. Proximity to urban areas, lack of adequate employment opportunities and poverty have driven them even to prostitution. According to women of Chikapar resettlement village of Upper Kolab Project, In the last three years at least six girls from the area have become commercial sex workers in the nearby towns of Koraput, Jeypore and other towns bordering the state of Andhra Pradesh.[87]

Tribal women thus become only subordinate workers under their husbands and begin to be considered exclusively in the housewife's role. We could think that subordination is the key aspect in Sanskritization. In most tribal societies Sanskritization involves changeover from bride price to dowry, from adult marriage through choice of partner to arranged marriage, at times child marriage. During field work in West Midnapore I was informed that child marriage is being performed; this practice is widely prevalent among the Baiga tribe as well, while in Kalahandi divorce and widow remarriage are beginning to be looked down upon. Arranged marriages are coming to be accepted as the norm.[88]

Development-Induced-Displacement: Marginalization of Tribal Women and Gender Justice

In the Indian context one of the best-known method by which displacement has taken on a massive scale is Development Induced Displacement. It has an inherent bias against the ethnic communities. Developmental schemes provide little spaces to the ethnic groups particularly the tribals to voice their presence or to contest, and, it takes no cognizance of the presence of ethnic groups either. Most of the time developmental projects are imposed upon, rather than taking into account prior consent of the ethnic groups and thus causing a fundamental dispossession or exploitation of the 'fourth world' of the first people, the indigenous or tribal people. Further, developmental projects are decided not in cultural setting of ethnic groups rather 'outside their realm'—the realm lies either in the capital cities or in the western multilateral institutions. These projects are imposed or introduced in a straightjacket manner without however taking into consideration locality or cultural settings of ethnic groups. Finally developmental projects are not backed by a proper rehabilitation policy.[89]

In the case of India's development model, displacement caused by large projects has actually resulted in a transfer of resources from the weaker sections of society to more privileged ones. Post-independence development policy and planning have largely followed the utilitarian and Benthamite logic of 'the greatest happiness for the greatest number'. This has allowed for millions to be displaced in the interest of the 'common good'.[90] Mega dams, in particular, create victims of development—mainly tribals who never share the gains of development. No reliable data exists so far on the extent of displacement in the name of 'public purpose'. But who constitutes the 'public'? And how is 'public purpose' defined? Even, The country lacks a comprehensive resettlement and rehabilitation (R and R) policy. Several studies have documented the qualitative consequences of forced development. This occurs along the following crucial dimensions: landlessness, homelessness, joblessness, food insecurity, social disarticulation, loss of common property, increased morbidity and mortality.[91]

Now the focus is on some key issues related to tribal women, displacement and people's struggle (for displacement see Table 1.1). First, it asks whether tribal women experience displacement differently from men. Second, it explores the role of tribal women in struggles against displacement. Third, it looks at biases against tribal women in resettlement policies and finally, it locates displacement and resettlement issues within wider debates of development, globalization and privatization, which offer the overwhelming context for displacement and pauperization in today's times.

Tribal women do experience displacement differently. Tribal women are deeply related to nature and natural resources; they are the food providers in a tribal family and

Table 1.1 Displacement between 1951 and 1990 (in lakhs)

Sl. No.	Type of projects	Total displaced and percentage	Tribal displacement and percentage	% of tribals to the total
1	Dams	164.0 (25.0%)	63.2 (25.0%)	38.5
2	Mines	25.5 (25.5%)	13.3 (24.8%)	52.2
3	Industries	12.5 (30.0%)	3.1 (25.6%)	25.0
4	Wildlife	6.0 (20.8%)	4.5 (22.2%)	75.0
5	Others	5.0 (30.0%)	1.3 (20.0%)	25.0
	Total	213.0 (25.4%)	85.4 (24.8%)	40.1

Source: As quoted in Planning Commission, 'Report of the Steering Committee on Empowering the Scheduled Tribes for Tenth Five-Year Plans', 2001, Ministry of Rural Development (p. 3).

that is why their concern is for preventing displacement in order to survive and sustain the livelihood pattern to give security to the family, whereas the tribal men tend to see it as an exchange on fair or unfair terms of property owned by them.

Why do we often see women at the forefront of struggles against forced displacement? Women's realms especially in the non-monetized tribal societies, more than men's, are largely located in non-market relationships. This perhaps allows them to understand certain things better than men, such as, soil erosion, destruction of greeneries, shortage of food, fodder, portable water, and so on. For example, when Bhutia tribal women of Chipko Movement (1972–1978) protested against the felling of the trees, the men opposed them because the men were employed to cut the trees. The men not only opposed them in fear of losing their jobs but also for the fear of not being provided with jobs in the army since the women compelled the government to retreat. But participating in struggle exposes women to state oppression and biases in ways never encountered before. They have been the victims of state-sponsored rape and abuse.[92] *'Mati Devata, Dharam Devata'*—the soil is our Goddess; it is our religion.' These are the words of adivasi women of the 'Save Gandmardhan' movement, as they embraced the earth while being dragged away by the police from the blockade sites in the Gandmardhan Hills in Odisha. The forests of Gandmardhan are a source of rich plant diversity and water resources. It would be desecrated by the Bharat Aluminium Company (BALCO) to mine for bauxite.

Although knowledge about the overall impacts of displacement has exploded in the last two decades, the gendered dimensions of displacement have so far remained a neglected area in resettlement research. The first step towards resettlement is social impact assessment (SIA) that usually is undertaken at the beginning of the project to identify project impact. The second step is compensation. Generally tribal women do not have ownership of or control over land, though they may often be its prime users. They are therefore not compensated for the loss of land. Even if substantial land is often worked, owned and inherited by the women in many cases, compensation is provided to the head of the family, almost invariably a man.[93] Though it accepts the claim of an 'unmarried adult son' to be treated as a separate family for the purposes of compensation, this definition makes no similar provisions for unmarried adult daughters, and leaves divorced, deserted and widowed women out forcing them into dependency upon male relatives.[94] The selection of the resettlement site affects women because tribal identity can be at stake if the new area is physically, climatically, socially and culturally completely different from their own. Reconstructing livelihoods after relocation is the final step. This is particularly problematic for the tribal women because of their dependence on CPRs and they lack legal titles (*patta*) to these resources. As a result, the acquiring agencies give preference to the CPRs, which provide tribal women with a major source of their earnings, and do not compensate for their losses.[95]

A job per displaced family is a scheme which has recently been proposed by many industrialists. But it has many serious shortcomings especially when its application is extended to the tribals. First, only one job per family is given when in fact the family often has several adults and that is bound to lead to conflicts within the family. Second, land records are not brought up to date. Third, almost all the jobs the Displaced Peoples (DPs) are given are of the unskilled variety, oftener than not temporary in nature since a large number of tribals are illiterate and do not have the technical skills or training required by the project. The NALCO unit of Damanjodi is among the few to give semi-skilled jobs to a few tribal men because a voluntary agency trained them in some skills. Even in this case no woman got a job.[96] In the Jagannathpur mines of Talcher in Odisha and the Piparwar mines of Palamau in Jharkhand, a family is entitled to a job for every 3 acres of land lost. Later the Piparwar mines reduced it to 2 acres for providing a job if the claimant had completed matriculation.[97]

Among the tribals even boys cannot hope to get technical training, women's situation is worse. If cash compensation is paid in lump sums to oustees, then that is without any advice on proper investment or help in channelizing it. The deprivation is more intense. After the enforcement of The Provisions of Panchayats (Extension to Scheduled Areas) Act (PESA) 1996, it is now compulsory for the government to consult the gram sabhas. But my experience says that in many adivasi villages, people do not even have knowledge of PESA to be able to demand decision-making rights. In recent land acquisition process pursued by Sterlite Industries in Lanjigarh, Odisha, we found that women were never consulted. Since negotiations did not succeed in addressing gender issues, adivasi women opposed with strong determination new projects whether in Kasipur (Odisha) where Utkal Alumina Plant has been proposed, Rayagada (Odisha) where L & T, JK Paper Mills and other industries are located, Nimmalapadu and Chintapalli (Andhra Pradesh) where calcite and bauxite mining is proposed, or Nagarnar (Chhattisgarh), where adivasis are opposing the Steel Plant of NMDC. Moreover, mining activities have a particularly negative impact on adivasi women's livelihood security, employment opportunities and rights. For example, the tribals in Odisha displaced by NALCO were forced to migrate across state borders in Andhra Pradesh and are living as 'illegal encroachers' on forest lands.[98] In the Upper Indravati Power Project, Odisha, a study of gender-specific issues revealed that tribal women, in particular, were seriously affected. Their displacement led to reversal in their socio-economic autonomy and status. These were formerly linked to forest-based, non-market economic activities. The dislocation of their communities, their resettlement and the flow of cash for compensation and rehabilitation into the hands of men, has left women with diminished control over resources.[99] Several landowning families affected by the Upper Indravati Project and resettled in Panasduka have been reduced to daily wage earners because of an inadequate rehabilitation package, compensation and soaring land price. While these families were landowners prior to their displacement, and at present, women from most of these families earn a living by cutting stones. They earn ₹7 for a small container of stone chips that they cut. Pregnant women and children are exposed to health hazards, as they inhale the dust and small particles that are produced while chipping stones in the quarry. One of these women said, 'With no other option left we have adopted this kind of work and life'.[100]

The similar situation prevails in Mahanadi coalfields (Odisha), Coal India mines of Jharkhand, Western Coalfields of Maharashtra, the bauxite mines of Damanjodi (South Odisha), the Singareni coalfields (Andhra Pradesh), and so on. The cash flow to which tribal women had access, from the sale of forest produce and raising livestock, has diminished. Instead these women are forced to migrate to the cities, serve as domestic maids in the township, casual construction labourers, petty traders and hawkers, and commercial sex workers (hitherto unheard of in tribal communities). They work with toxic and hazardous substances without any access to safety measures in the construction and mining sites with low wages, no paid holidays during pregnancy or any worksite facilities like toilets are provided to them. The impact of industrial displacement has thus meant a complete transformation and degradation in both the economic and social status of tribal women.

From 1951 to 1995, development projects in Odisha displaced and affected an estimated 1,500,000 people—42 per cent of whom were tribals. While only 32 per cent of the total number of displaced were resettled, this rate falls to 25 per cent among tribal populations and women are the hardest hit.[101]

VOLUNTARY VERSUS INVOLUNTARY DISPLACEMENT

Tribal migration challenges assumptions about the 'voluntary' character of migration and the involuntary character of displacement. I argue that this 'willingness' to be displaced stems from the structural dilemmas that confront poor tribal migrants in the cities, who are systematically denied access to secure employment and legal housing and who are resisting displacement and forging alternative solutions to their predicament. Categorizing displacement into 'voluntary *vs.* involuntary' might be too simplistic in understanding the process at work. More often than not, the 'voluntariness' of the displaced people is questionable as people are forced to shift due to factors over which they have no control. Thus the focus is on a reconceptualization of the nature of displacement (see Table 1.2).

Table 1.2 Displacement by Some of Odisha's Biggest Dams, Mines and Factories

	Estimated no. of villages displaced	Families	Persons
Hirakud Dam	285	22,144	180,000
Rengali Dam plus irrigation	287	11,725	
Upper Indravati Dam	99	5,301	40,000+
Balimela Dam (Illustration 22)	91	2,000	60,000
3 Subarnarekha Dams	75	5,214	
Upper Kolab Dam	49	3,179	14,000
Khadkei	36		
Lower Sukhtel Dam	32		
Ib Dam	29	3,092	
Ong Dam	29		
Lower Indravati Dam	25	1,462	
Ramial Dam	22		
Pilasalkhi Dam (near Phulbani)	17		
Ranupur Dam	16	1,634	
Talcher Coal Mines	61	1,790	
T.S. Thermal Power, Kaniha	53	1,940	
Rourkela steel plant	30 [64]	2,367	[23,000]
Ib Valley Coal Mines	18	1,353	
Nalco smelter, Angul	40	3,997	
Nalco refinery, Damanjodi	19	788	3,000

Source: Felix Padel and Samarendra Das, 2010. *Out of this Earth: East India Adivasis and the Aluminium Cartel* (New Delhi: Orient Blackswan): 354.

There was hardly any attempt to mitigate the trauma and profound injustice of displacement. Instead the government has often denied recognizing their rights by terming them as 'illegal encroachers' or 'people out of place'. So, we should re-examine *the politics of recognition* within the displacement debate. The debate on displacement has worked with an uncritical understanding of displacement as an 'involuntary' process. Anthropologist Liisa Malkki notes that 'people have always moved—whether through desire or through violence'.[102] Yet desire and violence are sometimes hard to disentangle, because one 'big' displacement is followed by a series of small but continuous displacements. This makes it difficult to classify displacement strictly as 'voluntary' or 'involuntary', as what appears to be voluntary, when seen in a historical context, may be involuntary—the only choice in a situation of limited opportunities.[103]

Now, what is the objective that compensation is meant to achieve? Dev Nathan holds that, in a normal, voluntary sale of land, it is sufficient (fair) if the seller receives the market price of land. But dispossession is an involuntary sale of land. Land in this case represents to the unwilling seller not its price as land, but a source of livelihood.[104] But the forced destruction of traditional ways of producing and living brought about by involuntary displacement brings to the fore the question: should indigenous peoples have the right of refusal? The right of refusal is closely connected to another point: the right of refusal is necessary for indigenous peoples to bargain for a better deal, one that allows for a reconstruction of their livelihoods in an equal if not improved position. The bargaining position of indigenous communities, however, is weakened by invoking the principle of eminent domain.

As Ranabir Samaddar points out, the rational choice framework informing migration studies that is able to clearly categorize the reasons for migration into the binary of 'push' and 'pull' factors, and thus distinguish between voluntary and forced migration, fails to do justice to the complex play of subjectivity that informs 'choice'.[105] When the decision to move is throughout informed by the paucity of affordable housing (read land) close to one's place of work, and by the overwhelming threat of state repression if tribals were to resist, can the process be termed 'voluntary' resettlement? This lack of meaningful choices makes the displaced tribal migrants to protest against several industrial and mining projects all over India. The process of land acquisition and resettlement take years to complete, but the population are deprived of livelihood activities and basic infrastructure in the interim.

In Dumka district of Jharkhand, Santhals are the major tribes comprising 40 per cent of the population of the district. Here displacement had a lot of implications on gender roles and spaces. The Masanjore Dam, built in 1955–1956 with Canadian assistance on the river Mayurakshi, displaced 144 villages in Dumka district. When the notification for displacement was first issued, all adivasis were promised 'land for land'. They were brought in trucks to the new locations and allowed to choose their new home site. The total value of the land holding in their original village was calculated on the basis of the quality of land: thus *dhani* 1 was valued at ₹2,200/acre, *dhani* 2 at ₹1,600/acre, *dhani* 3 at ₹1,300/acre, *bari* 1 at ₹800 per acre and *bari* 2 at ₹500/acre.[106] The entire land at the new site, however, was accessed as being *dhani* 2 and valued at ₹1,600/acre. As a result, the total land that the displaced people received in the resettlement village was much less than their previous holdings. Apart from the loss in total holdings, such classification has also had specific gendered implications. Previously, dhani or paddy growing land was seen to be under men's control. In contrast, women's rights of use over *bari* or homestead land were clearly recognized. Now, bari no longer exists as a category, so women's rights to land have been wiped out without any compensation. So, the lands allotted to the Santhals were uncultivable wastelands. They were not given a choice, but had to accept this land.[107]

Resettlement and Rehabilitation packages tend to treat both individuals and households as autonomous units, with a clearly identifiable set of interests, and thus fail to take account of their embeddedness in a network of social relations. The sudden movement reduces the possibility for tribal women to negotiate their traditional rights within the 'rehabilitation package'. The World Bank Resettlement Policy Draft of 2001 (December) covers only 'involuntary', and not voluntary, resettlement. As a result, voluntary resettlement financed by the Bank lacks any procedural or substantive policy requirements.[108] Thus the draft introduced a perverse incentive for project planners to characterise projects as 'voluntary' and thereby avoid the social safeguards that are at the core of the involuntary resettlement policy. In this way project affected people are required by the authorities to give their 'consent' to resettlement in order to receive benefits. Their 'consent' would, in turn, remove their rights to protection under World Bank policy.

Colonialism and capitalism transformed land and soil from being a source of life and a commons from which people draw sustenance, into private property to be bought and sold and conquered; development continued colonialism's unfinished task. Peter Berger has described development as the 'spreading condition of homelessness'.[109] The creation of homelessness takes place both through the ecological destruction of the 'home' and the cultural and spiritual uprooting of peoples from their homes. In this way organic communities give away to slum dwellers or urban and industrial jungles. dams leave behind wastelands and uprooted people. This was an essential part of colonialism then and of development now. The famous Odisha poet Brajnath Rai writes:

> Miles of cocoa
> and cashew plantation,
> countless, luxuriant

> betel-vines
> draw green artistic designs
> on the carpet of brown sand.
> ....
> infused into hearts
> of working people
> an eternal hope to live.
> But, today, suddenly,
> covetous eyes of a power-mad hunter
> has fallen on your green body
> To cut it to pieces,
> to drink to heart's content
> fresh red blood.[110]

In a specific context, at a point in time, sudden mass displacement is indeed traumatic, while in the long run, the impact of the gradual displacement may be as severe, as the alienation of tribal lands has led to the occupational displacement as well. This has undermined the economic role of adivasi women in the forest-based economy. R and R policies have not paid cognizance to the crucial factor of paying compensation to the adivasi women for the loss of their income earned through the collection of the minor forest produces. The role of the adivasi women in the forest-based economy has been overlooked totally by policy makers and increased their dependence on their menfolk. The long-term impacts on women can be highly damaging. In fine, the categories like 'voluntary' and 'involuntary' are increasingly blurred in a globalizing world, wherein the process of forced displacement and migration are accelerated.

NOTES

1. Engels, *Origin of the Family, Private Property and the State*: 82.
2. The pre-class society was organized into tribes. There are still visible remnants of tribal society in India as among the Munda, Oraon, Bhil, Toda, Kadar, and Santhal tribes. E. Sreedharan, 2007. *A Manual of Historical Research Methodology* (Kerala: The Centre for South Indian Studies): 35.

3. Vinita Damodaran, 2007. 'Tribes in Indian History', in *Situating Environmental History*, edited by Ranjan Chakrabarty (New Delhi: Manohar): 127–57.
4. Ramchandra Guha, *Savaging the Civilised*: 123.
5. V. Elwin, *Aboriginals*: 29.
6. Ghurye, *Aboriginals So-Called and Their Future*.
7. The famous ecological romanticists are William Wordsworth, John Ruskin, Wiiliam Blake, Coleridge, Shelley, Keats, and so on.
8. M. Assadi, 2004. 'Karnataka: Forest Encroachments, Left Adventurism and Hindutva', *Economic & Political Weekly* (henceforth *EPW*) (28 February): 885.
9. Govinda Chandra Rath, ed., 2006. 'Introduction', in *Tribal Development in India: The Contemporary Debate* (New Delhi: SAGE): 38.
10. Archana Prasad, *Against Ecological Romanticism:* 108–09.
11. D.D. Kosambi, 2002. 'On the Origin of Brahmin Gotras', in *Combined Methods in Indology and Other Writings*, edited by D. Chattopadhyay (New Delhi: Oxford University Press): 98–188.
12. Kosambi, *Culture and Civilization of Ancient India*: 172.
13. G.S. Ghurye, 1992. 'Features of the Caste System', in *Social Stratification in India*, edited by Dipankar Gupta (New Delhi: Oxford University Press).
14. Dev Nathan and Govind Kelkar, eds. 1997. *From Tribe to Caste* (Shimla: Indian Institute of Advanced Study): 2.
15. M.G.S. Narayanan has coined this term in preference to the earlier used terms, like 'Aryanization' or 'Sanskritization'. While he has used this term with reference to the secondary caste formation in South India, the use of this term can well be extended to the process of primary caste formation in North India too.
16. Béteille, 1974. 'Tribe and Peasantry', in *Six Essays*.
17. André Béteille, 1998. 'The Idea of Indigenous People', *Current Anthropology* 39, 2: 187–91.
18. Crispin Bates, 1994. 'Lost Innocents and the Loss of Innocence: Interpreting Adivasi Movements in South Asia', in *Indigenous Peoples of Asia* edited by R. Barnes, A. Gray, and B. Kingsbury (Ann Arbor, Mi: Association for Asian Studies): 119.
19. Sumita Saha and Nilanjan Goswami, 2013. 'Religious Life and Belief System of the Santals—A Case Study in Solageria Village', *Man in India*, 93 (2–3): 313–32.
20. K.S. Singh, 1993. 'Hinduism and Tribal Religion: An Anthropological Perspective', *Man in India* 73, 1 (March): 1–16.
21. Sumit Sarkar, 'The Decline of the Subalterns', in *Writing Social History*: 88.
22. S. Das Gupta and Raj Sekhar Basu, eds., 'Introduction', in *Narratives from the Margins*: 6.

23. Peter Berger, 2002. 'The Gadaba and the 'Non-ST' Desia of Koraput, Odisha', *Contemporary Society: Concept of Tribal Society*, edited by George Pfeffer and Deepak Kumar Behera, vol. 5 (New Delhi: Concept Publishing): 69–71.
24. Nirmal Kumar Chandra, 2008 'Concept of Tribe in the Draft National Tribal Policy' *EPW* (13–19 December): 29–35.
25. Bhupinder Singh, 1990. 'Between Two Worlds, Five Ancient Tribal Groups of Andaman and Nicobar Islands', in *Tribal Transformation in India*, edited by Buddhadeb Chowdhury (vol. 1: Economy and Agrarian Issues) (New Delhi: Inter-India Publications).
26. D.D. Kosambi, 1955. 'The Basis of Ancient Indian History', *Journal of the American Oriental Society* 75; reprinted in B.D. Chattopadhyay. ed., *Combined Methods in Indology* (New Delhi: Oxford University Press): 308.
27. D.D. Kosambi, 1967. 'Living Prehistory in India', *Scientific American* (February); reprinted in B.D. Chattopadhyay, ed., *Combined Methods in Indology* (New Delhi: Oxford University Press): 30.
28. Shereen Ratnagar, 2008. 'Kosambi's Archaeology', *EPW* (July 26): 71–77.
29. Partha Chatterjee, 2008. 'Democracy and Economic Transformation in India', *EPW* (April 19–25): 53–62.
30. Planning Commission, 1981. *Report on the Development of Tribal Areas* (Sivaraman Committee), National Committee on the Development of Backward Areas, Government of India, New Delhi.
31. Mihir Shah, D. Banerji, P.S. Vijay Shankar and P. Ambasta, *India's Drylands*.
32. Mihir Shah, 2008. 'Structures of Power in Indian Society: A Response', *EPW* (15–21 November): 78–83.
33. Morris Godelier, 1978. *Perspectives in Marxist Anthropology* (London: Cambridge University Press): 71.
34. Susan B.C. Devalle, 1992. *Discourses of Ethnicity: Culture and Protest in Jharkhand* (New Delhi: SAGE).
35. Pathy, *Anthropology of Development*: 46.
36. Niharranjan Ray, 1972. 'Introductory Address', in *The Tribal Situation in India*, edited by K.S. Singh (Shimla: Indian Institute of Advanced Study): 21–22; Devalle, *Discourses of Ethnicity*: 50.
37. Sumit Guha, *Environment and Ethnicity*: 2–5.
38. Sanjukta Das Gupta, *Adivasis and the Raj*: 9.
39. I borrow this concept from B.B. Chaudhuri, 1994. 'The Myth of the Tribe? The Question Reconsidered', *Calcutta Historical Journal* 16, 1: 152; Vinita Damodaran, 2006. 'Colonial Constructions of the 'Tribe' in India: The Case of Chotanagpur', *Indian Historical Review* 33, 1: 44–75.

40   Asoka Kumar Sen, 2003. 'Conceptualization of the Hos of Singhbhum as a Tribe', in *Changing Tribal Life: A Socio-Philosophical Perspective*, edited by Padmaja Sen (New Delhi: Concept Publishing): 2.
41   Crispin Bates, 'Lost Innocents and the Loss of Innocence': 109–19.
42   Yogesh Atal, 2010. 'Anthropology in the Twenty-First Century: Need for Re-Orientation and Fresh Perspectives', in *Tribal Economy Crossroads*, edited by S.N. Chaudhary (New Delhi: Rawat): 33–54.
43   M. Bhadra, 2004. 'Status of Scheduled Caste Women: A Case Study of the Rajbansis of West Bengal', *Man in India* 84, 3–4: 285–301.
44   Swatahsiddha Sarkar, 2014. 'Tribal Detour in Darjeeling Hills', *EPW* 49, 32 (August 9): 25–26.
45   Sunil Kumar, *Tribal and Indian Society*: 28.
46   Claude Levi-Strauss, 1987. *Anthropology and Myth, Lectures 1951–1982* (Oxford: Basil Blackwell).
47   Gail Omvedt, 2000. 'Unfair Label', *The Hindu*, Sunday, February 13; David Hardiman, 1987. *The Coming of the Devi: Adivasi Assertion in Western India* (New Delhi: Oxford University Press): 13.
48   Morris Godelier, 1978. *Perspectives in Marxist Anthropology* (London: Cambridge University Press): 72.
49   Arthur Mawick, 2001. *The New Nature of History* (London: Palgrave): 217.
50   Manoshi Mitra, *Women and Class Struggle*: 55–56.
51   Ranajit Guha, *Elementary Aspects of Peasant Insurgency*: 132.
52   S.C. Roy, *The Mundas and Their Country*: 330–31.
53   K.S. Singh, *Birsa Munda and His Movement*: 163–64.
54   Custers, *Women in the Tebhaga Uprising*: 131–34.
55   Vasanth Kannabiran and K. Lalitha. 1989. 'That Magic Time: Women in the Telangana People's Struggle', in *Recasting Women: Essays in Colonial History*, edited by Kumkum Sangari and Sudesh Vaid (Delhi: Kali for Women): 188.
56   The Srikakulam peasant uprising occurred in 1967–1970, in regions of Srikakulam district, Andhra Pradesh. The Naxalbari movement of 1967 inspired the upsurge.
57   A few years ago when Amlasole hit the frontage of the media as the epicentre of starvation deaths in West Bengal, the Chief Minister admitted that 'Amlasole is not an isolated incident', *Times of India*, 8 July 2004.
58   On 2 November 2008, the West Bengal Chief Minister Buddhadev Bhattacharjee and the Central Iron and Steel Minister Ram Vilas Paswan went to Salboni to inaugurate the Special Economic Zone complex of the Jindal industrial house along with a huge police convoy. On their way back, there was a landmine explosion when the convoy of the Union minister was passing, as a result of which a police car was hit and some policemen were injured. Sometime before

the explosion, the convoy of the Chief Minister had passed away. Suspecting the incident as Maoist activity, the police and the CRPF unleashed a reign of terror in 35 villages encompassing the entire tribal belt of Lalgarh. They attacked and beat up the adivasi women. The people of Lalgarh launched a resistance movement against these atrocities and formed their own organization *Pulishi Santrash Birodhi Janasadharaner Committee* or PSBJC, i.e., People's Committee Against Police Atrocities or PCPA. Adivasi women had equal participation in the organization and led the movement in its initial phase. The movement was brutally suppressed by 2010. For more details see Amit Bhattacharyya *Singur to Lalgarh via Nandigram*.

59 'Adivasi in India', March 2010. *Update Series 18* (Kolkata: Update Publications): 33–34.

60 Anonymous and undated, *Fact Finding Report on 'Lalgarh: Paschimbanger Adivasi'* (Kolkata: Nagarik Mancha): 1–3; see also Subhendu Dasgupta and Sujato, *Operation Green Hunt*: 9.

61 Malabika Das Gupta, 2002. 'Objective Function in Economic Models of Decisions on Production: Evidence from Swiddeners in Tripura', *EPW* 37, 34 (August 24): 3559.

62 Arjun Appadurai, 2004. 'The Capacity to Aspire: Culture and the Terms of Recognition', in *Culture and Public Action*, edited by Vijayedra Rao and Michael Walton (Palo Alto: Stanford University Press).

63 Dev Nathan. 2005. 'Capabilities and Aspirations', *EPW* (January 1): 36–40.

64 Vijayedra Rao and Michael Walton, eds. 2004. 'Culture and Public Action: Rationality, Equality of Agency and Development', in *Culture and Public Action* (Palo Alto: Stanford University Press).

65 Dipak Bara Panda, 2008. *Amlasholer Janajati Shabar Ar ek Arambher Suchana* (Kolkata: Durbar Prakashani): 47–50, 61.

66 For a detailed discussion on the demands and appeals of the adivasi men and women of Lalgarh see the letters of PCAPA published 2011. *Rashtriya Santrash—Naxalbari Theke Netaigram*, edited by Swapan Kanti Ghose and Madhumay Pal (Kolkata: Padatik).

67 On the night of 30 June 2010, joint forces attacked the Sonamukhi village and seven housewives were brutally raped and many others were molested.

68 Sanhati, 2013. *Letters from Lalgarh: The Complete Collection of letters from the People's Committee against Police Atrocities*, edited and translated by Sanhati, Kolkata: www.sanhati.com and Setu Prakashani): 2, 116–17.

69 For details see Amit Bhattacharyya, 2010. 'Is Lalgarh Showing the Way? *EPW* 45, 2 (Jan 9): 17–21.

70 Amarendra Das and Samarendra, 2005. *Wira Pdika or Matiro Poko Company Loko* (Earth Worm, Company Man, in Kui/Odia with

English subtitles), available from sdasorisa@hotmail.co.uk accessed on 21 August 2013.
71. H.H. Rivers, [1906] 1973. *The Todas* (London: Macmillan).
72. Dalton, *Descriptive Ethnography of Bengal*.
73. Grigson, *The Maria Gonds of Bastar*.
74. Elwin, 'Tribal Women', in *Indian Women*, Devaki Jain, ed: 205–13.
75. Furer-Haimendorf, *Chenchus*.
76. Elwin, *Nagaland*: 104.
77. Elwin, *Baigas*, 235–36.
78. Furer-Haimendorf, *Naked Nagas*: 101.
79. Hutton, *Sema Nagas*.
80. Hunter, *Orissa*.
81. K. Mann, 1987. 'Is Matriliny a Symbol of Higher Status? A Case of Garo Women', *Man in India*, 67, 1 (March): 36–46; Firth, *Human Types*; G. Menon, 1995. 'The Impact of Migration on the Work and Tribal Women's Status', in *Women and Seasonal Labour Migration*, edited by L. Schenken-Sandbergen (New Delhi: SAGE): 110; Sachchidananda, 1978. 'Social Structure, Status and Mobility Patterns: The Case of Tribal Women', *Man in India* 58, 1.
82. Dev Nathan, 1988. 'Significance of Women's Position in Tribal Society', *EPW* (June 25): 1311–12.
83. Boserup, *Woman's Role in Economic Development*.
84. Walter Fernandes, ed. 1993. 'Transfer of Resources, Migration and the Impact of Sanskritisation on Tribal Women'. in *The Indigenous Question: Search for an Identity* (New Delhi: Indian Social Institute): 84.
85. CPR includes all such resources that are meant for common use of the villagers, such as, village pastures and grazing grounds, village forest and woodlots, protected government forests, waste lands, common threshing grounds, watersheds drainage, ponds, tanks, rivers, rivulets, water reservoirs, canals and irrigation channels. With the extension of state control over these resources and the resultant decay of community management system, CPRs available to the villagers declined substantially over the years. Today, in almost all parts of the country, the villagers have a legal right of access only on some specific categories of land and water resources.
86. Walter Fernandes, 2006. 'Development-induced-Displacement and Tribal Women', in *Tribal Development in India: The Contemporary Debate*, edited by Govinda Chandra Rath (New Delhi: SAGE): 122–23.
87. Ravindran Latha and Babita Mahapatra, 2009. 'Gender Issues in Displacement: A Study of Irrigation Projects in Southern Orissa', in *Beyond Relocation: The Imperative of Sustainable Resettlement*, edited by Renu Modi (New Delhi: SAGE): 240–68.
88. Fernandes and Menon, *Tribal Women and Forest Economy*: 121.

89 Muzaffar Assadi, 2011. 'Ethnic Groups/Tribals in the Midst of Policy Transfer: Displacement, Rehabilitation and Governance in India—A Critique', *Contemporary Anthropology*, edited by Nanjunda D.C. (New Delhi: Discovering Publishing House): 10–11.
90 Arundhati Roy, 1999. 'The Greater Common Good', *Frontline*, 16, 11 (22 May–4 June).
91 M.M. Cernea, 1997. 'The Risks and Reconstruction Model for Resettling Displaced Populations', *World Development* 25, 10: 1569–88; and also see M.M. Cernea and C. McDowell 'Risks, Safeguards, and Reconstruction'.
92 Ramkuwar, 2009. 'We will Never Forgive the Government—A Personal Testimony', in *Displaced by Development: Confronting Marginalisation and Gender Injustice*, edited by Lyla Mehta (New Delhi: SAGE): 271–81.
93 Biswaranjan Mohanty, 2005. 'Displacement and Rehabilitation of Tribals', *EPW* (March 26): 1318–20; Government of India (GoI), 2006. *Draft National Rehabilitation Policy*, para 3(1) (J).
94 S. Singh, 2006. 'Displacement and Rehabilitation: A Comparison of Two Policy Drafts', *EPW* 41, 52: 5307.
95 Fernandes, Walter and M. Asif (1997) *Development-Induced-Displacement in Odisha 1951–1995: A Database on Its Extent and Nature*, New Delhi: Indian Social Institute: 84; Fernandes, and Raj, 1992. *Development, Displacement and Rehabilitation*: 92.
96 Fernandes, 2006. 'Development-induced-Displacement and Tribal Women', in Govinda Chandra Rath ed., *Tribal Development in India*: 116.
97 Sherman, *People's Story: A Report*.
98 S.M. Patnaik, 2000. 'Understanding Involuntary Resettlement: An Anthropological Perspective', *The Eastern Anthropologist* 53, 1 & 2: 146.
99 World Bank, 1995. *The World Bank and Gender in India:* 19–20.
100 Ravindran and Mahapatra, 'Gender Issues in Displacement': 251.
101 Walter Fernandes, 2001. 'Development Induced Displacement and Sustainable Development', *Social Change* 31, 1 & 2: 91; Government of Odisha (GoO), 2006. *Draft Odisha Resettlement and Rehabilitation Policy* (Revenue Department): para 6.
102 L. Malkki, 1992. 'National Geographic: The Rooting of Peoples and the Territorialisation of National Identity among Scholars and Refugees', *Cultural Anthropology* 7, 1: 24–44.
103 Amit Mitra and Nitya Rao, 2009. 'Displacing Gender from Displacement: the Santal Parganas, Jharkhand', in Lyla Mehta ed., *Displaced by Development*: 34–58.
104 Dev Nathan, 2009. 'Social Security, Compensation and Reconstruction of Livelihoods', *EPW* 44, 30 (July 25): 22–26.

105 Samaddar, ed., 'Still They Come: Migrants in Post-Partition Bengal', in *Reflection on Partition in the East*.
106 Land of five qualities is recorded in the land settlement records: *dhani* 1 refers to lowlands suitable for paddy cultivation, often irrigated; *dhani* 2 refers to medium quality paddy lands; *dhani* 3 refers to uplands that can be used for rain fed paddy; *bari* 1 refers to homestead plots and *bari* 2 to more distant homestead plots, often wastelands, used for tree crop cultivation.
107 Mitra and Rao, 'Displacing Gender from Displacement: the Santal Parganas, Jharkhand', Lyla Mehta, ed., *Displaced by Development*: 34–58.
108 World Bank, Environment Department (2001) *Involuntary Resettlement, Draft Operational Policy* 4.12. available at http://www.ciel.org/Publications/redlineresettle.pdf, accessed on 7 April 2012.
109 Peter Berger, Brigitte Berger and Hansfried Kellner, 1974. *The Homeless Mind: Modernization and Consciousness* (New York: Vintage Books).
110 Mies and Shiva, 2010. *Ecofeminism*: 101–02.

CHAPTER 2

Changing Livelihood Pattern of Adivasi Women in West Bengal

THE FIRST PRIME Minister of India, Jawaharlal Nehru, once said that 'in the tribal people, I have found many qualities which I miss in the people of plains, cities and other parts of India. It was these very qualities that attracted me.'[1]

Compared to other categories, incidence of poverty is high (53%) in tribal populations and literacy is the lowest (16.35%). Realizing these inequalities, the constitution has provided certain privileges to the tribals under Article 275. Development is a complex concept encompassing upward qualitative and quantitative changes in the base and superstructure of any society.[2] Does adivasi economy mean forest economy? How do we relate the needs and interests of tribal women to the overall development perspective? What are the social constraints that prohibit tribal women from taking appropriate advantage of any developmental projects?

The question of the development of tribal women is also closely linked to this general debate over status of dependency of women and their exclusion from the mainstream development matrix. The tribal economy is forest economy. The tribals rarely follow one occupation exclusively; about 90 per cent of the tribal population depend on cultivation, including shifting hill cultivation, as landowners or as agricultural labour. L.P. Vidyarthi has classified the basic economic activities of the tribals: *(i)* food gathering including hunting and fishing; *(ii)* pastoral; *(iii)* shifting hill cultivation; *(iv)* settled cultivation; *(v)* handicrafts; *(vi)* trade and commerce; *(vii)* labour-work including agricultural and industrial.[3]

Tribal women are not economically homogeneous. This distinctiveness is quite evident in the four states and we will discuss this in detail. Studies show that in the predominantly urban areas tribal sex ratio is lower than that of the total population because their urban presence is mainly through single male migration; 92,916 (4.97%) tribal women were urbanized in 1991 against 103,396 (5.33%) men.[4] Their urbanization continues to be low in 2001.[5] Their lower sex ratio in the urban areas is one of many indications that the status of tribal women declines with modernization. It is true also in states like Odisha, Chhattisgarh and the Northeast.[6]

The majority of the adivasis in the country depend upon agriculture for livelihood. With the introduction of market economy and the monetization of exchange relations in the adivasi areas, they are forced into degraded land resources and subsist with low productivity and low investment. The introduction of cash crops indebted them and widened the class differences among the tribals. Several traders from far-off places have now settled in adivasi areas where cash crops are cultivated, to the great disadvantage of the adivasis. They get further marginalized as the liberalization policy of the government tries to link their lives with international market. The Government of India claims that they have introduced several schemes like Integrated Rural Development Programme (IRDP), Mahila Samriddhi Yojana, and so on, to inculcate the habit of thrift and to operationalize Development of Women and Children in Rural Areas (DWACRA), Jawahar Rozgar Yojana (JRY), Employment Assurance Schemes (EAS), Prime Minister's Rozgar Yojana (PMRY), and other such schemes to provide employment opportunities to rural and tribal folk, but have not been able to improve the availability of work during the post-liberalization period. The government has introduced several schemes including Large-size Adivasi Multipurpose Co-operative Societies (LAMPS), Primary Agriculture Society (PAC) and others that do not benefit the adivasi women in the way originally envisaged. The sectors in which they have an advantage (such as fishing, plate-making, mat-making, rope-making, poultry, beekeeping) have never been studied properly by scholars and policy makers to suggest policy recommendations. Data presented show that the flow of funds for the adivasi sub-plan has been declining after 1991.[7]

Racially, linguistically and culturally these tribals may be categorized into two broad groups—the plain tribes and the hill tribes residing in the Himalayan and sub-Himalayan regions. The tribes living in the plains belong to the Pre-Dravidian or Proto-Austroloid racial stock. The Santhal, Oraon, Munda, Mal, Bhumij, Lodha, Kora, Birhor, and some others come under this category. The languages that they speak belong to the Austric-Dravidian family of languages. Most of them migrated from the neighbouring states of Bihar and Odisha and settled in the districts of Medinipur, Purulia, Bankura and Birbhum. The tribal groups of the hilly regions of north Bengal (Darjeeling, Jalpaiguri, Dakshin and Uttar Dinajpur) belong to the Mongoloid racial stock. The dialects of the Lepchas and Bhutias belong to the Tibeto-Chinese family of the Tibeto-Himalayan group. The dialects of the Mechs, Garos and Rabhas belong to the Assam-Burmese group and the dialects of the Chakmas, Hajangs, Maghs belong to the Assam group. Majority of these communities have migrated from Sikkim, Bhutan, Assam and Nepal. Matrilineal system still exists among the Rabhas.[8]

The Santhals are the only community which can be called 'very large', covering more than 50 per cent of the total tribal population of the state. It is also most advanced among the tribes. The Oraon community, which forms more than 14 per cent of the state's tribal population, can be termed as a 'large' community. Two other communities, Bhumij and Munda, may be categorized as 'medium-sized'. Under the 'small' sized communities there are the Koras, Lodhas, Kherias, Mahalis, Bhutias and Sabars. Three tribal communities in the state are nearly extinct: Bihors of Bagmundi of Purulia district (its present population is 333), Totos of Totopara of Jalpaiguri (with a population of 1,391) and Lodhas of West Medinipur (according to the Lodha census of 2003 its present population is 60,136). With the exception of a very few gatherers, most tribes in West Bengal grow crops, some are craftsmen and others are labourers in collieries, industries and tea plantations. Only a very small number are engaged in trade, commerce and other services.

Tribal societies are generally economically undifferentiated and tribals practise little specialization: Those undertaking farming—settled or slash-and-burn—are involved also in other subsidiary occupations like animal husbandry, wage labour handicrafts, gathering of food and forest produce. Except for ploughing, which is essentially a male job, in all other agricultural operations, the females participate and traditionally, these are part of a female's job and thus the participation of tribal women is more than the men in terms of different operations in major economic activity.[9] Tribal women at the same time also carry out all the household chores. The role of tribal women in minor forest produce component is 60 per cent of the total tribal household income budget has not been precisely evaluated, but observers see it as preponderant.[10]

ADIVASI WOMEN IN AGRICULTURAL SECTOR
Khanpur of West Dinajpur

Khanpur is 14 km away from the district headquarters, Balurghat, West Dinajpur district, to which it is well connected by bus. There is regular bi-weekly market in the village. There is a high school, a primary school and a non-formal female adult education centre in the village. There are 13 castes, one tribal, Santhals, and one Muslim community in the village. Santhals were a part of the large-scale immigration which was taking place in this district in the mid-nineteenth century. Women joined the Tebhaga movement. They took the lead in propaganda work, and often led the men in the fight, facing the hirelings of the jotedars.[11] Seventeen sharecroppers were killed in police firing amongst them two were women—Josodha Burmani and Kaushalya Kamini and injured hundreds.[12] The Tebhaga movement continued from November 1946 to February 1947. In its last phase when Kisan Sabha retreated from the movement the women took up the leadership.[13] According to Charu Majumdar, 'The participant peasants in this movement numbered about six million'.[14] Rani Dasgupta, the women organizer of Dinajpur, said that not only in Hindu-Muslim unity movements but in any phase of national freedom struggle it was not possible to eradicate social discrimination between the caste Hindus, Rajbansi, Kshatriya, Namasudra, Mahishya, and the Santhal, Kol, Munda, Oraon. Tebhaga movement removed the distance.[15]

There were initially two types of Santhal female workers in the village: betisol khet majur (female casual worker) and betisol chuktidar (female contract workers). Betisol khet majur consists of two categories. The dadonee (one who took a loan) came under the 'beck and call relationships' with the landowners. In the lean agricultural seasons the female agricultural labourers took advance loans (dadan) from the landowners with the oral promise that they would work in the fields of the landowner concerned. As daily wages they got ₹100 plus 3 ser (1 ser = 700 gm) of paddy, whatever might be the market price.

Santhal women play a dominant role in the agrarian relations of the village. But the nature and extent of their participation in the agrarian social relations has not been the same. The party workers of the village tried to generate consciousness among the Santhal women of the village, including other female agricultural labourers. They organized a strike in 1984 by the female agricultural workers because the women were from the poorest section of the village and yet were put under wage discriminations and if the women went on strike the economy of the agricultural labourers' households would be partially affected. The demands of the striking labour were: *(a)* equal wages for males and females; *(b)* implementation of the Minimum Wage Act, and *(c)* a stipulated time of work. The landowners enhanced the wage of the male and female labourers by a mere 50 paisa. The women have been brought into the mainstream of political life through the process of adult franchise, political mobilization and political actions.[16] Santhal women now have joined the adult education school, they can move out of the village freely; the young girls go to Kolkata to join political meetings, go to the movies frequently, and prefer to talk in the style of higher-caste women of the village. Santhal women take loans from government sources for piggery and poultry, raise cattle and goats.

Kora Women in Cultivation

The Koras are widely distributed in the districts of Barddhaman (Barsul village), Medinipur (Shitli, Ranbania, Dudhebude villages), Bankura (Jharia, Birkham, Labdapara village) and Purulia (Raghunathpur, Gobindapur, Sanka villages). During 1990–1996 many Kora families of Paschim Amba village of Gokulpur, West Medinipur, lost their lands in course of the huge amount of land acquisition (about 700 acres of fertile land) for the establishment of two big industrial companies: Tata Metaliks and Birla Century.[17]

My visit during my field study, July 2012, to Nathsimahalla Korapara village, Pandua Block, Hooghly district, revealed that the Koras are mainly dependent on agriculture and wage-earning as day labourers. About 69 per cent of the families have their own land and most of them work in their own land as well as in others, on a sharecropper basis. Kora women do sowing, transplanting, weeding, harvesting, threshing, winnowing, husking, preparation of rice and reaping. An adult Kora male earns ₹500 on an average during agricultural season per month, whereas a Kora female worker earns ₹300 on an average per month on the daily wage basis.[18] Minor forest products are also collected both for personal consumption and marketing. The most important edible produce of the forest is the mahua flower. Tamarind is another important item collected for household consumption. Collection and sale of the sal leaves and bamboo has assumed a great importance in recent times due to increase in the manufacture of leaf-plate and basket making from sal leaves and bamboo sticks respectively. Fishing is also one of the seasonal food gathering activities of the Koras. Both men and women take part in fishing activities.

Koras are also found in Bichabhanga forest village of Matiali block of Jalpaiguri district. This is under Bichabhanga Beat of Gorumara South Range in Jalpaiguri Division. The village is very close to National Highway No. 31. Though the FRA of 2006 advocates for the right of patta, the villagers have not got its benefit so far. All the villagers are below poverty level (BPL). They speak in Kora and in Bengali.

As an alternative profession, both men and women are engaged with handicrafts, mainly jute-based. Jute craft was initiated in this village in 2004. The women make various products such as doll, toy elephant, bag, cushion, table mat and the Forest Department buys these from them, giving 50 per cent of price immediately and the rest is deposited in bank.[19]

ADIVASI WOMEN IN INDUSTRIAL SECTOR

Population growth and lack of land has led to large-scale migration of both men and women from rural to urban or industrial areas. After independence, several industries were established in different parts of the country, even in the remote tribal areas. These labourers drawn from the rural sector constitute mainly the unskilled category of labour force in the industries.

Plantation Industry of North Bengal

In the tea gardens in North Bengal large-scale migration of tribal men and women took place from Chotanagpur and Santhal Pargana in search of food and livelihood in the growing tea industries. In Jalpaiguri such migration started since 1873 and the bulk of the immigrants were Oraon, Munda, Santhal, Ho, Kharia. Gradually this tribal population settled in the region with families. They now constitute more than three-fourth of the total workforce in a tea garden and are called as *madesia* by the local people. Women have been the main workforce in the plantations. Traditionally migration of families was encouraged so that children could be kept as reserve labour force.

During the last few decades there had been a continuous decline in the number of working women in the organized industries in India due to technological changes in the manufacturing processes in which women are considered unsuitable. Plantation is the only industry where women's employment has not declined. In a tea plantation industry pluckers constitute about nine-tenth of the total workforce. The job of plucking is done mostly by tribal women and the strength of women labourers in a garden is almost equal to men.[20] The question may be asked that why is the number of women in tea plantations increasing?

The Chandmani Tea Plantation (CTP), established in 1922, is situated at the foothill region of Darjeeling district. Among the workers, the adivasis outnumbered the non-adivasis. The field operations of tea are comparable to that of modern agriculture. When the Sixth International Tea Day was celebrated on 15 December 2010, the focus was on housing and land rights for plantation workers in the context of the restructuring of plantations. Tea workers are mostly adivasis and dalits who were brought to the plantations as indentured labourers during the colonial period and have been kept along with families in a state of virtual bondage. Workers were made to reside in labour lines which were designated areas of residence in the plantations. Each of the labour lines was under strict surveillance and the mobility of workers was monitored. Those who tried to escape were punished. The management policies have motivated the workers to cut off social relations to a large extent from their native villages and land.

A planter prefers to employ women for he thinks that women are more committed workers than men. In every plantation there are standardized working hours and weekly rest-day. The employer provides housing and other welfare facilities such as, free quarter, free fuel and firewood, free health services, free grazing land, cultivable lands, maternity benefits, bonuses, which have, perhaps, made the conditions of employment more favourable. Recently turnover in plantations has come down to the lowest level. In 2011, the plantation workers were getting ₹67 per day in the plains and ₹90 per day in hills of north Bengal.[21] Besides plucking, a woman labourer also does some other jobs in the garden such as pruning, clearing. Plucking season starts from March and continues up to October-November.[22] Besides her work in the garden a woman labours with her husband in raising some minor crops in the plot of land given by the company. The tribal groups also maintain to some extent their respective ethnic boundaries in such an alien and heterogeneous environment with the aid of three major markers like rules of commensality, dialect and intra-ethnic marriage.

According to the West Bengal Tea Board, during 1998–1999 a lot of small tea gardens started in north Bengal. But the contemporary government did not maintain any statistics about the nature of the land or about the owner of the land. These tea gardens are not even notified to the Tea Board.[23] According to the Confederation of Small Tea Growers, there are more or less 21,390 small tea gardens in north Bengal and if declared illegal then nearly five lakh workers will lose their jobs and most of them are poor adivasis.[24] Since there were no alternative livelihood options, labourers depended entirely on the plantation management. Planters prevented them from doing any work other than on the plantations. The governments (both the centre and the states) while enacting land reforms exempted tea plantations and they were never broken up, distributed or shared with those who cultivated it. Tea workers remain the tillers but their right over the land has never been acknowledged. During field visits it was found that the benefits of government schemes such as National Rural Employment Guarantee Scheme and Indira Awas Yojana remain limited. For example, the skilled plantation workers often do not understand why they are made to dig ponds or break the stones under the National Rural Employment Guarantee Scheme (NREGS). In Terai-Dooars any tea garden may get closed without giving any prior notice. Workers of these gardens do not even get their daily wages, rations and other due payments. As a result they are deprived of all the facilities provided by the scheme starting from the job cards to unemployment allowances. Many people have not been provided with the BPL cards. In most of the cases owners desert the tea gardens without declaring lock-out or suspension of work officially, which means the workers do not get government aid which requires official closure of the gardens. Neither the trade unions nor the government nor the NGOs is taking any steps to eradicate the problem.

There are many reasons for the crisis in the tea plantations. One is the lack of experience of the owners conducting the industry who use the gardens as a source of making easy money. They use huge amount of pesticides and chemical fertilizers to increase the productivity artificially and as a result the soil gets poisoned, production cycle gradually gets shortened and the tea plants fall sick. The fund released by the Tea Board of the Government of India to open new gardens is expropriated. And when the tea gardens become dilapidated and thus profitless the owners abandon them and run away. Other reasons like refusal of repayment of the bank loans on the part of the owners and robbing the provident funds of the workers are also making the industry moribund. Nowadays an average of 14 to 15 tea gardens remains closed in the entire year. But the activities of the closed gardens are not halted completely. Tea plucking goes on under the supervision of Operating Management Committee or OMC. The OMCs are government-approved and have the right to sell the tea leaves in the market on a fixed price. It keeps the gardens partially opened and brings ₹35–45 to the workers on daily basis. But the OMC, an amalgamation of trade union leaders, committee members and middlemen, controls NREGS, distribution of government reliefs and rations and is often involved in corruption and embezzlement. The workers working under OMC are awfully underpaid and do not get any facilities provided by the PLA. The owners of the tea gardens buy tea leaves from the OMCs on cheaper costs. The system is imposed from the above.[25]

During 2003–2004 starvation deaths have been reported from several closed tea gardens. According to government data, in 2007 there were about 33 abandoned tea gardens employing almost 30,000 workers.[26] According to an estimate, more than 50 gardens closed between 2000 and 2007, affecting a huge section of the workforce. They leave behind huge unpaid salary/wage bills, and provident fund and gratuity claims due mainly to the tribal workers. Evidently, the 'enclave economy' of Jalpaiguri tea gardens provides very few alternatives to unskilled and semi-literate boys and girls. Such vulnerability exposes them to the well-built networks of trafficking agents working openly as 'placement agents' in and outside gardens. Surveys conducted in the tea gardens reveal a very grim picture of child and women trafficking, particularly from sick and closed tea gardens (see Table 2.1). The prime targets of trafficking are mostly adivasi children, both boys and girls, belonging mainly to the Oraon, Munda, and Santhal tribes. The low level of literacy of the tribal boys and girls prevents them from looking for alternative job options. Agents try to lure fathers by gifting them alcohol and/or cash as an advance. There are many instances of girls returning pregnant or with AIDS.[27]

Table 2.1 Number of Missing/Trafficked Children from Tea Gardens in 2010

Tea garden	Status	Girls	Boys	Total
Indong	Sick	5	6	11
Grassmore	Sick	5	4	9
Red Bank	Sick	7	5	12
Chulsa	Good	5	4	9
Nayasaili	Sick	5	5	10
Samsing	Sick	5	4	9
Bharnobari	Sick	5	1	6
Dheklapara	Closed	6	3	9
Radharani	Sick	4	3	7
Rahimabad	Sick	2	1	3
Raimatang	Sick	5	4	9
Satali	Good	2	5	7
Total		56	45	101

Source: Biswajit Ghosh, 2014. 'Vulnerability, Forced Migration and Trafficking in Children and Women: A Field View from the Plantation Industry in West Bengal', *EPW* 49, 26 & 27 (June 28): 58–65.

The government announced a rehabilitation package which included restructuring of outstanding bank dues, fresh working capital with an interest subsidy from government, waiver of outstanding loans dues to the Tea Board and settlement of the provident fund dues in instalments. But that is also yet to be implemented. Moreover, in Jalpaiguri and Malda few tracts in the tea gardens that belong to the tribals have been occupied by non-tribals who duped them.[28] But the state backward class welfare department is unable to restore them.

Case Study 1

My visit to the tea gardens of Jaldapara, Jalpaiguri district of North Bengal reveals a good deal of information on the ongoing movement in the plantation industry corroborated by the oral accounts of the Oraon women of the area who are working in the factory as well as in the tea gardens. Vrinda Oraon (35), a labour of Jayshree Tea and Industries Ltd., said,

> The authority never bothers to meet the demands of the protesting tribals ... [In]the thika system, one thika consists of 23 kg tea leaf. We are to pluck 23 kg tea leaf at a time and get ₹90 per day. Extra one and half kg leaf brings additional ₹4 ... The entire process requires a heavy labour. But we are being paid with a meagre amount, i.e., ₹94 per day ... It was stopped in 2001 ... Our major demands are: to increase our wages; to construct our houses; if not then compensate us with cash money or quarter; allow us to collect lakdi or fire wood; to give us potable drinking water and electricity, doctors, hospitals and other medical facilities; provide rationing facilities; provide bonus; Unfortunately not a single demand has been fulfilled by the authority...[29]

According to my field survey, October 2012, the adivasi women expect ₹200–300 as their daily wage.

NABARD and Indian Statistical Institute jointly conducted a research on tribal poverty by Dr Kunal Chattopadhyay in 2008–2010 (Table 2.2). Over 119 villages of 19 blocks in five districts of three eastern states have been covered: Purulia and Jalpaiguri of West Bengal; Koraput of Odisha and Dumka and Jamtara of Jharkhand. Altogether 1000 households have

Table 2.2 District-wise Starvation Scenario of Adivasi Families (%)

District	Starvation per year 0 days	Starvation per year till 30 days	Starvation per year till 180 days	Starvation per year more than 180 days
Dumka	60	35	5	0
Jalpaiguri	55	30	14	1
Koraput	96	3	1	0
Purulia	60	27	13	0

been covered.³⁰ It has attempted to uncover the situation under which 35 adivasis died in the closed tea gardens in 2013.

The report shows that as far as the water, fuel, electricity and sanitation are concerned, adivasi families are almost at the stage of the pre-independence era; fuel condition is worse than 1947. Though they are quite familiar with the words such as widow pension, Annapurna Yojana, NREGA, job cards, BPL, they are yet to enjoy these benefits. The more striking information the report provides is that the remarkable improvement in Public Distribution System in Odisha has drastically changed the poverty scenario of the KBK region (Koraput-Balangir-Kalahandi).³¹ The report also reveals that in case of starvation and economic poverty West Bengal is languishing far behind Odisha and Jharkhand (see Table 2.2).³²

Stone Quarrying Industry in Birbhum

A policy of development based on technology and with an emphasis on the private sector paves the way for a higher degree of concentration of capital and an extremely exploitative situation. The exploitation of tribal women working in the stone quarries in the town of Mallarpur in Birbhum district is a case in point. Mallarpur is around 50 km north of Santiniketan in the economically backward Rampurhat 1 block of Birbhum district. The only industry in the area adjoining Mallarpur in Rampurhat 1, Mayureshwar 1 and Muhammad Bazar blocks is stone quarrying. There are about 80–100 quarries and 400 crushers in Muhammad Bazar block. The quarries of Panchami are functioning for more than fifty years. By removing the upper layer of the earth high quality basalt stones are lifted. The boulders are brought to the crushers for crushing and making stone chips. The stone chips are cheaper in this region than that of Pakur. All these quarries and crushers work under the State Mineral Development and Trading Corporation, which means that the prohibited quarries are functioning within their notified area. In fact, the government did not compensate the adivasis for the acquisition of their lands to excavate quarries.

Quarries require unskilled workers and large numbers of quarry workers are Santhal women who are drawn from the desperately impoverished areas, taking jobs in these quarries at a very tender age. They are made to work 10 to 12 hours a day, paid a pittance and are not provided with mandatory safeguards such as masks. Each woman gets ₹24.00 per day for crushing one ton stones. A group of seven or eight women can crush an average of 60 ton stones.[33] They receive no medical treatment and no compensation if they are injured in the course of their work. The tribal women working here suffer from serious health problems, such as asthma, as a result of inhaling stone dust. All existing environmental laws and statutes of West Bengal are violated by the quarry owners.

Many of these quarries have been dug on land which belonged to the Santhals. As the Deputy Superintendent of Police (DSP), Birbhum, reports: 'The quarry owners occupied the lands either through deceitful means or through political influence from the tribals at a minimum cost violating the Indian constitution, which prohibits any transfer of tribal land in the form of sale or mortgage.'[34] Besides, the women workers as well as their teenage girls are sexually exploited by the rich owners. Generally the police collude with the quarry owners.

Air pollution has already been proved in two scientific investigations conducted by West Bengal Power Development Corporation (WBPDC, approved by the Government of West Bengal) from 1999–2001. The investigations were conducted into two phases, one, pre-monsoon, that is, from April–May, and another post-monsoon, that is, in December.[35] Those who work in the fields and live in the contiguous areas of the quarries suffer. The stone dust vitiates the soil of their land, big pieces of stones harm their huts when blasts happen and sometimes causes serious physical injury, it even does not spare their cooked food. The adivasis of Panchami of

Muhammad Bazar block are compelled to live in this situation. The tension arose when on 5 February 2010 in the evening a big blast took place and harmed six houses of the village of Talbandh. On the very next day a group of goons on bikes attacked the village with hand grenades. According to the villagers, the quarry owners hired goons in order to threaten the adivasis who were protesting against the illegal crushers since 2008 under the leadership of Birbhum Adivasi Gaonta (BAG) which was formed at Suri. After this incident, the adivasis of Talbandh, Bharkata and Hinglo gram panchayat assembled with the beatings of madal (adivasi drums) in thousands of numbers. Adivasi women also joined the protesters and closed all the crushers where they themselves had to work. And since then the movement is going on unabatedly.[36]

The stone quarries started in the 1970s, when the then government issued licence and bank loans to the newly released Naxals for constructing quarries as their rehabilitation package. These Naxals could not cope with the situation and left the quarries forever, but the quarries remained there and spread gradually to the adjoining areas as well. The entire plot is declared as tribal land, which cannot be sold according to the Indian constitution, yet they are able to get the permission from the government to construct a stone quarry. The adivasis of Birbhum have mobilized under BAG and Manjhi Pargana Baisi to launch a protest movement against the illegal stone crushers. Gaonta has initiated afforestation programme by planting sal, mahua, neem; they have started celebrating adivasi festivals like Gobardhan fair, Sohrai, Karam, Baha, for the rejuvenation of Santhal culture and tradition as an integral part of the movement; they have succeeded in demolishing hooch posts, send their children to school, encouraged fishing, maize cultivation, and so on. In Dholakata and Sholagoria village they have started cultivation on two thousand bigha land with the stored water of the closed quarries. They are also planning to start looms to weave their own clothes. They have taken the pneumoconiosis patients to the health department of the National Human Rights Commission.[37] Later a new adivasi organization named Hihidi Pipidi was formed and joined the movement. On February 22, the District Magistrate called for a meeting with both the quarry owners and the adivasis. The adivasis attended the meeting and demanded that the owners have to maintain all the governmental rules and regulations regarding the stone quarries and crushers. They said that the quarries that have legal sanction both from the government and the court will continue and those who do not have will be closed immediately. But the situation still is same. The workers of the adivasi organizations are tagged as 'Maoist'.

According to my field observation, September 2012, the stone quarry industry severely contaminates the topsoil as well as the ground water. The level of water has already decreased to 15 feet and the small ponds and water bodies have dried up. The dense forests stretches of Kanksa, Ganapur to Rampurhat are already under threat. The villagers fall prey of deadly diseases like tuberculosis, fluorosis and silicosis. The owners neither obey the Labour Act nor the Minimum Wage Act. In 2012 National Industries of Small Mines (NISM) of Kolkata has conducted a survey under the Science and Technology Project Government of India on health hazards in stone quarries and crushers. All the exposed females were Santhals within the age group of 15 to 45 years with history of exposure to dust for more than 5 years. Apart from problems in the stomach, chest and skin, dust exposure of the eyes resulted in diminished vision, loss of hearing and poor gynaecological health was reported. Sexually transmitted diseases (STDs) are on the rise.[38]

The NISM survey reveals that the tribal women of the area do not get any widow pension or old age pension,[39] BPL cards have not been issued, and the adivasis are not even getting rice of two rupees in spite of government declaration. Following the closure of around 220 stone-crushing units by Gaonta in Rampurhat's Barpahari, Baromesia and Dighol pahari areas on 17 October 2011, the district administration called a tripartite meeting on the issue. At the meeting it was decided that the crushers and mines which have no legal documents will be sealed by the district administration. But the BAG leaders said that the administration has not taken any step against illegal mining.[40]

Topsoil is burnt to construct brick kilns, small water bodies are filled up to erect big buildings, factories are established across the paddy fields, and natural flow of streams and rivers is stopped to build highways—all these require stone-chips. Within fifteen years, the nature of the economy as well as the environment of Nalhati-Murarai-Rampurhat-Muhammad Bazar-Panchami-Hinglo of Birbhum was transformed drastically. Paddy fields, water bodies, people of the contiguous villages, everything was covered under the dust and the loud noise of the quarries. Big trucks pass by the road the entire day loaded with heavy stones. Non-tribals are intruding the tribal areas with the support of this industry. The forests of Sonthsal-Kashthagada-Habrapahari-Harinsinga are lost. The adivasis are fighting for *jal-jamin-jangal* since time immemorial,[41] and the movement in Nandigram and Lalgarh did influence the adivasis of Birbhum considerably.

Alternative Development Programmes in Bankura

Amarkanan village is in the heart of Jangal Mahal has witnessed miraculous social revival over the past few years. Established in 1996, the Shamayita Math is an international woman's religious centre situated on a hillock at Ranbahal in Bankura District, about 1 km from the Amarkanan bus stop. In the Math Adivasi women are key figures who have worked for development ranging from a convent school of adivasi girls to a 25-bed hospital that has an operation theatre. The organization seeks to add the idea of a personal and social reawakening to the tangible signs of development. The convent school has reached out to nearly 600 adivasi girls from neighbouring villages and brought the fruits of an English medium institution affiliated to the Central Board of Secondary Education to less fortunate sections of society who are otherwise taught to depend wholly on reservation.[42] Shamayita has brought essentials like water, electricity, education, health and sport and has indeed changed lives.

The next case is The West Bengal Tribal Development Cooperative Corporation Limited (WBTDCCL) that looks after the economic interest of the tribals. By 1984, 121 Large-Sized Adivasi Multipurpose Co-operative Societies (LAMPS), 2 Mahila Samitis, a Labour Contract Cooperative Society are affiliated to WBTDCCL. Since the 1970s, several projects have been initiated in some of the tribal districts of West Bengal. For instance, in Bankura the first women's collective called the Grameen Mahila Shramik Unnayan Samiti was formed in Jhilimili, a village in Ranibandh Block of Bankura District, in 1981. Ranibandh is part of the least developed region of Bankura with a large concentration of tribal population. Originally a part of the vast area known as Jungle Mahal, it used to be inhabited mainly by Santhals. Over the last few decades, thousands of men, women and children had taken to seasonal migration to the green revolution districts of Hooghly and Barddhaman.[43] The Centre for Women's Development Studies (CWDS), New Delhi, played a leading role in organizing the women here.[44]

Deforestation had left them no option to migration. Alternative employment was found in the collection of tendu and sal leaves from the adjoining forest, sold by the samiti to the local unit of LAMPS. The guarantee of a minimum price acted as a tremendous spur for the women. The success attained by this samiti led to the formation of two more Mahila Samitis in Chendapathar and Bhurkura. In Bhurkura, about 7–8 acres of land were donated to the samiti provided employment for a prolonged period. They planted arjun and asan trees and breed tassar silkworm on wasteland. Thus, the success of one project spawned off others.[45] In 1986 that the Nari Bikash Sangha (NBS) was formed to function as an apex body to coordinate the activities of the Mahila Samitis in the villages. The CWDS report says, 'The Bankura project has reached a plateau. After 16 years of great hardship the women are still happy with the little prosperity that they have won and with their new found social status.'[46] The 24 samitis cover a little more than 60 villages and 2,500 members.[47]

By the end of 1987 it was clear to the NBS leadership as well as to the CWDS that wasteland development through women's organization along with at least two support services like adult education and childcare, and training in organizational management of women were needed. A component of training in legal literacy was added later to inform women about their rights and responsibilities as citizens. By 1996 the NBS had expanded its outreach to two adjacent districts and acquired more than 600 acres of wastelands with thriving plantations of 2 million tassar host trees and babui grass, diversifying into new activities like the manufacture of synthetic footballs and leather footwear, sale of cheap cloth, running a public distribution shop and production of tassar seeds for its members. Another activity initiated since 1986 is of storing a very popular forest produce, mahua.[48] Between 2000 and 2003 the NBS made three other great strides. In collaboration with CWDS, it successfully implemented a three-year long programme of tassar culture supported by the UNDP, Central Silk Board and State Sericulture Department The NBS is a good example of how a women's organization defines empowerment.[49]

Since 1990 the NBS has taken a special initiative on the sustainable use of forest resources and for regeneration of forests. When the state Forest Department introduced the Joint Forest Management (JFM) programme in 1989 by organizing Forest Protection Committees (FPC) in each village, the NBS noticed that the government resolution excluded women and it made a representation to the state forest minister. Ultimately, NBS was successful in setting up a federation of FPCs in 1996 known as Ranibandh Banabasi Sangha (RBS) with certain environmental and developmental objectives. In the 1990s the NBS turned its attention to the issue of the optimum use of land. The process of land reclamation that has had a widespread impact in regenerating wastelands, creating employment and income for women, and building women's organizational and leadership skills. By 1988, there were twelve samitis with a membership of more than 1,500 women engaged in land reclamation and income-generating projects. As a result of their efforts, 100 hectares of former wasteland were reclaimed and regenerated. By linking conservation with employment and income-generation, as was done in Bankura, participants' ensured that short-term survival needs were met along with long-term conservation goals.[50]

From the very beginning, the NBS and Mahila Samitis took a non-party stand. Individually, their members generally supported the four political formations of the region—the Indian National Congress, the Trinamool Congress, the CPI and CPI(M) combine, and the various factions of the Jharkhand movement. The region, however, was the arena of chronic political rivalry between factions of the Jharkhand movement and the CPI(M). Within this political scenario, the NBS and its affiliated Mahila Samitis steadfastly resisted attempts at co-option by any political party and has contributed to the maintenance of political and ethnic harmony. Thus, the NBS been instrumental in creating a new social space for women, so far hardly regarded as their right.[51] My field study, February 2012, shows that the migration caused immense trouble to them. They thought that if there could be irrigation resulting in double or triple cropping, they would get enough employment. They would not have to go to distant areas for work and income.

Coal Industry of Barddhaman

The coal mining industry of West Bengal, Barakar block and Ranigunge block of the Barddhaman district, pulled a large number of tribal labourers like Santhal, Oraon and, Munda from its adjoining districts. The figures of Census of India 1961 revealed that not more than 7 per cent (20,000) of their total strength is engaged in the coal mining occupations. Adivasis living in the vicinity of Chittaranjan and Hindusthan Cables have got employment mostly under contractors as manual labourers. Adivasi agricultural labourers of Ausgram II and Faridpur cannot keep themselves engaged beyond six months in a year. Hence they have to search for work in the coal mining industry.[52] In the early stage of coal mining industry these tribal labourers worked underground and cut coal with the help of hammer, pick and crow bar. Below the pit the tribal women were employed to carry the coal on their heads to the foot of the shaft.[53] These labourers came to mines with their male members and were engaged in piece-rate system and also maintained their link with their natal villages.

There are mainly three categories of labourers: *(a)* a group of labourers who come daily from their neighbouring villages to mine site; *(b)* a group of labourers who are settled there as migrants; and *(c)* a group of labourers who are almost permanently settled in the mining proximity. They either live in the *dhowras,* residential quarters, erected by the management or in villages formed by the tribal group of workers at the vicinity of the coal mines. This industry provides them with ready cash by which they meet their daily necessities.[54]

The condition of these working women in the coal mines has never been assessed though there are some notable works on the miners as a whole. A good amount of their earnings are spent for consumption of country-made liquor thereby leaving a small amount at their disposal for maintaining the daily need of a week. Their diet is of poor quality. They are very often dependent on local moneylenders who impose a high rate of interest. The mechanization of the coal mines during the recent period has very naturally affected the status of women workers. There are some welfare schemes for the betterment of the living and working conditions of women and children. The coal mines' Labour Welfare Fund is the oldest statutory fund in India for the conduction of welfare activities.[55]

Santhal women constitute only 35 per cent of the casual labour force of the Chittaranjan Locomotive Works (CLWs).

Since tribal men have become engaged in different types of work related to the industry, agricultural work has been vested mainly on the womenfolk. Before establishment of the CLW, the Santhals could not depend wholly on their own land for subsistence. They worked as agricultural labourers or sharecroppers in the fields owned by other Hindu castes in the locality. The wage for the agricultural labourers is less than that of an industrial labourer and lack of irrigation facilities is a hindrance to the security of farm production.

When women came to the new spheres of work in connection with coal mining they became fully unskilled.[56] Their status in the economic arena of this industrial sector is almost equal to the men. But their involvement in the new arena of economic pursuits also brings up a socio-cultural barrier in their society; some disorganization like the introduction of immoral traffic; financial constraints due to dependency on moneylenders, a portion of wages is given as donation to local leaders, and so on. Most of the time, change has not been a healthy one. They are found to be very rigid in their customary rules especially in marital alliance and maintenance of their ethnic boundary.[57] These tribal women labourers maintain a link as unskilled labour force for agro-industrial economic avenues. They are especially preferred for transplanting and weeding. The cultivation of aus, aman and boro varieties and their high yielding seeds require more manpower in transplanting, weeding and harvesting. Tribal women's existence in the working force has not only benefited the tribal agricultural labour families, but it has also made the tribal sharecropper families economically more viable.[58] Mining is a hostile environment for them and they prefer their traditional occupation of agriculture.

TRIBAL WOMEN IN HUNTING-GATHERING SECTOR

The forest dwellers, both men and women hunted for food and for sport occasionally, but the representatives of the state, ancient, medieval and colonial, brought up on the ideology and traditions of shikar, hunted wildlife, as a mark of status, prowess and manliness.[59] According to K.S. Singh, unlike the huntress, women's role as gatherers shows a remarkable continuity. From gathering roots and tubers and other forest produce to maintaining the family in the early period, women today apart from performing this role also collect fuelwood and fetch water to keep hearth burning and play a considerable role in gathering and marketing what is called non-timber produce or minor forest produce. Women are the major beneficiaries of various experiments in reforestation.[60]

Some small hunter-gathers nomadic tribal communities seem to be frozen in time since 1871, when the British government 'notified' certain tribes as 'criminals' and passed the notorious Criminal Tribes Act.[61] Till 1944, amendments to this Act saw new areas and new communities included, all of whom lost livelihoods with the introduction of the railways, roads and outsiders entering their lives. In 1952, the government of India officially 'denotified' the stigmatised ones but made no provisions for their livelihood. In 1959, it passed the Habitual Offender's Act, which was not much different from the Criminal Tribes Act, 1871. Since 1961, it has, through state machinery, been publishing state-wise lists of 'Denotified and Nomadic Tribes'. The Lodhas, Sabars, Birhors and Dhikarus are some of the denotified tribes in Purulia, Bankura and West Medinipur districts. Birhors are strictly confined into three blocks of Purulia, Bagmundi (Bhupatipalli, Bareria, Baredi villages), Balarampur and Jhalda.[62]

Till date, the police and vigilante mobs continue to target these unfortunates.[63] Between 1979 and 1982, according to author and activist Mahasweta Devi, 42 denotified Lodha tribals were lynched by mobs—not for crimes committed but for being born 'Lodhas'. Eighteen Lodhas were killed at Patina in 1979, 6 killed and 4 maimed at Gonua in January 1982, 2 killed at Jhargram-Nunnunigerya in February 1982, 1 killed in Khejurkuti in June 1982, 6 killed in the three villages of Saro, Baghjhanpa and Chakua in June 1982.[64] Between 1960 and 1998, more than 50 Kharia tribes have been killed by the police or lynched by mobs.[65]

Kharia Women of Purulia

Data collected during my field study of September 2011 shows that the Hill Kharias are generally classified as hunters and gatherers. In most of the places they have been hard put to sustain life through hunting and gathering because the forest resources have dwindled or vanished altogether. Consequently, they are now taking recourse increasingly to wage labour. Hill Kharias live constantly under the shadow of hunger and privation. Totally landless and basically forest-dwelling, they get agricultural labour work for only three months as Purulia is drought-prone and has a monocrop system. Denudation of forests for timber and large scale plantation of eucalyptus have deprived them of their main livelihood—collecting and selling minor forest produce and eating fruits, roots, tubers.

A large number of tribal women are engaged in collecting minor forest produces. Similarly in LAMPS many tribal women are engaged in collecting Kendu leaves, oil seeds (sal, mahua, karanj, kusum, neem, haritaki), Mahua flowers, Sabai grass, Bahera, and the LAMPS are procuring these things by paying attractive collection rates to them. It may be mentioned here that the Kharia women of Purulia district along with their men applied modern techniques, blending the same with their traditional one for producing these crafts and the District Science Centre, Purulia has played a vital role towards transfer of such modern techniques in accordance with the skill and aptitude of Kharia men and women of the area. In other words, transfer of technology has been done keeping in view the power of assimilation and absorption of the Kharias and by supplementation of their existing technology and not by substitution.[66] As the forest receded Kharias settled and shifted from several villages finally settling down at the outskirt of village Kulabahal.

The present generation have taken to agricultural labour for a decade and half.⁶⁷

Sabar Women of Purulia

The difference between primitive tribal Sabars and predominantly land-owning Mahatos is stark—symptomatic of a stubborn adherence to feudal ways even as the rest of the country has moved on after independence. Being a Sabar is a kind of social stigma. The unwritten law in tribal villages of Purulia is that if a house is robbed, a Sabar must be guilty. The small village of Garasagma of Barabazar block of Purulia seems to be frozen in time since 1871. Among its 421 people comprising around 69 households, the Sabars are in the majority but the Mahatos possess pucca houses and employ Sabars to work in their homes, often for nothing in exchange. Work under the Mahatma Gandhi National Rural Employment Guarantee Act goes to the Mahatos who own agricultural land and supply minor forest produce like sal leaves and babui grass to the markets. Day after day, the rich prosper and the poor sink deeper into misery in Garasagma. The Sabars have become used to injustice and deprivation. Naked, hungry Sabar children have no right to take admission in the Garasagma Primary School just because they are Sabars, whereas the Mahato children are given admission and uniform as well. These malnourished Sabar children were 'born criminals'. Twelve years ago, a school in Garasagma was donated by the Ramon Magsasay Foundation, due to the initiative of Mahasweta Devi. Sabar children were given books and uniforms. Most importantly, they were given a mid-day meal every day.⁶⁸

Located in the foothills of two mountains, Amjharna is an isolated village under Kuchia gram panchayat in Bandwan near the Jharkhand border and about 100 km away from Purulia town. It boasts of about fifty residents, most of whom are from the Sabar tribe, one of the most impoverished groups that have resorted to extensive deforestation to earn a livelihood. The soil in Amjharna is infertile. Every day, a majority of women in Amjharna village trudge 40 km through dense forest and high rocky stretches, carrying timber for sale at a weekly haat in Galudih, Jharkhand, for which they get anything between ₹150–200. This pittance is expected to sustain them for the next seven days.[69] Their earnings from this practice are spent to buy salt, oil and vegetables for the family. Most of the villagers suffer from malnutrition. There is no alternative other than selling timber for their survival. The community lives in a despicable condition. Their huts have broken mud walls, poorly thatched roofs and practically no windows and doors. None of them have ever availed of the Indira Awas Yojana facility to build pucca houses. The villagers have to walk 2 or 3 km. to fetch drinking water. There is another signboard near the village that states Amjharna has been electrified under the Rajiv Gandhi Grameen Vidyutikaran Yojana. The electricity line was disconnected long ago since the villagers could not pay the bill. No child has been to school since the nearest one, a primary school is too far.[70]

Akarbaid village under Manara gram panchayat, 30 km. from Purulia town, is another such Sabar village referred by the police as 'crime village'. It was an isolated place with some hundred residents of a most impoverished denomination. The soil was infertile and most of the village's inhabitants were illiterate. They had no opportunity for employment and were ostracized by the rest of the villages in the district. Prasanta Rakshit, coordinator of the West Bengal Kheria Sabar Kalyan Samiti, an NGO, alleges that no government official has visited the place to take stock of the plight there. He said, 'Most of them had nothing to wear, including the women, in 2002. Women came and met me, one at a time, since they only had a single sari of sorts that they wore in turns. Despite the Centre having introduced the Forest Rights Act in 2006, to distribute lands to tribals, till now only 300 families within the community have been given land in the district.'[71]

Between 2002 and 2004 Rakshit's NGO set up community hall after community hall until there were 26 across several remote areas of the district. Rakshit arranged for the distribution of different traditional instruments to locals—from drums, flutes and cymbals to reed instruments—and they learnt to sing and dance. Off evenings, the youth would gather in the hall and sing along to beating drums and soaring flute music. In the morning, informal classes are being held and in the afternoon people from the clan receive handicrafts training to give them skills. The community halls have helped in dropping the crime rate among the Sabars.[72] The central and the state governments have sanctioned funds worth crores of rupees for improving the community and yet they remains in the doldrums.

Lodha Women of West Medinipur

The Lodhas are known as denotified tribe, formerly recognized as a criminal tribe. Due to the Forest Preservation Act the Lodhas were driven out of the forest and, as a natural consequence, they were uprooted from their basic economy. Finding no other alternative to maintain themselves they had to embrace antisocial activities like thefts, dacoities, and ultimately they had been branded with the stigma of criminality.[73] Chandan Sinha has observed that Lodha villages of West Medinipur are the most vulnerable because of the scarcity of irrigation and the lack of ownership of land. They have been brought out of the jungle and have settled on the worst possible land available.[74] Men play an important part in all major economic activities. On rare occasions, they also cook or attend to minor domestic duties. Women do not catch snakes, collect tassar cocoons or plough. Lodha women collect forest fruits like mahul, kendu, bhalia and different mushrooms (parab, bali and rutka chatu) from forests in March-April and weave sal leaves in the form of plates and bowls (khali-khola). The Lodhas of Nayagram also make ropes with babui grass.[75]

Most of the PTGs of Jangal Mahal were supposed to have moved out of the area.[76] My field survey of November 2011 shows that the PTG population of Lodha and Sabar—the traditional dwellers of the deep forests of Nayagram, Keshiary, Narayangarh, Jhargram, Salboni, Binpur I and Binpur II—was not depleted. It is the Mahato and Santhal communities who have fled the region. The PTGs—at the bottom of the pyramid—had simply nowhere to go and stayed back. Patta (under FRA 2006) distribution in Khajra, near Narayangarh, has created an unbridgeable divide between the Lodhas and the Santhals as the Santhals have been given pattas while the former's land rights have been ignored.

The Lodha women as members of denotified tribe enjoy less freedom in the outside world because of their stigma of criminality which is still prevailing in the minds of their neighbours. But at home their roles are highlighted by a number of essential indoor activities. The uprooted economic life and unbalanced mode of living compelled the Lodha women to maintain the day to day familial activities with profound hardship. Lodha men were associated with anti-social acts and, as a necessary consequence, they used to move outside. They had very little time or inclination to look after the household. In consequence of the repeal of the Criminal Tribes Act and subsequent rehabilitation of the Lodhas the situations has not improved much as the Lodha men are reluctant to do any responsible job. Owing to their husbands' reputations Lodha women do not easily get work in Hindu houses.[77]

Finally, the women who have struggled to get themselves educated and employed feel a tremendous pressure. While they get alienated from their own kind, they are not easily accepted at par by other communities. This was the tragedy of Chuni Kotal, the first woman Lodha graduate, who found it difficult to cope with these pressures and committed suicide. Chuni Kotal was the first woman from a primitive tribe to have passed the Higher-Secondary examination. In 1983, she was appointed a social worker at the Jhargram

ITDP office. From childhood, despite starvation, working in the fields and having no money to purchase books, she doggedly continued to study. In 1985, she graduated and in 1987, she was appointed superintendent of Rani Shiromoni SC and ST Girls' Hostel in Medinipur. That she was a Lodha, a hated name in the district, clung to her like a stigma; some of the hostel staff were against her because of her origins. Matters became worse when she enrolled herself at the local Vidyasagar University as an M.Sc. student in anthropology. From the very first day, a certain male professor started calling her a member of a criminal tribe who had no right to study for an M.Sc; he failed her twice. Then she became a victim of the inner politics between the members of the faculty. The enquiry commission set up to probe her complaints did nothing. Cornered from all sides she committed suicide on 16 August 1992.[78]

In 1988, Government of India adopted the policy of participatory management of forests. In West Bengal, the Joint Forest Management policy was implemented by a government order in 1989 and the first Forest Protection Committees (FPCs) were formed in 1991 under the initiative of the forest department. FPCs are village-based committees with representation from each household, which protect and manage the forests. For this they hold regular meetings in the presence of forest department staff or by themselves. In West Bengal, women were not roped in adequately in the beginning. Later, in November 1991, an amendment to the State Government Order of 1989 was passed which bestowed joint FPC membership on the husband and wife. In spite of this there has been little active participation of women in the decision making or functioning of the FPCs. The 1991 Amendment does not deal with situations where a man has more than one wife or where either the husband or the wife is simply not present (due to death, divorce, abandonment). There is no provision for the representation of women in the executive committees. Yet the necessity of soliciting women's active participation in the FPCs is acknowledged.[79] The JFM policy has helped tribal women on the whole because they have got free access to non-timber forest produces (NTFP) and to fuel.[80]

Several attempts have been undertaken by the Lodha Sabar Kalyan Samiti for the upliftment of the conditions of the Lodhas. Government documents will show that the Lodhas have been provided with lands, in reality they are provided with low quality of land which is worth nothing. A letter sent to the Chief Minister in 2003 demanded, *(i)* BPL ration cards for Lodha families; *(ii)* pattas of the government *khas* lands for the landless Lodha families; *(iii)* ensure the supply of electricity and portable drinking water facilities for the villages; *(iv)* mobile medical services in every village at least once a week; *(v)* special privileges for PTGs like Lodhas. This indicates that even in 2003 the Lodhas were deprived of all these facilities. The letter mentioned that in 1987 lands were taken from 29 Lodha families for the Subarnarekha Barrage Project without compensating them. In January 2009 a letter was sent to the district administrator saying that Lodhas are very poor and dependent on the collection of firewood and different kinds of leaves as their livelihood. The people of the community are dying out of poverty, malnutrition, deficiency and inability. In this letter the Lodha Sabar Kalyan Samiti had provided statistics from 1979 to 2010 about police atrocities, arrests, rapes, arsons and murders. In February 2010 another letter was sent to the district administrator explaining the displacement took place in 1987. It also informed the concerned authority that in Kharagpur Block-I Tata Metaliks and Rashmi Metaliks Companies grabbed lands of 67 Lodha peasants in 2004 and 2005 respectively. They still have not given them any compensation.[81]

Rabha Women Gatherers of Jalpaiguri

The Rabhas of North Bengal are a forest dwelling tribe that is matriarchal. Women are the owners of the ancestral properties. If a woman dies then her younger daughter will be the next owner. But now the Rabha society is transforming from matriliny to patriliny. Rabha economy is entirely dependent on the collection of minor forest products. They still practice *tangia* cultivation or shifting cultivation in some of the pockets of north Khairbari Forest.[82] In the sphere of economy the contribution of the Rabha females is somewhat significant though not many take part in direct sources of income. In the forest bastee only the males are employed. The females mainly work as agricultural labourers. Rabha females also collect fuelwood, roots, tubers and fruits from the forest; bring drinking water, cook, and so on. In Madhya Manasi village only 20.45 per cent Rabha workers are females. Among them 16.11 per cent are in cultivation, 27.78 per cent in labour, 5.56 per cent in sharecropping and the rest in other occupations. In Dakshin Manasi also only 21.74 per cent of the Rabha women work and of them only 26.67 per cent are engaged in cultivation, 33.33 per cent in sharecropping and the rest 40.00 per cent in other occupations.[83]

As mentioned earlier, the Forest Rights Act (2006) is not implemented properly in North Bengal. The Forest Department continues imposing previous schemes that contradict the Act, behaves very badly with the local people and defeats the very purpose of the FRA. Thus, Rabhas are compelled to collect firewood and other non-timber forest produces which are illegal according to the prevailing of laws, and thus face many types of exploitation by the forest guards, who sometimes kill them.[84]

A number of movements have been taken up by the tribals to arrest the FRA's faulty implementation as well as to organize forest villagers within its provisions, including mass petitions by the forest villagers at the block level, forest beat-wise campaign to establish people's control over the forest resources, and, most importantly, the dissolving of Gram Sansad-based Forest Rights Committees (FRCs) and replacing them by Gram Sabha-based FRCs.[85]

From 2009 to 2010 three adivasi youths were killed by the forest guards: on 13 November Suresh Rabha (25) at Uttar Poro village, on 22 January Suraj Kheria (16) at Newlands and on 12 April Sarju Cheria (36) at Mendabari village. Besides, on 18 April 2010 three Rabha women, Pavan Rabha (25), Radha Rabha (30) and Raman Rabha (30) were severely wounded. The lower portion of the bodies of both Pavan and Radha has been disabled due to the injury. All were tortured on the suspect of being a wood thief. But these kinds of incidents are not new in the Rabha villages of North Bengal. On 2–3 April of 2005 a public meeting was organized, by Rashtriya Vana Jana Shramajivi Mancha, NESPON and Disha, at Rajabhatkhawa of Jalpaiguri district regarding the Buxa Tigar Reserve. Justice Samaresh Banerjee, the Executive Chairman of State Legal Services Authority, West Bengal, headed the meeting with other lawyers and social scientists. More or less 700 adivasis were present to speak about the police atrocities perpetrated on them. The grievances were the dearth of primary schools, there is only one and it is without mid-day meals; villagers lack ration cards, BPL cards and voter ID cards; absence of health centre; elephant depredations; random unwarranted arrests; women harassed over collecting firewood, accused of trespassing, theft obstructing government officials, murder.[86] The situation remains the same and one of its reasons is the non-implementation of Forest Rights Act of 2006.

Munda and Oraon Women of North Bengal

Kalamjote village situated near Kwakhali is about five kilometres from Siliguri town. Munda and Oraon tribals live here as well. Munda houses are made of clay, complete with a stable for cattle, a place for offering prayers to their deities and a small patch at the back for growing vegetables and other plants. The men work as stone gatherers in the Balason's dry river bed and at the end of a month they earn about ₹6,000. In the monsoon, however, this income is reduced by half as the river bed swells with rain. The women remain at home, engaged in domestic chores and farm work, in addition to taking their children to school. Mundas, especially those who are Hindus, pay dowry and worship the Goddess Bishohari or Manasa Devi. Goddess Bishohari is equated with Mother Earth. The Mundas, both men and women, are also good fishermen.[87]

Magurmari forest village is situated at Rajadanga Gram Panchayat, Mal block under Kathambari beat of Apalchand range, Baikunthapur Division. Kailashpur Tea Estate is very adjacent to this village. There are 34 families in the village. All of the inhabitants belong to tribal group such as Munda and Oraon. All the villagers are below BPL. They speak Kurukh and Bengali. They drink handia (made from from fermented rice). The forest villagers subsist mainly on agriculture and employment in forestry including timber operation, plantation, re-plantation, mulching, transplanting, hoeing, intercropping, cleaning. They collect maximum NTFPs from November to May each year. Range of average income varies from ₹600 to ₹1,250 per month. In some cases both husband and wife becomes members of Village Forest Protection Committee in this village which is an important feature of the village.[88] The girl child of the family looks after the household and her younger siblings. Thus, it can be said that tribal women's lack of access to education is one of the causes of their large families. In West Bengal too, linked to low tribal literacy is child labour. To the tribal parents a child is not just a mouth to feed but two hands to work with.

NOTES

1 Shashi, Nehru and the Tribals: 23.
2 Hollis et al. *Structural Change and Development Policy;* also see Griffin Keith, *Political Economy of Agrarian Change.*
3 Vidyarthi, *Tribal Culture of India.*
4 Registrar General and Census Commissioner, 1992. *Census of India 1991: Series 1, India: Final Population Totals* (New Delhi: Controller of Publications): 664–96.
5 Registrar General and Census Commissioner, 2001. *Census of India 2001: Series 1, India: Paper 1: Provisional Population Totals* (New Delhi: Controller of Publications).

6. Fernandes, Chetri, Lama and Sherry, 2012. *Progress: At Whose Cost?* 87–88.
7. Annual Report, Ministry of Social Justice and Empowerment, Government of India, 2004–2005.
8. *Bulletin of Cultural Research Institute*, 1997, 22, 1: 1–5.
9. Chaudhuri, 1985. 'Tribal Women and the Economy', in J.P. Singh et al, eds., *Tribal Women and Development*: 47–57.
10. Ratna Gupta, ed., 1990. *Profiles of Tribal Women in West Bengal* (Scheduled Castes and Tribes Welfare Department, Government of West Bengal): 93.
11. R. Chakravarty, *Communists in Indian Women's Movement*: 87.
12. The Khanpur events are described, amongst others, by Sunil Sen, *Agrarian Struggle in Bengal, 1946–47* (People's Publishing House, New Delhi): 63; and extensively by Kali Sarkar in his contribution to the book *Utter Bonger Adhiyar Bidroh o Tebhaga Andolen* ('The Sharecroppers' Rebellion and Tebhaga Movement of North Bengal') (Malda, 1984, publisher unknown): 97. Chabi Ray in *Banglar Nari Andolen-Shongrami Bhumikar Der Sho Bochor* ('The Women's Movement of Bengal-One Hundred Fifty Years of Struggle-Policy'), (Calcutta, nd.): 162, a second woman was killed in the same incident, Pagli Kolkamar (Saotali).
13. Peter Custers, 1986. 'Women's Role in Tebhaga Movement', *Economic and Political Weekly* (henceforth *EPW*), (Oct. 25): WS 101. Also see Custers, *Women in the Tebhaga Uprising*: 131–34.
14. Charu Majumdar, 1965. *Eight Documents*; this is the Second Document, available at http://www.marxists.org/reference/archive/majumdar/index.htm accessed on 19 July 2010.
15. 'Tebhaga Andolaner Subarno Jayanti': 48–49, 'Saler Dwitiya Parjayer Andolan', in *Kalantar*, 20 January 1997.
16. Singha Roy, 'Socio-Economic Changes among Santal Women in a Rural Setting in West Bengal', in Singh, Vyas and Mann eds, *Tribal Women and Development*: 187–93.
17. Abhijit Guha, *Jami Adhigrahan Unnayan*: 29–36.
18. Jana *Ethnohistory of the Koras of Bengal*.
19. Paul and Bhuimali, *Forest Resources and the Poor*: 136–75.
20. *Tea Board of India*, 1976 and 1981–82, Tea Statistics, Calcutta.
21. *The Statesman*, 12 August 2011.
22. Pranab Kumar Das Gupta, 1978. 'Tribal Women in Industrial Context', in *Tribal Women in India* (Calcutta: Indian Anthropological Society): 192–94.
23. *Anandabazar Patrika*, 1 August 2010.
24. *Anandabazar Patrika*, 28 December 2010.
25. A Fact Finding Report, 2009. *Uttarbanger Cha Bagan Ek Anischit Bhabisater Pratikhha* (Kolkata: NESPON and Nagarik Mancha): 10, 16, 18. The survey was conducted from Oct. to Dec. 2008.

26. *The Statesman*, 29 December 2010 *Anandabazar Patrika*, 9 November 2012.
27. Biswajit Ghosh, 2014. 'Vulnerability, Forced Migration and Trafficking in Children and Women. A Field View from the Plantation Industry in West Bengal', *EPW* 49, 26 & 27 (June 28): 58–65.
28. *The Statesman*, 4 July 2012.
29. Interview with Vrinda Oraon, on 6 October 2012.
30. 'Impact of Economic Reforms on Tribal Poverty' by Dr Kunal Chattopadhyay, funded by NABARD, the project was started in 2008–2009 and completed in 2013–2014). This is an unpublished Externally Funded Project Report lies with the Economic Research Unit of Indian Statistical Institute, Kolkata.
31. Mihika Chatterjee, 2014. 'An Improved PDS in a "Reviving" State: Food Security in Koraput, Odisha', *EPW* 49, 45 (Nov. 8): 49–59. Using a sample of 793 households (60% are adivasis) in the district of Koraput in Odisha, this article reviews the performance of the PDS in the district, focusing primarily on BPL and AAY households. The aim of this article was to highlight the progress made in food grain distribution through the PDS in the deprived district of Koraput, while delineating areas of deficiencies in the system. A major achievement of the PDS is that it effectively distributes rice and inspires confidence among the beneficiaries. It is highly utilized, specifically vis-à-vis rice, and is perceived as essential to the overall welfare of beneficiaries.
32. *Anandabazar Patrika*, 31 July 2014.
33. *Anandabazar Patrika*, 21 July 2013.
34. *Report submitted by the Deputy Superintendent of Police, Birbhum, to the Women's Commission, Government of West Bengal*, July 2002.
35. *Anandabazar Patrika*, 9 February 2011.
36. *Anandabazar Patrika*, 30 March 2010.
37. *Anandabazar Patrika*, 18 September 2012.
38. Rupak Ghosh, 2012. 'Health Hazards among Tribal Females Working in Stone Crushing Units—Md. Bazar Block of Birbhum District, West Bengal', in *Bulletin of the Cultural Research Institute*, 24, Nos. 1 & 2 (Backward Classes Welfare Department, Government of West Bengal): 45–49.
39. *The Statesman*, 21 February 2011.
40. *The Statesman*, 20 October, 24 November, 5 December 2011.
41. A term coined by Myron Weiner in his path-breaking work, *Sons of the Soil: Migration and Ethnic Conflict in India* (Princeton: Princeton University Press, 1978).
42. *The Statesman*, 23 January 2011.
43. Narayan Banerjee, 1985. 'Women's Participation and Development: A Case Study from West Bengal', CWDS, Occasional Paper No. 5.

44. D. Bandyopadhyay, 'Travails of Tribal Women', *Mainstream*, 14 June 1980.
45. Anuradha Chanda, 2005. 'Tribal Women', in *Changing Status of Women in West Bengal, J. Bagchi,* ed.: 137.
46. Chanchal Sarkar, *'Tilting against Odds'*: 48.
47. Ibid.
48. Vina Majumdar, 1989. 'Peasant Women Organise for Empowerment: The Bankura Experiment', Occasional Paper No. 13 (New Delhi: CWDS): 1–35, available at http://www.cwds.ac.in/OCPaper/PeasantWomenVM.pdf downloaded on 18 August 2011.
49. Narayan Banerjee, 2004. 'Nari Bikash Sangha: Towards Empowerment', *Indian Journal of Gender Studies* 11, 2 (May-August): 179–203.
50. International Labour Organisation, *The Bankura Story*.
51. D. Bandyopadhyay, 'Travails of Migrant Tribal Women': 11–12.
52. 'Sub-Plan for the Tribal Areas of Barddhaman, West Bengal', Asansol Planning Organisation, November 1978. Tribal Development Project No. 31 and 32, Development and Planning (T and CP) Department (Government of West Bengal).
53. Sukumar Banerjee, 1978. 'Tribal Women in Coal Field Area', in *Tribal Women in India* edited by Indian Anthropological Society, Calcutta.
54. Amitabha Sarkar, 1990. 'Tribal Women in Industrial Arena', in *Profiles of Tribal Women in West Bengal,* Ratna Gupta, ed: 70–72.
55. R.M. Sarkar, 1990. 'Tribal Women in the Coal Industrial Setting', in *Profiles of Tribal Women in West Bengal,* Ratna Gupta, ed.: 55–66.
56. P.K. Dasgupta, 1978. 'Tribal Women in Industrial Context', in *Tribal Women in India*: Indian Anthropological Society. Also see 'Impact of Industrialisation on Tribal Life', in the *Bulletin of Anthropological Survey of India* 13, 1: 1964.
57. Debi Bharati, 1978. 'Tribal Women A Study of Modern Conditions and Future Prospect', in *Role and Status of Women in India* edited by Renowned Scholars (Calcutta: Firma KLM).
58. Satyabrata Chakrabarti, 1978. 'Santal Women in Agriculture: Observations in a Barddhaman Village', in *Tribal Women in India* edited by Indian Anthropological Society, Calcutta.
59. Feldhaus, Malik and Bruckner, eds., 1997. *King of Hunters, Warriors and Shepherds: Essays on Khandoba by Sontheimer, Gunter-Dietz,* New Delhi: Manohar.
60. K.S. Singh, 2004. 'Re-thinking Forest, Forest Dwellers and Ecological History', in *Tribes, Forest and Social Formation in Indian History* edited by B.B. Chaudhuri and Arun Bandyopadhyay (New Delhi: Manohar): 44–46.
61. P.C. Jain, 1999. *Planned Development among Tribals: A Comparative Study of Bhils and Minas* (New Delhi: Rawat): 116.

62 For detail information of Birhors of Purulia see Arun Kumar Mukherjee, 1991. *Birhor* (Kolkata: Cultural Research Institute, Scheduled Castes and Tribes Welfare Department, Government of West Bengal, Special Issue). 36. Also see Bhabesh Chakraborty, 1990. 'The Women in a Prefarming Tribal Society: The Birhor of West Bengal', in *Profiles of Tribal Women in West Bengal* Ratna Gupta, ed., Bulletin of the Cultural Research Institute Scheduled Castes and Scheduled Tribes (Welfare Department, Government of West Bengal, Special Series No: 34): 39–45.
63 P.K. Bhowmik, 1994. *Primitive Tribal Groups in Eastern India Welfare and Evaluation* (New Delhi: Gyan Publishing House): 54–55.
64 Mahasweta Devi, 1983. 'The Lodhas of West Bengal', *EPW* 18, 22 (28 May): 947.
65 *The Statesman*, 26 August 2012.
66 'New Directives on Forest Management in Tribal Areas', 1980. (Department of Forest, Land and Land Reforms, Scheduled Castes and Scheduled Tribes Welfare and Board of Revenue, Government of West Bengal).
67 Dikshit Sinha, 1978. 'The Status of Women among the Hill Kharia', in *Tribal Women in India* edited by Indian Anthropological Society, Calcutta.
68 Soma Basu, 'Brutal Inheritance', The report has been written under the aegis of the Akshaya Patra—One World Media Fellowships on Hunger, *The Statesman*, 26 August 2012.
69 *The Statesman*, 15 July 2012.
70 Ibid.
71 Ibid.
72 *The Statesman*, 24 March 2013.
73 P.K. Bhowmick, 1961. *The Lodhas of West Bengal* (Calcutta: Punthi Pustak).
74 Chandan Sinha, 2013. *Kindling of an Insurrection*: 164, 197.
75 Subrata Kumar Mukhopadhyay, (no year is mentioned; information gathered somewhere in 2001), *Change: A Dying-Art of the Lodha Tribes of Subarnarekha Basin* (Paschim Medinipur: Ashirbad): 10–11.
76 The Primitive Tribal Groups are identified generally by following three norms: *(i)* pre-agricultural level of technology; *(ii)* low level of literacy; and *(iii)* a stagnant or diminishing population. Based on the aforesaid criteria, 75 tribal communities are identified as PTGs spreaded over in 17 states and one Union Territory.
77 Shampa Sarkar, 1994. 'Status of Tribal Women in Three Socio-Cultural Dimensions', *Man in India*, 74, 1 (March): 49–57.
78 Kumaresh Ghosh, 1992. 'Chuni Kotal', *Desh*, 31 October.
79 Sarin, *Who Is Gaining? Who Is Losing?*
80 Chanda, 'Tribal Women' in *The Changing Status of Women in West Bengal*, J. Bagchi, ed.: 138.

81 Subhendu Dasgupta, *Prantaparer Katha*: 12–16.
82 Saumitra Das, 2012. 'The Rava Tribes of North Khairbari Forest', in *Exploring the Conditions of Tribal People and Their Culture in West Bengal* edited by K. Mishra and Amrita Dutta (Kolkata: Rachayita): 50–57.
83 Manis Kumar Raha, 1990. 'Status of Women in the Rabha Society', in *Profiles of Tribal Women in West Bengal*, Ratna Gupta, ed., *Bulletin of the Cultural Research Institute*: 31–38.
84 Ghosh, Ray Chowdhury and Dasgupta, 2009. *Banadhikar Ayne-2006: Laraier Hatiyar*, translated version of Forest Rights Act—Weapon of Struggle by Saumitra Ghosh (Kolkata: Nagarik Mancha, Rashtriya Vana Jana Shramajivi Mancha and NESPON): 18.
85 Sourish Jha, 2010. 'Process Betrays the Spirit: Forest Rights Act in Bengal', *EPW* 45 (33) (14 August): 24–27; *The Telegraph*, 7 January 2010.
86 S. Dasgupta, *Prantaparer Katha*: 45–54.
87 *The Statesman*, 9 November 2014.
88 Paul and Bhuimali, *Forest Resources and the Poor*: 101–35.

CHAPTER 3

Adivasi *Rejas* in Bihar

WHILE THE BIHAR government is busy doling out schemes for the empowerment of *Maha Dalits*, it seems to have been completely forgetful of the problems plaguing Bihar's tribal population. As a result, even after the state's bifurcation in 2000, policy makers remain clueless about the extent of its tribal population. The state does not even have a tribal commission. This, along with the Centre's equivocal overtures, has only compounded the misery of Bihar's tribal population of about 20 lakhs. The problem is that central and state government have not taken into account the addition of nearly 12 lakh tribals in the state after the 2001 Census. This number mainly comprises three tribes—Gond, Santhal and Tharu. While some of them live in scattered pockets, the majority is concentrated in 14 districts. While the fault may lie at the centre's door for this omission, the state government's apathy towards its tribal population is intriguing. It seems that after Bihar's bifurcation with the creation of Jharkhand, government officials and policy makers have impressed upon themselves that there is no adivasi population in the state.

The Fifth Schedule covers tribal areas in nine states: Andhra Pradesh, Jharkhand, Gujarat, Himachal Pradesh, Maharashtra, Madhya Pradesh, Chhattisgarh, Odisha and Rajasthan. Under this, villages and panchayats with a tribal population of more than 50 per cent are notified as Scheduled Areas. While this is true for other states, it has not yet been put to effect in Bihar's 14 districts where the population is most densely concentrated. This induced miscalculation has deprived the state's tribals of almost all of the Centre's schemes.

Officials seemed utterly indifferent about enforcing the Forest Rights Act in the state which was not implemented until 4 February 2009, then too after it had been brought to their notice by the State Tribal Forum organized by activists of the Hunger Free Bihar campaign. Lack of a database has ensured that their cries have gone unheeded. Nobody knows how many of them have died of starvation or what are the atrocities committed against them. Moreover, there is no record of the impact of Integrated Child Development Services (ICDS) in tribal clusters. Landless tribals in the state are of two types, namely, those who do not have land for farming and those who do not have land for housing/shelter. *The Hindu* reported that while the government is obliged to grant a minimum of 4 decimal and a maximum of 12.5 decimal of *rayati* (privately owned) land to the tribal families, it has not done so as it does not have a record of landless tribals. As the tribal does not have the permission to sell his own land, he does not know the actual price and hence is mercilessly cheated by unscrupulous brokers. The 11th Five-Year Plan is equally nebulous about the clauses pertaining to the progress of Bihar's tribals. For instance, it is just not clear whether there would be a separate hostel for SC, ST, OBC children or whether they would all be accommodated together. There are no tribal hostels, secondary schools or colleges for tribal boys and girls.[1]

While about the 4 lakh tribal families in the country have been covered under the Jan Shree insurance scheme Bihar's Asur, Kokha, Birhor and other tribes have not been able to avail themselves of its benefit. There is not a single mobile medical dispensary in any tribal cluster across the state. The state does not have a single Tribal Cooperative Marketing

Development Federation of India (TRIFED) building, which has severely impeded tribals' development, due to which they are routinely exploited. The central and state governments must involve NGOs to carry out these surveys. The Bihar government does not even need a matching grant while the centre is ready to provide the funds. It is also reported that a passing gesture in which ₹125 crores (125,000,000) were sanctioned by the Nitish Kumar government in January 2009 for the benefit of the Tharu tribe has been diverted to the betterment of the Tiger Sanctuary in that district instead. Only after a demand for a tribal 'mega tribunal' was made in the presence of state officials has the deplorable condition of the tribals finally come to light.[2] It is up to the state now to reconsider its policy quickly on tribals by beginning with a headcount.

ECONOMIC CONDITION OF TRIBAL WOMEN IN BIHAR

In the Census of 1891 the British authorities classified almost all of the tribals of Chotanagpur and Santhal Pargana as Hunters, Forest and Hill Tribes, and Cultivators.[3] Stuart Corbridge has calculated Weaver's Combination Index for each of Bihar's tribes using 1961 data and given a very different picture (Table 3.1).[4] Many tribes now record significant numbers of agricultural labourers in their ranks, with the Bathudi and Savar being predominantly of this occupation. Other tribal groups record a credible rate of participation in mining and manufacturing industries, which speaks again

Table 3.1 The Occupations of the Scheduled Tribes of Bihar, 1961

Scheduled tribe	Males	Females	All
Asur	C	C	C
Baiga	C, Ag	C, Ag	C, Ag
Banjara	Mg, C, O	Mg, O, C	Mg, O, C
Bathudi	Ag	Ag	Ag

Adivasi Rejas in Bihar

Scheduled tribe	Males	Females	All
Bedia	C	C	C
Bhumij	C, Ag, O	C, Ag	C, Ag
Binjhia	C	C	C
Birhor	HHI, C, Ag	HHI, C	HHI, C, Ag
Birjia	C	C	C
Chero	C	C, Ag	C
Chik Baraik	C	C	C
Gond	C	C	C
Gorait	C, Ag	C	C, Ag
Ho	C	C	C
Karmali	C, MQ	C, Ag	C, Ag
Kharia	C	C	C
Kharwar	C	C	C
Khond	C, Ag, MQ, O	C	C, Ag
Kisan	C	C	C
Kora	C, Ag, MQ	C, Ag, HHI	C, Ag, MQ, HHI
Korwa	C, Ag, MQ	C, Ag	C, Ag
Lohara	C, HHI, Ag	C, Ag, HHI	C, HHI, Ag
Mahli	C, HHI	HHI, C	HHI, C
Mal Paharia	C	C	C
Munda	C	C	C
Oraon	C	C	C
Pahariya	C, Ag	C, Ag	C, Ag
Santhal	C	C	C
Sauria Paharia	C	C	C
Savar	Ag	Ag	Ag

Key: C-Cultivators; Ag-Agricultural Labourers; MQ-Mining, Quarrying; HHI-Household Industry; Mg-Manufacturing; O-Others.
Sources: Stuart Corbridge, 2004. 'The Ideology of Tribal Economy and Society: Politics in Jharkhand, c.1950–1980', in Stuart Corbridge, Sarah Jewitt and Sanjay Kumar, *Jharkhand: Environment Development, Ethnicity* (New Delhi: Oxford University Press): 46.

of the scale and pace of regional economic transformation in tribal Bihar. The dependence of scheduled tribe males and females on the agricultural sector is much greater than that of others. But if the male and female are considered separately then the picture does not hold good. In tribal society, the percentage of female agricultural labour is much higher than that of female cultivators. On the other hand the percentage of male cultivators is much higher than that of male agricultural labourers. With improvement in economic condition women workers tend to withdraw from outdoor work in agriculture and allied activities. Tribal girls, however, tend to go up for education and thus they can join the tertiary sector of economy or take up more prestigious occupations later on. Decline in the participation rate of women in a growing economy can therefore be looked upon as a transitional phenomenon to a certain extent. It would, however, be a mistake to consider all declines in the participation rate as a mark of withdrawal on prestige considerations. Some decline is also related to the disappearance or reduction of the sex specific occupation role of women in the wake of rescheduling the resource utilization pattern or of introduction of technological innovations.

Technological change in agriculture has not radically altered the social arrangement. There are two aspects of technological change: mechanization and introduction of high yielding varieties along with ancillary inputs, particularly assured water supply. Mechanization has reduced the workload of men in preparing the soil, as has power-operated irrigation. But these two together have contributed to the increase in the total workload in agriculture. Where the time gap between two crops is short, mechanization has made multiple cropping possible. At the same time multiple-cropping along with introduction of high-yielding varieties in rice-growing areas increases the quantum of work in sowing, transplantation, weeding, harvesting, transport and threshing. Almost everywhere the first three are predominantly work of the women; the last three are mixed operations.

The status of women in tribal Bihar varies along with the differences in the level of socio-economic development. There are conspicuous inequalities between the sexes in all walks of life. Ninety per cent of the tribals in the state are concentrated in this area. Most of the tribal communities in Bihar have the patrilineal nuclear family as the basic unit of socio-economic life. But tribal women have a wide freedom. The importance of tribal women is apparent in the organization of tribal agriculture where the women maintain a high participation rate. Tribal women participate in different agricultural operations such as sowing, transplanting, weeding, harvesting and threshing. But with the introduction of modern technology, these traditionally female operated jobs are being gradually taken over by men and machines.

According to the 1981 Census the percentage of tribal female workers to total tribal females in Bihar is found to 19 per cent. Their male counterpart comprises nearly 55 per cent. Among the tribal female workers, as high as 91 per cent are in agriculture or in the unorganized sector as against 87 per cent of the male tribal workers. The proportion of female workers per thousand male workers in Bihar is only 174. While in rural areas it is 187, in towns it is as low as 79. The position of tribal female workers is better than that of general female workers (115) and worse than that of scheduled caste female workers (363) (Tables 3.2 and 3.3).

Notwithstanding the fact that a tribal woman works shoulder to shoulder with men in agriculture and contributes substantially to economic activities, she is deprived of inheriting landed property of her father or husband. They try to maximize the income they can earn, going down the line to low income activities, like collecting, carrying and selling head loads of fuel wood. The compelling factor is the gender division of responsibilities, where household food security is very much in women's domain. Failure to provide food can even lead to women being victims of men's domestic violence, besides being socially stigmatized. As a reaction to men's alcoholic violence adivasi women across

Table 3.2 Percentage of ST Workers in Different Categories in Bihar

	Total	Rural	Urban
Cultivation:			
Person	63.06	65.71	12.41
Male	67.54	70.55	13.67
Female	50.17	51.96	7.69
Agricultural labour:			
Person	23.20	23.86	10.69
Male	17.88	18.35	9.49
Female	38.51	39.50	15.20
Household industry etc.:			
Person	1.79	1.84	0.96
Male	1.72	1.76	0.95
Female	2.00	2.05	1.02
Other occupations:			
Person	11.94	8.95	75.94
Male	12.86	9.33	75.89
Female	9.36	6.49	76.09

Source: *Census of India* 1981, Series-1, India, Part II-B (III) Primary Census, Abstract, Scheduled Tribes:. xx–xxi.

Table 3.3 Proportion of Female Workers per Thousand Male Workers in Bihar

Place	All workers	SC workers	ST workers	General workers
Total	174	363	347	115
Rural	187	377	352	124
Urban	79	197	267	56

Source: *Census of India* 1981, Series-1, India, Part II-B (III) Primary Census, Abstract, Scheduled Tribes:. xx–xxi.

the country have responded with movements to ban alcohol consumption.

From production for self-consumption the new system of global market economy shifts to production for sale in the market. This fosters privatization of the access to productive resources, chiefly land. Consequently, the growth of external markets for various forest products, for example, non-timber forest products (NTFPs), has often been accompanied by the rapid depletion, even disappearance, of these products. Thus, adivasi women are losing their viable source of income. Moreover, with the opening up of the mines and growth of industries in tribal areas of Bihar, a large number of women have been drawn into occupations hitherto unknown to them. Their status in labour market has changed. They are employed in such jobs which give them ready cash. They now work at times in isolation from their own men. This has led to abuses and ushered in the trade of women's bodies. In many cases they have been subjected to sexual exploitation. Even, prior to independence, women were subjected to sexual abuse and assault, but only occasionally and exceptionally, certainly not systematically and calculatedly as now with the advent of the contract system and forced displacement of the work force.[5]

They have to work under private contractors who get contract work from industrial units. These women leave their home early in the morning and go back late in the evening. They remain out of home for more than twelve hours. They are required to follow this schedule for two reasons. First, the number of female workers exceeds the work available. Because of this, they try to come as early as possible so that they get work. Second, they are required to trek down a long distance from home to their place of work, consequently they leave home early and come back late. Most of them work to supplement family income. In some cases they are the only earners in their families. As the availability of workers is disproportionate to that of the jobs, they are treated harshly and become the victims of all sorts of exploitations.[6]

Premarital sexual relationship within the same clan is not forbidden in tribal communities of Bihar. But nowadays sexual relationship even beyond one's own tribe is established and it often leads to excommunication. The major predisposing factors leading to the sex workers' profession were unhappy family relationship, bad influence of relatives and friends, sexual desire, deception, poverty and high ambition.

Dev Nathan and Govind Kelkar have raised some questions: What has been done to change women's gender identity of subordination, including that of sexual subordination? Have the progressive, gender-sensitive policies attempted to use the threat point to dismantle patriarchal powers and structures that deny poor, rural and indigenous women control over their lives? According to them, the only way to understand this particular form of trade of women's bodies is to understand this practice as an aspect of masculine domination. In pre-capitalist class society, only the nobility and gentry had access to harems; landlords to peasant women; the lords' 'right of the first night'; upper-caste men to lower-caste women; priests and merchants to temple prostitutes, and so on. The spread of the market economy, however, transforms sexual service into a commodity like any other, available to anyone who can pay the price. At the same time, among adivasi women, the destruction of indigenous welfare systems of reciprocity and the rupture of access to productive resources, push them, with their continuing responsibilities for household food security, into selling their bodies for sexual services. In this arena of masculine domination among adivasis with relatively more equal gender systems, it is pertinent to mention that, there has also been a counter-movement of women's resistance to gender inequalities. For instance, among the Mundas in Bihar the produce of swidden is understood to be more the domain of women. But rice is exclusively men's province. Women cannot take out rice from the storage bin; not even for household food needs. If the man is absent, women will borrow rice from neighbours but not touch the household rice bin. Wet rice is then quintessentially man's domain, and a strengthening of masculine domination is historically associated with the spread of wet rice cultivation.[7]

TRIBAL *REJAS* OF BIHAR

With the advent of industrialization particularly in and around Bihar a huge labour force was needed to cope up with the growing requirements at various labour centres. Those engaged in industrial activities came out with a wide publicity to deploy a large number of labourers through their agents or sub-agents. With the result the tribal people of Bihar with an intention to supplement their incomes took to the work of labourers in different areas of the state. In the beginning it were men who joined first to be followed by women and thus the entire area started humming with the bustling of tribal woman labourers termed as *reja*. These tribal rejas were deployed at various labour centres like brick kilns, building constructions, industrial complexes, transportation of materials and the like, giving an emergence to a unique class of tribal woman labourers, popularly known as tribal rejas, a new concept of labour force altogether. This very labour force comprising the tribal rejas is, so to say, a new phenomenon in the tribal life of Bihar in the wake of industrialization as well as urbanization. Oraon and Munda, well-known tribes of Bihar form the majority of the tribal rejas besides that of the Lohra tribe which has also the credit of contributing some rejas.

Sexual asymmetry is a universal phenomenon. It is nowhere as carefully developed in nature as among human beings. Constituting a dependency class, women are described as the 'second sex' and the 'second creature' who live on surplus, their very existence being parasitic on the men who rule them. Women are 'burdened with cumulative inequalities as a result of socio-cultural and economic discriminatory practices which until recently have been taken for granted as though they are part of the immutable scheme of things established by nature'.[8]

One important manifestation of the subordinate status of women is to be found in the division of labour that provides a cheap and ready source of labour and presents the organization of marginal groups to further their common goals. Division of labour between sexes is culturally imposed and it ignores individual endowments. Although tribal males are still the major breadwinners of the families, in recent times the economic contribution of the tribal women has also assumed significant role due to various reasons. With the opening up of mines and growth of industries in tribal areas, large numbers of women have drawn into occupations hitherto unknown to them. Now women are not only employed inside the mines but also outside the mines.

Urbanization and industrialization have caused widespread changes in occupations. The traditional tribal economy which rested mainly on agriculture is no longer the only source of income. On account of a large number of factors, such as the opening of the tribal country, growing industrialization, growth of education and the impact of Christianity, opportunities for diversification of occupation as well as social mobility have multiplied. The building up of roads and development of fast communication has led to a large number of tribal women taking to petty trading and other commercial activities in some area of the country.

In areas where a lot of constructional activity is being carried out such as in industrial areas in Bihar, Madhya Pradesh, Odisha, tribal women are lifted on trucks from the tribal villages and nearabouts by the contractors. In the evening they are usually taken back to the villages.[9] In some cases the tribal women even migrate outside their villages, district and state to some distant places for period ranging from 2 to 6 months for working in the brick kilns, agricultural fields, tea estates.

Tribal women also feel inclined to go in for such short- and long-term employment avenues because these provide them ready cash which they prefer spending on clothes, new fashion ornaments, and other items of daily use. Besides the monetary gains, they also cherish the pleasure of daily outing which is actively associated with such occupations. But in many of the industrial projects, the employment of women has led to several forms of physical and economic exploitations, paving the way for physical exploitation: and to be more precise—sexual exploitation. This has ultimately led to break-up of family ties, conjugal relationship, erosion of the authority of the village headman and a general weakening of the social sanctions of the traditional social structure which provides certain distinct status of tribal women.

For providing empirical facts on the various socio-economic and socio-political issues behind the working tribal women in a larger society hitherto unknown to them, a study of the tribal rejas of Bihar has been undertaken. In the present study the term 'reja' refers to those tribal women labourers who represent the wage earner class among the tribal communities of Bihar inhabiting different districts in Chotanagpur division. They fall in the age groups of 5–10 years to 60 years. Though the word 'reja' commonly refers to those wage earners who are dependent on some semi-skilled jobs, the term 'reja' essentially refers here to those tribal women labourers who work with the contractors or independently at the various labour centres and are engaged in brick kilns, construction works, transportation of materials, industrial complexes, the conditions of the tribal women labourers (rejas) are still worse. Illiteracy, lack of awareness of local and other redress processes and unscrupulousness of the employers add to their miseries.

In agriculture, tribal women labourers suffer from sporadic and seasonal employment and also from disparities and discrimination in wages. Tribal women are generally employed on daily wages in sowing, transplantation, winnowing, crushing and harvesting and all jobs commonly rated as unskilled and less-skilled. After agriculture, tribal women are employed in various industries, trades, services. The vast army of unorganized tribal women labour force faces a battery of insurmountable problems accentuated by their vulnerability, acute poverty, pressing needs for themselves and families. These problems range from insecurity of employment, lack of standards of minimum wages, excessive hours of work and absence of welfare amenities and various other forms of exploitation. Some new industries and crafts, in the recent times, have developed in the backdrop of the tribal women labour force, without having been brought under the purview of labour laws. With callous immunity, many of the unscrupulous employers circumvent or openly violate almost all pieces of labour legislation—whether the Bidi and Cigarette Act, 1966, the Inter State Migrant Workman Act, 1979, the Minimum Wage Act, 1948, the Factories and Industrial Disputes Act, the Contract Labour (Regulation and Abolition) Act, 1970, and the like.

The worse victims are the tribal rejas who work as daily wage earners at different labour centres engaged in brick kilns, construction works, transportation works, industrial complexes, get their employment either by the contractors or direct by the management or owners of the labour centre. They have neither the benefit of minimum wages nor the protection of the labour laws. The reja as a profession has not only brought significant changes among the tribal society, but it also brought about many more new types of social and economic problems. Different types of peoples from different corners of the state started working together in a new situation. This not only stretched the contact but they also were exposed to many new types of situations which brought significant changes in their life and culture. Besides working at the various labour centres in districts of Bihar, the tribal rejas are sent to some remote corners of the state and out of the state also. The rejas are often subjected to exploitation either at the hands of their contractors or employers or other associates. The profile of the tribal reja is depressing and the lack of inadequate social security and welfare measure has engendered in her feelings of fear, insecurity, alienation and frustration. They are too weak to rebel because of their poverty, ignorance and illiteracy and the employers know how to manipulate the loopholes of legislation; how to evade their obligations to exploit them for weakness and how to circumvent the law.

This study is based on the data collected from among the tribal rejas of Ranchi district. The other cities of Bihar:

Bhagalpur, Patna, Gaya have more or less the same area under the municipal boundary. Since the study necessitated collection of the first-hand information on the various socio-economic aspects of the tribal rejas working in different occupational categories like construction work, brick kilns, transportation of raw materials, industrial complexes, field work was conducted in various labour centres. Information has been gathered from both the documentary and field sources through observation, interview, schedules, photography.[10] I have used observations and schedules' techniques supported by interviews as basic tools of field investigation. The whole study is supported by case studies and life histories. In most of the interviews notes were taken side by side and doubtful information counterchecked.

Tribal rejas have been attracted by the prospects at distant places like Siliguri and Burdwan. These women are lured by agents called sardar or sardarni for jobs at distant places, which results in migration. In the course of the field study such migrant labourers came to light. For the tribals of Bihar winter is a time when they face their annually recurring choice between starvation and brutal exploitation.

In the tribal belt of Bihar land is undulating and acidic, hence productivity is at its lowest. The agricultural season is short (between June and October) and runs out soon after the monsoon ends. The little usufructs which they have are hypothecated to the sahus (moneylenders) against earlier incurred loans. There are no irrigation facilities, electricity or proper roads and thus the tribals can produce only one crop annually. The forest land, which belongs to the government, is also out of bounds for the poor tribals, the government contracts out the forest lands to the highest bidder. Besides this, parts of the tribal belts of Bihar have been occupied by industrialists and trading communities for commercial interests because the areas are full of minerals and raw materials. The tribals can only provide unskilled labour and contractors bring in labourers from outside because they can be easily manipulated.

Around September agents of brick kiln owners come to the tribal belt of Bihar in search of cheap labour; they establish contacts with sardars and sardarnis, local sub agents also known as *arkatia* in the lingua franka of local tribals, and the Mundas mean this as seller of human beings. They are, sometimes, themselves tribals and have worked for several years in many brick kilns (there are more sardarnis than sardars and most of the people recruited from these regions are woman rejas). Once recruited, the tribals are paid *dadoon* or advance. The sardarni accompanies them to the brick kiln. Once the tribals reach the brick kiln they are categorized and work begins. The work of carrying bricks from where they are moulded to the furnaces, where they are baked, is usually done by women and children. Each reja receives just enough money to buy about 4 kg of rice every week. This is normally taken with salt and this is all they have to sustain them through the long period of their hard work. Children (between 8 to 13 years of age) face no better fate. In fact, they are paid less, largely because their output is not as much as that of adults and have to make do with rice and salt as their daily diet.

The trade of adivasi labourers through contractors or agents generally passes through three to four tiers. Mostly the contractors trap the tribal leaders for the job, who are given some commission. These tribal leaders, generally of the status of Munda chiefs, known as Maniks, command good respect among the tribals and encourage them to go with the contractors for work. After being escorted up to the railway station they are handed over to other contractors who take them to the work sites at distant places by train. The conditions are no better than that of animals which are loaded onto trains or trucks. Outside the state there are certain strategic places from where the labourers are sent on to different places like Siliguri, Hashimar, where the third contractor or middleman receives them and then take them to different work-sites. On reaching the work-sites, these labourers are finally handed over to the real master which is the fourth tier of this labour-trade. The labourers construct temporary huts. They work for 12 to 16 hours a day. Besides, the women labourers—rejas—are subjected to various kinds of physical, social and sexual exploitations.

Both the terms 'reja' and 'coolie' are widely known as unskilled labour. Coolie is an established term for male labour throughout the country. The term 'reja' is largely known as female unskilled labour in the district of Keonjhar, Jharkhand and in the mining and industrial areas of the eastern region. But the term 'coolie' is never used in agricultural farm labour in the eastern region.

There are different types of jobs which require tribal woman labourers: brick kilns; construction work; transportation of raw/building materials on trucks; industrial complex; and in miscellaneous types of work. The rejas who are engaged in brick kilns mostly do the work of loading and unloading the bricks. The rejas are sent to Chapra, Purnea, Patna, Hazaribagh, Jamshedpur and out of the state to Uttar Pradesh, Assam, Tripura, Nagaland, Punjab, Haryana, Andaman and Nicobar, Delhi, Andhra Pradesh, Madhya Pradesh, West Bengal. The deployment of rejas from one state to another is helpful in establishing the labour force which leads to steady completion of any work. They prefer to employ outstation labourers as the latter often leave aside their jobs to some other places for even minor gains. These contractors act as intermediaries between the management and the rejas. Whether in Kalyani of Nadia district or Talabir brick kiln in Mogra in Hooghly district, West Bengal, or in any district in Bihar, the sardarni accompanied the rejas to the brick kiln.

Construction works may pertain to buildings, road making or repairing, stone quarries, river projects. One can see a number of rejas standing in a line with their heads wrapped in a dirty piece of cloth against dust, passing bricks upto masons who are building a house. Although neatly clad with a piece of chadar tied around their waist these rejas are seen carrying cement, lime and mortar in large bowl shaped receptacles (karahi) on their heads. Generally contractors prefer employing the rejas of where the construction works are in progress or being undertaken; the contractors' assistant, known as munshi, visits the nearby tribal villages.

In transportation, the loading and unloading are done by those rejas who are kept reserved exclusively for this purpose. When an order is received, the suppliers first arrange to muster. First the driver of a truck collects the rejas from their respective villages and brings them to the site and on completion of the work they are reached back by the trucks A set of seven-eight rejas are attached with a truck.

Rejas are absorbed temporarily in industrial complexes through the contractual companies for doing casual work like head-load-carrying, mortar making, water fetching. Through the contractors they have the privilege of rendering duty as per the normal working hours which, unfortunately, is not the case with the rejas engaged in other trades.

The work of brick kilns generally starts from late October and goes on to May because this being the dry season there is no obstacles in brick making business. During the rainy season the rejas work as casual agricultural labourers, maidservants, selling vegetables. Rejas working independently may also be termed as free-lancers who set out early in the morning from their villages in quest of any type of job in the township so as to make both ends meet. These rejas can be used for any type of jobs in view of their capabilities. The rejas who work independently mostly prefer to work near their respective villages. A number of tribal women directly approached the owner of the brick kilns and started loading and unloading the bricks on a temporary basis because they are free to leave the job and go in search of other jobs.

WAGES

The availability of work in trucks is higher than any other work available to them. They perceive construction work as less strenuous and stressful but the availability of work is not

Table 3.4 Rejas Weekly Average Income (in Rs)

Reja engaged in brick kilns	Reja engaged in transportation of raw/ building materials on trucks	Construction works	Reja engaged in industrial complex
250–350	200–350	150–240	250–350

Source: Data available from field study.

as good as on trucks. On an average, rejas get hardly 15 days of work in construction in a month. The senior and married women prefer to work in construction and transportation because it allows them to look after their children and family.

The level of income difference varies from ₹150 to ₹350 per week (Table 3.4). The level of variation is higher in transportation work where as the income generation is lowest in construction work. The uncertainty of income is much higher in case of transportation and construction work. They are not given any training and by regular working and watching the senior rejas they gain expertise. Unfortunately, rejas specialized in certain works are not paid any additional remuneration but find it easier in getting jobs.

Tribal rejas are kept in the most inhumanly state. Small huts of bricks covered with the sheets of tin or with straws are provided where health, hygiene and sanitary aspects are very poor. There is also a total absence of electricity arrangements in the brick kilns. They are allowed to attend a weekly market from where they make purchases. The employer has someone keeping a watchful eye on them.

In their home area, their earnings mean they are of higher status as compared to other women. It has been observed that above all a sizeable number of the rejas were engaged as domestic servants because the jobs of maidservants are very easily available in urban society for which they do not have to struggle. That is why the tribal rejas engage with different labour centres and bring about more income to their families. The parents or guardians of the rejas have also no objection because they are supplementing their families with their income. Likewise in some cases husbands found that pecuniary helplessness debarred them from preventing their wives to be rejas. It is needless to say that with increased income the status as well as the standard of living grows by leaps and bounds. The highest contribution is made by the rejas who are engaged in brick kilns. They contribute 80 per cent of their total income to the family. The rejas try to copy the ways of life of the non-tribals who are working with them either in the capacity of employer, munshi and other associates other than that of the non-tribal communities. The rejas who are engaged in construction and transportation works, have more opportunities to move in urban areas and their expenditures on clothes, refreshments, cosmetics, entertainments are more in comparison to other rejas.

As the rejas cannot take time to do their household chores, which fall on the other members of the family: their own parents, brothers, sisters, husband, children, which cause much anger against them. Most of the rejas are found to be under stress because of the differential and preferential treatment of their employers. Having been fully engaged in jobs, the rejas can hardly please their spouses and thus a sort of tension prevails in husbands and wives which disturbs their family life altogether. It is evident that a good number of rejas are separated or divorced.

Urbanization and industrialization have greatly influenced the living conditions of the tribal rejas of Bihar who chiefly come from the Oraon and the Munda tribes, besides a few from the Lohra community as well. While studying their living conditions it has been noted that the houses of the tribal rejas are of traditional styles but many of the items relating to household have changed. Likewise their dress and ornamentation have not remained untouched; they have almost forsaken their traditional dress and instead donned sarees, blouses, petticoats, ribbons. Moreover, it has also been noticed that unlike their parents or some old members in their families the tribal rejas speak non-tribal languages. Those who are in contact with the Hindu society have been greatly influenced by the Hinduism and even the Christian rejas have taken to Hindu lifestyle.

Great changes are also noticed in their opinions and attitudes. The majority prefer to be treated by the doctors instead of ojhas. They now believe in imparting education to their children which they previously opposed. Karma and Sarhul festivals are still observed by them with gaiety just like other tribals, and also Dussehra, Deepawali, Holi. they participate in the festivities ungrudgingly and enjoy the fun mirthfully.

ECONOMIC EXPLOITATION

Employers or the entrepreneurs seldom maintain a regular system of payments to the working rejas. Those who are committed to weekly payments to their rejas, often fail to stick to weekly payment system and try to make certain excuses for delays in payments. If such system of payment is carried out in conformity with the Minimum Wages Act, then there would not be any resentment or dissatisfaction among the rejas. Since 80 per cent of the rejas are illiterate they very easily fall prey to the hands of such exploiters and hardly understand such intricacies and have to rely on their employers. In this way the ignorance and the innocence of the rejas are exploited to an undesirable extent. They are also made to work beyond the standard and prescribed 8 hours a day.

SOCIAL EXPLOITATION

A large number of rejas remain unmarried because their parents delay or avoid getting them married in time for fear of losing a substantial income source. Moreover, their society looks at the rejas from scornful and derogatory angle because the male tribals prefer to marry non-reja tribal girls as reja girls are held to be unchaste. Second, there are examples that husbands have deserted their wives who became rejas. These women have worked for the betterment of their respective families but are being subjected to much stress. It is better to earn money than to die of starvation yet their husbands want them to give up the work and look after their homes instead.

PHYSICAL EXPLOITATION

There is evidence of several cases of physical exploitation, especially those rejas who have been working under contractors in brick kiln, construction work and also those who come from outside Bihar from different places in India. They live under the clutches of the contractors, sardar or other intermediaries and on the mercy of their employers. In Bihar the tribal labourers, both male and female, have been brought from distant places to work in brick kiln. There are no proper arrangements for drinking water and toilets. Medical facilities are also missing. Regardless of the kind of labour, all tribal rejas engaged in different types of work are also subjected to physical exploitation. Sometimes it leads to suicide and other criminal assaults also. Tribal rejas belonging to the age-groups, 5–10 and 11–15 years, are working assiduously in brick kilns, transportation work, construction sites. But the greatest humiliation that the tribal rejas have to face pertains to sexual exploitation. It is not uncommon for a tribal woman to be locked up and beaten if she refuses to yield sexually to her employer or local toughs. The tribal female labourers who were subjected to torture are very innocent and poor and that is why they do not dare to seek help of officials or police due to the threat of the employers or perhaps they feel ashamed.

About 30–40 women have disappeared every year from Lohardaga region. As many as over 2000 minor or major girls are enticed away to brick kilns or other working centres every year; beautiful or attractive girls are generally sold to the market of prostitution. But the contractors do not give full account of the labourers to the labour department of Bihar. Hence there is no record of the tribal women who are economically and morally exploited by them.

PSYCHOLOGICAL EXPLOITATION

Psychological exploitation occurs in the rejas' day-to-day workings. The rejas are psychologically depressed. When engaged by brick kiln owners, managers, sardars, drivers, they are subjected to sexual exploitation. Rejas are also watched so that they may not escape.

In fine, it can be said that despite the existence of a lot of regulations pertaining to labour welfare, there is a staggering gap in regard to their effective implementation. It can be possible only if a monitoring cell exists at the nodal level to check the effective implementation of the existing legal safeguards for the labour in general and the tribal female rejas in particular.

Case Study 1

We interviewed two Birhor women who are dwelling in a slum of south Kolkata and work as domestic labour. In every winter Ranja Majhi (35) and her mother in-law, Titri Majhi (60), go to their village Ghoshbari (P.O. Champapur, P.S. Bakhtiarpur, District-Patna), to work in the brick kilns. Ranja explained to us the process of making bricks. She said, first a clay mould is attached to a wooden base. Once the mould is in the base, it is then left to dry and harden. This takes a minimum of a week. Once the investment is dried, the base is removed. Then it is again left to dry in the sun heat. The work of brick making goes on for eight months, from October to June. The work remains stopped for three months, from July to September, that is, during monsoon. The labour force constitutes equal number of men and women. The wages are paid only after the completion of the entire work; ₹4,000–6,000 rupees every month. During the monsoon they often migrate to the cities like Delhi, Kolkata, or to others in Uttar Pradesh and Haryana to work as domestic labour or as labour to erect big buildings. She said that they are first approached by an agent of the contractor with 50/100/500 rupees as an advance. They are taken to the kilns and got engaged in the work. Titri Devi said that the labourers are severely underpaid. The contractors exploit them through various means. Though the women earn a good amount of cash money, they have to face humiliation not only in the workplace but also, as mentioned earlier, within their respective families. She wants her granddaughter (Sangeeta Majhi, a class IV student) to be educated and not to work as a reja.

More or less 30 thousand children migrate to the brick kilns in different seasons. They migrate annually with their families from Jharkhand and Bihar to Barddhaman, Murshidabad, North 24-Parganas, and Howrah of West Bengal spend months working under miserable conditions for a meagre pay. But brickfield owners, real estate developers who buy bricks and government officials who are supposed to be watching them all say they are not aware of any problem of child labour. They get paid for each 1,000 bricks they mould but it is not much. An adult can make 500 bricks a day; a kid can make 200 to 300. Children start to work when they are about nine or ten years old. Their education gets hampered badly. No government thinks about starting bridge courses for these migrating children. They are 'nowhere children' often called as 'brick boy' or 'brick girl'. From Jharkhand alone, more than 77,000 children seasonally migrate. Seven out of ten of these are destined for brick kilns; most of them are headed for West Bengal.[11]

Case Study 2

Pukoro Rain (33) has a job to deliver freshly moulded bricks to the furnace in a brick kiln in Hooghly district of West Bengal. Pukoro, from Jharkhand, divorced her husband a long while back because he was a drunkard and would often beat her up. She has a 16-year-old daughter. She is presently training her daughter as a brick kiln worker. Several other women do the same tedious job and their husbands smash hard raw materials with hammers, packing the mix into brick moulds and delivering these to the furnace. They work for between 10 and 12 hours a day and end up with monthly incomes around 1,500–2,000 rupees a month. Sukoro Rain (23), also from Jharkhand, shares the same fate with her one year old son. It is found that the women working with their children as labourers are doubly disadvantaged as it takes a toll on their health and also ruins the chances of education of the children. Women have to bear the physical assault of their alcoholic husbands. Women's continuous exposure to heat and mud gets them infected with silicosis, a disease caused by inhalation of dust, and this is marked by inflammation and characterized by shortness of breath, cough, fever and a bluish skin.[12] The bricks are used to build offices, factories, call centres and cityscapes of a booming economic miracle, but have sadly failed to bring an iota of change in the lives of these people who give shape to the dreams of millions.

NOTES

1. *The Hindu*, 16 August 2009.
2. Ibid.
3. *Census of India* 1891, vol. III, Lower Provinces of Bengal—Provincial Table XVI.
4. Weaver's Combination Index is a simple measure designed to convey the most accurate classification scheme—or intervals—to describe a given body of data: in this case to determine the degree of occupational specialization of a given tribe. For a brief discussion of the technique, see J. Hammond, J. and M. McCullagh, 1974. *Quantitative Techniques in Geography* (London: Longman): 27–31.
5. Shachi Arya, 1998. *Tribal Activism—Voices of Protest (with special reference to works of Mahasveta Devi)* (Jaipur: Rawat Publication): 119–20.
6. B.B. Mandal and Kanika R. Sahoo, 1992. 'Status of Tribal Women in Bihar', *Man in India* 72, 3: 281–92.
7. Dev Nathan and Govind Kelkar, 2012. 'Civilizational Change: Markets and Privatization among Indigenous Peoples', in *Adivasi Question: Issues of Land, Forest and Livelihood* edited by Indra Munshi: 337–67.
8. Alfred D'Souza, ed., 1975. *Women in Contemporary India: Traditional Images and Changing Roles* (New Delhi: Manohar): ix.

9. Sachchidananda, 1978. 'Social Structure, Status and Mobility Patterns: The Case of Tribal Women', *Man in India* 58, 1 (Jan–March): 9.
10. For a detailed study on tribal rejas see Sushama Sahay Prasad, 1988. *Tribal Woman Labourers: Aspects of Economic and Physical Exploitation* (Delhi: Gian Publishing House).
11. *The Statesman*, 12 June 2013.
12. *The Statesman*, 18 May 2014.

CHAPTER 4

Adivasi Women and Land Rights in Jharkhand

IN COMMON WITH the food gatherer or even agriculturist economies, where the agriculture is not the intensive one with the heavy plough, women do a major part of the labour, not only in the home but also in the field or forest. As elsewhere in the eastern region, tribal women do not have ownership rights on land. Till the coming of the British the tribes of Jharkhand had clan ownership of land. The family right to land was only usufruct. Descent even then was patrilineal. And marriage was patrilocal. After the Permanent Settlement of 1793, land became alienable, and the property of the male head of the household. The clash between the residual usufructory right of tribal women (important in the case of widows) and the men's absolute right of ownership is perhaps what is behind the transformation of witch hunting from mere stigma or expulsion from the village to a killing of the women concerned. Whatever accumulation has taken place has been in male hands. But there is one important respect in which the control over female labour has not become absolute. Women still retain the right of their earnings, whether from sale of the forest produce, other commodities produced with their labour, or by wage labour. For that reason, the subordination of women in tribal society is not complete and they still retain some autonomy within the family. Male domination increases with the coming of the settled agriculture.

CONTESTING NOTION OF *WED* WITH SARAIKELA KHARSAWAN

Despite the growing dissatisfaction amongst academics with romantic ecofeminist and 'women, environment and development' (WED), generalizations about a special women-environment link, these ideas continue to be accepted uncritically by development planners and government policy makers. In particular, the translation of ideas about women as the primary natural resource users and victims of environmental degradation into discourses on women-as-environmental-custodians continues to justify a strong emphasis on women's participation in environmentally-oriented (particularly sustainable development) programmes. A number of authors, such as Bina Agarwal and Cecile Jackson, are particularly critical of the essentializing and homogenizing tendencies of ecofeminist ideology which romanticize the pre-modern period. They have rejected the view of women and men as unitary categories—undifferentiated by class, age, ethnicity, region and wider political economy/ecology factors. They have called for the replacement of WED by more robust 'gender and development' (GAD) and 'gender, environment and development' (GED) perspectives.

Let us first discuss the limitations of WED/ecofeminist approaches, which stereotype the role of adivasi women, and discuss the relationship between gender and environment by drawing upon my field study in adivasi-dominated villages in Jharkhand. The collected information is based on primary and secondary data compiled from relevant sources using different methodological tools of observation, interview, schedule, focus group discussion, case study and content analysis. The field work was conducted in the adivasi-dominated Chatarma village of Nimdih block of Saraikela Kharsawan district in September 2011, and some information was collected from secondary sources[1] on two other villages, namely, Ambatoli and Jamtoli of Ranchi district to compare the situations prevailing there. The three main sample villages have fairly similar ethnic compositions and environmental characteristics. Chatarma village is dominated by Santhal and Munda tribes, whereas Ambatoli and Jamtoli have predominantly Oraon. One of the main differences between the two sets of sample villages is their system of forest management, which have an important influence on gender variations in forest use and management and silvicultural knowledge system more generally.[2]

It is widely accepted in the WED/ecofeminist literature that forest use (especially fuel wood collection) and management in the developing world are predominantly female activities. Vandana Shiva states that women play the key central role in the forest economy, identifying men with hunting and women with gathering. She said that women provide up to 80 per cent of the daily food, whereas men contribute only a small portion by hunting.[3] On management of forest resources Shiva says, 'it is primarily women who use and manage the produce of forests and trees.'[4] From this hypothesis one would easily anticipate that tribal women of Jharkhand possess extensive ecological knowledge. But Kelkar and Nathan's study indicates that forest use is rather more evenly divided between women and men than many WED/ecofeminist accounts suggest. Their findings also show that silvicultural knowledges and forest-based management systems are strongly male dominated in Jharkhand compared to Shiva's account of the situation in north India.[5] According to Dev Nathan, the mistakes made in Vandana Shiva's analysis are first to take the contribution of hunting at that time of the year when it is at its lowest, and then to identify women entirely with gathering. Adivasi women earn some money by selling forest produce. Increasing the income from forestry will thus help strengthen the position of women within the family.[6]

In both Ranchi and Singhbhum districts, the fuelwood collection season starts in late October, when the main agricultural season is over, and finishes by the start of the monsoon in June. In the area under study and also within Jharkhand, fuelwood collection and the gathering of NTFPs like fruit, seeds, mushrooms, twigs, leaves and small branches, animal fodder are regarded as jobs for women and girl children. They bring sal leaves or sal toothbrush twigs (datun), ranu (herbs used in rice beer fermentation), chiraita or sataur (jhareebooti or medicinal herbs). They make sal leaf plates and press seeds for oil. Other jointly conducted activities include the inoculation, cutting and scraping of lac (for making shellac), cultivation of tassar cocoons, collection of honey, wax, gum, resin and gungu leaves for making raincoats and umbrellas.

Timber cutting, on the other hand, is a male-dominated activity, although this seems to be for strength-related reason. Cattle grazing is also strongly male-dominated. With the exception of hunting and madwa (the thatched stage where marriage rituals are performed) and timber collection, there are no specific taboos restricting different forest-related activities to men or women. Even, the taboo against women hunting is sometimes broken amongst adivasis in the area under study with the ritual Jani Shikar (women's hunt) that takes place every twelve years. There are also taboo against women carrying items on their shoulders (which is done by men only) rather than on their heads. Indeed, the method by which adivasis carry items is so sex-specific that one way of asking about the sex of a new born baby is 'to ask whether the child will carry on the head or the shoulder'.[7]

Regarding the collection of large timber, gender divisions of labour are rather more pronounced in Munda villages where only men go to the forests to bring wood for the construction and repair of buildings and agricultural implements. It has been found during the field work that although adivasi women spend more time collecting subsistence-related forest produce than adivasi men, the total number of hours spent in the forest by men and women is roughly equal.[8]

Reflecting wider taboos that restrict women's control over the production process, it is common in Singhbhum for adivasi women to be allowed to collect large timber only when male household members are either indisposed or away and even then they can only bring limited numbers of small diameter poles. When no male household members for the collection of such items are available and large timber is required, Munda women have to rely upon the madad system whereby male villagers from the same community provide labour in exchange for a specified amount of food and rice beer per person per day. In Oraon areas, by contrast, there are significantly fewer cultural restrictions on women collecting large timber from forest areas.

In addition, there are many examples of women doing men's work and men doing women's work. Environmental degradation and economic hardships have made it necessary for men to help women and force women to act as heads of households while men migrate. Thus, in the entire study area men and women from all tribal communities participate fairly equally in timber cutting and fuelwood collection and also in any replanting work. Kelkar and Nathan argue that in Jharkhand: 'there is a considerable sharing of jobs with some, not very rigid, division of labour. Gathering activity engages the whole family'.[9] The items most commonly gathered by men are economically valuable tree-borne oil seeds such as sal, mahua and piyar. The marketing of these products is also usually carried out by men whereas women tend to gather and sell less valuable fruits, leafy vegetables, sal leafs and sal twigs.

A major theme within ecofeminist ideology is the idea that women's silvicultural knowledge exceeds that of men. But the evidence collected during field survey suggest that even in the most female-dominated tasks such as fuelwood cutting, it is men who possess the greatest silvicultural knowledge.[10] In contrast to Vandana Shiva's view that indigenous forest management is 'largely a women's domain for producing sustenance',[11] studies on community and joint forest management initiatives throughout India indicate that the 'job of (forest) management is essentially a male one' as it is men and not women who have the greater role in village-level decision making.[12] Significantly though rarely, when adivasi women do speak out in forest management committee meetings, they look very assertive and outspoken and they are quite forthright in their views about forest decline and the problems of fuelwood collection. But it is also a cruel truth that, most witchcraft accusations are directed against women who appear to transgress existing social norms by asking for greater role in the decision-making process or property ownership rights. Needless to say that, if joint forest management gives women primary responsibility for forest management, there might be an increase in witchcraft accusations as men seek to re-establish their traditional control over forest resources. One important exception to male dominance is the village of Maheshpur in Anghara Block, Ranchi district, where a self-initiated, all-women forest protection committee took over from the former male-dominated committee when disputes arose in 1991. The tribal women's committee has between 400 and 500 members and meets weekly. In addition to its role in forest protection, the committee also operates a kind of bank to which members contribute a small amount of money per week and from which they can, if required, take loans.[13]

In Munda-dominated villages, decisions are taken by the gram sabha of traditional panchayats which is an exclusively male domain. One possible reason why female-dominated forest protection committees are more common in Oraon areas may stem from the greater participation of Oraon women in agriculture, which makes them more aware of forest and village boundaries than their Munda counterparts.

CASE STUDY 1

A report published by *The Statesman*[14] describing an exceptionally brilliant mission conducted by the Santhal women of

Jharkhand to protect the local wildlife by saving the forests, which have been fast vanishing due to the havoc caused by the timber mafia in the area, is a landmark in the theory of WED. A part of the Maoist movement's red corridor, Saraikhela Kharsawan has seen insurgency, with many of the local poverty-ridden villagers drawn into the armed struggle. It is one of the most backward districts of the country and has been given special status as one of the central government's Backward Regions Grant Fund Programme. According to the state government's Forest Department records, over a period of two decades Jharkhand as a whole has gradually lost 50 per cent of its 'protected' 24-lakh hectare forest.

Chami Devi Murmu aged 42, of Barisai village, which falls in the Rajnagar block of Saraikhela Kharsawan, has mobilized adivasi women from over 40 villages to plant sal, eucalyptus and acacia trees, among others, to replenish the heavily depleted green cover. The eco-brigade of Self Help Group women has planted more than a million trees and has also developed watersheds to help raise the ground water levels in the region. Their organization, the Sahyogi Mahila Group, a cluster of various SHGs, is now planting trees and also protecting them. The reforestation drive started ten years ago, keeping the needs of the local people in mind. The group began by planting acacia trees that are best suited for firewood. These were followed up with the hardy neem, sal, sagwan and sheesham that are useful in building homes and making furniture. Mango and Guava trees were planted for their fruit. The land, that had been barren due to very poor irrigation facilities, is now yielding paddy and arhar dal (yellow lentil) because of local efforts to build watersheds in the area. Women started making diversion canals, small sheds, float bindings, and water harvesting tanks to save water.

The movement started in 1988 is getting bigger. The women brigade is now conducting rallies in villages to mobilize more women to join them. So far, they have 3,000 dedicated volunteers and together they connect more than

45 villages. The volunteers do not just keep a track of the trees planted; they look for an area where there is a need for dedicated watersheds. In fact, villages like Pandugiti, Bagraisai, Jaharkani and Mochisai have their own version of small dams to save water and irrigate the fields. The group has also been able to persuade men to get back to farming paddy and contributing in the household with other work. On their part, the adivasi women are chipping in with extra income by making the tendu and sal leaf plates and selling them in the local markets. Chami Devi Murmu says 'Jharkhand' means 'the land of forests' and in our local Santhal language it also means 'a piece of gold'. Our survival is dependent on our ability to save our forests.'[15] Govind Kelkar has given an example of the impact of climate change on adivasi women's livelihoods in Khuti district of Jharkhand. Gradually with the assistance of a local NGO called PRADAN (Professional Assistance for Development Action), the adivasi women introduced new seed sticks of lac, brought from Chhattisgarh and Andhra Pradesh. But due to erratic rain and fog in the month of March they are sceptical about the result of these efforts. This example shows that unless the adivasi women are helped to adapt to climate change, progress in social and economic development is likely to be blocked.[16]

TRIBAL WOMEN IN INDUSTRIAL SECTOR

The arrival of technological advancement has brought both the villages and cities into new socio-economic structures leading to a new process of change—industrialization. Agriculture, which was one of the major traditional economies and the only source of income in India, is being rapidly supplemented by the other economy, industry. There is continuous social change due to a large expansion of industrialization in Jharkhand, which is experiencing industrialization after signing MoU between the state government and about one hundred private sector undertakings in the past few years. The process of industrialization in Jharkhand began in

1856 with the expansion of the coal mining industry in Jharia and Karnapura area of Dhanbad district. Industrialization which awakened the tribals of East Singhbhum district started spreading in the beginning of the twentieth century with the installation of Tata Iron and Steel Company (TISCO) at Jamshedpur in 1907. Since then, Jharkhand has been caught by industrial revolution and rapid industrialization.

With the advent of industrial forces and transmigration of various populations these tribal folks were exposed to new cultural experiences which resulted in giving them some sort of a cultural shock. The bureaucratic machinery managing Indian social planning in the 1950s thought that the only answer to the total eradication of poverty was concentrated effort towards industrialization. Tribal communities were now facing the challenge of machine technology; which demanded not only a change in an economic pursuit, but a total reorientation of their socio-religious lives and also disturbed the established political order and gave vent to social conflict. The forces of modernization have also produced changes in the thinking of tribal women. Although tribal women contribute substantially to the agricultural activities they are debarred from trade or service which require greater mobility and contact with outsiders. Only in primary sector of employment tribal women have got more employment than non-tribal women. But in secondary and tertiary sectors their employment is negligible.[17]

CASE STUDY 2

What was the impact of the introduction of a large steel plant at Bokaro upon the life of the industrially affected Santhal tribe? The entire core of the Bokaro industrial zone covering about 167.25 sq km of land was characterized by agricultural low land (*don*), upland (*tanr*) and scattered villages and the main occupation was agriculture. Rain was the primary source of irrigation with kuccha wells and tanks as the subsidiary sources. All the industrially affected villages had one single crop with rice as the chief crop. Daily wage labour under landlords, mukhias and other rich persons was also practised as the substitute economy. Pucca and kuccha wells were the main source of drinking water.

I visited nine industrially affected villages of Bokaro-Gorabali, Ranipukhar, Sangjouri, Kamaldi, Telidi, Ritudih, Dumro, Maango and Khutri. The dominant tribals are the Santhals. Gorabali village is just adjacent to the steel plant. Most of the tribals asserted that their stable traditional economy was completely disrupted; the majority of the tribal women were working as rejas under the contractors for the survival of their family. The majority of the tribals felt that the Bokaro Steel Plant had affected their culture adversely. The Santhals said their economy was destroyed, family destabilized and most of the cultural elements were lost. No proper displacement facilities have been provided as yet. The same view was persisting among the tribals of Ritudih village as well. In Kamaldi and Khutri villages the Santhals were angry that the Bokaro Steel Plant authorities had not provided adequate employment facilities, and agitations continue against it.[18]

The situation in Gumia village in Karmatand industrial complex of Chotanagpur plateau is similar. Their peaceful life was disturbed by the government's decision to establish Indian Explosives Limited (IEL) in their vicinity. Suddenly a structure of expectation was created both at the individual's level as well as at the planner's platform. The tribals thought that the factory would provide them regular source of income and that is why they surrendered their lands and accepted whatever monetary compensation was offered to them in a lump sum. The villagers were assured that at least one member of each household would be absorbed as a permanent employee in the factory. But since an industry like IEL requires the service of trained and technically skilled personnel, the natives of Gumia could attain jobs in the factory only as casual labourer that neither provided good income nor ensure regular employment.[19] Cultural contact coming from urban areas with industrialization brought some tokens of modern means of communication, clothing, language, but this failed to promote the level of education, health and hygiene.

CASE STUDY 3

In Noamundi, Barajamda and Gua in West Singhbhum district, a large number of iron ore mines of varying sizes and proportions are in existence. Other industries have also developed in this district due to its richness in mineral deposits and forest products. Iron ore in this area occurs in huge surface deposits and thus there is open cast mining. Before the mines came into existence (mostly after the independence), this area was heavily clad in forests, interspersed with villages with predominant Ho population. Production in most of the mines is labour intensive and is dependent primarily on an unskilled labour force. Ho labourers from the immediate tribal hinterland compose the bulk of the labourers with a sprinkling of Mundas and Santhals. A large number of tribal women are also employed as unskilled labourers. In a small iron ore mine which was surveyed, the total work force was about 490 of which 370 were men and the rest 120 were women. These mines provide some subsidiary income to the tribal peasants during off season and the rate of absenteeism among the labourers in these mines is very high. One of the significant consequences of involvement of the tribes in industrialization is the removal of a large section of male labour force from the primary sector, and dependence on women in maintaining the agriculture, because women are instrumental in maintaining this agro-industrial economic pursuit.

Jhinkpani shows how the Ho cling both to agriculture and industrial occupation and women play the vital role in the maintenance of the dual economic involvement. The factory and township of the Chaibasa Cement Works (C.C.W.) is located at Jhinkpani, district, West Singhbhum. The Ho constitute about half of the total workforce of the industry concerned. Women are mainly engaged in the limestone quarry. In Jhinkpani women are the main farm workers. We find that polygyny is significantly high in the town in comparison to that in the villages. One of two wives from a polygynous marriage lives in the village and looks after the agriculture whereas the other manages the town household.

In many private industries the recruitment of women is sometimes discouraged and they are encouraged to retire voluntarily under voluntary retirement schemes with a lump monetary incentive, newly introduced by the company. One of most important cultural barriers is marriage between tribal girls and non-tribal boys which is highly disliked and resented by the tribals. In Chittaranjan, six cases of irregular sex union of Santhal girls with members of other communities were reported where all the girls were excommunicated. Later in Jhinkpani the night shift for the women workers was stopped.[20]

IMPACT OF INDUSTRIALIZATION ON TRIBAL WOMEN

In and Out Migration

The integration of tribal societies of eastern India with the colonial system, coupled with the influx of population from the mainland, led to many far-reaching consequences, which ultimately resulted into serious tribal movements. Along with the loss of control over land, forest and other resources, the threat to their cultural system have stirred up the tribals deeply. The close proximity with the new settlers led to the acculturation or Sanskritization process. It posed a potential threat to their culture, which had allowed womenfolk to have a very open and free working space in the agriculture-cum-forest economy so far. Since colonial rule had already initiated certain process affecting tribal life, the deviation from the traditionally accepted economic-social role by becoming labourer in mines, construction work, brick kilns, plantations, and migrating to far-off places led to the tribal woman losing social status within tribal society. In Jharkhand, the system of male inheritance prevalent among the major tribes has somewhat affected their position, which is economically weak, dependent and insecure.[21] Besides, there existed certain taboos restricting women's free movement in certain essential areas of agricultural production.[22] Though women's participation in wage work has been equal to that of men, agricultural wages paid to them have almost always been lower. In spite of several legislative enactments, the discrepancies in wage structure continue to haunt them. In the industrial sector gender discrimination operates in obtrusive ways in many industries and mining. The majority of the women labourers in Chotanagpur, after being marginalized from agriculture and industries or mines, have started working as casual labourers.

According to Shashank Shekhar Sinha, postcolonial migrations have both intra- and inter-state dimension and some distinctive features as well. First, they are relatively temporary or seasonal in character. Second, the migrations will be directed along two routes: from rural areas to urban or industrial areas. These migrations have more of a male component or at times, also inter-state to cater to the demands of an ever-expanding construction industry (which has a substantial female component). Third, men migrate to the urban areas leaving behind their womenfolk to look after the agricultural operations in the villages. Thus male labour force is getting removed from the primary sector and therefore greater dependence on women in doing the agricultural work. With their men away, women are left alone to deal with exploitative elements like the moneylenders, landlords and businessmen. Adivasi women in areas with low female literacy are particularly susceptible to these elements leading to land alienation, being cheated in weighing and pricing and also being sexually exploited. The expansion of the construction industry led to the tribal migrations in the 1970s and this is the period when development-induced dispossession was peaking up in the Chotanagpur region and tribal women faced nightmarish working conditions in industrial sites.[23] This exploitation continues even after the enactment of the Inter-State Migrant Workman (Regulation of Employment and Conditions of Service) Act, 1979, which calls for better service conditions, accommodation and wage structure for the migrants.[24]

Alpa Shah has given an idea about tribal migration which is completely different from the prevailing notions. She has worked in the village of Tapu, less than 50 km from Ranchi, situated in the undulating landscape of forest of the Chotanagpur Plateau.[25] There are scheduled tribes like Munda, Oraon, Badaik and Maheli and other lower-caste people live in the village. Alpa Shah has said that from the point of view of the migrants of Tapu, migration to the brick kilns (Daisy Brick Factory, Jharkhand) did not just represent a way to earn money, nor was it seen as the torture and drudgery that much of the scholarly and activist literature portrays. Payment was at piece rates—₹22 for carrying 1,000 unbaked bricks, and ₹32 for 1,000 baked bricks. Payment took place at the end of the season. A monthly sum of money was given to each worker to cover living expenses, and subtracted from the final pay. Labourers expected that, after paying their living costs, hard-working couples could take home 8,000–9,000 rupees for the six-month season. It was far more common to hear of individuals who manage to save only 2,000 rupees. The major reason for this shortfall was cheating on the part of employers and contractors.

It is not contradictory to view labour migration to the kilns as exploitative, while also appreciating that most migrants not only view their movement as a choice but also as temporary, space away from the social constraints back home. According to Shah, the migrants themselves rarely stressed economic motivations. They saw the brick kilns as a space in which they could do certain things and be certain people away from home. These are important dimensions of seasonal, casual labour migration which are rarely considered as a primary impetus for migration in the scholarly literature and which have generally been ignored by the activists. She has surmised that from the migrant's point of view, economic motivations may be less important than liberation from the constraints of village life—obligations of kinship, domestic disputes, and a narrow-minded and oppressive environment. One of the most important constraints is amorous relationships in the tribal villages are strictly prohibited.

As Shah has stated clearly, premarital sexual relations are common among the Mundas in Tapu. The restriction on such relations, however, is that they must not become permanent. Marital partners should not be chosen by the boy or girl, but by their parents. While it was not necessary for a bride to be a virgin, marital partners should not have previously engaged in sexual relations with each other. Premarital lovers who want a more permanent relationship commonly use the tactic of leaving for the kilns. Frequently, they return after the woman is several months pregnant. The increasing brahmanical and Christian influence has led to the disappearance of the dhumkuria (youth dormitory) and the decline of the akhra (dancing circles) in some areas. It seems perhaps, brick kilns have become a functional surrogate for the spaces of freedom from the brahmanical constraints that were once provided by the akhra or the dhumkuria. Migration also provides the space to explore unions within a clan or between tribes and castes that are prohibited in the village, as well as postmarital affairs. This is not to say, however, that every young person who goes to the kilns engages in amorous relationships. It was also very common that when a woman is being accused of witchcraft, the brick kilns provide a welcome space of escape from the malicious village gossip.

Living in the city normally holds the promise of diverse employment opportunities and access to public spaces for women. For tribal women, however, their access to urban spaces and work opportunities is mostly limited to domestic work, which engaged almost 78 per cent of the total migrant female population in the village of Nawadih in Gumla district.

These work opportunities are based on the assumption that women need not acquire special skills to carry out domestic work in the cities. A deep-rooted nexus exists between local job contractors and unregulated placement agencies and is instrumental in the exploitation of domestic workers. For many tribal women migrants, the only way out of the village is through migrating for domestic work in the city.[26]

Industrialization not only increased cultural contacts between tribal and caste societies and exposed the latent contradictions in the tribal societies but also created new structures of oppression and control. Sanskritization emerged as a dominant process of assimilation of the tribal societies into caste societies. But as compared to Hinduism, conversion to Christianity was more complete and comprehensive. The forces of industrialization and urbanism also loosened many of the traditional moorings and cultural norms, while simultaneously providing for new and gendered situations of work. Tribal girls acquired new dress habits, dominant language, pre-puberty marriage, marriage with non-tribal men, going to the cinema, consuming country liquor, tobacco; and dhumkuria, community dance, consumption of rice beer gradually became non-existent. There was also the emergence of prostitution that was evidenced by the case of Bokaro industrial region.

Dispossession

We have to look at dispossession from the wider perspective of developmental activities. Displacement becomes a problem because of the dispossession that results from it. In the name of 'development' for 'national interest', the Jharkhand area is witnessing not development but the rape of its people and of its natural wealth through a process of colonialist and capitalist exploitation (Table 4.1). The brutality inherent in the process of industrialization, the plundering of its mineral wealth, and the decimation of its forests which provided much of the livelihood for its people, have not only reduced

Table 4.1 Tribals Displaced from 1950 to 1990 (in tens of millions)

Project type	Displaced	Resettled	Backlog	Backlog percentage
Dams	53	13.15	39.86	75.21
Mines	12	3	9	75.00
Industries	2.6	0.65	1.95	75.00
Animal Sanctuaries	5	1.25	3.75	75.00
Others	1.5	0.4	1.1	73.33
Total	74.1	18.45	56.26	75.92

Source: A. Minz, 2000. 'Development and/or Destruction in Jharkhand: Growing Fascism' Update Collective quoted in Prakash Louis, 'Marginalization of Tribals' *EPW* (Nov): 4088.

the majority of its inhabitants to destitution, but has also brought the area to the brink of an ecological disaster.[27]

Nirad C. Chaudhuri had a few meaningful points to make about the exploitation of adivasis. In *The Continent of Circe*, described as 'an essay on the peoples of India', Chaudhuri wrote, 'In my own life I have seen the march of industrialisation into the aboriginal's territory—I am quite familiar with the spot where it established its first base, and began the conquest with its most typical feature—cooperation between Indian capital and American technical guidance. This happened at a place in the Singhbhum district of Chotanagpur, which came to be named Jamshedpur.'

Chotanagpur Plateau is one of the richest areas in the whole country, rich in minerals with huge reserves of coal, iron ore, mica, bauxite, and china clay and has considerable reserves of copper, manganese, limestone, atomic minerals. A report of the Centre for Science and Environment (CSE) has focused on mining and extensively documents the state-wise environmental impact of mining in India. For Jharkhand, the report notes that, 'feeding minerals to meet the nation's insatiable appetite has turned large tracts of forests into wastelands'. The proposed scale of some of the projects in terms of land acquisition by the Mittals, the Jindals, and the Tatas is an indication of things to come (Table 4.2).[28]

Table 4.2 Forest Cover in Mining Districts of Jharkhand, 2005

Districts	Percentage of state forests in the district	Percentage of area in district under forest cover	Major minerals produced
Hazaribagh	9.19	34.81	Coal
West Singhbhum	16.78	38.47	Iron ore, manganese
Ranchi	8.25	24.36	Coal
Gumla	11.28	28.24	Bauxite
East Singhbhum	4.06	26.13	Copper
Chatra	7.87	47.91	Coal
Dhanbad	0.92	6.94	Coal
Bokaro	2.56	30.12	Coal

Source: Centre for Science and Environment, 'Rich Lands, Poor People': 163.

But the natural wealth of this area contrasts vividly with the desperate poverty of the people, among whom 85–90 per cent of the total population are adivasis, who inhabit it. In Hazaribagh, the requirement of Environmental Impact Assessment, which has been mandatory since the 1970s, was undermined by a 2001 draft notification where a carte blanche was given to mining projects with a lease of up to 25 hectares, widening of highways, and modernization of irrigation without the displaced people's prior informed consent or public hearing. To date, the statistics show that 50 per cent of the mining leases were below 25 hectares, thus excluding them from Environmental Impact Assessment. It has been estimated that 50,000 adivasis will be displaced in Jharkhand alone.[29]

According to M. Areeparampil, the basic phenomenon that characterizes the situation of indigenous people of Chotanagpur Plateau is that of dispossession through deprivation of their land and denial of benefits of development.[30] They are dispossessed of their political autonomy and their communities are being broken up in the name of 'development' and 'national interest'. 'They are dispossessed of their cultures, their values, and their very identity through well-planned policies, such as those of integration and assimilation, of bringing them to the so-called 'national mainstream'.[31] Almost all the major steel plants in India are located in what was once tribal land. These factories attracted men and women from all parts of the country who soon began to encroach on the homes, hills, fields and jungles of the adivasis. Everyone has done well save those who were once owners of the land on which the factories stand. But it was in Jamshedpur, the brightest jewel in the Tata crown, that the history of pauperization of the primitives began in right earnest. When once in a while someone like Shankar Guha Neogi in Bhilai-Rajhara or Nirmal Mahato in Jamshedpur has emerged to make the tribals aware of their stolen rights and the need to retrieve them, they have been silenced—the former shot in his sleep, the other done away with likewise as he stepped out of the Tisco guest house in Jamshedpur.

One of the major causes of land alienation and displacement in the area is the mining industry, particularly coal (Table 4.3).

Table 4.3 Number of Families Displaced and Number of Jobs Provided by Coal India Ltd.

Sl. No.	Company	No. of families displaced	No. of jobs provided to one member of the family
1	Eastern Coalfields Ltd.	14,750	4,915
2	Central Coalfields Ltd.	7,928	3,984
3	Western Coalfields Ltd.	6,232	2,250
4	Bharat Coking Coal Ltd.	3,481	752
	Total	32,751	11,901

Source: Report of the Committee on Rehabilitation of Displaced Tribals due to Development Projects (1985), New Delhi, Ministry of Home Affairs, Government of India.

The pioneering industrial concern of the region is Tata Iron & Steel Company that caused virtual disappearance of the original tribal inhabitant. According to the Dhebar Commission Report, 1,231 Scheduled Tribes families were displaced for the Rourkela Steel Project from 8,158 acres of land and only 843 of them of them were settled on land; for the Mandira Dam 817 ST families were displaced from 4,225 acres and only 447 of them were settled on a total area of 1,696 acres.[32] The Heavy Engineering Corporation Limited, established at Hatia in 1958, displaced 2,198 families or a total population of 12,990. These families belonged to Oraon and Munda tribes and some Hindu castes. Bokaro Steel Plant displaced 12,487 families, 2,707 of them were tribals.[33]

CNTA AND SPTA

The Chotanagpur Tenancy Act (1908) (CNTA) and Santhal Pargana Tenancy Act (1949) (SPTA) were enacted specifically to protect tribal land from being expropriated by non-tribals. Sections 46 and 47 of the CNTA clearly restrict the transfer of land in the Chotanagpur region, only to a member of the same caste/tribe as the original raiyat, who should also be a resident of the same police station area. This law was an impediment to the new industrial-urban development. As a result, the CNT Act was amended in 1947 by the addition of Section 49, so that tribal land could be acquired for the purposes of urbanization and industrialization and for developmental projects, including mining. Section 53 in the SPTA allowed acquisition of land for mining and some other specified purposes. But this section had been declared ultra vires by the Patna High Court in 1969 in the case of Buddinath Mishra *vs* State of Bihar and others (civil writ jurisdictions case no. 738 of 1967). There is a certain ambiguity here, as the SPTA has not been amended by then and there was no provision under SPTA which allows land to be acquired for mining in the Santhal Pargana's region. But there are lawyers who argue that the 1969 verdict itself is invalid in the light of the later constitutional amendment removing the right to property as a fundamental right.[34]

Recently CNTA, 1908, Amendment Bill of 2016 has been arbitrarily passed in the Jharkhand Legislative Assembly without even proper discussion and debate. Moreover, some changes were made in the Santhal Pargana Tenancy Act, 1949 as well. This has paved way for unbridled corporate loot and plunder of adivasi land and livelihood. These Amendments empower the government to usurp land for 'non-agricultural purposes', to make commercial use of their land, something that was prohibited till now. Also, it will adversely affect the pro-adivasi/marginalized provisions of the Panchayat Extension to Scheduled Areas (PESA) Act, 1996, The Right to Fair Compensation and Transparency in Land Acquisition, Rehabilitation and Resettlement Act 2013, Forest Rights Act 2006, and so on. The Jharkhand government has been consciously attempting to enact policies for serving the interests of the corporations.

Right to Fair Compensation and Transparency in Land Acquisition, Rehabilitation and Resettlement (LARR) Bill 2013 passed by both Houses to 'reduce forcible acquisition and help tackle Naxalism in mineral rich areas'. But with Coal Bearing Areas Acquisition and Development (CBA) Act 1957, Land Acquisition (Mines) Act 1885, and Damodar Valley Corporation (DVC) Act 1948, along with 10 other laws, exempt from the Land Bill, the central government has its own acquisition in mineral rich areas such as Jharkhand out of the law's purview. Some adivasi areas like Latehar, Palamau and Garhwa do not even come within the purview of the tenancy acts.

The cement dust from the ACC cement factory at Jhinkpani in Singhbhum is polluting the air and making vast areas of agricultural land practically useless. The red oxide from the slag dams at Noamundi iron ore mines has destroyed vast areas of paddy fields during the rainy season in several villages around them. The influx of the dikus and the gradual criminalization of the society due to prostitution, communal riots, robbery, and so on, are other reasons for the simple adivasis to opt out of such areas. For instance, into the composition of the government in the early years after the formation of the state, one would find that almost every important portfolio, from finance to labour and from health to housing, was in the hands of the diku.

According to *Directory of Mines and Mine Leases* published in 1976 by the Indian Bureau of Mines, there were about 300 mines operating in Singhbhum and more than 151,000 acres of land were leased out, owned mostly by private agencies. The Uranium Corporation of India Ltd. (UCIL), situated at Jadugora in East Singhbhum is the only producer in the country of the vital nuclear fuel needed in all atomic reactors fed by natural uranium. Exact figures are not yet available about the extent of land alienation and displacement due to uranium mining and allied activities.[35] The Jharkhand state cabinet has recently approved the second lease renewal of the UCIL, which had been pending since 2007.[36] During flash floods in June 2008, radioactive uranium waste dumped into a tailing pond in Jadugora reportedly spilled over into nearby village ponds, wells and fields, and destroyed crops as well. It has been found that children in many villages close to the uranium-bearing Jadugora region are born with congenital disability, which is a matter of grave concern for the state.

The tribal areas are not completely free from the threat of fresh displacement. The government often tries to revive those projects, which had earlier been discontinued following protests. For example, the local tribals vehemently opposed the Koel-Karo Hydro Electric Power Project, under which two dams were proposed to be set up at Basia (Gumla district) and Lohajimi (Ranchi district) in Jharkhand in 1975. This culminated in a pathetic incident on 2 February 2001, in which nine protesters were killed and 22 seriously injured when a large contingent of police force opened fire on a 4,000–5,000 strong crowd.[37] In a film entitled, *Development Flows from the Barrel of the Gun*, this case of police barbarism has been shown.[38] It is common knowledge that many of the adivasi elected political leaders or village elders contribute to their continued enslavement and degradation by direct or indirect collusion with the politician-civilian-capitalist-contractor combine (see also Chapter 3).

CASE STUDY 4

Nagri village, about 20 km from the Jharkhand capital of Ranchi, has been in the eye of a storm for several months now. Without consulting the inhabitants of the village, the government of Jharkhand acquired 227 acres of tribal land to construct a Central Law University, an Indian Institute of Management and several institutes of information technology. The adivasis of Nagri claim that the land is agricultural, and has been so for generations and, therefore, the government should look elsewhere for the proposed educational hub. Ranchi city was in grip of protest by the villagers under the leadership of the popular tribal leader, Dayamani Barla of the Adivaasi Moolvaasi Astitva Raksha Manch (Forum for the Protection of Tribal and Indigenous People's Identity). She had been leading several campaigns against displacement of tribals.[39] Nagri might well inflict a similar blow like Singur and Nandigram in West Bengal.

CASE STUDY 5

The Jharkhand government approved construction of the dam on the Chata River at Jabra village in Karra block of Khunti district that would submerge 365 hectares of about 100 tribal families. But Triveni Engicons Private Limited, the company that begged the tender, did not follow procedures before starting the project. Unsuspecting people got a rude shock on 10 December 2010 when they saw vehicles driving onto their land and contractors performing *bhoomi pujan*. Soon, heavy machines trooped in and construction began. Angry over the forced acquisition of their land, people staged several protests. What followed were arrests by the police and the abduction of two local residents. Here also the movement was led by Dayamani Barla who filed three RTI applications—with the state water resources department, its Khunti district office, and the land acquisition cell of the revenue department.[40]

TRIBAL WOMEN IN AGRICULTURAL SECTOR IN WEST SINGHBHUM

It is true that the problem of technologically stagnant and rain-fed agriculture, low cropping intensity (monocropping) and yields, a marketing system cornered by middlemen, lack of institutional credit facilities and heavy indebtedness gravely afflict the tribals: per capita land holdings and income have been declining slowly and steadily.[41] More and more tribals are reduced to the ranks of sharecroppers or migrant agricultural labourers, a large proportion of whom are women migrants in both seasonal and long term migration stream.[42]

My field work was carried on in Mirra village in September 2011, in the south of West Singhbhum district, surrounded by a Protected Forest Block. Previously all the lands were forested but today they have been brought under cultivation. Deforestation is rampant in these areas. Singhbhum is very rich in mineral resources. More than a quarter of the total mining activity in India is carried on in this area. But the poor tribals of this area have hardly benefited from this massive industrialization and urbanization. The Ho tribals of Singhbhum share many common features with the Mundas, Santhals, Oraons, Kharias. Today Hos are settled agriculturists. The Ho villages of Singhbhum still lack good roads, schools, electricity, irrigation facilities and consequently low productivity of agriculture. Cultivation is completely dependent upon natural rain and failure of monsoon causes scarcity of food. Thus, the adivasis are compelled either to rest on the collection of minor forest produces or to migrate as casual labourers in mines, construction industries, brick kilns and other worksites.

My field work in Raghunathpur village of Jhinkpani Tehsil, West Singhbhum in September 2011, revealed that 90 per cent of the total labour in tribal villages is performed by the womenfolk. The tribal economy functions primarily on the basis of women's labour. It is interesting to note that ploughing is one task that is strictly prohibited for the women to perform. It is believed that if a tribal woman touches the plough it would cause drought. If there is no man in the family to pull the plough, the women of the family have to hire male labour. This taboo indicates the male control over the land, though women perform more tedious jobs like breaking lumps of earth with a hoe, prepare manure from cow dung compost, transplanting of rice, hand-threshing, harvesting, carrying the grains from the fields to the house, and weeding. Women also build embankments, take care of irrigation, and water drainage in the fields in the absence of menfolk. Women collect firewood, medicinal herbs, wild fruits, sal leaves (for plate making). During the lean season they have to sell the firewood when the stock of rice is exhausted. Thus the women also go to the market in Chakradharpur or Rourkela, usually in a group, to sell the products. There they conduct barter activity, exchange grain, poultry, lentils, mahua fruits, oilseeds, for soap, salt and oil. Even though Ho women are more active than men in agricultural and marketing activities, they have to do all the household work without much help from men.

Childcare is mainly a woman's responsibility. When infants are breastfed, women often carry on their backs while going to work in the fields or for gathering in the forest. Health care facilities are unavailable in these villages that has affected the child mortality rate. Men perform hunting, ploughing, building roofs, but there are several reasons for men's labour contribution being low amongst the Hos and most other tribal communities. The Ho tribe was patrilineal and patrilocal even before transforming into settled agriculturists, although the absence of developed forms of private property helped prevent it from being as heavily patriarchal.

Writing on the inheritance right of the Ho women, Madhu Kishwar described her experience about the customary laws of the Ho tribe.[43] She said that the Hos continue to be governed by their customary law in inheritance which results in tribal women not being maintained by the men's labour, but getting the right to cultivate a portion of the land in their lifetime. After their death, it reverts to men of the family. This, as discussed earlier, is called a usufructory right. As soon as a daughter marries, she loses her limited usufructory right over parental land, even if the marriage turns out to be a nominal one. A discarded woman cannot claim any permanent right on her parental land, while an unmarried woman has the right to work on and be maintained from her family's land. But she does not inherit as a son does. She is not even given an equal portion of land with sons and only given a piece of land for her maintenance which is much smaller than the ones sons get. If an unmarried woman has a sexual relationship with a non-tribal man, she loses her usufructory right. A widow's usufructory right in her husband's land is similar to that of an unmarried woman. She does not inherit the land but has a right to be maintained from it. In practice, very few women's customary rights are honoured. If she remarries, she loses her usufructory right over her dead husband's land which goes to her sons, or if there are no sons, to the husband's male agnates. Women do not have rights on the domestic animals as well. Ho women's land rights as wives are the most precarious of all. At no point of her life can a woman claim a share in her husband's land in her own right. The concept of joint property is totally unknown. The wife's status is in many ways similar to that of a landless labourer. The male members of a tribal family can mortgage their family lands without consulting the female members who have a usufructory right in these lands because the lands are registered in their names.

This gives rise to a culture of son preference. Daughters are valued chiefly because of their work capacity. A Ho woman's work burden is overwhelming if she has no daughters to help her; girls fetch a bride price instead of taking a dowry, so they are not perceived as a burden on the family. Single women and childless widows are among the most vulnerable. If a woman does not surrender her usufructory right, she may become the target of different kinds of violence and the most common is in the form of witch killing. Although it is generally believed that lack of modern health care facilities makes tribals fall prey to the superstition that various diseases are the result of witchcraft, we should not forget the economic reason behind it and that is to take away her land by any means. Another form of violence is social ostracism. A woman who has been ostracized will not find anyone to plough her fields or thatch her roof.

The denial of equal land rights to Ho women is often justified on the grounds of patrilocal family structure. It is argued that because a woman shifts to her husband's home and village on marriage, she will not be able to cultivate land in her natal village, so there is no use her inheriting parental land. Ho wives have a very uncertain kind of rights on their husbands' lands. There are a high proportion of unmarried women among the Hos, because they have at least a right to subsist on their parents' land. According to the Census 1971, approximately 11 per cent of all Ho women 45 years of age or above had never married.[44] In contrast, the all India percentage of tribal women above 45 years of age who had never married is less than 1 per cent, approximately the same as the all-India figure for all communities.

Although most Ho men who find jobs outside the village do not contribute to work on the land, they manage to keep control over it by virtue of their near exclusive rights over it. An unmarried sister or a wife continues the subsistence agriculture in the village while the brothers or husbands function somewhat like absentee landlords. The land is an important source of security for men. After returning he can easily take over the land from his wife, sister or daughter, because the village community supports the man's right.

TRIBAL WOMEN'S ALTERNATIVE DEVELOPMENT INITIATIVE IN EAST SINGHBHUM

In East Singhbhum district of Jharkhand, some NGOs are successfully working for the development of the Primitive Tribe Groups (PTGs), like Bharat Sewa Ashram Sangha of Ghatsila, Vikas Bharti of Gumla and Society for Participatory Action and Reflection (SPAR) of Ghatsila. East Singhbhum is one of the PTG inhabited districts. The Sabars usually work as agricultural labourers and the families having agricultural land are negligible. They mainly depend on the forest for the collection of wood and other products. SPAR is presently working among the Sabar community inhabiting in four villages (Kendua, Lakhaidih, Bomro and Chatanipani) of Dumuria block.[45] SPAR promotes and forms Self Help Groups (SHGs) to organize and empower the Sabar women on group dynamics and management, savings and credit management, communication skill, production and marketing management.[46]

There has been 20 per cent increase in women's participation in Gram Sabha, women are taking part in decision-making process, resisting plunder of natural resources, contributing to gram sabha resource management. Villagers themselves prepare micro-planning: Gram Sabha Resource Management Plan and diversion channels have been developed in three villages. This will help the villagers to get water for additional two months. Thus SPAR ensured the participation of tribal women in management committees.[47]

TRIBAL WOMEN'S LAND RIGHTS IN JHARKHAND

The customary tribal land inheritance systems among the tribals of Jharkhand are patrilineal in order to prevent the land alienation, as we saw with the Ho women. Among the Munda and Oraon, the widow and the unmarried daughters are given the maintenance lands till the death the former and the marriage of the latter. After the marriage of the daughters their lands are divided among their brothers. But if the daughter is the only surviving child in the family, she is entitled to her father's property till she gets married, after which it goes to the closest male agnates of her father. But neither her husband nor her sons are allowed to inherit her father's landed property. A widow with grown up sons and daughters is given a plot of land, generally equalling a younger son's share, for her maintenance. Some money and grain is also given to her to see through till the next harvest. She enjoys a lifetime use of the produce of her land, which is generally cultivated by one of her sons at whose house she chooses to live. Should this son meet her funeral costs, he is entitled to this land after her death. Otherwise it is distributed equally among her sons. But if a widow remarries, she forfeits everything at her deceased husband's place and can take away only her clothes and jewels. A widow without sons is allowed a life interest in the property of her dead husband.[48] Among the Santhals, daughters have special privileges in sharing their father's lands. If an unmarried woman's father dies leaving no widow, sons, brothers or male agnates, she either shares his land with her sisters, or if here are no sisters, she inherits it entirely.[49]

According to Nitya Rao, land is not merely as a material asset but also as a 'key element in the identities of indigenous people'.[50] Women recognized the symbolic and historical significance of land to adivasi identity in general and kin identity in particular.[51] 'Women are unable to act as autonomous individuals in relation to land,' thus compromising their ability to fulfil a positive social identity through owning and cultivating land.[52] In the absence of a son, women can get married under the *gharjawae* custom, wherein the husband foregoes his land claims and moves to the wife's home, and thus inherits his father-in-law's land.

Activists claimed that if a widow is given land, she might be harassed. No one is able to cite cases of daughters asking for partition of land, but people may employ various 'tricks' to give property to their daughters, such as selling land and then buying it back in the daughter's name. There is also a practice of gifting a married woman some land in her natal village as maintenance by her father, brothers or other male agnates. But if it can be shown that an adivasi is sufficiently Hinduized, she/he may come under the provision of the Hindu Succession Act where women can inherit land. The grounds for the decision may be the practice of cremation rather than burial, the form of marriage, religious practices, and even social practices such as prohibition on women touching the plough. In case of marriage between tribal woman and non-tribal man or tribal man and non-tribal woman, the tribal community takes decision on the recognition of the matrimonial alliance and approval of the marriage and thereby inheritance.

At present the tribal people of Jharkhand suffer greatly on account of land alienation, and the ecological degradation is at its worst on account of the non-sustainable development process. The destruction of the eco-system for others' profit and not the adivasi's that began in the colonial period was aggravated in the postcolonial era of 'development'. Today 14 per cent of the land in Jharkhand is covered mostly by degraded forests. In the 1970s, a fierce conflict ensued between the adivasis and the forest department.[53] Although the Approach Paper to the draft Ninth Plan states that preference should be given to women in distribution of ceiling surplus land, it is not clear to what extent women as individuals have received land distributed by the Government of Jharkhand or Bihar.[54] Ever since the New Economic Policy ushered in the 1990s, the economic scenario of the country changed drastically. Jharkhand promptly brought out the 'Jharkhand Vision 2010' and 'Jharkhand Industrial Policy', both aggravating the plight of the tribal people. That is why as many as 74 Memorandum of Understanding (MoUs) have been signed by the Jharkhand government in the last few years giving 3,000 acres of land to Jindal Steel at Ghatshila and 25,500 acres to Tata Steel for Green Field Project at Manoharpur and Chandil in East Singhbhum to mention a few.⁵⁵ A review of the land distribution in Dumka during 1998–1999 reveals that the land distribution is absent in the largely adivasi and forested blocks of Kathikund and Gopikandar. In 1994–1995, in line with the Eighth Plan call to allot 40 per cent of ceiling-surplus land to women, but this focus is not reflected in the land distribution data. A related issue is in terms of issuing joint pattas to men and women. Progress in this too has been tardy. Government initiative in terms of redistribution does not seem to have touched women much in real terms, but has contributed to the discourse around the legitimacy of women's land claims.⁵⁶ Work participation rates for adivasi women in Jharkhand are much higher in comparison to that for the general female population in the state or even for India as a whole. While in India 74 per cent of women were classified as non-workers in 2001, the ratio at 65 per cent is much lower for Dumka district, 40 per cent of whose population is adivasi. For the scheduled tribes, women classified as non-workers are even lower: 59 per cent for Jharkhand and only 53.5 per cent for Dumka. Interestingly, the Census of 1991 ranked Dumka third in terms of female work participation rates in the then Bihar state, following the districts of Gumla and West Singhbhum, both with adivasi-majority populations.⁵⁷

CASE STUDY 6

Forcible occupation of tribal land in East Singhbhum district took place. Phulo Baske, a tribal woman, purchased a small piece of land (0.6 acres) from Chandu Ho by virtue of registered sale deed No. 6431, dated 20 September 1966. She got her name mutated and began to pay rent to the government. But Pagla Gwala, a non-tribal, forcibly occupied 0.2 acres of her land. Phulo Baske filed a restoration case in the court of LRDC, Dhalbhum, at Jamshedpur on 19 September 1989; her R.P. case number was 7–10/91. Pagla Gwala's tribal wife Raiban Ho claimed that she had also purchased the occupied land from the original Khatiyani Raiyat. After the inquiry in the court it was found that the land was truly transferred to Phulo Baske by the competent authority. Consequently, the land was restored to her as per the Order-sheet (Misc. case no. 86/87 under Section 46 of the Chotanagpur Tenancy Act 1908). The land was restored to Phulo Baske on 10 July 1992. The court ordered the CO to ensure that the delivery of possession is effected within 7 days of the receipt of the order. But Phulo Baske had been harassed by the CO and other officers. Eventually she lost all faith in the efficacy of the administration and hope of getting her land back.[58]

TRIBAL WOMEN AND LABOUR FORCE PARTICIPATION IN RANCHI

I discuss the impact of the poverty alleviation programmes and employment generation programmes on tribals as a whole and tribal woman in particular, of the rural areas of Ranchi. This consisted of three community development blocks: Burmu, Angara and Kara. The tribals of Ranchi use traditional and primitive technology in agriculture. There is high incidence of landlessness and there is no large-scale prevalence of leasing system in the tribal villages. Access to irrigation facilities among the tribals is low. They do not even have traditional farm equipment, such as wooden plough or sickle. They are very poor and take up any kind of economic activity, which is survival strategy for them. This is evident from the higher participation rates both among the males and females in the age group of 5–15 years and above. In the age group of 15 years and above, labour participation rates are almost equal to the male one because even those women who do not find time to work as full-time workers take up some kind of secondary activity. According to the criterion of extended labour force more than 80 per cent of the tribal women participate in economic activities,[59] and children supplement the family income through part-time work.

The tribals are mainly subsistence level cultivators; they also participate in other economic activities, because the share of surplus generated is very small. It results in lower wage rate for agricultural labourers, which is lower than even the wage rates prevalent in other parts of Jharkhand. In this connection, there are two noteworthy features of tribal peoples: the majority also participate in wage work in agriculture which was traditionally not so widely prevalent, and in rearing of domestic animals which was also traditionally not so common. Non-farm self-employment activities are generally of low investment and primitive technology-based. Trade of agro-products and minor forest products are the main activities. Here there is evidence of gender differentiation and discrimination. The tribal males participate in more remunerative trade such as selling of fuelwood and coal, while the tribal females take up less remunerative trade such as selling of grass, leaf plates, and so on. Earnings per day are higher for the males than for the females in all the activities. There is gender discrimination in wage payments as well—the wage rates of the females are much lower.[60] Livestock is increasingly becoming more important among tribals. Piggery and poultry are very common among almost all the tribal communities. Livestock rearing is mainly performed by the females and the young children.

The Integrated Rural Development Programme (IRDP) is the only self-employment programme being implemented in these villages by the District Rural Development Agency (DRDA). Even after selection, the beneficiaries face many hurdles before the actual disbursement of loans and other infrastructural help. An overwhelmingly large number of the beneficiaries do not know the provisions or facilities available under the IRDP, which works as a major hindrance in its successful implementation. Jawahar Rozgar Yojana (JRY) and its various components like Million Wells Scheme and Indira Awas Yojana are not as much prevalent as the IRDP in the tribal villages of Ranchi. There is also evidence of gender discrimination in wage payments under these programmes. Women get ₹5–10 less than the minimum wage rate prescribed by the government of Jharkhand (₹30–50) which is paid to the men.[61] Social forestry, so important for the tribal region, has not been given its due importance and so are the small schemes of irrigation in the rural areas which are also very important for agricultural development. There is significant scope for social forestry in the region.

BIRHOR WOMEN IN HUNTING-GATHERING SECTOR IN HAZARIBAGH

Birhors are one of the most important PTGs in Jharkhand, in mainly Hazaribagh, Ranchi, and Giridih districts, comprising 0.12 per cent of the total tribal population, with a population of 8,159 in 1991 (Census 1991). They are mainly divided into two types: settled Birhor (Janghi Birhor) and nomadic Birhor (Uthlu Birhor). In recent years a third category from Uthlu Birhor has emerged that is semi-nomadic Birhor, locally called Baslu Birhor.

Birhors mainly reside in villages like Banaso, Burhachanch and Sidhbara of Hazaribagh district. Birhors of Hazaribagh district of Jharkhand are nomadic in nature. Their close intimation with the forest has created a specific well-integrated man-nature relation. They live in small hamlets known as tanda which the Birhors can establish instantaneously. According to Vinita Damodaran, the Birhors, in the extreme east of Singhbhum, were a wandering community who lived by snaring monkeys and by collecting the fibre of the *Bauhinia vahlii* creeper.[62] Birhors pursue quite a number of occupations, of which rope making is the primary one. They also carry on hunting, which does not contribute much to their total economy. Besides household organization Birhor economy also involves band organization: a group of interrelated households moving and camping together. The major economic activity at such level is the pursuit of hunting monkeys and other wild game.[63]

Birhors exclusively depend on three different items of the forests: fibres, jungle roots, tubers and wild animals. The jungle infested regions in Hazaribagh district more or less provide these essential items.[64] These people face tremendous problems due to large scale deforestation throughout the Chotanagpur plateau. Using a kilogram of jute, they make five ropes which sell at 4 rupees per piece, enabling them to earn 20 rupees per day. If the *Bahunia* creepers had been available in the forest, each rope-maker would have been able to make a profit of ₹40.[65]

Although Birhors are called a nomadic tribe, now they are becoming settled and leaving their traditional pattern of migration. The population is getting redistributed as a result of the dismantling of their traditional modes of economy. The 1960s witnessed a major shift in their workforce structure. As the forests were no longer able to supply the raw material for rope-making, it declined in importance, and a large number of workers moved to work as agricultural labourers. The direction and intensity of the change in workforce structure took a different turn during the 1970s. A sizeable segment of agricultural labourers reverted to one of their traditional occupations of forest gathering. Though the alternative economic activity for the Birhors has been agriculture, ignorance of agricultural practices and low quality of land has been the major hindrances in adopting these activities. Thus they have gone back to rope-making.[66]

As a member of the hunter-gatherer tribe with wandering activities the Birhor women are specifically responsible for keeping the household materials in the right position during the transit of the band. Moreover they are responsible for maintaining the family duties. Collection of fire woods, fetching of drinking water as well as collection of jungle roots and tubers are the female jobs and the Birhor males are greatly dependent on them for this. The Birhor women are allowed to move freely in the neighbouring forests but they are debarred from cutting chop fibres—the essential raw materials for the preparation of ropes. Mahua liquor is one of the important liquors of the Birhors. Authority lies in the hands of the father, husband or an older male member, according to the composition of the household.⁶⁷ The basic economy of the Birhors rotates round the nuclear family. In this family the wife is the pivot and thus she is respected by all the family members.⁶⁸ Thus, women possess comparatively high position in the Birhor society.

ASUR AND PAHARIA WOMEN

The Asur is one of the primitive tribes in Jharkhand and is confined to Netarhat Plateau of Chotanagpur. The Asur have three economic and territorial sub-groups, namely, Soika, Birjihas and Jat Asur. They are patriarchal, patrilocal and patrilineal. They prefer early marriage. Divorce cases are absent. The socio-economic status of the Asur women is higher than that of other primitive tribal groups in Chotanagpur. The economy of Asur was dependent on shifting cultivation and iron ore smelting. But after the banning on the use of forest they were forced to take up agriculture in the new economic situation. They were engaged in daily wage labour and seasonal migrant labour in the Forest Department and mining along with their existing agriculture and collection work.⁶⁹ Rice beer or handia is prepared by women.⁷⁰

The main economy of the Paharias pivots around the kurwa or slash and burn cultivation and collection of forest produce. Both genders participate in field preparation. A man ploughs and the women sow the seeds from behind the plough. Women participate in collection of forest produce and cattle rearing. Both genders sell folk medicines in local hats. Women also do bee-keeping. Paharia men and women work as labourer at the crusher and get ₹20 to 35 per day as wages depending on the number of baskets of stone chips they loaded.⁷¹ Paharias have now become agricultural labourers as they lost their land in due course of time. The women are engaged in the collection of forest roots and fruits, bamboo work and lac cultivation. They do basketry as well.⁷²

BAIGA WOMEN AS SHIFTING CULTIVATORS IN GARHWA

The Baiga is one of the most important PTGs in the state of Jharkhand, inhabiting Garhwa district. Many make medicines by profession, though their chief traditional occupation has been shifting cultivation. The Baiga dwell in the remotest regions of the state and it becomes very difficult for the people of the urban world to reach out to them. Most of them are found to reside in the forested regions and hilly areas of Jharkhand. Baiga subsistence depends on a combination of gathering, hunting and swidden cultivation practices for their survival. Of these, swidden cultivation is considered the cornerstone. Gathering, hunting and bewar are bound together in a precarious balance by a fragile seasonal rhythm, whose success was intrinsically dependent on the success of the bewar cycle. Therefore, shifting cultivation system is difficult to sustain without the existence of hunting and gathering.[73]

The swiddening practices of the Baigas are similar to those of the Khondhs of Odisha. Baigas believe that tilling the soil with a plough is akin to scratching the breast of Mother Earth. Generally they start to prepare for it by late May. They sow 16 varieties of seed, mostly coarse grains and minor millets—an enviable diversity of native crops including paddy, wheat, pulses, oil seeds. Women process the maize, rice and coarse grains with the traditional instrument called 'jata'. They also do the preservation work. They process liquor from mahua flowers. The same plot produced less in the second and third years. The old bewar was then allowed to lie fallow for tree re-growth during the next ten to fifteen years, before being cut again.[74]

In the second year, there is more time for hunting because fewer crops have to be sown and harvested, but since there is enough food, the people lived on the bewars. It is only in the third year that the diet has to be supplemented with the forest products and game from hunting. This is true even as bewar forms the fulcrum of the seasonal cycle and enjoys a dialectical relationship with hunting and gathering, without which bewar itself would become unsustainable.[75] There is also the need to maintain the fallow cycles of bewar in order to replenish the nutrients of the soil. If the undergrowth fails to appear, it is impossible for the cultivator to do bewar cultivation on the field.[76]

Gathering is not a gender-specific task. Both men and women do the gathering for the local agrarian market. Men also gather roots in times of drought and famine. Mahua and sal seeds are collected by women and used as food or for brewing tadi (country liquor). Marketing of goods and articles of daily necessity are done by both men and women.[77] Today with massive commercialization of minor forest produce a change is taking place. The commercial establishments are appointing their collecting agents from outside, resulting in the loss of an important economic role of the women.

Male members of the community control the technology and the means of production. For example, the women are not allowed to touch the axe. After the marriage of the son, the father gifts an axe to him. The male child's access to the axe, bows and arrows give him power and is a recognition of his dominance as a future patriarch.[78] The Baigas are presently in a transitional phase. With the transformation from swidden cultivators to settled cultivators, Baiga women have started acquiring a greater role in the fulfilment of the Baiga needs. Baiga people are exposed to outside people and culture; the results can be seen in their customs, culture and society.

Forest economy is, to a great extent, women's economy. On an average, women and girls work in shifting cultivation for more than 200 work-days a year as against 60 days work done by men. Reports available on Chotanagpur show that 60 per cent of the women head loaders are in the age-group of 15–30 and 34 per cent are in the age group of 31–40 and the rest 6 per cent are above 40 years of age.[79] It is pertinent to mention here that no theories of western patriarchy and ecofeminism are entirely applicable in the Indian situation, although by seeing the situation outlined above, it is necessary to draw attention towards the need for highlighting the role of adivasi women in the natural economy and their vulnerability in the context of an ecological crisis, which is always there. Women depend more on non-market access to environmental products and services because they have less access to private property resources, such as land, and because of the gender division of labour which makes firewood or water women's work. Against the 'chrematistic' man,[80] we find the ecological-economic man. Today, on several counts, as with women's exclusion or token presence in many forest committees, it is necessary to change such institutions towards equality, both for justice and for effectiveness.

NOTES

1 Stuart Corbridge, Sarah Jewitt and Sanjay Kumar, 2004. *Jharkhand: Environment, Development, Ethnicity* (New Delhi: Oxford University Press): 112–74.
2 As agriculture is the cultivation of fields (*agra*), silviculture is the cultivation of forests (*silva*). Silviculture is the domain of foresters who are trained in the systems used to maximize the volume and value growth of forests. Silviculture also has to do with sustained yield and keeping the forest productive through multiple rotations (life spans of trees) for wildlife habitats, clean water and recreational uses as well as forest products.
3 Vandana Shiva, 1988. *Staying Alive: Women, Ecology and Survival in India* (New Delhi: Kali for Women): 50.
4 Ibid.: 60.
5 See Kelkar and Nathan, *Gender and Tribe*.
6 Dev Nathan, 2012. 'Women and Forests', in *Adivasi Question*, Indra Munshi, ed.: 195–202.
7 Kelkar and Nathan, *Gender and Tribe*: 58.
8 Jewitt, *Environment, Knowledge and Gender*: 279.
9 Ibid.: 57.
10 L. Fortmann, 1986. 'Women in Subsistence Forestry', *Journal of Forestry* 84, 7: 39–42.
11 Shiva, *Staying Alive*: 61.
12 Kelkar and Nathan, *Gender and Tribe*: 116.

13. Roy and Mukherjee, 'Status of Forest Protection Committees in West Bengal', in *Managing the Village Commons*, R. Singh, ed.: 113–16.
14. *The Statesman*, 23 September 2012.
15. Ibid.
16. Kelkar, 'Climate Change: Vulnerability and Women's Agency', in *Social Exclusion and Adverse Inclusion*, Nathan and Xaxa, eds.: 208–36.
17. Vinita Narain and Lakshmi, 1994: 'Self-Concept in Santal Women', *Man in India*, 74, 1: 15–20.
18. Awinash Chandra Mishra, 2009. 'Socio-economic Impact of Industrialization on the Santal Tribe of Jharkhand', *Man and Life*, 35, 3 & 4 (ISRAA, Bidisa): 99–104.
19. Shalina Mehta, 1992. 'Industrialization of a Tribal Belt: Some Observations', *Man in India* 72, 3: 271–80.
20. Pranab Kumar Das Gupta, 1978. 'Tribal Women in Industrial Context', in *Tribal Women in India*, Calcutta: Indian Anthropological Society: 192–99.
21. V. Das, 1992. *Jharkhand*: 79.
22. Ibid.: 76.
23. Shashank Shekhar Sinha, *Restless Mothers and Turbulent Daughters*: 113–16.
24. S.N. Ray, 1982. *Migrant Women Workers* (Ranchi: Bihar Tribal Welfare Research Institute).
25. Alpa Shah, *In the Shadow of the State, Indigenous Politics, Environmentalism, and Insurgency*: 131–61.
26. Neha Wadhawan, 2013. 'Living in Domesti-City Women and Migration for Domestic Work from Jharkhand', *Economic and Political Weekly* (henceforth *EPW*) 48, 43 (26 Oct.): 47–54.
27. Mathew Areeparampil, 2012. 'Displacement due to Mining in Jharkhand', in *Adivasi Question*, Indra Munshi, ed.: 239–50.
28. Centre for Science and Environment, *Rich Lands, Poor People*: 165.
29. Dias, *Kalinga Nagar, Before and After*.
30. Areeparampil, 'Industries, Mines and Dispossession', in *Development, Displacement and Rehabilitation*, Fernandes and Ganguly Thukral, eds.: 19.
31. Areeparampil, 'Industries, Mines and Dispossession of Indigenous Peoples', in *Tribal Movements*, Mishra and Paty, eds.: 142–68.
32. Dhebar, *UN Report of the Scheduled Areas and Scheduled Tribes Commission*, 1961, vol. 1, 1960–1961 (New Delhi: Ministry of Home Affairs, Government of India): 115.
33. *Report of the Committee on Rehabilitation of Displaced Tribals due to Development Projects* (1985), New Delhi, Ministry of Home Affairs, Government of India.
34. Ajitha Susan George, 2005. 'Laws Related to Mining in Jharkhand', *EPW* 40, 41 (Oct. 8–14): 4455–58; Nitya Rao, 2003. 'Life and Livelihood

in Santal Pargana: Does the Right to a Livelihood Really Exist?' *EPW* 38, 39 (Sep. 27–Oct. 3): 4081–84.
35. Areeparampil, Mathew (2012).
36. *The Times of India*, 1 October 2014.
37. Anonymous, 2001. 'Massacre of Adivasi: A Preliminary Report', *EPW* (March 3–9): 717–21.
38. Savyasaachi, 2012. 'Struggles for Adivasi Livelihoods Reclaiming the Foundational Value of Work', *EPW* 31 (Aug. 4): 27–31.
39. *The Statesman*, 27–28 September 2012.
40. *The Statesman*, 27 March 2011.
41. Goutam K. Sarkar, 1995. *Agriculture and Rural Transformation in India* (New Delhi: Oxford University Press): 208.
42. P.P. Ghosh and Alakh N. Sharma, 1995. 'Seasonal Migration of Rural Labour in Bihar', *Labour and Development*, 1, 1.
43. Madhu Kishwar, 1987. 'Toiling without Rights: Ho Women of Singhbhum', *EPW* 22, 3 (Jan 17): 95–101; 22, 4 (Jan 24): 149–55.
44. *Census of India*, 1971, Series 1, Part V-A (ii) Special Tables for Scheduled Tribes, 1977.
45. Suchismita Sen Chowdhury and Mahua Sengupta, 2012. 'Development of PTGs through NGO: A Case Study with Savars of Jharkhand', *Bulletin of the Cultural Research Institute*, 24, 1 & 2: 31.
46. Ibid.: 35–36.
47. Ibid.
48. Alex Ekka, 2011. *A Status of Adivasis/Indigenous Peoples Land Series—4 Jharkhand* (New Delhi: Aakar Books associated with The Other Media): 34–37.
49. W.G. Archer, 1984. *Tribal Laws and Justice: A Report on the Santal* (New Delhi: Concept Publishing Co): 142.
50. Nitya Rao, 2008. *'Good Women Do Not Inherit Land': Politics of Land and Gender in India* (New Delhi: Social Science Press and Orient Blackswan): 6.
51. Ibid.: 37.
52. Ibid.: 294.
53. M. Areeparampil, 1992. 'Forest Andolan in Singhbhum', in *Jharkhand Movement: Origin and Evolution* edited by S. Narayan (New Delhi: Inter India Publications).
54. *Approach Paper to The Ninth Five Year Plan (1997–2002)*, Planning Commission, Government of India, available at http://planningcommission.nic.in/reports/publications/app_nine.pdf downloaded on 24 August 2012.
55. Alex Ekka and Mohammed Asif, 2000. *Development-Induced Displacement and Rehabilitation in Jharkhand, 1951 to 1995: A Database on Its Extent and Nature* (New Delhi: Indian Social Institute): 33–38.

56. Census 199, Series 5 Bihar, Part-II-B (I) [Census 1991, Series 5 Bihar, Part-II-B (I); Census 1991, Series 5 Bihar, Part-II-B (I); Nitya Rao, 2012]. 'Displacement from Land: Case of Santhal Parganas', in *The Adivasi Question*, Indra Munshi, ed.: 122–23.
57. Nitya Rao, 2008. *'Good Women Do Not Inherit Land'*: 61.
58. Alex Ekka, 2011. *A Status of Adivasis/Indigenous Peoples Land Series*: 83–84.
59. Seema Singh, 1998. 'State Interventions and Tribal Workers', in *Empowering Rural Labour in India: Market, State and Mobilisation*, edited by R. Radhakrishna and Alakh N. Sharma (New Delhi: Institute for Human Development): 243–68.
60. R. Sharan, and H. Dayal, 1994. 'Discrimination against Female Farm Labourers in the Jharkhand Region of Bihar', *Indian Journal of Labour Economics* 37, 4.
61. Seeema Singh, 'State Interventions and Tribal Workers'.
62. V. Damodaran, 2007. 'Tribes in Indian History', in *Situating Environmental History* edited by Ranjan Chakrobarty (New Delhi: Manohar): 135.
63. Jyoti Sen, 1978. 'Status and Role of Women among the Birhor: A Nomadic Hunting and Gathering Community of Eastern India', in *Tribal Women in India* edited by Indian Anthropological Society, Calcutta.
64. B.K. Roy Burman, 1985. 'Challenges of Development and Tribal Women of India', in *Tribal Women and Development*, edited by J.P. Singh, M.N. Vyas and R.S. Mann (Udaipur: The MLV Tribal Research and Training Institute, Tribal Area Development Department): 19.
65. Sohel Firdos, 2012. 'Forest Degradation, Changing Workforce Structure and Population Redistribution: The Case of Birhors in Jharkhand', in *The Adivasi Question*: 169–81.
66. Ibid.
67. Ashim Kumar Adhikary, 1984. 'Society and World View of the Birhor', *Anthropological Survey of India*, Government of India: 21 and 28–29.
68. Sampa Sarkar, 1994. 'Status of Tribal Women in Three Socio-cultural Dimensions', *Man in India* 74, 1: 49–57.
69. Partha Das, and Nabakumar Duary, 2005. 'The Asur: A Study on their Changing Economy', in *Primitive Tribes in Contemporary India*, vol. 2, edited by Sarit K. Chaudhari and Sucheta Sen Chaudhari (New Delhi: Mittal): 43–48.
70. Pratibha Kumari, 2005. 'Asur of Jharkhand—A Glimpse of Their Material Culture', in *Primitive Tribes*, edited by Chaudhuri and Sen Chaudhuri: 49–59.
71. Pratibha Kumari, 2005. 'Sauria Paharia Economy in Time Perspective—A Case of Sahebganj District', in *Primitive Tribes*, Chaudhuri and Sen Chaudhuri, eds.: 69–84.

72. Channa, Kumar and Kapoor, 2005. 'Economy of a Primitive Tribe in Jharkhand', in *Primitive Tribes*, Chaudhuri and Sen Chaudhuri, eds.: 61–68.
73. *The Statesman*, 29 July 2012.
74. Rajesh K. Gautam, 2011. *Baigas: The Hunter Gatherers of Central India* (New Delhi: Readworthy Publications): 86–88.
75. Archana Prasad, 2004. 'Reinterpreting Tribal Livelihood Systems: Underdevelopment and the Local Political Economy in Central India, 1800–1940', in *Tribes, Forest and Social Formation in Indian History*, edited by B.B. Chaudhuri and Arun Bandyopadhyay (New Delhi: Manohar): 109–44.
76. Archana Prasad, 1995. 'The Political Ecology of Swidden Cultivation', *Tools and Tillage* 2, 4, Denmark.
77. A.K. Danda, 1978. 'Economic Role and Status of Women', in *Tribal Women in India* (Calcutta: Indian Anthropological Society).
78. Verrier Elwin, 1939. *The Baiga* (London: Oxford University Press): 78–79, 273.
79. N.G. Basu, 1987. *N.G.O. Report, Forests and Tribals* (Calcutta: Manisha): 94–104.
80. B. Agarwal, 1992. 'The Gender and Environment Debate: Lessons from India', *Feminist Studies* 18, 1: 119–58.

CHAPTER 5

Adivasi Women and Destructive Development in Odisha

ODISHA IS DEFINED in economic terms as one of India's poorest states, yet it is one of the richest in 'mineral resources', possessing the world's best deposits of the bauxite used in aluminium production, a process which requires the construction of dams to provide electricity. Many of these mountain ranges have complex sacred meanings attached to them by adivasis or are biodiversity 'hotspots' as defined by the International Union for the Conservation of Nature (IUCN). The agriculturally poor mining belt of Odisha, comprised Hos, Kols, Kharias, Mundas as the main working force, has large surplus labour and the poor wage structure. Tribal women and children are often found working in these mines. The women work in gangs, and are mainly involved in pit clearing, while children as young as eight are seen carrying waste underground.

With the acceleration of the forces of globalization since 1800, vigorous contestations for space and resources have taken place among adivasis, peasants, the state, and mining and other commercial companies. Since 1945, and much more since 1990, these contests have involved an increasing level of state and corporate violence against adivasis.

Adivasi Women and Destructive Development in Odisha 157

According to conservative estimates, 24,124 hectares of land (until 1999) have been deforested as a result of development projects in tribal areas including dams, mines, roads, railways and new industry.[1] The Kalinga Nagar massacre in Jaipur district in January 2006 appears to be a turning point in the breakdown of governance. A 35-year-old Ho woman, Deogi Tina, from a village in Champa Koila stood against illegal mining. The streams and hills were sacred to her and her kinsfolk. Deogi Tina was executed in cold blood by the Odisha police.[2] The Chief Minister Naveen Patnaik declared: 'No one, I repeat no one, will be allowed to stand in the way of Odisha's industrialization and the people's progress'.[3]

CASE STUDY 1

Centre for Research and Development Solidarity (CRDS), Odisha, conducted a field study in 2006, which partially aims to construct adivasi social movement perspectives on development and its implications in one hundred and twenty villages inhabited by Kondhs and Saoras of south Odisha. The study refers to the Adivasi Dalit Ekta Abhijan (ADEA). A Kondh woman leader expressed her sentiments as follows: 'The sarkar [government] and their workers think that we adivasis do not know anything ... To the government, we are of no significance. They are selling our forests ... our water ... our land and maybe they will sell us also.'[4] The ADEA movement's purposes are articulated at various forums employing different culturally-specific mediums of movement. Extracts of a lamentation of a song by three adivasi women follows:

> This forest, this mountain and this land is ours
> Given by our Gods to our ancestors.
> But people are destroying the forests,
> How can we depend on it if everything is gone?

TRIBAL WOMEN, LAND ALIENATION AND DISPLACEMENT

The status of tribal women in Odisha is mixed. Districts of Malkangiri, Rayagada, Nuapada and Kalahandi have a female literacy rate of less than 30 per cent. Gender disparity in education is further accentuated with only 31 per cent girls as compared to 51 per cent boys completing primary schooling (NFHS 2, 1998–1999). The Maternal Mortality Rate (MMR), that is, the number of maternal deaths in the age group 15–49 years per 100, 000 live births, has gone up from 361 in 1997 to 367 in 1998 in the state (*Human Development Report* 2004, GoO), whereas for all-India, it has declined from 408 to 407 in the same period. Overall 63 per cent of the women in reproductive age group (15–49 years) have some degree of anemia (NFHS 3, 2005–2006). Fertility continues to decline in Odisha. At current fertility levels, women will have an average of 2.37 children each throughout their childbearing years (NFHS 3, 2005–2006) down from 2.9 children per woman as per NFHS 1, 1992–1993. Crimes against women in Odisha have recorded an increasing trend.[5]

The Government of Odisha has enacted several important legislations for the development and welfare of STs, such as, Odisha Scheduled Area Transfer of Immovable Property (by Scheduled Tribes) Regulation of 1956, Odisha Survey and Settlement Act of 1958, The Odisha Land Reforms Act of 1960, The Bonded Labour System Abolition Act of 1976, The Land Ceiling Act of 1974–1975, PESA of 1996, Forest Rights Act came into force in 2008, and so on. The various legislations are based within the same matrix of colonial legal framework.[6] So, the continuation of the British pattern of policies stands today as an obstacle to social justice.[7] These laws have placed the landless tribals and non-tribal landlords on the same legal footing, a situation of utmost inequality. The role of the state continues the principle of 'Eminent Domain' from British rule, which has struck at the customary rights of the tribal people.[8]

The history of tribals has been one of deprivation, dispossession and marginalization. Tribals in Odisha continue to suffer land deprivation and dispossessions of different kinds despite special enabling provisions in the constitution, a legal framework for their implementation and several targeted public policy initiatives taken by the state government. The erosion of the tribal way of life and landownership system, imposition of the values and dominance of outsiders have ensured that the tribals in Odisha continue to be impoverished and dispossessed.

In the districts of Koraput, Kalahandi, Balangir and Sambalpur, more quantum of land has been distributed than in coastal districts. The tribals or the rural poor could not take full advantage of this because it was not followed by financial assistance for their cultivation.[9] There are no disaggregated data showing the number of tribal women beneficiaries, which indicates the absence of gender-wise break-up.[10] For all these reasons Odisha is witnessing series of tribal resistance movements in recent years: land conflicts between the tribals and the Bengali settlers in Gudari region of Rayagada district; Malkangiri district; and Nabarangpur district; then the ongoing conflicts over resources between tribals and non-tribals in Narayanpatna block of Koraput district; and the conflict between the Kondh tribe and Panas in Kandhamal district of Odisha.[11] The adivasis of Narayanpatna organized under the banner of Chasi Mulia Adivasi Sangha (CMAS) and are working on two linked issues: the illegal and fraudulent grabbing of adivasi land and alcohol addiction, and mobilized adivasis to take back land that they claim has been unfairly appropriated by non-tribals. Angered by police atrocities, 200 villagers along with CMAS leaders proceed to Narayanpatna police station, where the police indiscriminately opened fire at the people.[12] The Malkangiri Adivasi Sangha (MAS), another adivasi organization, is fighting fraudulent land alienation and arbitrary arrests.[13] In Kandhamal the two most disadvantaged communities, adivasis and dalits, had been incited against each other by political and fundamentalist forces.

Closely related to these are the corporate interests whose goal is the district's exceptionally rich resources: land, forest, water, minerals.[14]

The adivasi women's situation is worst among the marginalized and face displacement from multinational projects (Table 5.1). Re-settlement is inadequate.

Table 5.1 Displacement of Tribal Families

District	Name of the project(s)	Forest area covered (sq km)	No. of tribal families displaced
Koraput	NALCO and other industrial projects	2,000	—
	Machkund Hydel Dam	—	1,500
	Balimela Project	—	2,000
	Upper Kolab Multipurpose Project	—	7,092
Koraput/ Kalahandi	Upper Indravati Project	—	5,000
Keonjhar	Salendi Dam	—	965
Sundargarh	Rourkela Steel Plant	13,185	—
All Odisha	Sanctuaries (16)/ Parks (12)	7,395	—
	Mining	950	—

Source: K.G. Karmakar, 2002. *The Silenced Drums: A Review of Tribal Economic Development* (New Delhi: Northern Book Centre): 50.

CASE STUDY 2

During our field investigation in Damanjodi in October-November 2012 we came across an underground mine of Panchpat Mali Bauxite Mines at Kakiriguma in Koraput, owned by National Aluminium Company Ltd. (NALCO). With a single integrated plant in the country, NALCO has emerged as Asia's largest and world's seventh largest aluminium complex integrating bauxite mining, alumina refining, aluminium smelting and casting, with dedicated power generation, rail and port facilities. It was like a big city inside with excellent roads and big buildings. The giant trucks with full of bauxite were coming and going. A young officer, R.N. Sahoo, told me (3 Nov. 2012) that when NALCO started Koraput-Bolangir-Kalahandi was an underdeveloped region and NALCO has done a great job in developing the local area. A Corporate Social Responsibility (CSR) team is visiting the tribal villages within 7 km of the plant and making plans to develop them. NALCO is working for the upliftment of the tribal women as well. It is encouraging backyard poultry, distributing sewing machines, stitching machines, giving trainings on making terracotta figurines and sanctioning regular grants. NALCO profits two thousand crore (20 billion) annually and 2 per cent of that profit is being spent on the development of the tribal areas. The immediate motif of NALCO is 'prosperity among poverty'. NALCO has already built colonies, like B.R. Colony, Sahid Laxman Nayak Colony, for the displaced tribals and provided them with proper monetary compensation and jobs. All the 600 tribals who were once displaced have been rehabilitated satisfactorily. According to him, NALCO is the forerunner in making proper R & R policy for the displaced.

The project affected 26 villages directly and over 690 villages indirectly, most of which were tribal villages. As per the claims of the NALCO officials, 600 families were displaced out of which 597 were provided with housing in rehabilitation colonies; one person from each displaced family was provided employment at NALCO. The reality on the ground is that 60 per cent of the land acquired by NALCO at Damanjodi was tribal communal land and no compensation was paid for it. The tribal families were shown on to have been paper paid a paltry ₹6,700 per hectare. Land given to the tribal families as compensation was uncultivable, whereas the jobs NALCO promised benefited only the non-adivasis.

The estimates show that no fewer than 40 per cent of the Displaced Persons or DPs/Project Affected Persons or PAPs of five decades of planned development are from the tribal communities. In Odisha they are 22 per cent of the population, but account for 42 per cent of its DPs/PAPs.[15] Fewer than 25 per cent of the DPs seem to have been resettled during the first three decades of planned development.[16] It is recorded that only 35.27 per cent of the DPs in Odisha have been resettled between 1951 and 1995.[17] Even, after mechanization very few jobs are left for the women. Transport of minerals is fully mechanized and has created about 300 skilled and semi-skilled jobs that have gone to outsiders.[18] In Odisha, out of 266,500 families of DPs/PAPs for which data are available, the project has given one job per family to 9,000.[19]

An interview with a young tribal woman, who was displaced as a child from a tribal village to Amlabadi which is NALCO's main resettlement colony at Damanjodi, has been published. Her parents made sure she got a good education. She pursued an MA degree and got a teaching post in a village outside Damanjodi. NALCO would not give her a job despite their quota for displaced persons.[20]

Policymakers should know that the natural resources are also the common property resources (CPRs) for the tribals and the womenfolk do exercise a great amount of control over these resources. The denial of their rights will cause not only economic impoverishment but also the loss of their social status. In the shifting cultivation of south Odisha both men and women share the burden; the division of work is more gender-friendly in shifting cultivation than in settled agriculture. Since the land laws in India considered the tracts of shifting cultivation as state property, the women are left with no alternative to the livelihood lost. For example, in Odisha, out of 11 projects we may refer here to the two NALCO plants, one at Damanjodi in the tribal majority Koraput district and the other in upper caste-dominated Angul. In the former case, 58 per cent of all land taken over and more than 65 per cent of that acquired from the tribes constituted CPRs.[21] In Angul, it was only 18 per cent, much of it school, roads and other service areas. In neither of these cases was compensation given for their CPRs.

ADIVASI WOMEN IN AGRICULTURAL SECTOR

In the districts of Keonjhar, Koraput, Sambalpur and Sundargarh the tribal women form nearly 78 per cent of the workforce in agriculture. It would also be critical to the enquiry to focus on power struggles and contestations not in a socio-cultural boundary of gender alone but within the large unexplored territory of family, state and gender relations. Koraput tribes are Gadaba, Bondas, Gond, Kondh, Paraja, Koya, Pentiya, Saora and Bhuinya. Among these the Bhuinyas have a very low literacy level and are usually very poor. They are losing their distinct socio-cultural identity. The Gadabas, who are primitive though exogenous, still maintain their traditional political organization. The Gonds have a very superior socio-cultural ethos, though a section of the Gonds is losing it through marginalization.[22]

The Kondhs are the most primitive and also the largest tribe in Odisha. The Parajas or the 'common people' are isolated by nature. The tribals are both patriarchal and patrilineal. The hill slopes are locally called as 'dangar' lands and the very low lands with constant flow of water are known as 'jhola' lands, famous for paddy and vegetable cultivation. Most of the tribal women are either recorded as marginal or non-worker that ignores entirely their contribution to household management and livelihood.

The tribal inhabited villages of Koraput are, A. Malkangiri (Admunda Malkangiri is a village in Dasamantapur Tehsil in Koraput district in Odisha), Tentuliguda, Hardaput, Mundigura. The tribal villages of Sambalpur district are Birsinghgarh, Jharanpada, Kudamunda, Mahulipalli; of Sundargarh district Budhabahal, Baragada, Bijlikhaman, Chhentenpalli; of Keonjhar district Badaposi, Bayapandadhar, Kaliabeda, Tentuli. A majority of the women in India work in agriculture and agro-based enterprises. The men in these three districts admitted during village surveys that women are the real workforce in agriculture. They prepare the land, break the clods, sow the seeds, do the weeding operations, transplanting, beushaning (beushaning is used in dry seeded lowland fields to control weeds) operations, apply manure and fertilizers. They also help during harvesting, inter-culture operations, uprooting, plant protection, transporting, threshing and processing. They store the grain and market it.

Women's activities included land preparation, usually identified as a male work. They collect various forest products, conduct farming operations, sericulture, bidi-making (villages around Sambalpur town), forestry and post-harvest operations and have varied responsibility as head of farm household, farm manager, cooking and carrying food to the field and taking care of the children and cattle as well as other domestic animals. It has found that every household has livestock. The survey in the villages clearly brought out the heavy daily workload of tribal women. Wherever irrigation is available, there is multiple cropping, leading to heavier work load on women.[23] Decisions regarding use of implements, land development, use of plant protection measures and purchase of animals as well as irrigation are done with women's consent.

THE CONSTRAINTS

First, lack of improved farm implements: seed drills, threshers, iron ploughs. Irrigation facility should be developed. Second, training needs: female trainers should be appointed to train the women because the tribal women are not free to meet the outsiders; in their local languages. Women have specified few things as of importance to them and these are, production practices of cereals, vegetables (rainy season); disease and pest control; improved implements; fertilizers and manures; new crops and crop diversification; seed treatment; organic and biofertilizers; water management; poultry; mushroom;

horticulture; processing of forest produce; soil and water conservation, bunding and terracing; post-harvest technology including seed storage; sugarcane growing; weed control or safe use of weedicides; sericulture, pisciculture, dairy.[24] The other constraints are non-availability of fertilizers and pesticides, lack of good HYV seeds, absence of land development. When men migrate leaving women in charge of cultivation, they cannot avail of credit from the bank and need access to credit facilities. Access to inputs is a serious constraint for women. Women cannot access available resources. Inadequate fodder for cattle is a serious constraint. There are low food security, poverty, deprivation, low level of literacy, malnourishment of the tribal women, and children, poor health, inadequate avenues of alternate employment opportunities, attacks of incurable diseases, lack of adequate storage facilities at village level. Low value attached to literacy has confined the majority women as marginal workers in the field of agriculture.

Two other issues emerged from the field survey. The first was the increasing violence against tribal women. The majority of tribal men usually use a major share of their earnings for purchasing liquor. Wife battering seems to be the product of increased alcoholism among the tribal men, which is never reported. Field work reveals that there has been a steady increase in rape and other forms of sexual assault. There has also been an increase in sexual exploitation of tribal women by outsiders, the major reason being poverty. There is a lack of awareness among the tribal women of their legal and constitutional rights and gender sensitivity in the judicial system.

The second issue was that increasing migration of men to urban areas did not reduce the poverty levels as tribal women and children remained very much below the poverty line. Even, their wages were found to be much lower, in many cases 50 per cent of the men's. The tribal custom of bride price is disintegrating; decreasing income means it is difficult to pay. There were even a few cases of tribals demanding dowry, which explains the increased numbers of single women.

The Training and Visit System of Extension (assisted by the World Bank) has introduced largely needed improvements in the overall agricultural extension machinery. This, in turn, has been mainly responsible for introduction of modern agricultural technology that has bypassed half of the population engaged in agriculture, namely, tribal farm women. Tribal women's participation is neither acknowledged nor meaningfully incorporated in planning agricultural development. This is aggravated by the fact that male extension workers have a lack of faith in women farmers and there is a social bias of not coming into contact with tribal women.

Panchayats could only carry out developmental activities such as Jawahar Rozgar Yojana (JRY). While 33 per cent of these functionaries are women, most of them have been pushed into power by husbands and communities and cannot cope with their new roles. The state has kept women out of the development process; the patriarchal society has turned into a patriarchal state. All research has a male bias. Knowledge for tribal women remains peripheral. In keeping women out of the decision-making roles in farming by limiting their knowledge the state can be held responsible for the deteriorating state of agriculture in the tribal areas.

BONDA WOMEN IN AGRICULTURAL SECTOR OF MALKANGIRI DISTRICT

Bondas inhabit the Bonda Ghati Area (Bonda Hills) in the undivided Koraput district which now comes under Malkangiri district after 1992. Not mobile, they are therefore confined to that area. According to the Census 2001, the Bondas are about 6,000. They speak Remo. Agriculture and forest collection are principal sources of livelihood, both shifting cultivation (podu) and terraced cultivation, also gleaning, hunting, fishing, animal husbandry, and wage earning. Bondas are extremely aggressive in nature. It is their customary practice that a Bonda woman of the age group 16–20 years marries a male (boy) of the age group 12–14 years. This

Adivasi Women and Destructive Development in Odisha 167

is how a relatively mature woman (who happens to be older than her spouse) exercises control over the latter. Therefore, it is the women whose opinions get precedence over male members with regard to household matters.[25] There are specific dormitories meant for boys and girls for this purpose, which serve as matrimonial agencies to facilitate selection of spouses. Usually, older girls prefer to marry boys younger than them so that the latter would earn for them when they grew old. The way Bonda women dress is attributed to an episode in the *Ramayana*. Bonda women shave their heads and wear around their waist only a tiny piece of cloth called ringa, covering their torsos with strings of stunningly multicoloured beads. Abundant metal rings used to cover their necks and the bangles adorning their arms are more functional. The ornaments shield them from attacks by wild animals when they go for hunting.[26]

The Bondas largely rely on their women for survival. They wander in the forest for food, work in the fields and even hunt. The Bondas can be divided into two groups: Lower Bondas who have come down from the hills, live on the foot hills in the multi-tribal villages whereas the Upper Bondas territory is full of mountain ranges rising in most cases to more than 3,000 feet in height above the sea level.[27] As a result of development programmes introduced in the Bonda Hills, sale of vegetables, spices and other horticultural produce, wage labour and paid employment have become sources of income. Bonda women are conscious about their significant role in their economy.[28]

Bonda women play the main role in weekly markets. During their visits it is seen that the Bonda women are treated with utmost caution; they sometimes snatch away the items if they are not treated carefully. The management and economy of the household are the responsibility of the wives. They sell and buy in the weekly market: sell seasonal fruits, liquor, palm juice, leaf plates, and vegetables and they buy mostly dry fish, salt, cloths and cosmetics. They are experts in preparing liquor with all kinds of fruits and rice.[29] Fishing plays an important part in Bonda diet and ritual.[30]

Bonda Development Agency (BDA) was formed in the 1970s for development of the Bondas and community members came to work in its development programmes as wage labourers. This encouraged the community to switch from subsistence production to production for exchange. Consequently wage labour or buti replaced the earlier cooperative labour, *odja*, resulting in dilution of the domestic community. The Bondas lost their age-old subsistence mode of production and were pushed into the permanent web of the wage economy. Wage earning has become substantial source of income of the Banduguda village for women and girls because this village is very near to Mudilipada Project Area. The women are involved in government building constructions, road repair works and check dam constructions. As the idea of development was imposed on them from above, it destroyed their economic independence, made them subservient to an exogenous system and finally devalued their culture.[31]

As India celebrated its seventieth year of the Republic, what has become of these 'first citizens'—these people who live pretty much the way our ancestors did when they first came to India? Is there a way to give them the benefits of modern civilization while, at the same time, helping them retain their ancient identity and culture? The Bondas have fiercely resisted—perhaps more than any other tribal group—all attempts by the state to 'develop' them. A lot of the indigenous knowledge of the Bondas—like the use of the rhizome from a plant, 'black turmeric', to induce abortion—is at stake as the government forces its development programmes on them. Even Remo, an Austro-Asiatic language that they speak, is endangered under this onslaught. Most Bondas now speak, if not Oriya, a pidgin that has evolved from it. And the state has pushed Remo further into extinction by not evolving a text for the language that can be used by Bonda children.[32]

THE DIDAYI WOMEN OF MALKANGIRI

The Didayi is a little known Primitive Tribal Group of Odisha confined to Khairaput and Kondakamberu Mountain range and its foothills which constitute the part of the Eastern Ghat Mountain Range. In fact the hill range is known as Didayi land. The construction of Balimela Hydel Project (1962) changed their lifestyle and habitat. The people settled in the valleys were displaced as their lands got submerged in the reservoir water. Most of them shifted to the hilltop and some preferred to stay back at their own locality of the river bank. The cut off Didayi have lost their cultural identity because of their displacement and rehabilitation. They have even lost linguistic and socio-cultural identity owing to the influence of the Bengali refugees, Kondhs, Telugu businessmen and others.

Didayi Development Agency (DDA) was established in the year 1986 at Kudumulugumma of Malkangiri district. Didayis were aware of the difficulties of becoming displaced and had protested against the construction of the Balimela Hydro Electric Project. During interviews many of the Didayi burst into tears which indicate the depth of their agony. Didayis of plains are known as *Jhadi*-Didayi, the Didayis of hilltop are called *Konglo*-Didayi or *Ghati Duar* Didayi, and the Didayis of cut off sector are known as *Londia* Didayi.

The Didayi economic structure mainly revolves round the agriculture and forest produce collection. Their primary occupation is food production by means of settled and shifting cultivation while the secondary occupation involves wage earning, forest produce collection and other casual employment. Hunting and fishing seems to be a tertiary occupation The Didayi women understand the functioning of the Panchayati Raj system and some who have actively participated in political processes at grassroot level and got elected as Sarpanch, Naib Sarpanch and Ward Members. The women participants in the system are supported from not only the family members, but also of the community as a whole.

Didayis are patrilocal and thus patrilineal and patriarchal although a certain degree of female dominance is marked in several matters. Both nuclear and extended families have been found. Bride price is also in practice. The girl's family may reject the marriage proposal made by the boy's family. A large number of girls between age group of 15 to 35 years from plain and hilltop sector are found unmarried due to lack of suitable proposals pressed from the boy side. These girls live with their parents and support the family by wage earning. The plain boys with little education are only seeking alliances with educated working girls from other communities. Most of the PTGs of Odisha have youth dormitories either for boys or girls or for both. The Didayi dormitory is meant for only boys. It is known as gulisung and its socio-economic and cultural importance are lessening.

The District Rural Development Agency (DRDA), Malkangiri, has been implementing its various schemes. Development of women and children, a sub-scheme of IRDP was started in 1982–1983. It aims at collective endeavours of women groups providing additional opportunities for self-employment. Under this scheme Didayi women are organized in groups of 10–15 for taking of economic activities like broom binding, spice and turmeric powder making and tailoring. There are 11 DWCRA groups in operation in such different income-generating activities in the Didayi villages.[33]

Didayi womenfolk play a vital role not only in the household sphere but also assume responsibility in supplementing household income. Marriage for a woman cannot be performed without her consent. Their latent leadership quality has been manifested in the assumption of roles under Panchayati Raj institutions and they have become reasonably vocal to express their ideas for the betterment of the community. Their awareness level has enhanced their zeal to organize Self-Help Groups (SHGs), promoting a micro-financing network. Didayi women in the hill area and cut-off area are less advanced and need a special campaign to increase their awareness level.[34] A woman after marriage lives with her husband in a lineal extended family or in a neo-local residence according to patrilocal residential rule. In case her husband dies or leaves her at a young age she is free to remarry by leaving her husband's households with or without her children. They follow levirate so that a young woman can remarry her deceased husband's younger brother. Polygyny or plurality of wives is practised. and often requires maintenance of two households instead of one in order to avoid unhappiness.

THE KOYA WOMEN OF MALKANGIRI

The term 'Koya' means man. Koyas are concentrated in the southern portion of Malkangiri district. Since the 1960s the Government of India and the Government of Odisha started rehabilitating refugees from East Pakistan in their area, and the increase of population depleted the traditional natural resources of the Koya. The refugees possessed higher agricultural technology and had expertise in wet-rice cultivation, which made them prosperous. Their traditional pastures were converted to agricultural land by the government for the settlers, which led to the Koya pastoral economy suffering a major setback.

The Koyas are divided into five categories or sub-tribes: Gomin, Goti, Meta, Dartad and Manim. The Gomin Koyas inhabit the low land of Malkangiri, sandwiched between Sileru and Saberi tributaries of Godavari. They are mostly cattle herders. The Goti Koyas inhabit the plain lands and depend upon farming. The Meta Koyas occupy the hilly areas and practise shifting cultivation. The Koyas who earn a living through iron smithy are known as Dartad. The Manim Koyas are the ones who live on the western side of the Saberi River in Chhattisgarh. Meta Koyas reside in Malkangiri and Kalimela blocks. The Goti Koyas occupy the Podia block and the Gomin Koyas dwell in the Motu.

There are several weekly markets in the Koya area, which cater to the buying and selling needs of the Koya. Both men and women together carry out the transaction. Koyas mainly practise shifting cultivation as suitable land for plains and wet cultivation is scarce in their habitat. Harvest period is a busy time for them, when all members of the family go to the crop field to collect the crops. Ploughing or *udsinadi* of land commences after the pre-monsoon showers in the April or May. Ploughing is done with a simple ploughshare either by men or women. Women are totally forbidden from sowing seeds.

CASE STUDY 3

In November 2012 we visited to Malkangiri. I wanted to visit Bonda Market but it is restricted to the outsiders, as mentioned in the Particularly Vulnerable Tribal Groups Act of March 2012, enacted by the Odisha government that prohibits foreign travellers/scholars to visit the tribal areas at night, taking photographs, entering inside their houses or any kind of physical proximity with the tribal people. We started on our journey early in the morning. Malkangiri is fully covered with dense forests and is the Maoist heart land as well, the district falls under the red corridor. On our way to Bonda Market we covered the exact place where a land mine blast took place in July, 2008. It was a heavy explosion that took lives of 17 BSF jawans. My guide said that the mines are operated from inside the jungles. The road was closed for few years after the explosion and has been opened just the last year. The entire district has been covered with high security. There are BSF camps after each twenty km and more police stations than required. In front of the BSF camps there are security personnel on duty with arms.

We met the Didayis, the shifting cultivators of Malkangiri. One of them, Chandan Pujari, told me that their rights over the forest and forest products are still unrecognized. They have not been informed about the Forest Rights Act, 2006. Another Didayi, Buddhu Pujari, said that they collect mainly firewood and different kinds of leaves. On the way to Bonda

Market we met two Bonda women carrying liquor on their heads. They said that livelihood of the Bondas is a primitive form of agriculture, animal husbandry and hunting. The Bondas are still deprived of the minimum basic needs of life like drinking water, sanitation, education, communication. We reached Bonda Market, situated at Mundiguda village close to Khairaput Block, Mudulipada P.S. of Malkangiri. The market sold dry prawn and other fish, vegetables, chillies and saris and other garments. At the edge of the market the Bonda men and women were selling traditional country liquor. The women wear a lot of rings on their head, neck, ear, nose, hand-made with brass or nickel even in their day to day life; they wear it by boring the pins into their neck. Since their lives are so tough, perhaps they are hardened against pain. Lots of projects are being established in these areas by displacing thousands, such as Balimela Hydro Power Project (only 30 km) away from Malkangiri.

Tanginiguda village, Khairaput Block of Malkangiri has large areas of sal forests. The Bonda and Paraja women were going to the market with vegetables and fruits. We also found men digging the earth under National Rural Employment Guarantee Scheme. On our way back we visited Bhuniya Market of Boipariguda, a weekly market held on every Sunday used by the Gadabas, Bhuniyas and Parajas who sold dry fish, vegetables, garments, fruits and tobacco. Gadabas wear a two-piece nose ring whereas Kondhs wear a three-piece nose ring, and Bhuniyas wear a two-piece nose-ring, sometimes one-piece, and anklets as well. Lakshmi Puja was being performed by the tribal women and wearing white saris they were distributing prasad and putting on the vermillion tika. Many Bengali refugee families came from erstwhile East Pakistan and settled in Malkangiri and have had an impact on tribal culture.

More than 90 per cent of the households depend on agriculture, out of which more than 60 per cent depend on both shifting and settled agriculture; with 50 per cent depending on shifting cultivation alone. With the establishment of the

Bonda Development Agency there has been better involvement and participation of the local inhabitants. Women's consciousness has increased considerably in as much as some of them have started clothing themselves in a better way. (Field work in Koraput and Rayagadha was carried on during October-November 2012.)

THE KONDH WOMEN OF KORAPUT AND RAYAGADA

The Dongria Kondh is one of the officially designated PTG in Odisha.[35] They are the original inhabitants of Niyamgiri hilly region which extends to Rayagada, Koraput and Kalahandi districts of south Odisha. The theological pantheon is the earth goddess (Darni Pennu) at the apex and Niyam Pennu (Niyamgiri Hill) is believed to be the creator of Dongrias. The Dongria population is confined to three community development blocks namely Bissamcuttack and Munuguda of Gunpur sub-division and Kalyansinghpur block of Rayagada sub-division. They speak Kuvi, which is of Dravidian linguistic ancestry that has no script. Each Dongria Kondh village is situated in the centre chain of hills of Niyamgiris, which are inaccessible, hidden in the mountains, devoid of road and transport facilities. Dongria Kondhs are known for their deep knowledge and skill in horticulture. Due to development, their traditional lifestyle, customary traits of economy and political organization, norms, values and worldview have been drastically changed. Kondh women are considered assets because of their contribution inside and outside the household. For this reason the girl child is preferred over the boy child and fetch high bride price. The girls' dormitory is called *adasbeta* is a common practice. However, the family is patrilineal and patrilocal.

The Dongria Kondhs extensively practice *bogodo*, slash and burn (swidden) type of cultivation. The hill slopes are clearly marked by areas under swidden cultivation, organized in such a way as to ensure a regular supply of food over several months. Traditionally most tribes of Odisha grew around 26 varieties of cereals and pulses that matured during different months between October and February when forest produce like fruits and edible flowers became available. But because of deforestation and decline in resources, tribal families have become more dependent on shifting cultivation than in the past. The shifting cultivation cycle has changed to becoming more frequent because of soil degradation, from 6 years to 3 years. As a result of the shorter cycle, the forest does not regenerate, soil erosion follows and soil fertility declines.[36]

Kondh women display a vast knowledge of the agricultural, horticultural and swiddening activities. Women's expertise in the fields of crop management and housekeeping is significant. Dongria girls are particularly adept at embroidery, weaving the Dongria shawls, in house decoration and the making of paints and cosmetics. Dongria women are skilled at processing and preserving foodstuff and at distilling liquor, which is officially a men's task. They are efficient at gathering non-timber forest products. Both sexes operate on an equal footing in the market place. Women transport and sell the products at the market and are thus aware of basic commercial practices.[37]

Rayagada district is infamously known as the hunger pocket of Odisha. The district is inhabited by the hill tribes, nearly 90 per cent of the population depends on agriculture but the land area is too meagre, mostly with poor soil base and a large part faces drought with a wide seasonal variation in food consumption mainly in quality and quantity. Dongria Kondhs face acute shortage of food in the post-sowing monsoon period (July-September) and again around March when the kharif harvest has been exhausted.

The Primary Health Centres (PHC) situated at K. Singpur, Bissamcuttack and Muniguda are quite inaccessible, devoid of road and transport facility and often cut off en route with flowing canals and rivers; thus the Kondhs still consult their traditional medicine man at times of need. Kondh women are aware of certain medicines that are used specifically during birth, for contraception, abortion, and amenorrhea; and are familiar with remedies for common ailments, the knowledge being acquired from the medicine man's wife.

Dongria Kondh society displays marked sexual inequality, men occupying the dominant position in the social hierarchy. Women are denied certain social activities; despite their inferior status the contribution made by women in certain situations is quite substantial. Certain religious ceremonies require significant female participation. As in the neighbouring Lanjia Saora community, Dongria women also work as shamanins. There is also a discernible hierarchy among the women who work as priests or religious performers.[38]

Kondh customs of human sacrifice were performed principally to the Earth Goddess. She was called Darni Pennu, the main deity worshipped by most Kondhs, along with Bura Pennu or the Sky God. According to Kondh belief, human sacrifices were performed in response to Darni's demand for human blood to ensure the fertility of the earth. The victims of sacrifice were called *meriahs* and were of either sex. Kondhs bought meriahs, who were not Kondhs by birth from other lower castes. Between Bura and Darni Pennu there was perpetual strife. Some Kondhs held Bura supreme, and therefore performed no human sacrifices; instead they practised female infanticide, since they identified women with the evil principle. The bride price given for women in Kondh community was enormous. The Kondh woman used to change her husband whenever she wished and in that case the huge bride price which her first husband paid was to be repaid by her father. So, having a girl child was an expensive business and that is why most of the female babies were killed.[39]

CASE STUDY 4

We visited Bhatpur village, Bissamcuttack Block, Rayagada district inhabited by Kondhs. A linear village, which is only inhabited by Dongria Kondhs who speak Kui. There are two Self Help Groups in the village. In a micro finance scheme women have made a banana plantation. There was a community house, a remnant of a dormitory or ghotul where young tribal boys and girls lived together and were sexually active; now it is abandoned. There was also a sacrificial ground, probably influenced by the Hindu culture. Kanchana Hemrika (28) took me home. There was a photograph of the Hindu goddess Lakshmi, the household goods were hanging from the roof. Baskets, sarees, utensils, and pails—all scattered. The children were found reading books in Oriya in the courtyard. Houses are being built with the funds released under Indira Awas Yojana, but the houses do not suit tribal culture.

The Rayagada tribes' staple food is a gruel prepared from ragi or finger millet locally called 'mandia' which contains iron, calcium and protein, offering richer nutritional value than rice. Flavoured with a pinch of salt and a handful of rice or maize corn thrown in, the rather flat tasting gruel is taken for breakfast, lunch and in the absence of rice, for dinner too, without variation; it is the first solid food for babies too. Each family gets between 120 to 160 kg of millet and the same quantity of rice again in the second cropping. Selling a portion to cover cash expenses, the rest lasts for four months. In the monsoon the women may pick wild gurundi leafy greens and work for daily wages.

Their main sources of income are agriculture, collection of forest produce and occasional wage labour, which lets a family of five members, at best, survive for six months. By mid-monsoon the millet and rice produce have been consumed. Wage labour is hard to come by. The tribals were BPL card holders, but the performance of Annapurna Yojana was not satisfactory at all. Malaria is virulent; sapping their immunity and diarrhoea lays them to further waste and even death, a death that is often represented as 'starvation death'.

At the Dongria Kondh Development Agency (DKDA) of Rayagada, I interviewed the DKDA officers, M.K. Karkaria, Bhagirath Sahoo, Karno Kausaliya, Janak Bag, S. Trinath

Rao and Ramesh Nalla. They said that in 1964 the Odisha Government started the Agency with the Purchase and Sale Fair-Price Shops scheme through which the indigenous produce of the Dongria Kondh were being purchased at a reasonable rate and the daily necessities like salt, kerosene, tobacco, match box and cheap garments were provided at a fair price. They introduced me to Kondh women. The women showed their ornaments mainly hair clips, one knife kept within the hair-knot, 25–30 earrings, khagla or necklaces with beads, nose rings of mainly gold or brass and little tattoos. Government projects and funds for the development of the Dongria Kondhs are utilized through the Agency. The Odisha Welfare Service cadres help the government to implement the projects properly. Driven by the need of sustainable farming they cultivate several indigenous varieties of pearl millet, brinjal, sesame, bottle gourd and legumes. The DKDA has its own plans related to the cultivation of the seasonal crops such as, pineapple, jackfruit, mango, papaya, black pepper, coffee, lemons, orange. DKDA gives training on how to grow crops on both the hill terrains and plain lands and which crop has to be cultivated in which season so that the women can go to their villages and carry on the process learnt here. The DKDA is also training Kondh women to make different types of handicrafts, especially designing shawls which sell for ₹700–1,000.

Our next destination was in Khojuri village, Bissamcuttack Block, Rayagada district inhabited by Kutia Kondh and Dongria Kondh. Tribal women also work under National Rural Employment Guarantee Scheme. They are getting ₹126 per day as wages. Many want the NREGS withdrawn as the benefits were not fully percolating to the community. The daily diet of the Kondhs consists of millet, gruel, dry fish, rice, chicken, and vegetables. Their occupation is mainly in primary sectors: agriculture and domestication of animals and horticulture. They have no land in their name. The Kondhs practise bride price instead of dowry but that is in kind and not in cash.

Then we visited tiny Titijhola village, in Kumbhikota Gram Panchayat under Sadar block at the tail end of Rayagada district bordering Koraput, which is inhabited by the Jharia Paraja community. There is no Self Help Groups in the village. We found the shifting cultivation tracts extensively under swidden cultivation for maize and rice. We entered the Titijhola Primary School, an upgraded school both for girls and the boys. The little Kondh and Paraja girls were wearing three-piece nose rings. They sang the prayer song before us and ended it with 'Jana-Gana-Mana'. When asked about the mid-day meal programme we were told that on Wednesday and Saturday they are served with eggs and in the rest of the days with khichris (a blending of rice, dal and vegetables). Titijhola is a classic example of official apathy on electricity front. Rajiv Gandhi Grameen Vidyutikaran Yojana (RGGVY), a scheme for providing access to electricity was launched by Union Ministry of Power on 18 March 2005. But when I visited Titijhola in November 2012, there was no electricity connection.

We moved to Jhigidi and Ghasi Sahi of Jhigidi Gram Panchayat, Muniguda Tehsil, Rayagada where we visited the luxury goods markets at Jharia Paraja Market. The artisans were preparing dokra using a once lost-wax technique, a process by which the metal sculpture is cast from an artist's sculpture. Charms, pendants, rings, necklace, different types of idols, ornaments, are just a few items that can be made.

We went to Gadaba village of Rayagada block, Rayagada, The villagers make and sell different types of pottery. Our next destination was the village Janiguda, Laxmipur Tehsil, Koraput. The village is inhabited by the Bodo Paraja tribal community which has been recognised as PTG. This is the only tribal community that still bears matriarchal culture. There are two SHGs and undoubtedly need more supervision on the side of the government. Janiguda is situated very near to Narayanpatna but there were strict restrictions on entering the block since security forces were posted to handle any kind of unrest.

THE HOLVA AND SAORA WOMEN OF KORAPUT

The tribal society of Koraput presents a picture of a stable, tolerant, gender-cooperative, gender-non-discriminatory, and humane society. Though the tribal society here is a closed society having a primitive life style and attitude, they are natural feminists. According to the 2001 Census, in Koraput, the tribal population comprises almost half (about 49.62%) of the district's total population. Among all tribes of Koraput, no discrimination is known to be made on the grounds of sex. According to the 2001 Census, out of 8,145,081, total number of scheduled tribe population in Koraput, the female population (4,078,298) outnumbers the male population (4,066,783).[40]

Holvas have undergone a process of 'Sanskritization.' They are mainly found in Undivided Koraput and Kalahandi districts of Odisha. They speak a dialect called 'Halvi,' but are also capable of speaking Oriya language without difficulty. The pattern of dress and ornaments among the Holva is the same as that of their Hindu neighbours. The Saoras are known as one of the oldest tribes in Odisha. They are known for their artistic skills and traditional panchayat system, which is responsible for maintaining law, order and solidarity in the village.

So far as following the guidelines of an Institutional Review Board (IRB) or Ethics Committee (EC) is concerned, the tribal chieftains (Gamango/Buyya in case of Saora tribe) of the respective tribes were consulted and were intimated about our intentions. The places where the interviews were conducted are Saora Guda (for Saoras), and Umeri (for Holvas). Saora Guda and Umeri were found to have the respective tribes in a sizable majority. In the absence of modern day varieties in the composition of the population of the two tribes, only age, sex, and to some extent education were taken into consideration while taking interviews. The responses of the Holva women, in sharp contrast with the Saoras, indicate that they have shown more interest in raising their status vis-à-vis their male members. The Holva tribe encourages widow remarriage. A widow can remarry the younger brother of her deceased husband. In a similar way, Saoras practise both sororate and levirate forms of marriage, that is, a man can marry his deceased wife's younger sister and women can marry her deceased husband's younger brother. Saora women retain their family name after marriage.[41]

Male and female members in both the tribal communities are economically self-dependent. Both male and female consume country wine. Both males and females dance together during their community festivals. Dhemsa is the most popular form of dance among tribals of Koraput where both male and female dance together, keeping their hand on each other while singing in a chorus. Even if today female members are given some political offices through the Panchayati Raj Act, it does not make any difference in the status and position of the women. They prefer to work and live in cooperation with their male members. Gradually tribal women are increasingly enrolled as members of the SHGs. This has been a means to enhance the economic condition of tribal women. However, the benefits and responsibilities of the SHGs are also regarded as a partnership between males and females in tribal community. In the villages inhabited by Holva tribes, institutions like Youth Centers, Kirtan Mandali and Mahila Samitis (Women Organizations) are found to exist. Women take up issues concerning them in these centres.

THE GADABA WOMEN OF KORAPUT

Gadaba society in India has gone through rapid socio-economic transformation in recent days under the impact of both traditional and modern factors of social change. In Odisha, they are distributed mostly in five different districts: Koraput, Malkangiri, Nabarangapur, Kalahandi and Rayagada. However, Koraput has the highest Gadaba population among the districts (Census 2001). Keeping this in mind the study has been conducted at the micro level covering three Gadaba dominated blocks of Koraput district—Pottangi, Nandapur and Semiliguda—to analyse the socio-economic transformation process.

With the introduction of forest laws now in force the Gadabas lost their traditional forest land on hill slopes and were driven down to the flat fields below. The Gadabas had to cultivate the low land. Land alienation has become evident in Gadaba villages due to industrialization and inflow of non-tribals. The traders and businessmen of urban area now have acquired the lands of these people by paying a very small amount. Thus a majority of Gadabas, who do not have any knowledge about the land tenure laws, found themselves increasingly deprived of the very land that was their source of livelihood. The construction of the hydroelectric project in Machakund and the multipurpose dam in upper Kolab have taken away lands from the Gadabas without giving them anything in return. Due to the setting up of Hindustan Aeronautics Ltd. (HAL) factory at Sunabeda and the NALCO at Damanjodi, the Gadaba and Paraja territory has been invaded.[42]

The major occupation of tribals of Koraput district can be classified as: (a) forestry and food gathering; (b) shifting cultivation: (c) animal husbandry; (d) settled agriculture; (e) wage labour; (f) household industry; and (g) miscellaneous occupation. With the decline in output from forest produce, as well as shifting cultivation, tribals are increasingly becoming dependent on seasonal wage labour, both as agricultural and unskilled construction workers.

In matters of marriage, observation of rituals and arrangement of feasts, the husband and the wife take decisions jointly. Though the position of women has improved, it is still not at par with men, especially in ritual, education, political aspects. The change in Gadaba women's status is perceptible more in urban than rural areas, more among educated than uneducated women and more in Christian than non-Christian women. Female literacy has slightly gone up due to free education up to high school, scholarships and establishment of residential schools for girls. Education has helped the women to improve their social position within the family and provide opportunities for performing new roles outside.

In Gadaba society there are women with magic power who is called 'Gurumai' or 'Bejuni'. She performs rituals to stop the evil spirits causing ill health to an individual or a family out of the village.

CASE STUDY 5

We visited to two hundred acres forest land of coffee plantation on the foothills of Deo Mali in Semeliguda Block of Koraput which is densely populated by the Gadaba tribe. The forest was covered by the cash crops: coffee, black pepper, silver oak trees. These cash crops provide employment to the tribals for nearly six months. The coffee plantation of Koraput employs men and women who take part in fertilizer application, weeding, bush management, nursery maintenance, harvesting and coffee processing. The workers receive their wages as per the rule of NREGA: 120 rupees per day. The produce from Koraput is exported to places like Chennai and Mumbai for marketing. At Dangarachhini Gram Panchayat of Jeypore Block Gadaba women were preparing the leaf plates for a funeral meal. They said that the dead bodies are cremated, but in case of unnatural death they bury the dead bodies by the river bed. We found a sacred grove called sarna where tribal goddesses are worshipped with a banyan peepal or jackfruit tree; there was a mark of vermillion on a big rock a sign of Hindu influence on the tribals. The villagers said that sorcery is still being practiced by the jani or janguru in most Gadaba villages and believe that janis can suck the spirit.

Our next destination was Maliguda village of the Gadabas, Jeypore, close to Boipariguda. In this village, Mali, the sub-tribal group, live with the Gadabas as well. We found a place with a large platform. It was a community gathering place where the Gadabas hold meetings and perform Demsa dance.

Gadaba women use different types of hairpins, wear earrings, nose rings and finger rings made with coins, brass bangles. Bride price (jala dabu) prevails in their community though. Gadaba society is going through transformation of their whole socio-cultural milieu. Now, one can hardly find a Gadaba woman wearing Kerang sarees. Many customary festivals and rituals are decaying, animal sacrifice is frowned on.

BHUYAN-JUANG WOMEN OF KEONJHAR

Extensive deposits of minerals resources like iron and manganese ores have also made this district quite an important one in the resource map of Odisha and India. The Bhuyan-Juang Pirh (abode of the hill tribes) is a mountainous country with two broad divisions: the Bhuyan Pirh to the west and northwest of the Keonjhar town; and the Juang Pirh to the south of the town. Juangs live a largely communal life and revenue is paid by the village altogether, But Bhuyans have become individualistic, do not share, and rich and poor are distinguished.

CASE STUDY 6

We also visited Patrapura village of Jeypore Block, Koraput, a Bhuyan village, not linear but circular in nature. Shifting cultivation, locally known as kamani, continues to play a dominant role in the household as well as their village economy. Somari Parajoni, a Bhuyan woman said that they have no land in their names. She gets widow pension that has increased from ₹200 to ₹300. She is a BPL cardholder and gets 25 kg rice through PDS. She also said that bride price is paid in kind. The Bhuyans speak Oriya and have adopted the local Hindu culture more extensively than the Juangs who, though speak Oriya, have a dialect of their own. Till recently, the latter were considered to be a semi-nomadic race unlike the Bhuyans. There are more than 12 sub-divisions among the Bhuyans. Each group considers itself to be the superior one and does not intermarry.[43]

The geo-physical location and climatic condition of the Pirh have attracted many development agencies operating for last few decades in mining exploration, tea plantation, and so on. The Gandhamardan Iron Ore Mining of Odisha Mining

Corporation is working in a contiguous area of 5,751.25 acres since 1963 for a projected time period of 200 years. This has so far affected 1690 acres of forest land, 121 acres of non-forest private land, and 397 acres of non-forest government land. Surrounding villages like Suakati, Danala, Upparjagar, Luapada, Upper Kainsari, Nitigatha and Ichinda has been highly affected due to the impact of mining activities with respect to their forest, economy, sources of employment, cultural life and institutional patterns. The second major development project is a tea garden owned by a private company at Tamarkanta near Bansapal by IPICOL, Government of Odisha and one private company of West Bengal in 1982. The tea garden has deforested an area of 2200 acres of forest land, of which 800 acres was given on lease to a private company. The land was largely dominated by sal trees. The tea garden has been closed since 2002. The third major factor affecting the Pirh is the construction of National Highway-6 during 1980s linking Calcutta with Bombay, as a result of which thousands of trucks go through Bhuyan Pirh. The construction of roadside dhabas and hotels has resulted in prostitution, child labour, sexually transmitted diseases.[44]

The Juangs are found in large numbers in Keonjhar and Dhenkanal districts. The Juang economy has been based on shifting cultivation. Women are forbidden to take part in ploughing, sowing and storing grains, but women do participate in all other work. Saora women of Sambalpur district unlike many tribal women are allowed to use the plough. Almost in every hill tribe community women dominate in household affairs (but not in village matters); they are earnest in family matters and more strongly attached to their family than the males.[45] Some of the common taboos like women must not plough are based on the perception of difference between masculine and feminine nature while some others owe their origin to purely socio-religious concepts.[46] Women's contribution to the household income is that that they constitute 50 per cent or even more of the working force.[47] But women do not inherit land and property though a widow can be allowed to inherit the homestead land. This creates a major problem for them after the death of their husbands unless they have male children, and they become destitute without a husband or son.

Juangs used to wear only leaf-dress even during the nineteenth century and were hence known as Patra (or leaf) Saora or Pattoa. Almost all large and smooth leaves were used for this purpose and the 'dress' was changed daily.[48] The Juangs still practice toila or jhum cultivation. The right of the forest belongs to the community as a whole and is divided by mutual consent.[49]

Juang Development Agency (JDA) was constituted in 1970s for the development of the Juang under the 'Tribal Sub-Plans'. But in the name of creating new scope for economic growth of the tribe, the JDA forcibly diverted the community from their age-old shifting cultivation to commercial exploitation of the forest wealth. Later on, when the forest department enforced restrictions on use of forest resources, these tribes were pushed back to the condition of virtual landlessness.[50] On the economic development of the survey and settlement operations during 1965–1985 helped demarcate forest blocks clearly and a number of these DPFs (Demarcated Protected Forests) were then proposed to be declared as Reserve Forests. One such PRF (proposed reserve forest) is the Gandhamardan Hill forest where mining is taking place. Bharat Aluminium Company or Balco started mining in north Chhattisgarh and disrupted the lives of thousands of adivasi. In February 1986 people from both sides of Gandhamardan set up a blockade on the mining road. Women played a crucial role at this point and placed their babies on the road, right in front of police and mining vehicles. By June 1986 the blockade had completely stopped work at the mine.[51] Usually the whole area of Bhuyan-Juang Pirh was considered to be under shifting cultivation since there was no control over it in this area. Previously when the customs were strictly adhered to in context of shifting cultivation, the impact on environment was negligible;

the rotation of 22 years has come been reduced to 5 years sometimes.[52]

DANDAKARANYA DEVELOPMENT AND TRIBAL WOMEN

The present KBK region consists of the undivided Koraput, Bolangir and Kalahandi districts, which was reorganized into eight districts in 1992–1993 as: Kalahandi, Nawapada, Bolangir, Sonepur, Koraput, Malkangiri, Nawarangpur and Rayagada. The KBK region along with the contiguous Gajapati and Khandamal districts is considered one of the poorest in the country. Scheduled tribes like Bonda, Didayi, Lanjia Saora and Dongria Kondh inhabit this area. The tribal population suffers from high morbidity on account of undernutrition as well as endemic malaria and other localized diseases.[53] Sanjay Kak has stated, 'In a terrible twist, this land, traditionally fertile with the nutrients that flow down its many bauxite rich malis, became emblematic of the endemic poverty of Odisha ... there have been terrible famines since the 1960s.'[54]

In 1957 the Ministry of Rehabilitation carved out a contiguous area of about 80,000 square miles stretching over Koraput district of Odisha and Bastar district of Madhya Pradesh (now in Chhattisgarh) for the policy towards rehabilitation of the Bengali Hindu refugees from East Pakistan, which was given a mythical name: Dandakaranya. The Ministry proposed to leave half the area as forest and keep the other half for the settlement of four million persons, of which half may be the local adivasis and the other half displaced persons. The Dandakaranya Development Authority (DDA) was set up by a Resolution of the government dated September 1958 to look after the project. The area covers the areas belonging to Bastar and Koraput.

The rehabilitation project planned to build new colonies over 200–300 villages for the settlement of 35,000 displaced families and 6,000 tribal families. The project started to face aberrations around 1966, when a large number of settlers left for West Bengal. Another exodus also took place between 1972 and 1978. By the end of 1984, it was estimated that there were altogether 36,513 families in the rehabilitation sites, but this number was reduced to 25,153 after the exodus.[55] The settled groups acquired more benefits from the project compared to the tribals. This caused severe unrest among the tribes. In course of time, the DDA left implementation of tribal welfare to the two concerned state governments and primarily functioned as an agency for rehabilitation of the refugees.

The tribals did not react negatively while the settlement process was on. Neither did the government feel the need for obtaining tribal consent for the settlement nor did the tribes feel any necessity to react to it. When the bulldozers of the Dandakaranya Development Authority started cleaning the jungle, out of insecurity the tribals ran away into the deeper forests. When the settler acquired their land, the tribes did not protest, as they knew that they could reclaim more land by cleaning the forests, which they did. But the settlers once again grabbed that newly reclaimed land of the tribals. Many of the families in the settlers' communities increased their landholding to up to 50 acres through this process. The tribals now became landless and started working in the fields of the settlers as agricultural labourers.[56] Besides the land, the tribals gradually lost control over community resources such as forests. At a later stage, Joint Forest Management Committees (JFMCs) were formed with the villagers as members, to take care of the distribution of income from forest produce among the village community. The settlers acquired the dominant position in these committees by manipulating the process and selected those tribals as representatives who had been working in their houses as servants. This helped them to alienate the local tribe from such resources. The settlers are now higher up on the ladder of progress. Their children have acquired education. Those who are educated have got good jobs in the government. There are engineers and doctors from this community but one can rarely find even a clerk from the tribal community.

Fernandes reported that 432.20 sq km of land were deforested for the Dandakaranya Project in Nowarangpur, Jeypore and Malkangiri Divisions.[57] Koraput's thick forest cover dwindled rapidly in the course of major developmental projects like the Indravati Hydro Project, which evicted 5,000 families. The movement against the project was effectively suppressed in April 1992 when police lathicharged and arrested 28 or more protesters, who were taken to Nowrangpur jail.[58] They are still waiting for rehabilitation.[59] The local tribes of the area are deprived of irrigation facilities; instead, water from the dam is allowed to flow to many distant parts of Odisha. A number of private industrialists established paper mills in the district, which led to depletion of forests due to mindless cutting of bamboo.

The forest cover of Koraput is a mixture of sal and bamboo. Once the bamboo is taken away, it destroys the thickness of the forest, resulting in high temperatures, going up to 45°C in summer. The liberalization process of the government encouraged many multinational companies to take interest in the area. All these projects would displace many thousands of people. Against these forceful displacements when resistance is increasing, the response of the government is highly repressive. Tribal protestors of Maikanch village in Kashipur block of Rayagada district are protesting against Utkal Alumina International Limited—a joint venture of Alcan of Canada and Hindalco of India (UAIL).[60] The Prakritik Sambad Suraksha Parishad (PSSP) has been spearheading the struggle against UAIL.[61]

CASE STUDY 7

In November 2012, I visited Utkal Alumina Ltd. at Kashipur. Our first place of visit was Karajhola village of Sankarada Gram Panchayat, Kashipur Block, Rayagada. The women's contribution along with the loans provided by the government is being utilized to grow mango and mustard. Tribals here are dying of diarrhoea because of polluted drinking water combined with an inefficient public health care system that is responsible for a high mortality rate in this area. Even the NGOs failed to perform efficiently. The villagers talked about the incidents of starvation deaths in Kashipur. A large number do not resort to any treatment for diarrhoea. Most will consult the dasari or traditional doctor first, who stays virtually next door and who may prescribe an herbal remedy. We went to visit the Karajhola Primary School. There were no toilet facilities not even for the girls and this is the situation in almost every school. The school teacher, an exception, is committed to teach in this extremist affected area.

We then moved to Utkal Alumina International Ltd. situated at Tikiri. In April 2007, Alcan declared that it is withdrawing from the project by divesting its stake to Aditya Birla group by June 2007. The project aims to mine bauxite through open-cast mining from Baplimali (in Maikanch panchayat), a hill regarded as sacred by the tribal people. The extracted bauxite would be transported to a refinery at Doraguda near Kucheipadar, where it would be processed for aluminium in an alumina plant. The processed aluminium is to be transported to Tikiri by trucks, for onward transport to Visakhapatnam seaport by train for export to different parts of the world. The entire industrial complex is surrounded by Niyamgiri Hills with ostentatious quarters. Security did not let me enter the company. So I talked to the local adivasi women of Kucheipadar who felt that it is their natural surroundings and environment that is being threatened by UAIL. Sumani Jhoria and Mukta Jhoria said, 'For us, the lands, forests, hills and the rivers of Kashipur are the source of livelihood and also our Gods. We will continue to protest.'

In Lanjigarh of Kalahandi district 34 tribals were arrested in April 2006 because they opposed forceful occupation of their land by Vedanta Alumina Company of UK. One of the tribal woman leaders was Maladi Majhi who led the movement with others. At one village called Chatrapur, downstream from Vedanta's refinery, villagers have complained several times of contamination in the local Vansadhara River. An Odisha Pollution Control Board Report confirmed that toxic waste from the factory had been dumped into the river during 2007. People also complained that they were not getting jobs they had been promised by the company.[62] The traditional beliefs, values, norms and religious practices like the Meria festival of sacrifice are dying. A woman said, *Amoro devata ke bi nashta kole*—they even destroyed our deities—referring to the Dharni vali (Earth Goddess stones) that form the centre of a Kondh village, which has been crushed to rubble along with the houses.[63]

Local residents face repression for opposing POSCO. In Sambalpur and Jharsuguda district of west Odisha, tribals are opposing sponge iron projects because these plants contaminate water bodies and air. People also faced brutal police repression in Dhenkanal in December 2005 and in Bolangir in May 2005 when protesting against Bhusan Steel Company and Sukhtel Dam project respectively. Plans for a lower Sukhtel Dam in Bolangir are almost certainly linked to the plans for mining Gandhamardan. Inhabitants of villages due for submergence have been virtually forced into signing agreements to accept compensation. Tribal women and men were severely beaten and harassed by the police for taking part in demonstrations.[64] Since August 2008, the Odisha government has started a similar scheme like the Salwa Judum of Bastar, of deploying 2000 armed tribal youths as special police officers in five districts of Odisha particularly affected by Maoist violence: Kandhamal, Gajapati, Rayagada, Koraput and Malkangiri.[65] According to Satnam, 'In Bastar, different kinds of fires burn—the fire in the empty belly, the fire of the jungle, of the revolution.'[66]

Koraput had been the original home of various tribes for centuries. From 1961 onwards, settlers expanded their material base in the lands of the tribe, took away their lands and forests, displaced them from state politics and dominated in the sector of government jobs. The tribals of Koraput, under the leadership of their educated sons, started a demonstration against the settlers over the issue of preservation of land and forests in the tahsil town of Umarkote. They stopped the illegal felling of the trees. In June 2001, the movement turned into a violent clash between the settlers and the tribals. The police firing at Rayagada block headquarters led to deaths; the movement gradually gained strength and the tribals attended meetings armed with their traditional weapons like bows and arrows. The movement also led to political mobilization among the tribes and created a new state of Chhattisgarh.

In Rayagada the Dandakaranya Jagaran Morcha, constituted by the local people, has now demanded patta rights on the land that has been in their possession since a long time. Militant organizations like the Kui Chasi Mulia Samiti and the People's War Group (PWG) have become active in creating political consciousness safeguarding tribal rights to land, forests and water. Earlier the PWG worked in a zone comprising the tribal areas of Andhra Pradesh, Chhattisgarh and Malkangiri, but now they have included all the tribal areas of Koraput as a separate zone for their action. There is also an adivasi women organization called Krantikari Adivasi Mahila Sangha (KAMS) or Revolutionary Adivasi Women's Organization.[67] In the Dandakaranya region an alternative model of development has been introduced by CPI (Maoists). The Dandakaranya Special Zonal Committee of CPI (Maoists) supervises the developmental activities of Dantewada, Bastar and Kanker districts of Chhattisgarh and Gadchhiroli district of Maharashtra.[68]

Action for Welfare and Awakening of Rural Environment or AWARE is a non-governmental development organization involved in the overall development of this region. In 1992 AWARE adopted many villages in the Dandakaranya region covering Andhra Pradesh and Odisha states. It works through Village Associations, Mahila Mandalis, and Youth Associations by creating awareness through motivation and organization. A survey report has been published on development process initiated by AWARE from 1992–1996.[69]

The basic education for the girl child is one of the important national level objectives as well as AWARE's target. Nearly 95 per cent of the women in AWARE villages want their girl child to be educated as compared to 28 per cent in the non-AWARE villages. AWARE efforts to bring a change in the attitude towards a girl child have given the desired results. Nearly 70 per cent of women feel that there are no atrocities in AWARE villages while it is less than 34 per cent in non-AWARE villages. AWARE is playing a significant role in savings schemes which cover over 60 per cent of AWARE families.

The survey report further talked about the Mahila Mandalis of the Dandakaranya region. Mahila Mandalis play an important role in forming a concerted effort to mobilize women. They meet more frequently based on the concerned issues, conduct training camps to discuss nutrition aspects, population, education, use of local resources, taking an active role in awareness regarding their development in all aspects. Mahila Mandali plays an important role in solving the conflict among members. More than 70 per cent of them indicated that in cases of trouble, they make them sit together and solve the problem. In some instances, they caution them and even impose fine on them. The Mahila Mandali members also meet with other associations like Youth Associations, Village Association and offer some help.

Chaitanya Shakti members visit the villages as part of rural development efforts. These visits are expected to offer more confidence and empowerment for women. The major achievement is strengthening the unity among women. The report indicates that more than 50 per cent of the respondents are in favour of reservations to women. The Mahila Mandali members meet frequently the District Collector, concerned MLA, police, and other district officers. Women empowerment is the strategy of AWARE. The strength of women in

AWARE villages is derived particularly from connecting with other women through their own medium of Mahila Mandali.

TRIBAL WOMEN IN RESISTANCE MOVEMENT IN ODISHA

The foundation stone for the first of Odisha's new steel plants, near Gopalpur was laid by Prime Minister Narasimha Rao on 30 December 1995 was thwarted by a strong people's movement. The factory threatened to displace about 25,000 people from 25 villages, who stood to lose a rich agricultural economy, and swiftly established a Gana Sangram Samiti to fight the plant. Tribal women formed a *Nari Sena* (women's army), and came to the forefront of protests when about 6,000 armed police were sent to curb resistance in August 1996 and arrested hundreds of men and women. Police invaded the area again in March 1997, and meeting strong resistance again, opened fire, injuring four severely. People set up 14 gates to prevent entry by company officials and police, erecting a pillar inscribed with the words: 'Water, land and environment belong to us and no one else has any rights to them.' The movement managed to stop the plant and a dam on the Rushikulya River 120 km away, which would have displaced about 5,000 adivasis. Yet TISCO displaced several of the Gopalpur villagers, enclosing 5,000 acres with a high wall, though till now, this land has remained unused.[70]

The Kalinganagar complex of steel plants is conveniently close to Sukinda of Odisha. In May 2005, police lathi charged a protest against a bhumi puja being performed by Maharashtra Seamless Steel. The Additional District Magistrate ordered seated adivasi protesters to disperse, after which police disarmed and then attacked them.[71] On 2 January 2006, hundreds of adivasis from 25 villages heard that Tata was about to start construction on their land near Champakoili village. For 23 days, the adivasis had blocked the state highway at Kalinganagar, protesting against the takeover of their farmlands by TISCO. The police was brought in to forcibly clear the highway.[72] Police took six bodies away immediately afterwards, and when these were returned to their families, it was found that the police had cut off their hands, the men's genitals and the women's breasts.[73]

Pohang Steel Company of South Korea (POSCO) was also drawing up plans for a contentious steel plant at this time, on the coast near Paradip Port, in Jagatsinghpur district. The primary aim was to get a lease for mining iron in north Odisha, including the deeply forested Khandadhara Mountain in Sundargarh. People of the Pahari Bhuiya tribe were preparing to resist this invasion. The farmers of the district threatened with displacement were 22,000 people from 3,700 families in 11 villages. People erected barricades and formed POSCO Pratirodh Sangram Samiti. Pro-POSCO goons threw bombs at a crowd consisting largely of women.[74] A Khondh woman of Putsil village, close to Deo Mali, Odisha's highest mountain, where both the Ashapura Minechem Ltd. and Bhushan Steel Ltd. have been angling for clearance, spoke on how the adivasi women took part in the movement against mining, 'On 8 March 2008 we were going to Boro Manjili. On the same day the MLA was passing by car. We stopped him and asked him: 'Where are you going?'

'I'm going because of the mining. Don't worry—I'll make sure you Putsil people get work, and others of this area, and I'll feed you in my own house'.

> 'Why have you sold our mountain to the company?'
> Finally he said, 'As long as I'm MLA I won't allow any mining.'[75]

A month after this event, the villages around Deo Mali organized a meeting at Upara Kanti, the village after Putsil (13 April 2008). They said, 'We have to protect our area from being destroyed ... We won't give our mountain, Deo Mali ... Our cattle, buffalo, sheep and goats would die. We won't let them have our precious fields ... We won't sustain as construction and mine workers. When the government comes we'll tell them, 'If you want to kill us, just kill us, but we all Adivasis and Harijans won't let you mine our mountain. We mustn't let them divide us. That'd make it easy for them, to sell Deo Mali like they've sold Mali Parbat [to Hindalco, that is, Birla] ... If we lose our land where will we go?'[76]

The adivasi women of Narayanpatna have set an example by keeping themselves in the forefront of the struggle while patiently putting up stiff resistance to the inhuman attack on the agitating villages and arrest of the agitators by the police. Using traditional weapons and the home-made chilli powder they have been able to withstand the police and played a key role in cracking down on the hooch manufacturing units and made Narayanpatna liquor-free. When all the male members, the CMAS leaders, are forced to go in hiding, the remaining children, and women took up agricultural activities.[77] In the wake of police firing on 20 November, the police arrested Kumudini of Polapat village, a woman leader of the CMAS. Police arrested the husbands of Sirka Bina and Sonia Hikoka on suspicion of aiding the Maoists.[78] They formed a separate women's organization named Biplabi Adivasi Mahila Sangha (BAMS), Revolutionary Tribal Women's Organization. BAMS have have achieved considerable success in its endeavour.[79]

A part of this chapter is based on Debasree De, 'Development-Induced Displacement: Impact on Adivasi Women of Odisha', *Community Development Journal*, 50 (July 2015): 448–62 (Oxford University Press).

NOTES

1. Behura and Panigrahi, (2006) *Tribals and the Indian Constitution:* 192.
2. Vinita Damodaran, 2010. 'Globalization and Tribal Histories in Eastern India', in *Environmental History: As If Nature Existed,* edited by John R. McNeill, Jose Augusto Padua and Mahesh Rangarajan (New Delhi: Oxford University Press): 179 [From the field notes of Richard Grove who visited Kalinga Nagar in March 2006, Damodaran has cited Richard Grove's accounts of his field visit in her article.]
3. This was a statement made by the Chief Minister of Odisha, Naveen Patnaik, which was on Oriya (Odisha) TV news on 5 December available at http://www.minesandcommunities.org/article.php?a=3931, accessed on 18 June 2012.

4 Chana Kapoor, 'Adivasi Social Movement in Odisha', in *Dissenting Voices and Transformative Actions* Debal K. Singha Roy, ed.: 510, 511.
5 Hans, Patel and Das, *Violence against Women in Odisha*.
6 Viegas, *Encroached and Enslaved*: 34. Walter Fernandes, 1996. 'Land Reforms, Ownership Pattern and Alienation of Tribal Livelihood', in *Social Action* 46, 4: 433.
7 Walter Fernandes, 1996. 'Land Reforms, Ownership Pattern and Alienation of Tribal Livelihood', *Social Action* 46, 4: 433.
8 L.K. Mahapatra, 1999. 'Tribal Rights to Land and the State in Odisha' in *Contemporary Society: Tribal Studies*, edited by Deepak Kumar Behera and Georg Pfeffer, vol. 3, *Social Concern* (New Delhi: Concept Publishing): 135–51.
9 P.K. Agrawal, *Naxalism: Causes and Cure*: 153.
10 Bina Agarwal, 2002. '*Are We Not Peasants Too? Land Rights and Women's Claims in India*', in SEEDS, Issue-21 (New York: Population Council) the article was downloaded from http://www.binaagarwal.com/downloads/apapers/are_we_not_peasants_too.pdf on 15 July 2012; see also 1994. *A Field of One's Own: Gender and Land Rights in South Asia* (Cambridge: Cambridge University Press).
11 Jagannath Ambagudia, 2010. 'Tribal Rights, Dispossession and the State in Odisha', *Economic and Political Weekly* (henceforth *EPW*), 45, 33 (August 14): 60–67.
12 A fact finding team of DSU (Democratic Student Union) of the students of Delhi University, JNU and IGNOU published a report in a booklet after visiting the area from 11 April 2011 to 16 April 2011: 2012. 'Flames of Narayanpatna: Two Reports on the Narayanpatna Struggle in Koraput, Odisha' (Chandigarh: Charvaka): 15–16.
13 *Tehelka*, 6, 50 (19 Dec. 2009).
14 Padel and Das, *Out of This Earth*: 403.
15 Fernandes, and Asif, *Development-Induced-Displacement*: 112.
16 Hansda, 1983. 'Agricultural Development in Tribal Areas', in Mishra and Singh eds., *Tribal Area Development*: 23.
17 Fernandes and Asif, *Development-Induced-Displacement*: 135.
18 Gopabandhu Pattanaik and Damodar Panda, 1992. 'The New Economic Policy and the Poor', *Social Action* 42: 2 (April–June); 201–12.
19 Fernandes and Asif, *Development-Induced-Displacement*: 137–39; Fernandes, and Raj, *Development, Displacement and Rehabilitation*: 141–44.
20 Padel and Das, *Out of this Earth*: 360–61.
21 Fernandes, and Raj, *Development, Displacement and Rehabilitation*: 90.
22 Satnam, *Jangalnama*: 96–97.
23 Hans, *Tribal Women A Gendered Utopia*: 29.
24 Adivasis have a tradition of animal husbandry, though not of profitable dairy husbandry. The Operation Flood programme to replicate

the Amul pattern has from the start—as the National Dairy Plan has done now—self-selected only 'milk shed districts', i.e., western India (from Punjab down to Kerala) with an extant tradition of profitable dairying. As a result, the entire adivasi belt of central India has remained excluded. The Vasudhara cooperative is a classic case of the 'reinvented' Amul pattern, ideal as the model to launch India's second White Revolution to empower adivasi women and strengthen their livelihoods. See Tushaar Shah, Yashree Mehta, Shilp Verma and Amit Patel. 2015 'Vasudhara Adivasi Dairy Cooperative: Model for the Second White Revolution?' *EPW* 1, 7 (February 14): 15–18.

25 Panda, *Bonda Banabasinka Vivaha Pratha Parab*, 104–08.
26 Debarshi Dasgupta, 2010 'Being Remo: For the Bonda Tribals of Odisha, a Constant Struggle Is On—with State and Custom', in *Outlook* (1 February).
27 Patnaik, Chowdhury, Das Patnaik, *The Bondos and Their Response to Development*.
28 Jhansi I. Rani, and K.E. Raj Pramukh, 2009. 'Bondo Women and Their Economic Organization', *Man and Life* 35, 3&4: 31–34.
29 Ramesh P. Mohanty, 1992 'Belief and Practices in Liquor Preparation among the Bondo Highlanders', *Man and Life* 18, 3&4.
30 Elwin, *The Bondo Highlanders*.
31 Nanda, *Contours of Continuity and Change: The Story of the Bonda Highlanders*.
32 *Outlook*, 1 February 2010.
33 B. Mahapatra, *Development of a Primitive Tribe*: 152–53.
34 Final Report on 'In Search of a Strategy to Build a Field Model': 102–05.
35 The term 'primitive' is derogatory, wrong and dangerous. Since 2006, the Government of India has recommended that the term be avoided and that tribes, such as the Dongria Kondh, should be referred to as Particularly Vulnerable Tribal Groups. Internationally, the use of the term has been discouraged for many years. Back in 2007, the Association of Social Anthropologists advised that the use of the term' primitive' is damaging and is used as a pretext for depriving people of their lands and rights.
36 Fernandes, Menon and Viegas *Forests, Environment and Tribal Economy*: 251–53; Fernandes, and Menon, *Tribal Women and Forest Economy*: 76.
37 Mihir Jena, Pathi, Dash, Patnaik, Seeland, *Forest Tribes of Odisha: Lifestyle and Social Conditions*: 122–25.
38 Ibid.
39 For detail see Padel, *Sacrificing People*.
40 Saran, *Final Population Totals: A Brochure of Odisha*.
41 Mohanty, Mohapatra, Samal, *Tribes of Koraput*: 94.
42 Padhi, *The Gadaba Tribe of Odisha*: 148–49.
43 N.K. Bose, 1929. 'Juang Associations', *Man in India* 9.

44 Nilakantha Panigrahi and Rashmirani Balabantaray, 2012 'Tribal Society, Women and Social Inclusion', in *Social Exclusion & Gender: Some Reflections*, edited by Rath, Chinara, Mohanty and Mohanty: 325–46.
45 Verrier Elwin, 1948. 'Notes on the Juang', *Man in India* 28, 36; also see *Bonda Development Agency: Baseline Survey & Needs Assessment and 10th Five-Year Action Plan for 2002–03 to 2006–07* (March 2002): 39.
46 Elwin, 'Notes on the Juang': 36.
47 *Lanjia Saora Development Agency: Baseline Survey & Needs Assessment and 10th Five-Year Action Plan for 2002–03 to 2006–07* (March 2002): 44–45.
48 E. Samuels, 1856. 'Notes on a Forest Race called Puttooas or Juanga, Inhabiting Certain of the Tributary Mahals of Cuttack', *Journal of the Asiatic Society of Bengal* 25: 296–97.
49 Roy and Roy, *Hunger and Physique*: 21–22.
50 A.E. George, 1982. 'Tribal Development: A Visit to the Juang', *EPW* 3 July: 1095–96.
51 *Telegraph*, 13 November 1986.
52 Elwin, 'Notes on the Juang', 51; Saradindu Bose, 1961. 'Land Use Survey in a Juang Village', *Man in India* (July–September): 174.
53 *The New Indian Express,* September 11, 2009.
54 Kak, Sanjay, 2010. 'The Bauxite Mountains of Odisha', *EPW* 45, 38 (September 18): 30–34.
55 R.K. Barik, 2006. 'Faulty Planning in a Tribal Region: The Dandakaranya Development Authority', in *Tribal Development in India*, Govinda Chandra Rath, ed.: 97–98.
56 B. Singh, 1984. *The Saora Highlander: Leadership and Development* (New Delhi: Somaiya).
57 Fernandes, Menon and Viegas. *Forests, Environment and Tribal Economy*: 6–10, 63–84.
58 Pradhan and Council of Professional Social Workers *State of Odisha's Environment: A Citizens' Report*: 144–45.
59 Manipadma Jena, 2008. 'Food Insecurity among Tribal Communities of Odisha', *EPW* (February 9): 18–21.
60 Padel, and Das, *Out of this Earth*: 122–23, 126.
61 Debranjan Sarengi, 2005. 'Shallow Grave: Odisha's New Labs of Horror', *Tehelka*, 23 July.
62 *The Statesman*, 10 October 2010.
63 Binay Kumar Pattnaik, 2013. 'Tribal Resistance Movements and the Politics of Development-Induced Displacement in Contemporary Odisha', in *Social Change* 43, 1: 53–78.
64 D. Sarengi, 2006. 'Odisha: Paradise for Private Players', *Frontier* 39, 5 (August 20–26).
65 *Indian Express*, 30 October 2008.
66 Satnam, *Jangalnama*: 38.

67 Amit Bhattacharyya, 2010. 'Maoist Movement in India and the Alternative Model of Development in Dandakaranya', in *Discourses on Naxalite Movement*, Pradip Basu, ed.: 268–80.
68 For detail of this model of development see, Bhattacharyya, *Janaganer Unnayan*.
69 V.B.N.S. Madduri, 1997. 'Sustainable Development of Dandakaranya Tribals: Methodological Issues', in *Sustainable Development in Tribal and Backward Areas*, Kohli, Shah and. Chowdhary, eds. 85–95.
70 Shiva, and Jafri, *Stronger than Steel: People's Movement against Globalisation*: 4. Also see Birendra Nayak, 2000. *Voices of Gopalpur*, an English language bulletin edited by Birendra Nayak from 1996 and published from Berhampur with Prafulla Samantara.
71 Nayak, and Kujur, *State Aggression and Tribal Resistance*: 9, 15.
72 C. Kartik Dash, and Kishore, C. Samal, 2008. 'New Mega Projects in Odisha: Protests by Potential Displaced Persons', in *Social Change* 38: 4: 627–44.
73 Amita Baviskar, 2008. 'Pedagogy, Public Sociology and Politics in India: What is to be Done?' *Current Sociology* 56, 3: 425–33.
74 Padel, and Das, *Out of this Earth* 408; also see *Update*, edited by Suvro Mallick, Series-13 (January 2007), Kolkata.
75 Ibid.: 563.
76 Ibid.: 564–65.
77 Amitabha Kar, 2012 'The Invincible Flame of Narayanpatna: An Interview with Dandapani Mohanty', Sanhati: Fighting for Neo-Liberalism (18 November 2012), available at www.sanhati.com downloaded on 11 December 2013.
78 'The Flames of Narayanpatna': 92–93.
79 Ibid.: 43.

CHAPTER 6

Increasing Marginalization of Adivasi Women: The Process of Cultural Silencing

> The low, flat-topped hills of south Odisha have been home to the Dongria Kondh long before there was a country called India or a state called Odisha. The hills watched over the Kondh. The Kondh watched over the hills and worshipped them as living deities. Now these hills have been sold for the bauxite they contain. For the Kondh it's as though god has been sold. They ask how much god would go for if the god were Ram or Allah or Jesus Christ?
>
> —Arundhati Roy

THE TERM 'GENOCIDE' was first used in 1944–1945, to describe the Nazi treatment of Jews. 'Genocide' means killing a people, race or tribe. There are two levels to what was killed: the physical extermination, and the killing of a culture. 'Cultural Genocide' means essentially the killing of people's culture by uprooting them from their ancestral lands. Underlying this cultural genocide is the invaders' total disrespect for adivasi people's traditions and cultures. This is nothing but a deeper psychic death. The starting point of this extermination is the process of cultural silencing of the most vulnerable section of the adivasis: adivasi women, who are the marginal of the marginals and I have termed this very process as 'peripheralization'.

Let us attempt to delineate the tribal culture by segregating the colourful sides of its life: mythology, arts, crafts, songs, dances. Let us deal with drudgery, hunger, malnutrition, illiteracy of women, increasing domestication that curbs their autonomy, sexual victimization, brutal killing of suspected 'witches', commodification of their labour by converting them into domestic maids or mine workers. The issues of representation and the politics of identity—body politics in particular—lead to questions of culture, gender and power.

The word 'silence' can be of two meanings: First is simply ignoring their voices: the 'culture of silence' initiated by the process of Sanskritization or Hinduization. On the one hand the voices of the tribal women were continuously culturally silenced by the manipulation of the state elites and the state system and on the other by the forces of patriarchy. The culture of silence causes a cultural memocide, killing of memory of resistance and creative excellences and aesthetics. Dispossession and forced migration have remained chronic, leading them to extreme poverty, exploitation, oppression and dehumanization culminating into cultural silence that debilitates and destroys not only personality, but also the creative genius of the ethnic groups. Eventually, these adivasis lost their cultural strength and were forced to adopt the dominant norms. Pashupati Prasad Mahato has termed the process as *nirbakization* or cultural silence, which embodies the same process of what I called peripheralization.[1]

The application of the word 'peripheralization' can be questioned because we are more conversant with the word 'marginalization'. Both the words are synonymous. Then how does the difference follow, reader will ask? 'Marginal' means the people who live on the edge of society and 'periphery' denotes an outer boundary or an outer world. The 'outside' is important because it positioned territory and people in an oppositional relation to the dominant Centre. The notions of accessibility and remote rurality are attached to the term 'periphery'. Centre, as an opposite, was always there, but the periphery has been constructed everywhere. Centre is the first world and periphery is the third world. Centre is the exploiter, periphery is the exploited. Both these are constructed opposing identities. Centre forces the periphery to abide by its rules and commands, but periphery sometimes revolts and prepare their own alternative model of development. Centre conquers periphery, uproots it by applying impunity, jailing, mass rape. Periphery protests, retaliates, and faces brutal repression of the Centre but always remains there. The adivasis see the culture of the Centre or the culture of the mainstream as peripheral.

Adoption of the mainstream culture by the adivasi women leads to their invariable subjugation. Mainstreamization may take place in two ways: 'being mainstreamized' and 'doing mainstreamizing'. 'Being mainstreamized' means when the adivasi women consciously or unconsciously, however deliberately, take up the culture of the women of the dominant caste society. With the introduction of land as private property, the growth of trade and the market economy, spread of modern education, opening up of new occupations, and modern communications adivasis are experiencing economic and social structural changes. They are not ready to give up their ST status. And needless to say, the reason is the politics of reservation. Prima facie mainstreamization actually confirms the permanent peripheralization of the adivasis by denying their right to embrace modernity. Next is the issue of 'doing mainstreamizing'. The very first step towards mainstreamization could be the recognition of the fundamental rights of the adivasi communities to be the citizens of this country. And that can be done through enumeration of all the tribal groups in the Census. But the parliamentary committee on welfare of scheduled castes and scheduled tribes has found that 18 tribal groups in two successive censuses—1991 and 2001—remained non-accounted. These tribal groups are Gutob Gadaba, Kutia Kondh, Kondh Sabar, Bonda Paraja, Parenga Paraja in Andhra Pradesh; Cholanaikayan in Kerala; Abujh Maria, Bharia and Hill Korwa in Madhya Pradesh; Maria Gond in Maharashtra; Chuktia Bhunja, Dongria

Kondh, Kharia, Kutia Kondh, Lanjhia Saora, Paudi Bhuyan and Saora in Odisha; and Toto in West Bengal. These groups have been termed as Particularly Vulnerable Tribal Groups (PTGs).[2]

According to the state, massive industrialization will bring the adivasi societies into the 'mainstream'. Henry George in his phenomenal work *Progress and Poverty* (1880) said that natural resources are the key to understanding our economy, and the failure of others to see this has led to increasing poverty and environmental degradation. Henry George has very truly stated, 'Where the conditions to which material progress everywhere tends are most fully realized—that is to say, where population is densest, wealth greatest, and the machinery of production and exchange most highly developed—we find the deepest poverty, the sharpest struggle for existence, and the most of enforced idleness'.[3] When the Supreme Court stalled the Vedanta Group's bauxite mining project in the Niyamgiri Hills of Odisha on 18 April 2013, till the gram sabhas clear it, several sections of society asked are the adivasis of Niyamgiri going to be segregated from the mainstream forever? Won't they take part in the mainstream development initiatives? If they are substantially compensated then everyone may gain from the project! The Supreme Court specifically said the villagers would decide whether the proposed mining would cause harm to their religious rights of worshipping Niyam Raja at Hundaljali hilltop, about 10 km from the identified mining site. The apex court added that the Forest Rights Act has been enacted conferring powers on the gram sabha constituted under the Act to protect community resources, individual rights, cultural and religious rights; the Court cited the 'religious freedom guaranteed to Scheduled Tribes and the Traditional Forest Dwellers under Articles 25 and 26 of the Indian Constitution'.[4] According to the adivasis, the bauxite-rich rocks are lying at the top of the Niyamgiri Hills and sustain the rain water for the whole year. The water flows down like streams and supplies drinking water to the adivasi hamlets of the region. For the mainstream bauxite means aluminium; but for the adivasis bauxite means river, water and water gives life.

The easiest way to expose the adivasis to the real world is to impart education which helps them to get a better life. But here also the government fails miserably. Most of the tribal children hardly understand the dominating alien languages through which education is being imparted. Thus they lose interest in education. Take, for example, the case of Amrita Baro, an Oraon tribal girl found in the tea gardens of Jalpaiguri. She came here with her father from Gumla district of Jharkhand in search of livelihood. Amrita goes to school and is very much willing to go to the college. But the major problem she faces is the lack of toilet facilities for the girls in the schools. She knows that sanitary napkins should be used instead of rags and open defecation is unhealthy (the initiative taken by the panchayat to sell low-cost sanitary pads has been proved a lie).[5] A study commissioned by the Sarva Shiksha Abhiyan, Ministry of Human Resource Development and Government of India in 2012, revealed the fact that in Odisha not a single sample school (20 schools were visited) had separate usable toilets for boys and girls. This was also the case in Bihar, where 75 per cent of the schools had usable toilets but most of them were locked for the use of teachers.[6] Adivasi boys and girls are being brought to towns to study in urban educational institutions so that they merge with the 'mainstream'.[7]

The other meaning of silence is 'silence' itself. It is often said that the silence of the tribal women should be read or sensitized. If they do not answer any particular question and choose to remain silent then we should try to find out the probable causes of their silence or try to read from their expressions. This is, I believe, more harmful than the former one because then it justifies that 'subalterns cannot speak'. We, the non-tribals or caste people, can never be an appropriate representative of their silences. Will an adivasi woman, the most vulnerable group of our society, agree to share her secrets with an unknown male researcher?

For example, when you ask women about witch hunts they usually remain silent about it. This is not because they are afraid to speak but perhaps they do not want to involve outsiders. If they are asked why they still practise black magic or go to ojhas for curing diseases, they may have no answer perhaps because they know that this is their custom or rule of their society. It is also very true that they have no other alternative, such as an expensive nursing home or doctors' clinic or a mere health centre! You must try to make them break the silence; you have to believe in that tribals can and will speak. Needless to say this is the most difficult task, though not impossible, than simply assuming different meanings of their silence. It is wrong to see the tribal women as mere passive victims. Indeed, they have been at the forefront of dynamic struggles against displacement and oppression (see Chapter 5). For this 'culture of silence' to be broken, we need to push for emancipatory politics that challenge gender biases both at the level of community as well as in wider state-directed institutions and policies. Still the basic questions remain unanswered, why have the development policies failed? Are the 'felt needs' of the tribals ever taken into consideration?

HISTORY OF CULTURE

History is constituted by culture—of the 'people'. Such culture is perceived to constitute an important seed-bed of tradition and heritage from which ordinary people derived their perceptions regarding their traditions. Cultural objects are not manufactured by the historian but by the people he/she studies. They give off meaning. All interpersonal relationships are of a cultural nature, even those we qualify as 'economic' or 'social'. The tribal world, for example, is their own world and here we are the intruders. Therefore, we can say by following Darnton that 'the third level (culture) somehow derives from the first two (economics, demography and social structure)'.[8]

I have attempted to adopt an anthropological mode of history writing. Anthropology has much to offer the historian: first, an approach which is to gain entry into another culture; second a programme that will try to see things from the native's point of view, and to seek out the social dimensions of meaning; third, a concept of culture as a 'symbolic world' in which shared symbols serve thoughts and actions mould classification and judgement, and furnish warnings and indictments.[9] The use of sources, for example, the witchcraft accusations can be the sole material of cultural study. They can rewrite the history of the movement in terms of a struggle for cultural power. In this way cultural studies affirm the normalcy of apparently exceptional forms of behaviour, and identify the rational in the irrational, the ordinary in the grotesque. It transfers attention from the study of 'objective' reality to the categories in and through which it was perceived, from collective consciousness to cognitive codes, from social being to the symbolic order.[10] Allen F. Repko suggests that, 'disciplines are fluid and their boundaries porous'.[11] Yet it can be said that the openness and fluidity of current academic fields undermines the main critique of the disciplinary system.[12] By focussing on the forms of representation it offers a common ground where epistemology and ontology, anthropology and ethnology, history and archaeology, language and literature, past and present can meet in conditions of rough equality. It encourages the historian to borrow freely from other spheres.

TRIBAL WOMEN'S SEXUALITY

Ajay Skaria once questioned why the emphasis on the unbridled sexuality of the Bhil woman in western India remained muted in the nineteenth century? His findings suggest that it was because the primary emphasis was on the exotic sexuality of the oriental woman, epitomized in South Asia by her for the upper castes. Thus there was the colonial fascination with sati, the practice of widow immolation amongst the upper castes. This fascination was to a large extent 'voyeuristic', stemming from the fact that sati enacted the 'powerful male fantasy of female devotion'. Because of this primary focus on exotic, orientalist sexuality, the primitive sexuality of the tribal woman was, with some important exceptions (as for example in the tea plantations of northeast India), not much dwelt on.[13]

Reference might be made to a whole series of collateral changes which, over the past forty years, have shifted the locus of historical inquiry from the study of social facts to that of the symbolic space they inhabit. One could instance the vast new literature on representation of womanhood and latterly on the idea of masculinity and the formation of sexual identities. Tribal women have their own modes of thought regarding conjugality, passion and privacy that might have been regarded as vulgar by 'civilized' people. Their privacy is of two types: privacy in their personal life and privacy within their community life maintained against the non-tribals. Writing on women's sexuality is attempting to extract meaning from the absences, silences and 'aporia'.[14] It attempts to interpret the visible by the evidence of things unseen by using the behaviour and mode of thought of the tribal women themselves and not by ours.

It was felt essential to study the dimensions of sexual behaviour of tribal women, because the tribes are a closed group community and due to their exposure towards urban area and mass media, the tribal women are becoming a vulnerable group for sexual exploitation and thereby subjected to psychological and physiological problems. (The field study was conducted in February 2012.) Earlier, their behaviour was mainly governed by their own culture and directions given by their elders but now all that is changing. Sexual behaviour has never been a taboo for the tribal people. In their society it is governed by their own cultural rules and regulations and they enter into relations within their community. For example, Santhals have their own customary law to regulate sex. It aims both at providing the greatest freedom as well as enforcing the strictest control. The main rules regarding regulation of sex are: *(i)* all premarital relations should be private. If a boy and girl are caught together a goat is exacted by the village and if does not end in marriage the boy has to pay a fine; *(ii)* intercourse should always be consensual; otherwise the girl can complain and the village will fine the boy; *(iii)* if post-marriage intercourse with another man is detected, the adulterer will have to pay a sum of compensation or double bride price and sometimes the costs of the wedding or take the woman or pay her divorce money; *(iv)* in no circumstances a Santhal can have sexual relations with any non-Santhal. Intercourse with the Santhals of the same clan is banned.[15]

As mentioned earlier, there was a dormitory system prevailing in tribal society's ghotul. It is separate for boys and girls. In this system boys and girls spend their night together under supervision of old men and women of the village. Due to the influence of NGOs and missionary schools, the ghotul is disappearing from tribal societies. But interestingly the custom of bride price is still prevalent in the tribal areas of eastern India. Pannan Hansda of Raipur block, Bankura district said that the amount of bride price is only seven rupees. Sometimes cows, clothes and ornaments are given to the father of the bride by the family of the bridegroom.[16] The amount has increased, varies from ₹2,000 to 5,000, paid in cash. According to W.G. Archer, 'It confirms the family's responsibilities for the girl's fidelity. It is way of formally recognizing a son-in-law. It stresses the conception of woman as property. The price is symbolic. It is a legal payment that acts as a foundation of the rights of the husband and his family.'[17]

Dongria Kondh in Niyamgiri Hills (Bissamcuttack and Muniguda, in Gunupur and Ksinghpur sub-divisions) has youth dormitories. Once unmarried boys and girls attain puberty they are sent off to the *Dhangara bassa* (boy's dormitory) and *Dhangiri bassa* (girl's dormitory) located at the far end of the village. The youngsters sing, dance and share experiences. In what could be termed a 'modern' move, girls and boys are allowed to forge relationships, including sexual ties, with those from other villages. The idea is that eventually their 'affair' will end in marriage. The boy usually proposes and his family gives the girl's family wine and buffaloes as offerings. If his feelings are reciprocated, then along with wine and buffaloes the girl's side provides other 'gifts' to consolidate the union. Unfortunately, not all liaisons have happy endings. Dongria girls who face rejection are not allowed to stay in the Dhangiri bassa and cannot even be part of dances or musical programmes during festivals, because they are considered 'rejects'. Tradition demands that these women are to live like widows and wait for the boy forever. They have to shave their heads, wear only light-coloured cotton saris, sport no ornaments and remain alone for the rest of the life. Practices like this are now posing a huge risk to their very existence and they are getting increasingly depleted by the day.[18]

According to the information gathered during my field study, tribal women today are more exposed to education and the outside world and are more aware of abortions and contraceptive methods.[19] Women, to fulfil their enhanced desires, need more money to get things from market. The women are now actually living in a transformational phase, trying to adopt a new lifestyle, which is very much influenced by transportation, consumerism, modernization, urbanization and migration to big cities for education and livelihood at the same time linked to their own culture. Due to exposure to outside world, they have become vulnerable to sexual abuse and many modern evils like HIV/AIDS.[20]

In tribal society only after the influx of modern education, migration and contact with non-tribal communities, some restrictions were imposed on the girls like coming back home before sunset, accepting a marriage settled by parents. All this happened as the young tribal girls started getting attracted towards non-tribal norms, culture and lifestyles. This made them vulnerable to many evils. Earlier the social behaviour of young boys and girls were limited up to dancing, singing, playing and chatting. They had sexual relations only with those whom they wanted to marry and settle down with. Due to exposure to mass media and to non-tribal communities, now the young tribal girls are not sticking to relations within their own community. Many tribal girls, who are studying and working outside, become sexually active within or outside the community, easier for them as social interaction with opposite sex is not a barrier for them.

Sexual harassment is unwelcome attention of a sexual nature. It includes a range of behaviour from mild transgression and annoyances to serious abuse, which can involve even forced sexual activity. Tribal women have frequently been observed as a sexual object by the 'civilised' men. Tribal communities have their own knowledge of indigenous methods of birth control.[21] They use several types of forest products and *jadi buties* (herbal) for controlling unwanted birth. Later new methods evolved in contraceptive technology like condom, pills, IUD, sterilization.

TRIBAL MEDICINES

As a forest-hunting tribe the Birhors have an age-old tradition in the domain of herbal medicine. Pressed by economic hardship, many of the experts in herbal medicine have approached the modern markets for selling these to the outsiders. The Birhor medicine men are called Mati or the Baiga. Birhor women also practise and train themselves in using tribal medical traditions. For Birhors the dream is a medicine too. According to the Birhor methods, khaksa root stops menstrual bleeding. Morom-dah and pathal-konda roots are very good in treating women's complaints. The best sexual stimulant is haser. There are cures for cancer and AIDS or other problem sicknesses ravaging the modern world.[22] In childbirth: mahua seeds, mahua liquor, mahua oil; for barrenness: imli with sugar, bark of ashoka plant, amarlata plant; for family planning: oil of neem and karanj, betel leaves and roots; for abortion: mahua flower, ginger and loaf sugar.

The risk factor associated with the traditional methods of preventing unwanted pregnancy and the pain associated with adopting them have diverted them towards modern methods of birth control.[23] Female sterilization is the most widely known method of contraception, followed by contraceptive pills. During my field study in West Medinipur I asked Lakshmimoni Mandi (Kopatkata village of Jamboni block) about whether there is any attempt going on for raising awareness about family planning she replied, 'Didimoni comes and talks about the use of *bori*.' I got to know that an Aganwadi worker comes in the village and talks about the use of contraceptives. The knowledge of contraceptives is higher among younger girls than older ones. But the women are not always convinced by her. The use of condoms is not very clear to them and they know very little about IUD/ Copper-T Loop and about male sterilization. They are still not fully aware of the need of a proper family planning.

Collecting information on matters related to sexual intercourse is a very difficult task. (The field work was carried out in November 2011). When I asked the women respondents specifically about pregnancies and abortions, they became reluctant to disclose anything. These issues are too personal and should be dealt with proper care. They declined coming before the camera until they were convinced that their names or photographs would not be disclosed at any level. They said that the medical plants which are mainly used by the tribes are: karand, karkati, padal, kena, betel leaves, betel nuts (kasaili), awala, baheda and bhagrud. For abortions, some hot medicinal plants are used in the form of paste, which is kept on the mouth of vagina and after that, sometimes malish (oil rubbing) is done on stomach with hot tisi oil. Sometime they use some particular stems, which are inserted in the vagina. All these are very painful.

Most tribal women are engaged in the unorganized sector working as domestic servants, brick kiln workers, daily wage workers (see Chapter 4). Most of them are sexually active at their workplaces. These women neither receive their full payment nor are physically secured as they are subjected to sexual exploitation and rape. Premarital pregnancies lead to unsafe induced abortion.

WITCH HUNT

Witchcraft is studied today in the light of gender and class, or as the limit case of strategies of subversion and resistance. Almost all tribal groups in India believe in witchcraft, Evil Eye and productive, protective and destructive powers of the spirits or gods and goddesses. When somebody in the family is sick, it is suspected that the evil spirit has attacked the individual. The sudden death of several animals at a time in a family or village is also considered to be caused by a witch. Thus, tribal women also have to face internal violence in the form of witch hunting. Mainu Hansda from Kopatkata village of Jamboni block, West Medinipur, talked about the witchcraft. (Field work was conducted in Purulia in September 2011.) She said two years ago a boy died in some unknown disease. The people of the village suspected that it happened due to black magic. In Hura block of Purulia district Mamoni Murmu was first suspected as a witch and then beaten to death. Sajani Soren of Sarenga block, Bankura district said that witch hunt is often performed in their village and they still have a deep faith on black magic.[24] If a person is ill for a long period and it is confirmed that his illness is due to witchcraft, the second step is to locate the witch. If the witch does not disclose the location of seeds of sickness that she has planted she is beaten up by the villagers and the village council drive the suspected witch out of the village. Vijay Tendulkar, a well-known Indian playwright, relates his personal experiences in 'Tribal and I'.

> Everything beneath looked like a dream with sounds of drums reaching us at the top. Then gradually, groups of tribals with gigantic dhols (drums) and coloured bodies and faces emerged out of the surrounding depths ... [they]

attacked a tribal woman among their own group ... the woman ran for her life. They chased her, caught hold of her and began to beat her with fists and legs. They pelted her with stones, fisted and kicked her in her abdomen, on her face, on her head, on her back.

Soon the body of the lone tribal woman lay prostrate on the ground—half dead? Dead? Some distance away, and the killer men and women returned to their clan and resumed dancing as if nothing had happened ... soon everything was normal, except that body lying motionless. According to the law of her clan members, she, a witch needed to be killed. Her body would be left to rot, and to be eaten by dogs and wolves.[25]

Tendulkar's rendering of the real drama of witch mobbing and torture is also enacted in Shivkumar Pandey's short narrative, 'Daakan' (The Witch).[26]

Soma Chaudhuri has connected witchcraft accusations to gender conflict. First, the 'witchcraft' (women's acting outside of established norms) that fuels the hunts can be seen as a rebellion against an established order of society, and second, the witch hunts are attempts by men to denounce the ritual knowledge of women and link it to evil, establishing their societal dominance over women.[27] But witch hunting is also a kind of class struggle.

Suffering imposed on a woman's body by inflicting physical violence, verbal assault, or rape has had precedence as a general norm in India. This is not necessarily motivated by sexual desire but very often as the outcome of women's supposed defiance of the system of power or kinship dispute—as vendetta.[28] In *Bortika*, Mahasweta Devi has mentioned several cases of witch hunting in tribal societies. Mahasweta Devi's exploration of the life of a young woman, Chandidasi, falsely accused of being the *Bayen*—one who practices witchcraft, is another story of women's forceful subjugation by the forces of patriarchy. According to Spivak, the subaltern womanhood cannot break itself away from internalized gendering, and accepts exploitation as it accepts sexism in the name of willing conviction; that this is how one is accepted as being a good and ethical woman.[29] And 'if women speak outside [the symbolic] order they will either not be heard or be heard as insane', says Patricia Waugh.[30]

It is important to note that both men and women are suspected as witches. Thus while both dayan (female) and *bishaha* (male) can be identified as witches, there is a greater likelihood of women, generally widows, being identified as witches. The tribals make a distinction between 'white magic' and 'black magic': the minister of white magic is known as ojha or diviner and medicine man, while one of black magic was known as dayan, or witch or sorcerer. The belief in the existence of witches was remarkably absent among the nomadic foraging communities (like the Birhor). Among the Santhals, witches are exclusively women while among the Munda, Ho and Oraon a witch can either be a man or a woman.[31] The fact that ojhas or in Mundari term *deoras* (traditional witch healers) are exclusively males reflects the extension of gender conflicts in the domain of witchcraft.

In 2012, in Dubrajpur village of Daspur-I block in West Medinipur the victims were Fulmoni Singh (62) and her daughter Sambari Singh (40) and another Sambari Singh (55). A meeting was called, then the *janguru* consulted. After that they summoned an arbitration assemblage and started beating the adivasi women with a heavy bamboo stick. Later the dead bodies were buried under the bank of Kangsabati River.[32] Dubrajpur has a primary school, a high school, and Narajole Raj College within three kilometres. Many educated people live there.

Why are childless, single, widow or unprotected women primarily the victims? Traditionally, witch hunt is a ritualized violence or simply a brutal custom perpetrated against women. In the post-independence period the erosion of the communality of traditional land holdings and replacing those with private ownership of land reinforced the gender dimensions of witch hunt. The displacement of the adivasis from their lands under 'development' further aggravated the problem. Vinita Damodaran argues that the rise in witch-hunting in the latter half of the nineteenth century and in the twentieth century was linked to the 'pressure of rapid ecological changes combined with the erosion of common property rights and deforestation'.[33] The clash between the residual usufructory right of women and the men's absolute right of ownership is perhaps what is behind the transformation of witch hunting from a mere stigma or expulsion from village to the killing of women concerned.[34]

Witches were made to walk naked, through the village, be gang-raped, have their heads tonsured or their breasts cut off, their teeth broken, or be forced to swallow urine and human faeces, to eat human flesh or the raw blood of a chicken.[35] But with the monetization of the witch trials suspected witches are now to pay a huge fine and very often ostracised.[36] An elderly couple, Robert Lakra (65) and his wife Colestina (60), were forced to eat excreta and drink urine, after they were blamed for the sudden death of cows and other animals in Puro village of Latehar district in Jharkhand. They were also beaten up for allegedly practising witchcraft.[37]

Rumour also plays an important role during the whisper campaign against the accused woman.[38] Tendulkar' said, 'She was a wife of one of them, a mother of his children. An elderly woman. Her husband must have been there among the dancing tribals with their coloured faces and torsos. Her children must have been there.'[39]

Under the impact of ecological and social crisis, even the strains generated by regular fluctuations in the agricultural cycle became difficult to sustain. The agriculturally lean periods would thus be particularly turbulent for the adivasis. It has found that most of the witch killing was committed between the months of May, June and September. May and June have traditionally been 'hunger months', when the strain of living bulks largely felt. The high incidence of witch killing in January could also be explained by the fact that there is a general sense of abandonment following the winter harvest. The fact that there was no witch killing in the month of transplantation, that is, August, also speaks a lot about the intricacies involved.⁴⁰ The traditional systems of health care and cure have fallen flat without a corresponding availability of modern health care facilities. 'Witches' thus are increasingly becoming scapegoats to ojhas failure to diagnose and cure many new diseases.

In the 1988 summer the tribal region of Bihar experienced an acute drought. In these inaccessible areas medical facilities were almost non-existent. The tribals lacked the wherewithal for a bare meal every day and their caloric intake was starkly inadequate. The tribals had to first go to the ojhas who exploited them by telling that their sickness was due to some black magic and demanded money to please the evil spirit. But the reality was that the doctors first failed to identify the disease and termed it as malaria. For around a week or so, the patients continued to be given antibiotics while the required medicine, gamaglobolin injection, was not supplied to the villagers.⁴¹

In an another case, branded as a witch, Sarathi Baske, a resident of Oltar village under Habibpur police station of Malda district of West Bengal, was attacked and forced to flee from home. The reason behind this incident was that the village had seen several baby deaths. Also, the villagers had been seen suffering from some ailments. Worried with the prevailing trend, the villagers led by Lolin Soren and Moti Murmu therefore visited the janguru. He labelled Sarathi as a 'witch' and held her responsible. The villagers stormed Sarathi's house. The incident was also linked to the property issue since Sarathi owned 10 bighas of land.⁴² This poignantly exposes and mounts a scathing attack on the bias that inheres in tribal women's gendered location dented by a dual patriarchal onslaught.

Witch hunt thus forms a special and an institutionalized instrument of social discrimination. It is also conducive to the social process of controlling women. The threat of being declared a 'witch' certainly helps to restrict non-conformism. Witch hunt could therefore be seen as one of the many, though extreme, reflections of gender and social tensions; a sphere where struggle for power and resources were resolved through violent means.

Witch hunt is also reflective of some kind of distrust in women and a fear of their sexuality. Sexuality not only influences the constructions of witches but also accounted for women's invisibility from adivasi rituals and religion. Troisi says that the belief in dangerous potentiality of women to seduce evil spirits and wreck vengeance on their enemies means that all sacrifices were tabooed for women. Women were also not allowed to climb trees, as it was believed that the nearness of their sex would 'pollute the *bongas*' (the deities of the tribals).[43] Roy similarly says that the exclusion of Kharia women from religious festivals and ritualistic observances was due to the tribals' horror of the menstrual blood, which attracted evil spirits. For similar reasons, there were restrictions against women accompanying funeral processions to burial place or cremation ground or against their going to sarnas (sacred groves).[44]

There is a link between Christianization of the tribals and witch hunt. Christian conversion has been a topic of angry debates from the time of the Indian national movement up to the present resurgence of militant Hindu nationalism. Laxmi Murmu (50) of Mahishdhal (Bolpur, Birbhum district of West Bengal) had a very strained relationship with her brother-in-law's family. She was accused by them of being a witch and had been beaten up severely a few times. She was living with the fear of fresh attack on her while her husband, Balai Murmu, was almost dying of some incurable disease. Nobody stood beside her. She went to the village ojha to cure her husband. The ojha demanded a lot of things to propitiate the 'angry' god. But Laxmi could not meet his demands. She was also asked to perform a puja that would cost another heavy financial burden. At this point, a Christian neighbour suggested that she should visit the local church at Mokrampur. She grabbed the suggestion as a last resort. Her husband received care and treatment at the charitable dispensary run by the Catholic missionary and she became free from all threats of being a witch as well. Her husband recovered soon and they finally converted into Christianity. In another case it has been found that Mungli Tudu (25) of Balipara village (Shantiniketan, Bolpur) was driven towards Christianity because of the fear of branding as witches and evil spirits.[45] In 1991, there were 0.17 per cent Christians in Birbhum. According to the Census, 2001, this had increased to a mere 0.24 per cent

During the field survey in Birbhum in 2012, I came across certain causes deeply rooted within the Santhal society that serve as a catalyst for turning towards Christianity. Santhal villages in Birbhum are isolated. Government health centres and schools are in minimal functional conditions. Moreover, NGOs catering exclusively to the needs of the tribes are extremely rare. In such a dismal situation the Catholic churches with their imposing organizational structure and benign presence deliver the urgently required service in these areas. The most dominating fear psychosis of a tribal woman is being branded as witch, and by changing religion she can nullify the effect of all degrees of evil in one stroke under the protection of the Christianity. Sometimes, conversion to Christianity remains the only choice available for the Santhals, especially for women wishing to escape from the internal pressure of the community. Catholic missionaries also encourage the Santhals to educate their children, arrange books, tuitions and scholarships.

Once the identification of the witch is 'established', the accused is left with no alternative but to accept the charge. Patriarchy not only creates witches but also hunts them down. The woman had no other alternative except to plead guilty.[46] Ajay Skaria points out that many women in fact claimed to be witches maybe because of the resources and respect they secured or because it was one of the few means by which they could claim authority.[47] Tribal cosmology is replete with references to women being 'trained' as witches. It is held that the power of witchcraft is not inborn but is acquired through 'training in secret'. According to Shashank Sinha witch-hunting should be seen as acts of resistance as well. He said that, the world of witches, spirits and ojhas was a very vibrant and reflective one; it resonated with, yet contested the impact of colonial rule in myriad ways.[48]

A shift in focus from 'extraordinary moments of collective protest' to 'variety of non-confrontational resistances and contestatory behaviour'[49] could lead to a way of examining women's agency even while they belong to and participate in an oppressive patriarchal society.[50] The 'everyday forms of resistance' require little or no coordination, or planning; represent a form of individual self-help and typically avoid any direct symbolic confrontation with authority. Witchcraft could therefore be seen as an act of subversion, an attempt to create a space denied by/in society.[51]

It is important to say that adivasi women are gradually becoming stronger to fight against such injustice and superstitions. Punam Toppo of Namkumer Nayabusu village of Ranchi was once accused of being a witch. She is a graduate in economics. She started her protest first in Jharkhand then visited Odisha and Purulia with the aim to raise consciousness of the women against witch hunt. Her attempt was recognized in 2004 by the central government. She has presently started an organization called ASHA. More or less 30 to 32 organizations are working together with ASHA to form a network to help the victims of witch hunt.[52] North Bengal's Peoples Development Centre (NBPDC) is an NGO that is currently working on anti-witch hunt campaigns since 2003. The primary focus of the NBPDC in the Dooars expanded from women's problems to encompass the marginalized population in the tea plantation areas.[53] Liberal Association of the Movement of the People (LAMP) during 1984–1989 has reported about fifty cases of witchcraft and related punishment meted out to persons accused as witches in Bankura, Purulia and Medinipur districts.[54]

Another study carried out by the Bihar Tribals Welfare Research Institute on the number of cases registered in different police stations revealed that in West Singhbhum, between 1993 and 1998, out of 82 people killed on account of being suspected as witches, 64 were women, the rest men; and the situation is similar in Ranchi, Palamau and other district.[55] The number of people killed in West Singhbhum between 1993 and 1998, out of the 82 killed, 64 were women (P.C. Oraon, Bihar Tribal Welfare Research Institute, 1999–2000: 11, 13).

A significant component of the population in Ranchi, Palamau, Hazaribag, West Singhbhum fall in the list of a hundred most backward districts and are poverty stricken.[56] The situation has become so bad that the Bihar government passed legislation in 1998 to curb incidents of witch hunt.[57] But no such initiatives have been taken by the Government of West Bengal so far.[58]

HEALTH OF TRIBAL WOMEN: EVALUATING NATIONAL RURAL HEALTH MISSION

The three consecutively National Family Health Surveys (NFHS) conducted in 1992–1993, 1998–1999 and 2005–2006 lay elaborate emphasis on the level of deprivation regarding health and education. The level of such deprivation has been measured in terms of six variables: presence or absence of any adult literate member in the household as an indicator of lack of social and communicational access; house electrified or not; whether there is any arrangement of drinking water facility within the house; whether the household owns a radio, transistor, bicycle or television; ownership (or otherwise) of agricultural land; and whether residing in a house that is kuccha or otherwise. Higher incidence of deprivation is reported among the tribes of Bihar, Jharkhand and Odisha.[59]

Child mortality rates for tribals in rural areas have nearly stagnated. All-India data indicate that tribal babies are not more likely to get sick from diarrhoea or respiratory disease, but are much less likely to get treated. NHFS 2005–2006 reported that 55 per cent of tribal women have ever used contraception; a relatively smaller proportion of ST women reported three or more ante-natal visits; they also remained less likely to receive pre-natal care from doctors. Almost 80 per cent of tribal women give birth at home.[60] There is a deep rooted cultural chasm and mistrust between the largely non-tribal health providers and the tribal patients whom the former treats with little dignity.[61] Moreover, medical facility providers are reluctant to visit to the tribal areas. For a migrating or displaced tribal family immunization and ante-natal care is no longer a priority.[62]

Besides the biological causes, most of the ailments in tribal areas are caused by an unbalanced diet and starvation. In 2002, tribal districts like Kalahandi in Odisha, Palamau in Jharkhand, Shivapuri in Madhya Pradesh and Baran in Rajasthan reported starvation deaths. In this situation of food crises, children are prone to starvation death than the adult members of the community. In India the role of the state in health care system is only seven decades old and is unable to meet the changing health service demands of the people. Tribal health has a causal link with food security, which itself is highly dependent on the agro-forest economy as well as the health delivery system of the state.

The tribal districts are still lagging behind other districts of Odisha in terms of supply-side infrastructure like distribution of beds, health personnel, medicine and other facilities. Suggestions to improve the situation is new to development discourse: a health delivery system, which provides health infrastructure on the basis of incidence of poverty, malnutrition, infant mortality and morbidity, rather than the present criterion of density of population and location.[63]

In 2005 National Rural Health Mission (NRHM) was launched by the Prime Minister Dr. Manmohan Singh which seeks to provide effective health care to rural and urban populations with the special focus on the backward districts through. It seeks to integrate health and Panchayati Raj Institutions, Women and Child Development, Rural Water

Supply and Sanitation and Education. The main components of NRHM are Reproductive and Child Health II (RCH), Immunization, National Disease Control Programme and other initiatives.[64]

The health scenario of Odisha is not an encouraging one. According to the National Family Health Survey, 2005–2006, about 17.0 per cent females in the age group of 15–19 were married. Besides, 1.6 per cent females below 14 years of age were married; 14.40 per cent of women in the age group of 15–19 years have begun child bearing in Odisha. The adolescent thus is vulnerable and at risk of unwanted pregnancies due to ignorance and lack of access to contraceptives. Other reproductive health related problems such as STDs/HIV/AIDS and RTIs are also on the rise in the age group of 15–19 years. Anaemia affects 61.20 per cent of women as compared to 53.30 per cent in the country. The incidence of anaemia among the pregnant women is as high as 68.10 per cent.[65]

According to Odisha Human Development Report (2004), the nutritional status of tribal women is not much worse than that in the case of the general population or that of women belonging to other disadvantaged social groups such as scheduled castes and Other Backward Classes. However, the incidence of anaemia amongst tribal women is significantly higher than that for other social groups. There are two indicators of maternal health: extent of antenatal check-up and delivery care, where among tribal women, 37 per cent did not have any ante-natal check-up. While institutional delivery is low in the case of Odisha (22.7%), as mentioned earlier, it is even lower in the case of tribal women (8.7%). The incidence of anaemia among children is, however, much higher among the tribal population.[66]

The scheduled tribe districts of Odisha are characterized by high geographical inaccessibility and a population largely guided by their cultural practices and beliefs. These two major factors have largely influenced the accessibility of the tribal people and specifically the tribal women to the health services provided by the state. Therefore, the fruits of NRHM are yet to be translated into action and the people are yet to internalize the benefits since the programme has not considered people as a bio-cultural resource. Health providers while implementing various programmes of NRHM need to reconsider various institutional perspectives of tribal communities, their contribution in strengthening the health status of the tribal communities and to reduce the regional disparities in the achievements of health indicators.

CASE STUDY 1: PURULIA

Sirkabad in Purulia is a tourist destination. At about 304 metres above sea level, it is the main halt for tourists on their way to the Ayodhya Hills, about 12 km. away. But the village Bhuda of Sirkabad presents a picture of desperation and remains starved of clean water. During the field survey it was found that the stream is their sole source of water because there is not a single tube well in the village. There has not been one since independence. The increasing use of fertilizers in the fields through which the stream flows has turned its water toxic and yet there is no alternative. Diarrhoea and allied stomach ailments represent the resultant resident evil. The mid-day meal at the primary school, which caters to about 54 children, is cooked with water from this stream that also caters to the village cattle. The village is often rendered inaccessible by this stream.

Meals in the village are cooked with polluted water, as a result of which at least six children of the 54 in the school are absent everyday because of diarrhoea and other stomach infections. The villagers, mainly forest-produce collecting tribals, are unaware of the concept of chlorine treatment and their children get to eat meat and eggs only at school. The school has no proper toilets as well. The primary school apart, the village has no Integrated Child Development Services centres and the nearest primary healthcare unit is 9 or 10 km away. Most of the tribal women in Bhuda age fast. The school has children up to the age of 12 but almost all of them have stunted growth, brittle nails and a weak immune system.

Stunting is the result of prolonged food deprivation and disease or illness; wasting denotes acute malnutrition as a result of food deprivation or illness; and underweight is indicative of both acute and chronic malnutrition.[67]

In a study carried out to determine the prevalence of malnutrition among Santhal children of Purulia district of West Bengal, 442 Santhal children (216 boys and 226 girls) aged 5–12 years were taken from randomly selected schools of Balarampur and Baghmundi areas of Purulia. The prevalence of stunting, underweight, and wasting among Santhal children in Purulia district is 17.9 per cent, 33.7 per cent and 29.4 per cent respectively. The prevalence of moderate stunting among students of this community was found to be higher in girls (15.9%) than boys (9.7%).[68] The percentage values of severe stunting in both the sexes are similar: 4.17 in boys and 5.76 in girls.[69] In West Bengal, 54 per cent children (6–12 years of age) of the Oraon tribe suffer from severe malnutrition.[70] Another report entitled as Integrated Child Development Scheme—Annual Action Plan 2014–2015 prepared by the Social and Women Welfare Department pointed out that in West Bengal Purulia has the highest number of malnourished children (30.78%) followed by Barddhaman (29.42%) and West Medinipur (29.21%).[71] The government has failed to lure most of the children to schools with the midday meals and that is why they suffer from malnutrition. In some blocks there are hardly any health centres.

CASE STUDY 2: WEST MEDINIPUR

A field survey was carried out in 2006 and the report revealed the situation of the Munda settlers in the Keshiary block in two villages Sanjhaparia and Meghdumbur. All houses were made up of mud and not a single brick built house was found. The poor condition of the houses has some adverse effects on the health of the Mundas. Absence of proper drinking water facilities and drainage system result in accumulation of filth and mud. Sanitation was totally absent in these villages with endemic typhoid, fevers and so on, Anaemia has been found to be more frequent among the women maybe because of repeated pregnancy due mainly to the lack of nutritious food. With low income and more dependents many of them even cannot include pulses in their regular diet. Due to lack of government initiatives the Mundas rely heavily on magico-religious and herbal treatment.[72] Amlasole village of West Medinipur is in a miserable health condition too. A health check up was conducted of the students of Bera Bhenge School at Kengora, Amlasole. There were three communities: Sabar (Boys-8, Girls-9), Munda (Boys-10, Girls-11) and a non-tribe Singh (Boys-2, Girls-1), all severely malnourished.

STATE OF EDUCATION AMONG TRIBAL WOMEN

Education is regarded as the most important factor in the sphere of social change. In the development programme of the tribal people education plays an essential role specifically in the creation of various stagnant behaviour-patterns. We can put forward a couple of very sensitive research questions: (i) what leads to failure in achieving and qualitatively improving teaching and learning activities in tribal areas? (ii) what kind of measures are needed for improving the current situation? The District Primary Education Programme under the National Policy of Education provides physical and infrastructural facilities to all the primary schools in tribal areas. A large number of schools in the tribal areas have still not received essential teaching aids or teachers do not use them properly. Thus the problems begin at this stage.

The drop out rate of children is high and literacy rate of the tribal female (12.74%, according to the Census 1991) is lowest of all social groups.

The majority of educated tribal women see education as a means of getting employment and maybe due to the reservation facilities, almost all educated tribal women are government employees. Those women who were encouraged by their families did much better than those who were denied this. Maximum dropouts from the schools happen due to dire economic necessity. The majority of tribal women in West Bengal and Odisha choose general schools instead of tribal schools because they think that it helps them to move ahead. They strongly oppose the consumption of liquor and community dances because dances are associated with liquor and intoxication. This rational attitude is more prominent in the field of health and hygiene. Most of them always use modern medicine and doctors at the time of sickness. During my field study I found that most of the tribal women were in favour of education for their daughters.

Sometimes educated tribal women face problems in getting grooms. It is because educated boys, when they get good jobs due to reservation facilities, prefer to marry outside to get dowry or to connect with families of high social status. Educated women usually take up nursing and become health workers and that is why they face problems in getting grooms. In the tribal villages bride price is still the rule. But among the urban educated families in common with their Hindu neighbours dowry is a practice. Educated tribal women have begun to restrict their behaviour regarding pre-marital sexual intercourse. Only a few educated tribal women do not believe in witchcraft.

CASE STUDY 3: WEST BENGAL

In West Bengal, age-specific attendance rates of tribal children are 62.54 per cent and 52.15 per cent in primary and upper primary levels, respectively, which are even lower than the respective median rates (82.49%, 55.05%) in the country. School completion rates are 2.65 per cent and 16.18 per cent for primary and upper primary levels respectively which are much below the respective median figures (57.9%, 40.4%) in the country.

In 2011 the central government decided to introduce a special education loan scheme—Adivasi Siksha Rin Yojana—exclusively for the students coming from Scheduled Tribes communities.[73] A loan up to a maximum amount of ₹5 lakhs (5,000,000) would be provided if their annual family income did not exceed ₹40,000 in rural areas and ₹55,000 in urban areas. Under the scheme, loan would be disbursed through National Scheduled Tribe Finance and Development Corporation, a statutory organization controlled by the Centre. Repayment starts either after six months of the completion of the course or after securing employment.

The education gap is extremely serious as in 2003–04, 81,000 tribal habitations remain unserved as regards school facilities.[74]

CASE STUDY 4: ALIPURDUAR

The Totos are a primitive Indo-Bhutanese tribe residing in a small enclave called Totopara in Jalpaiguri district of West Bengal. Totos were nearly becoming extinct in the 1950s, but recent measures to safeguard their areas from being swamped with outsiders have helped preserved their unique heritage and also helped the population grow. According to the Census 2011 the total number of Totos is 1307 (at present their population is 1391). While measures to safeguard the population have been effective nothing has been done regarding the socio-economic uplift and growth of the tribe as a whole. The economic life of the Toto has been transformed to a great extent. About 95 per cent cultivate their own land. The women mostly help the men in the peak agricultural season. About 70 per cent of women are engaged in collection of firewood from the forest along with their usual household chores.[75]

During my visit to Totopara (in October 2012), I met Rita Toto (22) who is the first woman graduate, from Prasanna Deb Women's College, Jalpaiguri, and worked for TCS Company (IT). She said, 'I always wanted to be a teacher; English is difficult for me as is the computer. Also adjusting to Kolkata is hard. I have written to the state government for a suitable job but not received any reply.

Mr Ashok Toto (52) expressed Toto discontent regarding the movement launched by the Gorkha Janamukti Morcha (GJM). He said the demand was raised by the outsiders or people coming from Nepal and Bhutan. The Totos' principal demand is proper development of the community in every sphere of life.

Dhaniram Toto (60), the president of Toto Kalyan Samity said, 'The government is not providing "primitive tribe" certificate to the Totos, as a result, Totos have to compete with the major tribe like Bodos and also with the non-tribes like Nepalese and Gorkhas. Such uneven competition deprives them from all the opportunities especially in the field of employment.'

According to Amali Toto (23), there is no dowry system and girl child is welcomed in the family. There are 5–6 girl children in a single family, but the succession goes through the male line. There is a clear division of labour among them. All household work such as cooking, child care, giving fodder to the cattle and collecting firewood, is done by the women. Oranges are the principal cash crop that transformed the marginal economy of the Totos into a market economy. Toto women also work in the fields, collect marua (a kind of millet), and cultivate maize which is their principal food. Education of the girl child or even the boys is not a priority at Totopara. Women do not participate in political activities. She said that the women go to the panchayats but hardly speak in the meetings. Women do not hold lands in their names.[76]

Due to poor sanitation, food scarcity and lack of nutrition, Totas lead unhealthy lives: average male life expectancy is 35; prevalence of thalassaemia and anaemia is rampant, particularly among the women; also tuberculosis and skin diseases.[77] The tribe almost became extinct because of malaria and kala azar around 1865. For almost five months in a year, Totos depend on forest products or stored food grains. Once maize, kaoni and marua were eaten for about seven months, but now the staple food is rice. Beef and pork and dried meat are also eaten. Fresh vegetables are rare.

Totopara displays all the symbols of modern India like cell phones and some pucca houses. There are both Christian Totos and non-Christian Totos. There is a Grameen Bank too, but the grim fact is that the tribe is now struggling with land rights within its own village. Many Nepalese, Marwaris and Biharis have settled in Totopara and the rich are buying the land. Those Totos who can afford to do so are trying to build pucca houses to ensure that their rights to the land are held by them. The criminal nexus between the police and the timber mafias is causing massive deforestation in the area which is another problem for the Totos since non-timber forest produces play a crucial role in their day to day economic life. Totopara gets cut off during the rainy season, when the surrounding rivers get flooded. Transportation is a problem. Education, especially for women, comes far behind major concerns like food, health, shelter, transportation, employment and livelihood.

CASE STUDY 5: WEST MEDINIPUR DISTRICT

We will briefly analyse the impact of the development programme on Mahali, West Medinipur district, West Bengal. Field work was conducted in the village named Kotaigarh under Narayangarh Gram Panchayat, Kharagpur sub-division in November 2011. An attempt has been made to examine the various measures taken for the upliftment of the tribals in the field of education and health and their actual rate of success. There are at present two primary schools in the village. Both the primary schools hold classes from first to fourth.

Most of the Mahali children drop out of school at a very early age or simply do not go to school. There is no proper motivation by the government functionaries and gram panchayat body which force them to go to school. The children are engaged in basket making from a very early age, so their parents are reluctant to part with their help without a proper incentive. Among the Mahali, boys have so far been given the chance to get educated. This differentiation on the lines of gender probably has its roots in their culture. Girls are married off early and they are considered better at home. One Mahali was training for his B.Ed and another has joined the Railway Reserve Police Force. There is a primary health centre at Barakalanki in Kotaigarh village. It was established in 1968. There is no doctor and an acute scarcity of medicines.

CASE STUDY 6: MID-DAY MEAL PROGRAMME

In April 2001, the People's Union for Civil Liberties, Rajasthan, filed a Public Interest Litigation in the Supreme Court, arguing that the right to food was a fundamental right of every Indian citizen and demanding that the country's gigantic food stocks (about 50 million tonnes of grains at that time) should be used without delay to prevent hunger and starvation. It argued that the right to food should be seen as a corollary to the fundamental 'right to life' (Article 21) in so far as it was impossible to live without food. The Supreme Court has passed orders directing the Indian government to introduce hot cooked mid-day meals in all primary schools; provide 35 kg of grain per month at highly subsidised prices to 15 million destitute households under the Antyodaya Anna Yojana, a component of the Public Distribution System. An aim was to universalize the Integrated Child Development Services by increasing the number of centres from 0.6 million to 1.4 million; and identify schedule caste and schedule tribe hamlets/habitations for new ICDS centres on a priority basis.[78] The Supreme Court, in an interim order dated 28 November 2001, converted the benefits of nine food-related schemes into 'legal entitlements' and directed all state governments to fully implement these schemes.[79] However, implementation has been at the mercy of the ration dealers who have disregarded the norms completely.

A report of the Comptroller and Auditor-General (CAG) for fiscal 2009–2010 was published by *The Statesman* that pointed out that the Government of West Bengal lost a whopping ₹133.66 crore (13 billion) in food subsidy receivable from the centre as the finance department did not prepare the annual PDS accounts from 2005 to 2010. The government was never serious in doing its duty as regards the identification of the Antyodaya Anna Yojana beneficiaries in West Bengal.[80]

A study conducted by Pratichi Trust Organization in 2004 in West Bengal especially in Birbhum District funded by Amartya Sen found the presence of classroom hunger in Birbhum district to a large extent, particularly among the dalits and tribals. While the caste Hindus made a lot of complaints against the monotonous menu, the tribals such as the Santhals and the Koras mentioned that they did not bother much about the repetition of the menu. So, the percentage of enrolment and attendance increased more among the dalit and tribal students than the caste Hindu students.[81]

THE MARGINALIZATION OF TRIBAL LANGUAGES

Because tribal languages are not dealt with respect,[82] a kind of a limited 'linguistic terror' has been created among the tribals. We should listen to the competing voices struggling for narrative mastery and think of the social location and sexual identity of the voices competing for narrative space. In anthropological literature, tribes in general have been defined in terms of the distinctive features of language, culture, territory and government. For tribals, language and culture, now often referred to as ethnicity, matter the most and was hence the most pronounced marker of distinctiveness.[83] Tribes were invariably posited against the dominant regional community, which also happened to be a distinct linguistic and cultural community.

The Constitution recognizes the distinct cultural features of tribes especially in respect to language and, according to the Constitution, Article 350 A provides for facilities for instruction through the mother tongue at the primary stage of education. Yet, no effort whatsoever has been made so far by the federal state or the provincial states towards safeguarding tribal languages. The thrust is towards absorption, which entails their inclusion into the dominant society. The unstated state administrative practices both at the federal and state levels have been geared towards their absorption into the larger society. It has pushed the tribals towards the articulation for greater political power in the form of a struggle for autonomy, which has more often than not moved in the direction of a demand for a separate state either within the Indian union or even outside of it. The promotion and revitalization of tribal languages and the creation of primers, literature and even introducing the tribal language in primary schools has been voiced. Connected to it is the search or development of a script as has been the case with the Santhals or the Tripuri speaking tribes in Tripura. The choosing of the script from among scripts tribals are familiar with has also formed a part of identity articulation as with the Bodos of Assam.[84]

Though nearly half of the tribal societies still maintain a distinct language as a mark of their identity, a large section of them tend to switch over to the surrounding non-tribal languages as their mother tongue or retain both languages (ancestral and non-tribal) in home environments and various modernization processes have further accelerated the pace of assimilation. Tribal languages in this area are charged with minimum functional load (restricted largely to the home environment) and serving primarily as a mark of group identity. These languages, thus, are open to the pressures of assimilation from major regional languages. For example, many tribal languages do not keep the pace vis-à-vis the growth of the tribal community bearing the same name, such as, Kharia tribe. We have been actually institutionalizing the mass hara-kiri of the indigenous languages.

An intense degree of bilingualism is noticed in the East Indian tribal regions. Elicitation techniques in the Census favour the reporting of 'status' languages prevailing among tribals. Hence one notices the traces of under-reporting the most intimately known tribal languages of their own milieu. Prominent contact languages of the tribal origin, though claimed by smaller populations, in different states are: Santhali in Jharkhand, Bihar and West Bengal; Munda and Kurukh in Jharkhand and Bihar; Kui in Odisha. Kui and Kondh are two separate languages, raising the issues of language identity. Some regions have developed local creolized languages like Sadan/Sadri and Kurmali (hybrid forms of Bihari and Mundari, in Jharkhand and Bihar); Desiya (a tribal blend with an Oriya base in Koraput, Odisha).[85]

In Jharkhand, my field work was in September 2011, a strong current of the distinct identity has emerged around the lingua franca Nagpuria (with an Indo-Aryan base, commonly identified with the caste label Sadan/Sadani) by carving out a regional consensus over and above their Austric/Dravidian mother tongue identities. Such cultural synthesis can be described as 'grassroot Aryanization' where the Jharkhandi regional identity gets defined around the grasp of the Indo-Aryan Sadan/Nagpuria language. Persistent efforts are being made to develop a literary diction in Nagpuria written in Devanagari script.

Despite the provisions in Article 350(A) of the Indian Constitution, many states have denied giving efforts for developing tribal languages as preparatory media at the primary stage of education; textbooks are generally prepared in the dominant regional script (Devanagari, Bengali, Oriya). There has been a move to revive the indigenous Ol Chiki script for Santhali. Textbooks in Ho, Munda, and Kurukh are prepared in the indigenous Adi script, or in Devanagari or Roman. But at the secondary stage most of these languages are confined to the regional script. Tribal elites of Chotanagpur, Jharkhand, do not prefer Sadan and made Hindi as the medium of education. Similarly, a limited recognition is accorded to Santhali in primary education in West Bengal. In Bihar textbooks are prepared in Santhali, Kurukh, Mundari, Ho, Kharia but the state authorities have not shown great enthusiasm as far as its implementation is concerned. In the absence of a definite policy concerning the questions of orthographies for tribal languages, the preparation of textbooks in these languages has been considerably retarded.

MIGRATION AND TRAFFICKING

The tribals in India have inherited a rich culture from their ancestors. However, with the onslaught of industrialization, urbanization and modernization and the resultant migration of tribal men, women and girls to urban centres the age-old culture of these communities is on the verge of extinction.

Tribal women and girls have migrated from different tribal areas far away from the cities in which they settle; the 'Push-Pull' factors have played an important role. The significant push factors were very low rates of wages, unemployment and land alienation along with poverty and indebtedness. Women who are in marriageable age or have just married are migrating to towns and cities in search of jobs. It is worth noting that some of the women have never contacted their families after leaving the villages, and families fear that these women have been sold somewhere after trafficking.[86]

Other reasons reported included acquisition of land/house for development projects, repeated natural calamities like floods and famines, attraction of city life and education. Migration of tribal girls to big cities for education is very limited and hence negligible. It is, therefore, very clear that in spite of the facilities like free hostel facilities the tribal girls are not coming to big cities for higher education in sufficient number.

Tribal women and girls migrated to cities belong to different tribal regions of different states in India and as such they had different patterns of lifestyle. Migrant tribal women and girls had to gradually shift from their traditional lifestyle to the local lifestyle of the cities. The employment status, income range and level of exploitation (both financial and sexual) of the migrant tribal women and girls in cities should also be counted. Most of the migrant tribal women are domestic servants, some work as construction labour and industrial workers, and thus very frequently they have been the victims of sexual exploitation. The principal causes of financial and sexual exploitation of the migrant tribal women and girls in cities were poverty, lack of employment opportunities, misunderstanding of the local people about tribals being available for free sex and lack of community support to victims of sexual exploitation. Mental harassment is also frequent.

The tribal women and girls who migrate to cities from their hinterland in search of jobs have to face the problem of sexual exploitation by the middlemen who offer them good emoluments, good placement and work conditions and after they are taken to the workplace it is a different case. Many of the employer or their agents, after providing jobs to these tribal women and girls, take every opportunity to exploit them sexually. Many a time sexual contact is a pre-condition for giving jobs to these women and girls. Due to acute poverty and non-availability of jobs the tribal women and girls surrender themselves for sexual exploitation against their will. A Research Study Report, submitted to the Planning Commission, states the causes of exploitation of migrant tribal women and girls.[87] Good education and the courage to fight the exploitation are the only ways open for resisting exploitation. A study carried out by the NGO Pragati in 11 blocks of Sundargarh district of Odisha in 2010 revealed that 723 girls and women had been trafficked and had never returned to their homes, while 60 are missing and cannot be traced. It also highlighted 345 cases of sexual abuse, of which only 38 have been registered. To date, one trafficker has been punished and released on bail. According to the study, 56 girls travelled to Delhi with unknown people, and the identity of only 15 traffickers has been established so far. The study reported that around 85 per cent of the tribal women who left Sundargarh villages were being exploited. The majority of the girls are lured to leave Sundargarh for Delhi by relatives, neighbours, or friends. The tribal women's isolation in the city deters them from reaching out to their own groups. What is important to note here is that unlike other domestic maids living in the city, who are organized and come together for common causes, tribal women have been unable to do so because of social exclusion primarily due to the barrier of language, and their lack of confidence in a metropolitan setting.[88] The Census data may not fully reflect seasonal or circulatory migration, estimated to be up to 10 million by the National Commission on Rural Labour.

CASE STUDY 7

The number of people missing from Jangal Mahal in West Medinipur has increased manifold, triggering fears that more persons are being trafficked from the region than before. Social activists have blamed poverty, lack of job opportunities and political instability for the rise in the number of missing persons. The situation is alarming in Sankrail, Binpur-II, Gopiballavpur-I and Nayagram blocks of Jhargram since the geographic conditions of Jhargram is such that it forms an easy transit point for trafficking. Local people said that most of these people are trafficked by middlemen locally known as dalal or agents, some are by their near relatives or even family members. These people, mostly tribal girls between 15 to 18 years and their parents, become easy prey of agents who lure them with attractive packages and lifestyle. These trafficked tribal girls are subjected to worst kind of economic and physical exploitation at various metros in our country. It is strange that the administration has no proper information or data bank for these trafficked tribal girls. The local respondents also asserted that, during the tough periods when political clashes often occurred in tribal villages, many earning members of the tribal families were forced to join the armed camps. It seems that police are also responsible for increased trafficking as this issue is not prioritized enough.[89]

ADIVASI WOMEN IN BHADRALOK IMAGINATION

There is an indigenous Hindu Bengali view of history, rooted in the culture of Bengal, distinctively different and unique from several other concepts of history. The celebration of the 'peoples' culture' was an integral feature of the Swadeshi movement. But the limitations inherent in the romantic celebration of 'peoples' history' need to be kept in mind. The masses were eulogized as the custodians of the region's history and customs. It required urban, upper-class, often upper-caste, and educated scholars to speak up for and represent village traditions in a bourgeois public sphere shaped by print. It was perhaps inevitable too that the perception of what was considered to be peoples' culture would be coloured by caste, class and other cultural considerations unique to the urban Bengali literati.[90] It automatically raises the question that why does the figure of the dancing and singing tribals, specifically tribal women, appear so frequently in Bengali literature and films? Rajnarayan Basu's *Deoghar Diary* thus proceeds without any reference to Santhals, except one description of a Santhal dance staged by a local Bengali, on occasion of his son's first rice-eating ceremony.[91] This is also a kind of cultural silencing.

One of the big problems of writing tribal women's history is that there is not a single account written by the tribal women themselves, unlike for the dalits and Muslims. The only account that we find about a Santhal girl is, Sona. We know Sona's life better than that of any other convert, since P.O. Bodding wrote her biography, which is the most complete biography we have of any Santhal woman during the colonial period.[92]

In the construction of tribal identity as 'primitive', there were two attempts on the part of the Bengali literati that were made during colonial and postcolonial period. These were, first to integrate the tribals into the so-called mainstream caste society which can be regarded as an integral part of the nation building process, and the other tendency was portraying the tribal woman as a sexual object. Though the literature is not replete with the life stories of the tribal women, yet it is based on a very biased view of their sexual objectification.

It was with the railways that the Bengali bhadralok began visiting places like Santhal Pargana, as a holiday retreat. Bengali travel-imperative drew its competence from the

Increasing Marginalization of Adivasi Women 239

project of the colonial 'penetration' of interiors. In this paradigm of travel as penetration—of interior—spaces as well as of the depths of time—the land and the people of the land were equated. The penetrative competence staged the first-ever visualization of the 'primitive' as a discovery of a people who appeared not to exist prior to observation. The 'primitive' was thus denied his/her definitional antecedence, which could dislocate history itself by making the 'primitive' more originary to the nation than the 'historical'. In Santhal Pargana, for example, the colonial administration denied the right of some Bengali settlers precisely on the ground that the 'primitive' Santhals were more 'original' to this land than Hindus. And the politics of Bengalis in Deoghar became that of actively reclaiming the Hindu's tenancy rights over that space of the nation, which colonial administrative discourse had classified as purely 'primitive'.[93] This discourse of discovery also implied that there were lands within the nation which were as yet untouched by the stir of passing events to mainstream Indian society. This undid to an extent the claim of nationalism itself. If the strategy of spatial gathering was indispensable to the nation so that the 'primitive' could be integrated without disrupting the unitary narrative of history, it was this very strategy which also reproduced the nation in the colonial image of a fractured and stratified terrain.[94] The question whether tribes should unconditionally be integrated to modernizing mainstream society or should be protectively confined within spatialized and bounded 'culture gardens', thus, became an intractable problem for nationalism and still remains a disputed one.

As colonial modernity sought to commodify the tribals by making them pure bodies, they seemed to become increasingly larger than life, muscular (tribal men) and sensuous (tribal women) and desirable to the middle-class Bengalis. This produced the Bengali aesthetic imagination of tribals as sensuous and uninhibited figures—to be painted, sculpted, filmed, and desired. For example Sanjib Chandra Chattopadhyay wrote about the Kol women of Palamau in his memoires of Palamau, which was published as a serial between 1880 and 1882 in Bankimchandra Chattopadhyay's *Bangadarshan*. Bankim Chandra was his brother. He said that the Kol women appeared to him as unbearably beautiful and sensuous. He believed that even in old age, Kol women remained young.[95] He wrote, 'All of the same height, the same black colour of stone, bare-bodied, on their naked breasts mirrors sparkle in the moonlight. Wild flowers in their hair and ears, smile on their lips ... restless with pleasure.'[96]

Bibhutibhushan Bandyopadhyay's *Aranyak* reflects similar kind of romanticization of a tribal woman, Bhanmati. We can have a clear notion of a tribal woman imagined by a bhadralok intelligentsia (*Babuji*, as Bhanmati used to call Satyacharan) in the portrayal of Bhanmati: 'a slim and healthy young girl ... the garments she wore would not have been considered modest in civilised society ... she had a certain natural poise and an inherent sense of dignity.[97] Satyacharan further thinks that when she is affectionate and loving, it is as if the gates of heaven are opened on our earth. The dictates of refinement and the pressures of the civilised world had erased in her sisters the eternal woman that resided in Bhanmati.'[98]

In these descriptions of Bhanmati we find a stereotypical picture of a tribal woman replete with an unbound sexuality and passion. Though tribal history in British India was always a history of violent movements and protests, yet there are no such reflections found in the mentality or imagination of Bengali intelligentsia and their writing.

But with the appearance of the landmark character of *Draupadi* (*Dopdi*) the imagination of a tribal woman achieved a new horizon. Mahasweta Devi in most of her stories makes explicit the patriarchal appropriation and usage of women's body, her sexuality and gender identity, as cultural sites to create, revamp and contest its notions of normality and social respectability. Her stories usually foreground tribal woman as a doubly 'otherized' embodiment of exploitative patriarchal praxis that operates at the cross-section of class and caste, tradition and modernity, feudalism and capitalism.[99] In

Draupadi, Mahasweta Devi invites us to begin effacing the image in an inextricably mingling historico-political specificity with the sexual differential in a literary discourse. 'Draupadi' first appeared in *Agnigarbha* (Womb of Fire), a collection of loosely connected, short political narratives. Here she begins putting together a prose that is a collage of literary Bengali, Bureaucratic Bengali, tribal Bengali, and the languages of the tribals. The Naxalite movement and the severe state repression are the background of the story and it is the killing of this mistress's husband that sets going the events of the story. Dopdi was first apprehended and then brutally tormented by the police since she denied revealing the whereabouts of her comrades.

> Slowly the bloodied nailheads shift from her brain. Trying to move, she feels her arms and legs still tied to four posts. Something sticky under her ass and waist. Her own blood ... She senses that her vagina is bleeding. How many came to make her? ... How many? Four-five-six-seven—then Draupadi had passed out.[100]

Draupadi of the *Mahabharata* provides the only example of polyandry and thereby exceptional. But Mahasweta Devi's Dopdi also got exceptional when she was placed first in a comradely, activist, guerrilla warrior, monogamous marriage and then in a situation of multiple rape.

The strongest characterization of a tribal woman, Draupadi, comes out through the way she protested against the army officer who captured and degraded her.

> Draupadi, naked, walking toward him in the bright sunlight with her head high ... Draupadi stands before him, naked. Thigh and pubic hair matted with dry blood. Two breasts, two wounds ... She looks around and chooses the front of Senanayak's white bush shi ... for the first time Senanayak is afraid to stand before an unarmed target ...[101]

Thus, Dopdi crosses the sexual differential into the field of what could only happen to a woman that she emerges as the most powerful 'subject', who, still using the language of sexual honour, can derisively call herself 'the object of your search', whom the author can describe as a terrifying super-object—'an unarmed target'. Being a tribal woman Dopdi is not romanticized by Mahasweta Devi. There is a long tradition of writing on tribals as is evident from the work of famous writers such as Tarashankar Bandyopadhyay and Satinath Bhaduri. But there is a remarkable difference in their outlook and that of Mahasweta Devi. In an interview with Gayatri Chakravorty Spivak, Mahasweta Devi says:

> 'The tribals and the mainstream have always been parallel ... The mainstream simply doesn't understand the parallel ... They can't keep their land; there is no education for them, no health facilities ... they are denied everything ... That is why I started writing about the tribal movements and the tribal world ... I repay them their honour.[102]

Regarding the gendered politics, Colin MacCabe's comment appears to be closer to the heart of the matter, when he says: 'The force of Mahasweta Devi's text resides in its grounding in the gendered subaltern's body, ... The bodies of Jashoda and Dopdi figure forth the unutterable ugliness and cruelty which cooks in Third World kitchen to produce the First World feast that we daily enjoy.'[103]

New histories have been popularized as a way of demystifying the world of appearances, where media plays a very crucial part. In independent India, the major thrust of cultural policy is documentation and dissemination. Unfortunately media itself is stereotyping the gender dimensions of tribal society and it can rightly be called as the poverty of empiricism, because the reading or deciphering myth regarding tribal way of life is a new way of legitimizing bourgeois readership and bourgeois conceptualization.

Photography may show perhaps the original of what is today the faster growing area of 'alternative' critical practice of cultural studies. But here also the role of the photography and audio-visual media is not satisfactory at all in upholding their worldview. The movies made on tribal life portray a wrong image of its womenfolk. For example, the tribals have been portrayed as exploited people, as militants, as simple, gullible folk in the film *Mrigaya* (The Royal Hunt) of 1976 directed by Mrinal Sen. In this award-winning film the central female character is Dungri. She happens to be abducted by a local moneylender in lieu for the debt of ten rupees owed by her father. Santhal women have been shown dancing and singing. Portraying a hunter-gatherer tribal society somewhere in the Santhal Pargana, the character of Dungri fails to recognize the courage and the freedom inherent to a tribal woman.

The film *Aranyer Din Ratri* (Days and Nights in the Forest) of 1970 directed by Satyajit Ray, which is based upon the Bengali novel of the same name by Sunil Gangopadhyay, describes the escapades of four urban young men in tribal areas of Palamau and their attitude to Santhal women, which is deplorable. The entire sequence is interspersed with shots of tribal women dancing to primitive rhythm as the central characters are engaged in their primitive pursuits. The four young men from the city are not unlikable, but their treatment of the local tribal people reveals an unthinking arrogance that at times verges on brutality. One of them, Hari, gets close to a Santhal girl Duli when she approaches the group for extra drink. When Hari sees the rustic and attractive Duli, the tribal key to increase his self-esteem, he jumps at it. He does not like it when Shekhar pays the tribal women money for sweeping and swabbing floors for them. Duli has an untamed quality that enhances her appeal. Hari takes her into the forest and makes love with her. Though the film masterly juxtaposes the urban and tribal, yet the character of Duli gives a very negative idea about a tribal woman. This identification of adivasi women with pure Bengali bourgeois culture has also been pointed out by Prathama Banerjee: 'In films like Mrinal Sen's *Mrigaya*, Satyajit Ray's *Aranyer Din Ratri* and later *Agantuk*, the adivasi appeared as that marginal presence, on the frontiers of embourgeoised society, which haunted the nation as an embodied political critique. And yet, this critique always figured as the dancing, drinking, singing, "primitive", whose freedom and sensuality had the potential to turn, in a jiffy, to retributional violence'.[104]

As suggested by these divergent visual and textual accounts the bourgeois objectification of the tribal women indicates dehumanization in capturing the ethnic identities. Rabindranath Tagore, however, realized that the Indian intelligentsia needed to destabilize social prejudices, to allow India to flourish as a pluralistic postcolonial democracy. He wrote,

> The Santhal woman comes and goes
> Over the gravelled path under the shimool tree,
> Slender limbs draped by a coarse sari.
> Some heedless divine artist
> As he sat shaping a dark bird,
> Finds his elements in thunder and lightning,
> And creates unaware, this woman's form.
> ....
> My heart is touched with shame when I feel that the woman's service,
> sacredly ordained for her loved ones, its dignity soiled by the market price,
> Should have been robbed by me with the help of a few pieces of copper.[105]

At Visva-Bharati, Rabindranath instituted a new perception vis-à-vis India's indigenous peoples, which attempted, through hegemonic inter-cultural relations, to subvert the colonial separation of 'aboriginals' from mainstream Hindu India. As is evident in his poem, 'The Santhal', the agency of the subaltern is less easy to identify because Tagore positions adivasis and modernists on an equal footing, producing a new dynamic between 'real' and 'positional' subalterns.

In all these accounts the uniqueness of tribes, of their social structure and their worldview, their sense of harmony with nature and with one another, does not come through either. The tribes are not doomed to suffer for eternity. Tribal women, have broken the 'culture of silence' to demand equal rights. However, they continue to be marginalized. There is something in their society and their culture that has survived and endured and held them together in many parts of India. This story needs to be told.

NOTES

1. Mahato, *Sanskritization vs Nirbakization*: 17–18.
2. *The Statesman*, 29 August 2013.
3. Henry George, 1880. *Progress and Poverty* (New York: Robert Schalkenbach Foundation): 6.
4. Manipadma Jena, 2013. 'Voices from Niyamgiri', *Economic and Political Weekly* (henceforth *EPW*) 47, 36 (7 Sept.): 14–16.
5. *Anandabazar Patrika*, 12 November 2013.
6. Vimala Ramachandran, and Taramani Naorem, 2013. 'What It Means to Be a Dalit or Tribal Child in Our Schools: A Synthesis of a Six-State Qualitative Study', *EPW* 47, 44 (2 Nov.): 43–52.
7. Banikanta Mishra, and Sagarika Mishra, 2014. 'Mining and Industrialisation Dangerous Portents', *EPW* 49, 14 (5 April): 56–65.
8. Robert Darnton, 1984. *The Great Cat Massacre and Other Episodes in French Cultural History* (New York: Basic Books): 257.
9. Roger Chartier, 1985. 'Text, Symbols, and Frenchness', *The Journal of Modern History* 57, 4: 682–95.
10. Raphael Samuel, 1991. 'Reading the Signs,' *History Workshop Journal* 32, 1: 88–109.
11. Allen F. Repko, 2012. *Interdisciplinary Research Process and Theory* (2nd edition, London: SAGE): xiii.
12. For more details see Jerry A. Jacobs, 2013. *In Defense of Disciplines: Interdisciplinarity and Specialization in the Research University* (Chicago: Chicago University Press): 20.
13. Ajay Skaria, 1997. 'Shades of Wildness Tribe, Caste, and Gender in Western India,' *Journal of Asian Studies* 56, 3 (Aug.): 726–45.
14. In William Harmon, *A Handbook to Literature,* for example, aporia is identified as 'a difficulty, impasse, or point of doubt and indecision' while also noting that critics such as Derrida have employed the term to 'indicate a point of undecidability, which locates the site at which the text most obviously undermines its own rhetorical structure, dismantles, or deconstructs itself.'
15. P. Bandyopadhyay, *Tribal Situation in Eastern India*: 87–89.
16. From field work in February 2012.

17. W.G. Archer, 1984. *Tribal Law and Justice, A Report on the Santal* (New Delhi: Concept): 307–19.
18. Sarada Lahangir, 'Robbed of a Future', *The Statesman*, 7 July 2013.
19. Savara, M. and C.R. Sridhar, 1994. *Report on a Survey of Sexual Behaviour Patterns and Attitudes amongst Men and Women in Maharashtra* (Mumbai: Shakti).
20. Zelnik and Kanter, 1981. 'Confronting the Teenage Pregnancy Issue: Social Marketing as an Interdisciplinary Approach', *Journal of Human Relations* 38, 10: 983–1000.
21. Steven Polgar, and Ellen S. Fried, 1976. 'The Bad Old Days: Clandestine Abortions among the Poor in New York City before Liberalisation of the Abortion Law', *Journal of Family Planning Perspectives* 8 (3), May/June.
22. Bulu Imam, 1993. 'The Story of Kamli: A Birhor Medicine-Woman', in *Man in India* 73, 4: 377–85.
23. Nagda, *Social Correlates of Fertility*.
24. Field work conducted in Bankura, February 2012.
25. Vijay Tendulkar, 2007. 'Tribals and I', in *Vijay Tendulkar Omnibus*, edited by Makarand Sathe (Delhi: Amar Kumar Publishers): 268–82.
26. Shivkumar Pandey, 'Dakan', in *Bhagoria Ki Baat*: 123–31.
27. Soma Chaudhuri, *Witches, Tea Plantations, and Lives of Migrant Laborers in India*: 23.
28. Vanashree, 2010. 'Witchcraft: Pain, Resistance and the Ceremony of Punishment—Mahasweta Devi's Bayen', *Indian Journal of Gender Studies* 17: 2: 226.
29. Gayatri Chakravorty Spivak, 1988. 'Can the Subaltern Speak?' in *Marxism and the Interpretation of Culture*, edited by Cary Nelson and Larry Grossberg (Urbana, Il: University of Illinois Press): 287.
30. Waugh, *Metafiction*: 54.
31. Dalton, *Descriptive Ethnology of Bengal*: 198.
32. *Anandabazar Patrika*, 18 October 2012.
33. Vinita Damodaran, 2002. 'Gender, Forests and Famine in Nineteenth Century Chhotonagpur, India', *Indian Journal of Gender Studies* 9, 2: 147.
34. Dev Nathan, 1988. 'Significance of Women's Position in Tribal Society', *EPW* (June 5): 1311–12.
35. Archana Mishra, *Casting the Evil Eye*.
36. Upen Kisku, 2004. '*Daini*', in *Adivasi Samaj o Sanskriti*, edited by Dibyajyoti Majumdar (Government of West Bengal, Centre of Folk and Tribal Culture, Department of Information and Culture): 287–92.
37. *The Hindu*, 21 July 2012.
38. Soma Chaudhuri, *Witches, Tea Plantations and Lives of Migrant Workers*: 98.

39 Tendulkar, 'Tribals and I', in Makarand Sathe, ed., *Vijay Tendulkar Omnibu*: 68.
40 S.M. Naqvi, 1943. 'Santal Murders', *Man in India* 23, 3: 240.
41 Indu Bharti, 1989. 'Paharia Tribals' Plight and Government's Indifference', *EPW* (July 8): 1503–05.
42 *The Times of India*, 23 July 2012.
43 Troisi, *Tribal Religion*: 221.
44 S.C. Roy, 1937. 'The Kharias', *Man in India*: 120.
45 Moushumi Roy, 2011. 'Choosing to be Christian: An Analysis of the Causes of Conversion of the Santal Tribals', *Jadavpur University Journal of Sociology* 4, 4 (March): 43–52.
46 Palamau District Gazetteer: 165, available at https://docs.google.com/viewer?a=v&q=cache:xtLfSBsaaTQJ:palamu.nic.in/gazette/general_gazette.doc+Palamau+District+Gazetteer,+p.+165
47 Skaria, *Hybrid Histories*: 89.
48 Shashank Sinha, 2007. Witch-Hunts, Adivasis, and the Uprising in Chhotanagpur', *EPW* 42, 19 (May 12–18): 1672–76.
49 Haynes and Gyan Prakash, *Contesting Power*: 1–2.
50 Nita Kumar, *Women as Subjects*: 4.
51 Shashank Shekhar Sinha, 2006. 'Adivasis, Gender and the 'Evil Eye': The Construction(s) of Witches in Colonial Chhotonagpur', *Indian Historical Review* 33, 1: 134–35.
52 *Anandabazar Patrika*, 25 September 2010.
53 Shoma Chaudhuri, *Witches, Tea Plantations and Lives of Migrant Workers*: 137.
54 Pradip Bhattacharya, 1994. *Witchcraft Among the Santals* (Calcutta: Liberal Association for Movement of People [LAMP]): 21.
55 P.C. Oraon, 1999–2000. Janjatiya Kshetra Mein Dayan Pratha Ki Samasya Avom Samadhan (Ranchi: Bihar Tribal Welfare Research Institute): 11 and 13.
56 Shashank Shekhar Sinha, 2004. 'Gender Constructions and "Traditions": The Positioning of Adivasi Women in Twentieth Century Adivasi Chhotonagpur', *Indian Historical Review* 30, 1 & 2 (Jan and July): 69–70.
57 In Purulia district, movement against witch hunting was once very strong, but later it has died down. Lakshmindra Kumar Sarker has described the course of the movement in his book, 1991. *Puruliar Daini Birodhi Andolon* (Kolkata: Sachayan Prakashani). According to him, witch hunting is still prevalent in the tribal areas of West Bengal mainly because of illiteracy and poverty. There are numerous reports on witch killing published in newspapers. Let us mention some of them: 21 January 2010—Badli Mandi (50)—Balagarh in Hooghly—Driven out of her home *(The Statesman)* 16 October 2010—Ramsumari

Devi (35)—Majhaulia village in Sitamarhi of Bihar—Beaten to death (The Statesman) January, 2011—Sindri, Sasangdi and Jiling villages of Manbazar-Barabazar of Purulia– Ransacked the houses of the accused women and beaten *(Anandabazar Patrika)* 26 February 2011— Budhin Murmu (27)—Jaipur village of Mangalkot, Burdwan—She was fined with three thousand rupees. The villagers forcefully sold her cows and then ostracized her. *(Anandabazar Patrika)* 4 March 2013—Laxmi Murmu (50)—Fatesinghpur village of Chadrakona Road—janguru was called and after identifying her as a witch was beaten badly *(Anandabazar Patrika)* 18 February 2014—Amti Murmu (65)—Dogachhi village in the Gazole police station, Malda—The accused people are after the land bequeathed to the woman by her late husband and are bent on burning her to death by concocting stories.

58 K. Srinivasan, and S.K. Mohanty, 2004. 'Deprivation of Basic Amenities by Caste and Religion: Empirical Study Using NFHS Data', *EPW* (February 2014): 728–35.
59 Maitreyi Bordia Das, Soumya Kapoor and Denis Nikitin, 2012. 'Dying to Get Attention: A Closer Look at Child Mortality among Adivasis in India', in *Social Exclusion and Adverse Inclusion: Development and Deprivation of Adivasis in India* edited by Dev Nathan and Virginius Xaxa (New Delhi: Oxford University Press): 113–44.
60 A. Pandey, Nandini Roy, D. Sahu and Rajib Acharya, 2004. 'Maternal Health Care Services: Observations from Chhattisgarh, Jharkhand and Uttaranchal', *EPW* (Feb 14): 713–20.
61 Das, Kapoor and Nikitin, 'Dying to Get Attention': 113–44.
62 Motilal Mahamallik, Sunil Kumar Mishra and Minarva Dash, 2006. 'Health-Disease-Poverty Nexus among Tribals in Odisha', in *Tribal Development in India: The Contemporary Debate*, edited by Govinda Chandra Rath (New Delhi: SAGE).
63 Sabita Acharya and Abhijita Das, 2012. 'State of Health and Health Service Delivery System in Scheduled Districts of Odisha: A Look', *Journal of Indian Anthropological Society* 47, 1: 53–74.
64 *Key Indicators for Odisha from National Family Health Survey 3, 2005–06*, available at www.nfhsindia.org/factsheet.html, downloaded on 5 March 2012.
65 *Human Development Report Summary* (2004), Odisha, Government of Odisha, Bhubaneswar, Published by Planning and Coordination Department: 22, available at http://www.odisha.gov.in/pc/human-development/summary/Summary.pdf downloaded on 05.11.2013/
66 *The Statesman*, 2 September 2012.
67 Sutanu Dutta Chowdhury, Tarun Chakraborty and Tusharkanti Ghosh, 2007. 'Prevalence of Undernutrition in Santal Children of Puruliya District, West Bengal', Department of Human Physiology

with Community Health, Vidyasagar University, West Medinipur, West Bengal, also available in *Indian Pediatrics* 2008, 45: 43–46.
68. V.G. Rao, R. Yadav, C.K. Dolla et al., 2005. 'Undernutrition and Childhood Morbidities among Tribal Preschool Children, *Indian Journal of Medical Research* (July) 122, 1: 43–47.
69. Dutta Chowdhury, Chakraborty and Ghosh, *Prevalence of Undernutrition in Santal Children of Puruliya District*: 43–46.
70. *The Statesman*, 10 August 2014.
71. Abhijit Ghosal, and Sovan Chakraborty, 2012. 'Socio-Economic Impact on Health: A Study on the Mundas of Paschim Medinipur', *Bulletin of the Cultural Research Institute* 24, 1 & 2 (Government of West Bengal, Backward Classes Welfare Department): 57–63; Sudhangshu Chakrabarty, 2010. 'Mahal', in *Durbar Bhabna* 2, 2 (June) (Kolkata: Durbar Prakashani): 17, 20.
72. P.K. Sahoo, and B.C. Das, 2006. 'Primary Education in the Tribal Belt of Odisha', in *Tribal Development in India: The Contemporary Debate*, edited by Govinda Chandra Rath (New Delhi: SAGE).
73. *The Statesman*, 9 December 2011.
74. Ministry of Home Affairs, 2001. *Census of India* (New Delhi: Government of India): Eleven Five Year Plan, 2007–12, vol. 1, Planning Commission: 113.
75. Amitabha Sarkar, 1993. *Toto: Society and Change (A Sub-Himalayan Tribe of West Bengal)* (Calcutta: Firma KLM): 12.
76. Rajib Chatterjee, 2010. 'Life Among the Totos of Totopara: A Study in Continuity and Change', *The Oriental Anthropologist: A Bi-Annual International Journal of the Science* 10, 1 (Jan–June): 269–78.
77. *Supreme Court Orders on the Right to Food: A Tool for Action, August 2008* (2nd ed.), published by Right to Food Campaign, Secretariat, and printing support from Office of the Commissioner's to the Supreme Court (Civil Writ Petition 196 of 2001): 1–159, available at http://www.righttofoodindia.org/data/scordersprimeratoolforaction.pdf downloaded on 30 August 2012.
78. The schemes are: (1) Public Distribution System (PDS); (2) Antyodaya Anna Yojana; (3) National Programme of Nutritional Support to Primary Education, also known as 'Mid-Day Meals scheme'; (4) Integrated Child Development Services (ICDS); (5) Annapurna; (6) National Old Age Pension Scheme (NOAPS); (7) National Maternity Benefit Scheme (NMBS); and (8) National Family Benefit Scheme (NFBS). A ninth scheme, Sampurna Gramin Rozgar Yojana (SGRY), was not mentioned in this order but it did figure in the initial list of food-related schemes on which the Supreme Court requested affidavits from the state governments (on 17 September 2001), and SGRY became the main focus of the next interim order, issued on 8 May 2002. Ibid: p. 21.

79 *The Statesman*, 2 September 2011.
80 Sumita Saha, 2011. 'Mid-day Meals Program: A Boost to Primary Level Education in India', *Jadavpur University Journal of Sociology* 4, 4 (March): 26–34.
81 Pey de Garros, 1887. *Poesias* (Toulouse): 299.
82 Virginius Xaxa, 2005. 'Politics of Language, Religion and Identity: Tribes in India', *EPW* (March 26): 1363–70.
83 Script developed by the Santhals in known as Ol Chiki, Kak-Barok is the script developed and used for the Tripuri speaking tribes of Tripura. Among the Bodos, there is an increasing articulation for the use of Roman script in place of Assamese to mark off their distinct identity.
84 Lachman Khubchandani, 1992. *Tribal Identity: A Language and Communication Perspective* (New Delhi: Indus Publishing): 55.
85 Society for Regional Research and Analysis, 2010. '*Migration of Tribal Women: Its Socioeconomic Effects—An in-depth Study of Chhattisgarh, Jharkhand, M.P. and Odisha*' (October) Submitted to Planning Commission, Government of India, Yojana Bhawan, Sansad Marg, New Delhi.
86 Tirpude College of Social Work, Civil Lines, Sadar. A Research Study Report, 2003. '*A Research Study On Migrant Tribal Women Girls in Ten Cities: A Study of Their Socio-Cultural and Economic Reference to Social Intervention*', Submitted to Planning Commission, Government of India, New Delhi.
87 Panda, Smita Mishra, Ragnhild Lund et al., 2013. 'Gender, Mobility, and Citizenship Rights among Tribals of Khurda and Sundargarh, Odisha (India)', *Gender, Technology and Development* 17, 2: 105–29.
88 Report on Human Trafficking on the rise in Jangal Mahal, published in *The Statesman*, 4 April 2012.
89 Sumit Sarkar, 'The Many Worlds of Indian History', in *Writing Social History* (New Delhi: Oxford University Press): 22–24.
90 Rajnarayan Basu, 1995. 'Devgrihe Dainandin Lipi' [1879], in *Nirbachita Rachanasamgraha*, ed. Baridbaran Ghosh (Calcutta: College Street Publishers): 193. For more details see Prathama Banerjee, 2006. *Politics of Time* (New Delhi: Oxford University Press): 86–87.
91 P.O. Bodding, 1919. *Sona: En Kristen Santalkvindes liv oggjerning* (Copenhagen: Den Nordiske Santalmisjon).
92 Shashibhushan Ray, 1926. *Santal Pargana, Past and Present* (Deoghar).
93 Prathama Banerjee, 2006. *Politics of Time: 'Primitives' and History-writing in a Colonial Society* (New Delhi: Oxford University Press): 91.
94 Sanjivchandra Chattopadhyay, 1970. 'Palamau,' in *Sanjiv Rachanabali* Calcutta): 381.
95 Ibid.: 393.

96 Rimli Bhattacharya, *Aranyak of the Forest:* 151–54.
97 Ibid.: 181–82.
98 Rekha, 2015. *Gender, Space and Creative Imagination: The Poetics and Politics of Women's Writing in India* (New Delhi: Primus Books): 69.
99 Gayatri Spivak, *Mahasweta Devi Breast Stories*: 34–35.
100 Ibid.: 36–37.
101 Satyanarayana, *Plays of Mahasweta Devi:* 19.
102 Colin MacCabe, Foreword, *In Other Worlds*: xvi.
103 Prathama Banerjee, 2011. 'Culture/Politics: The Curious Double-bind of the Indian Adivasi', in *Subaltern Citizens and Their Histories*, edited by Gyanendra Pandey (New York: Routledge): 132.
104 Daniel J. Rycroft, 2006. 'Santalism: Reconfiguring "The Santal" in Indian Art and Politics', *Indian Historical Review* 33, 1: 150–74.
105 Rabindranath Tagore, 1935. 'The Santal Woman', in *Visva-Bharati Quarterly*, New Series, vol. 1, Part 1, edited by K.R. Kripalani (translated from Bengali by Tagore on 2 April 1935): 71–72.

Epilogue

> *The government is simply waiting for me to die ... My health is not good ... I pray to all of you, please help me stay alive.*
>
> —Soni Sori

SO UNFEELING A contrast provided by Soni Sori[1] to Bhanmati. Adivasi women—the poorest, hungriest and malnourished—are fighting patriarchy in their own communities and displacement, lacking access to education, health care or legal redress, mercilessly exploited and raped as matter of right by police and forest department officials. Their evictions from land and forests where they worked, lived and worshipped are not regarded as a feminist problem. Being disillusioned by the promises of the governments they have started looking for an alternative.

Chandra Talpade Mohanty in her essay 'Under Western Eyes' suggests that the formulation of autonomous, geographically, historically and culturally grounded feminist concerns and strategies is a key to third world feminist enquiry. The first project is one of deconstructing and dismantling; the second, one of building and constructing. While these projects appear to be contradictory, the one negatively and the positively, unless these two tasks are addressed simultaneously, 'third world' feminisms run the risks of marginalization or ghettoization from both mainstream (right and left) and western feminist discourses.[2] In this enquiry of not the third but fourth world, that is, the indigenous women, this concern is grounded in not only epistemological traditions but is located in construction of social reality. The complexities and absence of an indigenous theory tends to incline literature towards adopting ecofeminism, losing the strands necessary for enquiry into indigenous women and signifies the problematique faced in the field.

There is in India, as in most of the developing world a gendered division of labour. In India, agricultural workers are widely acknowledged to be women. This women's work has been invisible as the state does not include women's work in the fields as part of economic input. Both state and society largely discriminate against women. What is not very clear here is tribal women's status. Are tribal women considered equal to men? Is their work in the fields acknowledged by the men? Does this work convert itself into rights or enhance their power? What role does the state play in their lives? These were questions that confronted me when I began my research. Poor adivasi women commonly referred to as head loaders, walk miles through different conditions, collecting wood, gathering fodder, picking leaves, brewing liquor and selling them—the typical items of work are all characterized by monotony, hard physical labour, harassment and exploitation. The activities they predominantly engage in are such as manufacture and sale of products based on minor forest produce. These activities are typically low income, seasonal activities, and marginal to the economy. The liquor trade in tribal areas finds a predominance of adivasi women. This may seem a sharp contradiction when viewed in terms of the problems faced by adivasi women on account of male alcoholism. But when viewed in context of the limited availability of economic options and issues of survival, it is perhaps less surprising that such trade is taken up by women. In the few cases that employment is available to adivasi women, gender-based discrimination in wages both by government and contractors reinforces their economic marginalization.

Not only economic marginalization but also the field of adivasi politics, active or passive, has also remained largely male dominated. The feminization of domestic affairs precludes the process of politicization of adivasi women to a great extent. Their visibility in the politics by the constant attempt of vocalizing silences has been denied sometimes by their own men in various ways. For example, the first largest SEZ project was planned in Raigarh district of Maharashtra, spreading across 35, 000 acres. According to the Land Acquisition Act of 1894 this land was chosen for the establishment of industries. The villagers were completely unaware of the term 'SEZ'. When they got to know what it actually means 2,800 peasants had already sold their lands amounting to 12,000 acres. Later they decided to protest against the proposed SEZ. On 28 June 2006 an unprecedented dharna was organized in front of the Collector's office of Raigarh demanding the withdrawal of the notice of the land acquisition which was attended only by the women of the village, some with their babies on their laps. The way they protested was unprecedented as well, they sang folk songs composed by them to voice their dissatisfactions. More or less 35 women were arrested by the police during the protest and booked under various cases. The women had to spend several weeks in jail. After that an organization was formed named Chaubis Gaon SEZ Virodhi Manch (Twenty-four villages against SEZ). Quite surprisingly there was no place for the women in the organization. In 1984 when the land acquisition began for the Gopalpur project in Gajapati district of Orissa the first objection came from the women of the village. Lakshmi Amma and Erema Amma were killed in the police firing. The movement is still continued under the banner of 'Samaj Suraksha Samiti'. But the women of the organization are considered as second-class citizens.[3]

Recently Gobindapur villagers who have refused to give away their land to POSCO have formed a three-tier human barricade at the entry point. On 2 February 2013 the police attacked a human barricade composed of over 350 women. The indiscriminate use of force, which allegedly included lathi attacks on women and children, injured over 50 people. On 6 February, the district administration of Odisha was forced to halt the operation at around noon when hundreds of women and children formed a human barricade and told the police: 'Kill us first before you proceed further'.[4] But there is no woman in the leadership positions, neither in POSCO Pratirodh Sangram Samiti nor in Bhitamati Suraksha Manch nor in United Action Committee.

Although it has been emphasized time and again that villagers should be consulted on decisions concerning rural development, women are generally not consulted at all, or else their viewpoint is not accorded the importance it deserves. Thus, there is little understanding of the priorities and problems concerning half of the country's population. Women themselves were not really bothered being deprived of leadership. Needless to say any organization is the mirror of the society and its norms. We still have not granted power to the women to take decisions either in the family or in the society, how will the organizations do that?

It is noteworthy that the Lalgarh movement for the first time gave equal participation to the adivasi women with their male counterparts in the movement as well as in the organization. But even there they were visibly absent in the leadership positions. They formed a separate organization for the women called Nari Ijjat Bachao Committee. It is also unfortunate that most of the feminist and women organizations maintain a safe distance with the adivasi organizations like say the Krantikari Adivasi Mahila Sangathan of the Dandakaranya forest (with 90,000 members).

Therefore, the tribal scene today is very disquieting. The need for change was never greater than today. Positive policy by itself is not enough, although it forms the basis of what is to be done. In spite of positive policy and allocation of considerable funds, not much has been achieved during the last seventy years of independence. In the Twenty-Ninth Report (1987–1989 and submitted on 28 May 1990), the Commissioner, B.D. Sharma, finds it futile to make any fresh recommendations and said, 'What recommendations can be made when the foundation of the system itself is faulty? The law and system itself are against the spirit of the constitution and basic tenets of natural justice; moreover the right to life of ordinary people is being violated at every step. The whole report itself is one substantial recommendation.'[5] He has further stated that, 'In a hurry for development we have accepted the questionable premise of "development first" and given social equity secondary position. In this approach an important fact of the global system was overlooked that the "dustbin" of the third world was a necessary concomitant of the process of development in the first and second worlds. In the same continuation the third world now requires the "dustbin" of a fourth world.'[6] Tribals constitute this dustbin—victims of the mindless process of development: dispossessed, displaced and raped.

Let us strike one example of the attempt to short sell India's natural resources to the corporations with attendant kickbacks for our political leaders. 'I am forced to conclude that there is no valid gram sabha resolution under Section 6 (1) of the Forest Rights Act,' said the union minister of state for environment and forest, Jairam Ramesh, while granting final forest clearance to POSCO, ₹54,000 crore, 12 million ton integrated steel plant near Paradip in Odisha, barely three months after putting 60 conditions pertaining to pollution control and the captive port in the vicinity of the plant. The gram sabhas of Dhinkia and Gobindapur passed a resolution that the Odisha government had failed to implement the Forest Rights Act, which promises tribals and other forest dwellers legal land rights. The enquiry committee appointed by the ministry had described the project as an 'environmental disaster in the making and the Indian Council for Social Development in its summary report on the implementation of the Forest Rights Act has said: 'All the key features of this legislation have been undermined by a combination of apathy and sabotage during the process of implementation. Unless immediate remedial measures are taken, instead of undoing the historical injustice to tribal and other traditional forest dwellers, the Act will have the opposite outcome of making them even more vulnerable to eviction and denial of their customary access to forest.' Among 1,620 hectares of land spread over eight villages in Jagatsinghpur district, 1,253 hectares is forest land. The Odisha government suppressed the fact that the area was home to about 4,000 tribal families comprising more than 20,000 members.[7] Instead of certificates from gram sabhas, as required under the Forest Rights Act, certificates from the District Magistrate were relied on while granting clearance. Instead of treating this massive project as a whole, it was broken up into smaller units for purposes of granting clearance. It means that POSCO's gain is a loss to the nation.

'Deprivation', as would be clear from the above analysis, seems to be the key word: deprivation of land, forest resources, water, real freedom, education and of opportunities for participation in the developmental processes. Coupled with this is the feeling of disregard for their ethnic identities, which more than ever before is causing great distress as also a feeling of being let down. The question of statehood or autonomy is not related merely to the notion of ethnic identity but it also reflects the hope and conviction that once the tribals become partners in planning and are entrusted with the job of implementation, other problems will be automatically sorted out.

Adivasis, whether they are in different parts of India or in other lands, are faced with the common crisis of being denied their basic rights to livelihood, to traditional lifestyles and to an identity that is quite different from that of the 'outsider'. Everywhere they are displaced and marginalized; and everywhere they defy the arson and anarchy that governments unleash on them. Everyone save the adivasi seems to have prospered in greater or lesser degree in what was originally adivasi country. The worst insult which a self-respecting tribal has to swallow today in the name and game of development is the epitaph 'poor' given to him/her by the arrogant elite. It is being done on purpose so that they can project themselves as the well-wishers of the tribals and the born rebel is tamed by the subterfuges whose significance he/she can hardly realize. The bitter truth is that the tribal is not poor but disinherited.[8] Who knows better than the interlopers how they have robbed the adivasis of their land, forests and rivers, metals, minerals, languages and lifestyle, customs and ceremonies, gods and ancestors, their creativity and confidence, their pride and sense of self or of self-worth, and their deep-rooted communion with Nature, all in the name of introducing them to the democratic mainstream and the rule of law.

And when they challenge the authority of the mainstream, the mainstream expels them by calling it a 'threat'. Tribals have taken up arms to fight against poverty and disparity. We have nurtured such a heartless social system for these communities where death is more desirable than living. According to the statistics given by the National Commission for Enterprises in the Unorganized Sector, in our country 77 per cent people earn less than ₹20 daily and 5 per cent people live in indescribable prosperity. According to the statistics of National Nutrition Monitoring Bureau, 33 per cent people suffer from famine and starvation and languish in endemic malnourishment and thereby deadly diseases; 50 per cent members of SC and 60 per cent members of ST communities belong to this famine affected areas. Besides, in a draft report published by the Rural Development Ministry of the Government of India, it is said that 77 per cent dalits and 90 per cent adivasis are landless.[9] With the Forest Conservation Act of 1980 the adivasis lost their lands and rights over the forest and forest resources. Moreover, the tribals live in the mineral rich areas which are presently the target of the MNCs and are waiting for the mass eviction in the near future. How can there be two Indias—one hit by starvation and the other enjoying an excess of luxuries? A 'poverty line' that is based on calories can at best be called a 'hunger line'.[10]

The districts of Kalahandi and Rayagada in Odisha, where the mining company of Vedanta would have been situated, are very poor and this has been used to suggest why industry should be encouraged. Some of the arguments used by Vedanta's lawyers in the Supreme Court seemed completely spurious: that people were desperately trying to feed themselves and mining would help to alleviate this situation.[11] Most of the people in the area are hardworking farmers or food gatherers who value their land more than anything else. Many would not swap their land for any amount of money. 'We cannot eat money' as one Dongria Kondh woman said in a documentary film named *Cowboys in India* made by Simon Chambers.[12]

In the village Sindhekela of Bolangir district, Odisha, the very life-support system of the Kondhs, the forest, has vanished. The ownership of vast stretches of farmland all around is now with non-adivasis. In the Kalahandi-Bolangir-Koraput region in Odisha, the influx of non-adivasis started in the early nineteenth century. It is small wonder that, in the second half of that century, the region was hit by famine for the first time in history, which became a routine feature thereafter. Post-independence, the biggest casualty was that the dark and dense jungle was relegated to mere images, intriguing though, in folklore. Today, the Kondhs walk for more than three days (about 75 km) to Chhattardandi to collect a specific type of bamboo stick essential for the annual rituals. The Ganher trees, too, are few and far between. Their branches are used by people to make delicious cakes, one of the 16 items offered to the Goddess. Sindhekela points to the political economy of cultural appropriation in India as a tool for not only resource-grabbing but also internal economic colonialism.[13]

Economic colonialism was not possible, despite the blood, without cultural colonization. This was done broadly in two ways: by adopting the existing cultural practices of adivasis and gradually taking control of them; or by imposing one's own cultural and religious tenets by means of using royal power or by intimidating them with the divine 'superiority' of a new God, such as the spread of the Jagannath cult in which thousands of temples came up in remote, forested hinterlands, sucking them into an alien temple system. This has been the single-most lethal process of cultural colonization in Odisha.[14] Cultural appropriation led to a change of hands in controlling local resources around the new power centres—always in agreement with the dominant political order of the day—which resulted in sudden dispossession and perpetual deprivation of the adivasis. It is a travesty of history that the adivasis are the ones who today lend the region the dark identity of being hunger-ridden and backward.

Did tribal societies exist in a state of gendered equality and equity? By analysing the existing situation in several tribal districts of four states, it was possible to challenge this assumption. It has to be recognized that the women belonged to different tribes, spread across four large states in different parts of the country. These states are at different stages of economic and agricultural development. For example, Sundergarh district is more developed than Koraput in Odisha. Studies however indicated that in spite of these overall variations the tribal villages are transitional societies moving out from the primitive stage.

The favourable position of the women in a tribal community should not induce complacency. First, although the sex ratio is favourable, it is declining. The number of tribal women taking up employment is rising sharply which shows the extent of their pauperization and marginalization. There is resistance to the recognition of their right to land and placing their right to maintenance on the statute book. Female literacy is still low except in a few pockets. In some areas like mining and other occupations they have been replaced by men. The minimum wages for tribal men and women are not uniform. Adivasi women have been exposed most ruthlessly to the operations of market and other commercial forces and of unscrupulous elements that have flocked into the tribal areas for the exploitation of mines and establishment of industries.[15] The struggle for women's property rights and their ownership of land has been a subject of policy debate over the course of the twentieth century; and these rights have still not been achieved in our country. Women have lower levels of access to education and medical services and these differences are related to the differential control of household assets. Lack of control over assets also results in women's lower wages, and cripples their economic agency and decision-making power over assets.[16]

According to adivasi women in a national conference of adivasis at Ranchi, Jharkhand in February 2007, women's declining social stature within society and growing vulnerability over the past 60 years, can be attributed to the following: *(i)* increasing erosion in women's use and control rights to land and housing; *(ii)* lack of access to new technologies and agricultural extension services; *(iii)* human insecurity and displacement; *(iv)* lack of participation in decision-making processes on use of community resources (forests, pastures, water); and *(v)* inadequate knowledge and control over marketing. These are aggravated by lack of attention to such issues in development and the lack of basic amenities (education and health-care facilities) provided by the government, infrastructure, including communication information technologies, in women's communities and personal lives.[17]

Adivasi women negotiate patriarchy in everyday lives. One such area has been the struggle for land rights. In 2013 Krishi Ratna Award had been given to one farmer from each block of West Bengal. A total of 341 farmers were given the award among which only two are women—Chhandarani Karan (52) of Kolaghat and Fulmani Hansda (27) of Lalgarh. Fulmani expressed her concern over the issue of women's land rights, 'Women give the most back breaking labour to agriculture, though they are mainly unskilled jobs. They are deprived of modern technology like tractor or power tiller which are under men's control. So, women earn less than men. Women have no land in their names and without land how will they become farmer? Nobody knows how many women get kisan credit cards or membership in Krishi Samabai?'[18] On 25 April 2013 Reserve Bank Employees' Union organized a conference in Kolkata where Munni Hembram (40) from Dumka district of Jharkhand reiterated the problem of lack of land rights which is key to their autonomy.[19] Kanaklata Murmu (40) has emerged as a community leader by displaying the gumption to stand up for women's rights in the remote village of Kumari in Manbazar II block of Purulia district. Kanaklata joined a local organization called Purulia Zilla Banchita Jana Jagaran Adhikar Samity supported by Action Aid. She has set up a parallel justice delivery structure in her village to take decisions on disputes usually under the consideration of the male elders. She has been able to get drinking water, ensuring pensions for several widows and helped people access jobs under NREGS in her village.[20]

An empirical understanding of the tribal women in eastern India places them as unimportant cogs in the wheel of the state. In the process of modernization and development she loses whatever space she may have created for herself. Her marginalization is complete when neither society nor state considers her important to their existence. Poverty, deprivation and now the reduction of government expenditure on basic medical health facilities are reflected in the absolutely poor health condition of adivasi women and children. Maternal mortality was reported to be high among various tribal groups but no exact data are available. The main causes of maternal mortality were found to be unhygienic and primitive practices for parturition. The crude death rates are also very high. These adverse health indicators are largely due to inadequate access to the nutritious foods and lack of access to health care services. The lack of food supply through the TPDS is compounded by the fact that adivasis have no rights in forests that used to provide them with a variety of food. The solution of providing food for work (EGS) or free food would only take care of the immediate needs of the adivasis, but will not provide a long-term solution.[21]

According to the Asian Centre for Human Rights (ACHR),[22] despite constitutional provisions in the Fifth and Sixth Schedules that recognize tribal ownership rights over land and forests in Scheduled/Protected Areas, 'contradictory legal provisions and failure to implement or translate Constitutional Provisions into reality' undermine these rights of adivasis. Under the Forest Conservation Act (1980), the Wild Life Protection Act (1972), and the Land Acquisition Act (1994), 'The government has the sovereign right to evict people for undefined public interest or 'larger interest' but the affected people do not have the right to question the decision of the government on the forced evictions'.[23] In fact, until just recently, the Land Acquisition Act, which has been instrumental in evicting tribal peoples for more than a century, has had no provisions for resettlement and rehabilitation, not to mention right to free, prior, and informed consent (the Right to Information is a recent legal innovation in India). The New Economic Policy (NEP) of 1991 (neoliberal policy prescriptions to marketize, privatize and open up the Indian economy to foreign direct ownership/investment) has exacerbated the process of adivasi land alienation.

One can notice a clear case of wide variation in the formal frame of tribal rights over resources with extreme positions. For example, the traditional frame of 'community ownership and individual use' is continuing in khutkati (collective rights) areas in Jharkhand and extensive shifting cultivation areas in Odisha. Several tribal communities, particularly those that are relatively educationally advanced, have launched movements to conserve their ethno-cultural values and refurbish their ethno-cultural identity. In other words, this is a solidarity movement. Some of the tribal communities, for instance, the Santhal in Odisha, and several in the northeastern states of India equate their ethno-cultural identity with some kind of ethno-cultural sub-nationalism. The identity of self-image centres on their age-old hegemony over the natural resources in their habitat. Now there is increasing state control over these resources; and moreover, non-tribals have grabbed their resources in a large measure. Material deprivation led the leaders to form an ethno-cultural organization to promote ethnic solidarity and fight for the mitigation of their material deprivation. Thus 'identity mobilization' is an adaptive strategy for gaining access to strategic resources and power.

The tribal and the scheduled castes and the Other Backward Classes constitute more than two-thirds of Indian society. Relentless coercion and ignorance have reduced them to a beastly plight. If poverty is the linchpin of India's problems, it should be forthwith apprehended by the right distribution of Gross Domestic Product. If ignorance is ingrained in the Indian masses, it must be quickly driven away by the spread of education so that neither poverty nor ignorance can farther pass from generation to generation. If the segregation of women among indigent Indians is an insurmountable hurdle, it must be annihilated expeditiously. If disease in rural areas remains unchecked because of casual and insincere health services, serious steps must be taken against those responsible.

It is true that women were hardly positioned as equals in traditional adivasi societies. However, earlier they had formed an important cog in the traditional gender division of labour inside as well as outside the household. Under the impact of the colonial-capitalist regime, they were pushed to the margins of resultant political economies. In this book I have tried to investigate the invisible everyday forms of resistance and how adivasi women are related to the question of women's agency. Because accounts are largely by the intelligentsia using written records that were also created largely by literate officials, histories and social sciences are not always adequately equipped to uncover the silences and anonymous forms of struggle that typify the oppressed.

NOTES

1 Soni Sori, an adivasi schoolteacher from Bastar, was arrested and tortured in Dantewada police custody since she tried to stop local government corruption. She was stripped off, given electric shocks and stones were pushed up her vagina to get her to 'confess' that she was a Maoist courier. The stones were removed from her body at a

hospital in Calcutta, where, after a public outcry, she was sent for a medical check-up. At a recent Supreme Court hearing, activists presented the judges with the stones in a plastic bag. The only outcome of their efforts has been that Soni Sori remains in jail while Ankit Garg, the Superintendent of Police, who was named by her of ordering and supervising her torture and sexual violence against her, was conferred with the President's Police Medal for Gallantry on Republic Day.
2. Chandra Talpade Mohanty, 1991. 'Under Western Eyes: Feminist Scholarship and Colonial Discourses', in *Third World Women and the Politics of Feminism*, edited by Chandra Talpade Mohanty, Ann Russo and Lourdes Torres (Bloomington, In: Indiana University Press): 51.
3. *Ananda Bazar Patrika*, 24 August 2010.
4. See *Sanhati: Fighting for Neo-Liberalism* at http://sanhati.com/articles/3634/downloaded on 20 February 2013.
5. Verrier, *Tribal World of Verrier Elwin: An Autobiography*: xxiv.
6. Ibid.: iii.
7. *The Statesman*, 7 May 2011.
8. B.D. Sharma, 2010. *Unbroken History of Broken Promises: Indian State and the Tribal People* (New Delhi: Sahyog Pustak Kuteer): 98–99.
9. *Ananda Bazar Patrika*, 11 August 2010.
10. Very few people know about the incidents of starvation deaths in the tribal areas of western India. In the wilderness of Baran district in Rajasthan the Sahariyas, a primitive tribal group are often in the news for starvation deaths. The Sahariya women collect forest produce and work as agricultural labourers. They live in abject poverty and are debt-ridden and suffer malnutrition. See Syeda Hameed and Gunjan Veda, 2012. *Beautiful Country—Stories From Another India* (New Delhi: Harper Collins); Tejinder, 2004. *Dairy—Saga Saga* (New Delhi: Rajkamal Prakashan): 12, for the starvation deaths of Kashipur. see 66–67.
11. *The Statesman*, 10 October 2010.
12. *Cowboys in India*, a film by Simon Chambers, was shown on NDTV, 10 October 2010 at 1 pm.
13. *The Statesman*, 16 January 2011.
14. Subrat Kumar Sahu and Mamata Dash, 2011. 'Expropriation of Land and Cultures: The Orissa Story and Beyond', *Social Change* 41, 2: 251–70.
15. Mukhopadhyay, *Tribal Women in Development*: 7.
16. Govind Kelkar, 2014. 'The Fog of Entitlement Women's Inheritance and Land Rights', *EPW* 49, 33 (August 16): 51–58.
17. Kelkar, *Adivasi Women Engaging with Climate Change*: 12.
18. *Ananda Bazar Patrika*, 23 April 2013.
19. *Ananda Bazar Patrika*, 13 June 2013.

20 *The Statesman*, 9 February 2014.
21 Anonymous, 2006. 'Adivasi Women: Situation and Struggles', *People's March* 7, 7 (Aug–Sept–Oct).
22 Asian Centre for Human Rights (ACHR), 2005. 'Promising Picture or Broken Future? Commentary and Recommendations on the Draft National Policy on Tribals of the Government of India', available at http://www.achrweb.org: 4–5. Accessed 17 December 2017.
23 Ibid.: 9.

Bibliography

PRIMARY SOURCES

A Fact Finding Report, 2009. *Uttarbanger Cha Bagan Ek Anischit Bhabisater Pratikhha*, Kolkata: NESPON and Nagarik Mancha: 10, 16, 18. (The survey was conducted from October to December 2008.)

A fact finding team of DSU (Democratic Student Union), 2012. *'The Flames of Narayanpatna: Two Reports on the Narayanpatna Struggle in Koraput, Odisha'*, Chandigarh: Charvaka Publications.

A Research Study Report, 2003. 'A Research Study On Migrant Tribal Women Girls in Ten Cities: A Study of Their Socio-Cultural and Economic Reference to Social Intervention', submitted to Planning Commission, Government of India, New Delhi by Tirpude College of Social Work, Civil Lines, Sadar.

Annual Report 2008–09 of the Union Ministry of Home Affairs, Government of India, Chapter-II, 'Internal Security', available at http://www.satp.org/satporgtp/countries/india/document/papers/annualreport_2008-09.htm downloaded on 9 May 2011.

Anonymous and undated, Fact Finding Report on 'Lalgarh: Paschimbanger Adivasi', Kolkata: Nagarik Mancha.

Approach Paper to the Ninth Five Year Plan (1997–2002), Planning Commission, Government of India. Available at http://planningcommission.nic.in/reports/publications/app_nine.pdf downloaded on 24 August 2012.

Asansol Planning Organization, November, 1978. *Sub-Plan for the Tribal Areas of Burdwan [West Bengal]*, Tribal Department Project No. 31 & 32. Asansol Planning Organization, Development and Planning (T & C.P.) Department, Government of West Bengal, Bhabani Bhawan, Upper Chelidanga, P.O. Asansol (713304), Dist. Burdwan, West Bengal.

Bennet, Lynn, 2002. 'Using Empowerment and Social Inclusion for Pro-Poor Growth: A Theory of Social Change', *Background Paper for the Social Development Sector Strategy Paper*, April: 13.

Bonda Development Agency, March 2002. Baseline Survey & Needs Assessment and 10th Five-Year Action Plan for 2002–03 to 2006–07.

Census of India 1891, vol. 3, Lower Provinces of Bengal—Provincial Table XVI.

Census of India, 1971, Series 1, Part V-A (ii) Special Tables for Scheduled Tribes, 1977.

Democratic Students' Union [DSU], August 2009. 'State Repression and People's Resistance Experiences from the Lalgarh Movement, A Fact-Finding Report.'

Development Challenges in Extremist Affected Areas, April 2008. Report of an Expert Group to Planning Commission, Government of India, New Delhi. Chapter-5, No. 5.1.1, http://www.planningcommission.gov.in/reports/publications/rep-dce.pdf downloaded on 15 February 2011.

Dhebar, UN Report of the Scheduled Areas and Scheduled Tribes Commission, 1961, vol. 1, 1960–61, New Delhi: Ministry of Home Affairs, Government of India.

Draft of Bihar Rural Livelihoods Development Project, Tribal (Indigenous People's) Development Plan, 9 April 2007. ADRI, Patna, Bihar, available at http://brlp.in/admin/Files/Tribal%20Plan%20of%20Bihar%20Rural%20Livelihoods%20Project.pdf downloaded on 10 November 2012.

Elvin, Verrier, 1945. Supplement to *'A Brief Survey of the Aboriginal Tribes of the Districts of Ganjam & Koraput'*, Honorary Anthropologist to the Government of Odisha, D.O. No. 10/45 dated camp Kanakaraguda, to Mr. Nicholson (Dec. 25).

Elvin, Verrier, 1969. *Ethnographic Study of the Kuvi-Kandha*, 16 April 1969. Sukumar Banerjee, Anthropological Survey of India, Government of India.

Final Report on 'In Search of a Strategy to Build a Field Model to Ensure People's Participation for Sustainable Development: Case Study of the Didayi (A Primitive Tribal Group of Malkangiri District of Orissa)', 2001–02. Sponsored by the Planning Commission, Government of India, Council of Analytical Tribal Studies (COATS), Koraput, Odisha 2001–02.

Government of India, 2002. *Orissa Development Report*, Planning Commission, New Delhi: 466.

———. 2006. *Draft National Rehabilitation Policy*, para 3(1) (J).

———. Ministry of Coal and Mines, Department of Mines, *Annual Report 2003–2004*, available at http://www.mines.nic.in accessed on July 11, 2011.

———. Planning Commission, 1981. *Report on the Development of Tribal Areas* (Sivaraman Committee), National Committee on the Development of Backward Areas.

———.2010. 'Migration of Tribal Women: Its Socioeconomic Effects—An in-depth Study of Chhattisgarh, Jharkhand, M.P. and Orissa', Submitted to: Planning Commission, Yojana Bhawan, Sansad Marg, New Delhi: Society for Regional Research and Analysis (October).

Government of India, 1985. *Report of the Committee on Rehabilitation of Displaced Tribals due to Development Projects*, Ministry of Home Affairs.

———. *Selected Educational Statistics, 2004–05*, Ministry of Human Resource Development, at http://www.educationforallinindia.com/SES2004-05.pdf downloaded on 17 February 2012.

Government of Orissa, 1959. *Forest Enquiry Report*, Cuttack: Government of Orissa Press.

———. SC & ST Research and Training Institute, 1991–92. *Development Handbook for the Juangs of Juang Development Agency*.

———. 2005. *Draft Orissa Resettlement and Rehabilitation Policy*, Revenue Department.

———. 2004. *Human Development Report Summary*. Bhubaneswar, Published by Planning and Coordination Department, available at http://www.odisha.gov.in/pc/humandevelopment/summary/Summary.pdf

———. 2006. *Draft Orissa Resettlement and Rehabilitation Policy*, Revenue Department, para 6.

———. 2010. '*Keonjhar District Monitoring Visit Note on Banspal and Telkoi Block*', by Dr. Ashwani Kumar, Member, Central Employment Guarantee Council (CEGC), Tata Institute of Social Sciences, Mumbai (Feb. 4).

———. Scheduled Castes and Scheduled Tribes Research and Training Institute 2001. *Tribes in Orissa: A Data Sheet*, Bhubaneswar.

Government of West Bengal, 1990. *Profiles of Tribal Women in West Bengal*, edited by Ratna Gupta, Cultural Research Officer. Special Series No: 34, *Bulletin of the Cultural Research Institute*, Scheduled Castes and Tribes Welfare Department.

———.1990. *Profiles of Tribal Women in West Bengal*, Edited by Ratna Gupta, Cultural Research Officer. Special Series No: 34, Bulletin of the Cultural Research Institute, Scheduled Castes and Tribes Welfare Department, Government of West Bengal.

———. 2002. *Report submitted by the Deputy Superintendent of Police*, Birbhum, to the Women's Commission (July).

India Agricultural Policy Review, 2008. Agriculture and Agri-Food Canada (May), 4, 3 available at http://www.dsp-psd.pwgsc.gc.ca/collection_2009/agr/A38-3-5-1-1E.pdf

India Social Development Report, 2008. New Delhi: Oxford University Press.

International Institute for Population Sciences (IIPS), 2010. *District Level Household and Facility Survey* (DLHS-3), 2007–08, Mumbai: IIPS, Odisha, available at www.rchiips.org/pdf/rch3/report/OR.pdf accessed on 6 March 2012.

Key Indicators for Orissa from National Family Health Survey-3, 2005–06, available at www.nfhsindia.org/factsheet.html, downloaded on 5 March 2012.

Lanjia Saora Development Agency, 2002. *Baseline Survey & Needs Assessment and 10th Five-Year Action Plan for 2002–03 to 2006–07* (March).

Letters from Lalgarh, 2013. *The Complete Collection of Letters from the People's Committee against Police Atrocities.* Edited and translated by Sanhati, Kolkata: www.sanhati.com and Setu Prakashani.

Malhotra, A, S.R. Schuler, and C. Boender, 2002. 'Measuring Women's Empowerment as a Variable in International Development', Gender and Development Group of the World Bank (June 28).

National Family Health Survey (NFHS)-1, 1992–93, NFHS-2, 1998–99, NFHS-3, 2005–06, available at http://www.rchiips.org/nfhs all reports are scanned copies.

National Federation of Indian Women, 2008. 'Socio-Economic Empowerment of Women under NREGA', by Navjyoti Jandu. Report prepared for the Ministry of Rural Development. http://www.righttofoodindia.org/data/navjyoti08_employment_guarantee_and_women's_empowerment.pdf accessed on 12 April 2011.

Oxaal, Zoe, and Sally 1997 (rev.). 'Gender and Empowerment: Definitions, Approaches and Implications for Policy'. Briefing prepared for the Swedish International Development Office (Sida), Institute of Development Studies, Sussex (October).

Saran, M. 2001. *Final Population Totals: A Brochure of Orissa*, Orissa: Census of India, 2000.

Saxena, N.C. 2010. 'Hunger, Under-nutrition and Food Security in India', Chronic Poverty Research Centre, The Indian Institute of Public Administration, Working Paper 44, available at http://www.dfid.gov.uk/r4d/PDF/Outputs/ChronicPoverty_RC/CPRC-IIPA44.pdf accessed on 28 August 2012: 53.

Saxena, N.C., and Jayanti Ravi. 2007. '*Realising Potential of Panchayati Raj in India*', AGRASRI Working Paper No. 66 (January). http://www.esocialsciences.com/data/articles/Document1109200540.1757013.pdf accessed on 14 May 2011.

Supreme Court Orders on the Right to Food: A Tool for Action, August 2008 (2nd. ed.), published by Right to Food Campaign, Secretariat, and printing support from Office of the Commissioner's to the Supreme Court (Civil Writ Petition 196 of 2001): 1–159, available at http://www.righttofoodindia.org/data/scordersprimeratoolforaction.pdf accessed on 30 August 2012.

Tea Board of India, 1976 and 1981–82, *Tea Statistics*, Calcutta.

Vidyarthi, L.P. ed. 1981. *The Profiles of the Marginal and Pre-farming Tribes of Central-Eastern India*, Special Series No. 26, *Bulletin of the Cultural Research Institute*, Scheduled Castes and Tribes Welfare Department, Calcutta.

UNPUBLISHED THESIS

Chakraborty, Bidisha, 1997–98. 'Oral History: Scope, Method and Techniques', thesis submitted to School of Archival Studies, for Diploma in Archival Administration, New Delhi: National Archives of India.

Sarkar, Ayan, 2009–11. 'A Microscopic Tribe's Encounter with Colonialism: The Case of Totos in Colonial Bengal (1901–1947)', M. Phil. Diss. Rabindra Bharati University, Department of History, Kolkata.

Sen, Sharmila, 2004–06. 'Mahasweta Devir Golpe Narir Sthan: Pratibadi Swar', M. Phil. Diss., Department of Bengali, Jadavpur University.

MOVIES

Das, Amarendra and Samarendra, 2005. *Wira Pdika or Matiro Poko Company Loko* (Earth Worm, Company Man, in Kui/Odia with English subtitles), available from sdasorisa@hotmail.co.uk

Chambers, Simon, *Cowboys in India*, was shown on NDTV on 10 October, 2010 at 1 pm.

Toppo, Meghnath, and Biju Toppo of Akhra. 2003. *Development Flows from the Barrel of the Gun.*

SECONDARY SOURCES

Agrawal, P.K. 2010. *Naxalism: Causes and Cure*, New Delhi: Manas.

Ahmed, I. ed. 1985. *Technology and Rural Women*, London: George Allen and Unwin.

Alam, Jayanti. 2000. *Tribal Women Workers: A Study of Young Migrants*, New Delhi: Raj.

Altekar, A.S. 1962. *Position of Women in Hindu Civilization*, Delhi: Motilal Banarsidass.

Amin, Shahid. 1995. *Event, Metaphor, Memory: Chauri Chaura 1922–1992*, New Delhi: Oxford University Press.

Archer, W.G. 1984. *Tribal Laws and Justice: A Report on the Santal*, New Delhi: Concept.

Arendt, Hannah. 1970. *On Violence*, New York: Harcourt, Brace and World.

Arya, Shachi. 1998. *Tribal Activism—Voices of Protest (With special reference to works of Mahasweta Devi)*, Jaipur: Rawat.

Bagchi, Jasodhara, ed. 2005. *The Changing Status of Women in West Bengal 1970–2000: The Challenge Ahead*, New Delhi: SAGE.

Bagchi, Kathakali S. 1999. *Natural Resource Management: Eastern Region*, India Watch Monograph Series-1, New Delhi: Upalabdhi, Trust for Development Initiative.

Bandyopadhyaya, Bibhutibhushan. 2002. *Aranyak—of the Forest*, translated from the Bengali and introduced by Rimli Bhattacharya, 2002. Calcutta: Seagull.
Bandyopadhyay, Kalyani, 2000. *Nari, Sreni o Varna: Nimnoborger Narir Artha-Samajik Abosthan*, Howrah: Manascript India.
Bandyopadhyay, Pradip Kumar. 1999. *Tribal Situation in Eastern India: Customary Laws among Border Bengal Tribes*, Calcutta: Subarnarekha.
Banerjee, Anil Kumar. 2012. *Scheduled Castes and Scheduled Tribes (Prevention of Atrocities) Act & Rules along with Norms for Relief Amount and Notification on Uniform Definitions of Physically Handicapped*, Kolkata: Anima Prakashani.
Banerjee, Prathama. 2006. *Politics of Time: 'Primitives' and History-Writing in a Colonial Society*, New Delhi: Oxford University Press.
Banu, Zenab. 2001. *Tribal Women Empowerment and Gendered Issues*, New Delhi: Kanishka.
Barnes, R.H., Andrew Gray and Benedict Kingsbury, eds. 1995. *Indigenous Peoples of Asia*, Michigan: Association for Asian Studies.
Baske, Dhirendra Nath. 1987. *Paschimbanger Adibasi Samaj*, vol. 1, Calcutta: Subarnarekha.
Basu, N.G. 1987. *N.G.O. Report, Forests and Tribals*, Calcutta: Manisha.
Basu, Nirmal Kumar. 1973. *Some Indian Tribes*, New Delhi: National Book Trust.
Basu, Pradip, ed. 2010. *Discourses on Naxalite Movement 1967–2009*, Kolkata: Setu Prakashani.
Basu, Sajal. 1994. *Jharkhand Movement: Ethnicity and Culture of Silence*, Shimla: Indian Institute of Advanced Studies.
Bathla, Sonia. 1998. *Women, Democracy and the Media: Cultural and Political Representation in the Indian Press*, New Delhi: SAGE.
Baviskar, Amita. 1995. *In the Belly of the River*, New Delhi: Oxford University Press.
Béteille, André. 1974. *Six Essays in Comparative Sociology*, New Delhi: Oxford University Press.
Behera, Deepak Kumar, and Georg Pfeffer, eds. 1999. *Contemporary Society: Tribal Studies*, vol. 3, Social Concern, New Delhi: Concept.
Behura, N. and N. Panigrahi. 2006. *Tribals and the Indian Constitution: Functioning of the Fifth Schedule in Orissa*, New Delhi: Rawat.
Berger, Peter, Brigitte Berger and Hansfried Kellner. 1974. *The Homeless Mind: Modernization and Consciousness*, New York: Vintage.
Bhadra, Gautam, Gyan Prakash and Susie Tharu, eds. 1999. *Subaltern Studies*, vol. x, New Delhi: Oxford University Press.
Bhattacharyya, Amit. 2009. 'Singur to Lalgarh via Nandigram: Rising Flames of People's Anger against Displacement, Destitution and State Terror', Jharkhand: Visthapan Virodhi Jan Vikas Andolan, April, July and August, Update-I & II.

Bhattacharyya, Amit. 2007. *Janaganer Unnayan: Dandakaranyer Avigyata*, Kolkata: Radical Publications.

Bhattacharyya, Amit, and Bimal Kanti Ghosh, eds. 2010. *Human Rights in India: Historical Perspective and Challenges Ahead*, Kolkata: Setu Prakashani.

Bhowmick, P.K. 1961. *The Lodhas of West Bengal*, Calcutta: Punthipustak.

Bhusan, Anand, Ram Bhagwan Singh and Ram Kumar Tiwari, eds. 1999. *The Tribal Scene in Jharkhand*, Patna: Novelty & Co.

BJA and NBJK. 1993. *Social Impact: Piparwar and the North Karanpura Coal Fields*, Hunterganj and Champaran: Bharat Jan Andolan and Nav Bharat Jagruti Kendra.

Bleie, Tone. 1985. *The Cultural Construction and the Social Organization of Gender: The Case of Oraon Marriage and Witchcraft*, Bergen: Ch Michelsen Institute.

Bodding, P.O., ed. 1942. *Traditions and Institutions of the Santals*, Oslo: Oslo Etnografiske Museum.

———. 1925. *Santhal Folk Tales*, vols. 1 and 2, Oslo: W. Niggard.

Boserup, Ester, 1980. *Women's Role in Economic Development*, New York: St Martin's Press.

Bosu Mullick, S., Edwin Jayadas, Auto Akkara, and Anita Jaydas, eds. 1994. *Indigenous Identity: Crisis and Reawakening*, New Delhi: Navdin Prakashan Kendra.

Centre for Science and Environment. 2008. *Rich Lands, Poor People: Is Sustainable Mining Possible?* Delhi: CSE.

Cernea, M.M., and C. McDowell, eds. 2000. *Risks and Reconstruction: Experiences of Resettlers and Refugees*, Washington DC: The World Bank.

Chakravarty, R. 1980. *Communists in Indian Women's Movement*, New Delhi: Peoples Publishing House.

Chakrabarty, Ranjan, ed. 2007. *Situating Environmental History*, New Delhi: Manohar.

Chakrabarti, S.B., ed. 1988. *Social Science and Social Concern*, Delhi: Mittal Publications.

Chalam, K.S. 2011. *Economic Reforms and Social Exclusion: Impact of Liberalization on Marginalized Groups in India*, New Delhi: SAGE.

Chattopadhyay, B.D., ed. 2002. *Combined Methods in Indology and Other Writings*, New Delhi: Oxford University Press.

Chattopadhayaya, Devi Prasad. 1959. *Lokayata: A Study in Ancient Indian Materialism*, New Delhi: Sine Nomine.

Chattopadhyay, Pradip. 2014. *Redefining Tribal Identity: The Changing Identity of the Santhals in South-West Bengal*, New Delhi: Primus Books.

Chattopadhyay, Sanjibchandra. 1970. *Sanjib Rachanabali*, Calcutta.

Chaudhuri, B.B., and Arun Bandyopadhyay, eds. 2004. *Tribes, Forest and Social Formation in Indian History*, New Delhi: Manohar.

Chaudhuri, Soma. 2013. *Witches, Tea Plantations, and Lives of Migrant Labourers in India*, New Delhi: Foundation Books.
Chaudhury, A.B. 1987. *The Santhals: Religion and Rituals*, New Delhi: Manohar.
Chaudhary, S.N., ed. 2010. *Tribal Economy Crossroads*, New Delhi: Rawat.
Chowdhury, Arun. 2013. *Adibasi Jibon: Samaj o Sangram*, Kolkata: Gangchil.
Chowdhury, Buddhadeb, ed. 1990. *Tribal Transformation in India*, vol. 1. *Economy and Agrarian Issues*, New Delhi: Inter-India Publications.
Choudhury, Damina. 2000. *Tribal Girls—Aspirations, Achievement and Frustration*, Jaipur: Pointer Publishers.
Corbridge, Stuart, Sarah Jewitt and Sanjay Kumar. 2004. *Jharkhand: Environment, Development, Ethnicity*, New Delhi: Oxford University Press.
Custers, Peter. 1987. *Women in the Tebhaga Uprising: Rural Poor Women and Revolutionary Leadership (1946–47)*, Calcutta: Naya Prakash.
Dalton, Edward Tuite. 1973. *Tribal History of Eastern India*, Delhi: Replacement of Numeric Publisher Codes.
——— 1955. *Descriptive Ethnography of Bengal*, Calcutta: Beer Gatha Prakashan.
Das, Amal Kumar, and Ramendra Nath Saha, 1989. *West Bengal Scheduled Castes and Scheduled Tribes Facts and Information*, Special Series No. 32, *Bulletin of the Cultural Research Institute*, Scheduled Castes and Scheduled Tribes Welfare Department, Government of West Bengal, Kolkata.
Das, V. 1992. *Jharkhand: Castle Over the Graves*, New Delhi: Inter-India Publications.
Das Gupta, Sanjukta, and Raj Sekhar Basu, eds. 2012. *Narratives from the Margins Aspects of Adivasi History in India*, New Delhi: Primus Books.
Das Gupta, Sanjukta. 2011. *Adivasis and the Raj: Socio-Economic Transition of the Hos, 1820–1932*, New Delhi: Orient Blackswan.
Dasgupta, Subhendu, and Sujato Bhadra. 2011. *Operation Green Hunt*, Kolkata Book Fair.
Dasgupta, Subhendu. 2012. *Prantaparer Katha*, Kolkata: Nagarik Mancha.
De Beauvoir, Simone. 1973. *The Second Sex*, trans. E.M. Parshley, New York: Vintage.
Desai, Neera, and Maithrey Krishnaraj, eds. 1987. *Women and Society in India*, New Delhi: Ajanta Publications.
Desai, Neera, and Vibhuti Patel. 1985. *Indian Women: Change and Challenge*, Bombay: Popular Prakashan.
De Souza, Alfred, ed. 1975. *Women in Contemporary India: Traditional Images and Changing Roles*, New Delhi: Manohar.
Devalle, Susana B.C. 1992. *Discourses of Ethnicity: Culture and Protest in Jharkhand*, New Delhi: SAGE.

Dhali, Debendra Nath. 1987. *Toto: Paschim Banger Ekti Sankhyalaghu Parbatya Adibasi Goshthi*, special issue 31, *Bulletin of the Cultural Research Institute*, Scheduled Castes and Scheduled Tribes Welfare Department, Government of West Bengal, Kolkata.

Dias, Xavier, 2006. *Kalinga Nagar, Before and After*, Ranchi: Jharkhand Area Mines Coordination Committee (JAMCC).

Doshi, S.L. 1971. *Bhils: Between Societal Self-awareness and Cultural Synthesis*, New Delhi: Sterling.

D'Souza, A. 2001. *Traditional Systems of Forest Conservation in North-East India: The Angami Tribe of Nagaland*, Guwahati: North-Eastern Social Research Centre.

Dube, S.C., ed. 1998. *Antiquity to Modernity in Tribal India*, vol.1, *Continuity and Change among Indian Tribes*, New Delhi: Inter-India Publications.

Dutta, Naba. 2014. *Manusher Adhikar Chalaman Sangram*, Kolkata: Nagarik Mancha.

Duyker, Edward. 1987. *Tribal Guerrillas—The Santals of West Bengal and the Naxalite Movement*, New Delhi: Oxford University Press.

Ekka, Alex, and Mohammed Asif. 2000. *Development-Induced Displacement and Rehabilitation in Jharkhand, 1951 to 1995: A Database on Its Extent and Nature*, New Delhi: Indian Social Institute.

Ekka, Alex. 2011. *A Status of Adivasis/Indigenous Peoples Land Series 4 Jharkhand*, New Delhi: Aakar Books associated with The Other Media.

Elwin, Verrier [1939] 1986. *Baigas*, Delhi: Gyan Publication.

———.1964. *The Tribal World of Verrier Elwin: An Autobiography*, New Delhi: Oxford University Press.

———.1961. *Nagaland*, Shillong: The Research Department, Adviser's Secretariat.

———.1950. *The Bondo Highlanders*, London: Oxford University Press.

———.1944. *Aboriginals*, New Delhi: Oxford University Press.

Engels, F. [1884] 2010. *The Origin of the Family, Private Property and the State*, London: Penguin.

Epstein, T. Scarlett. 1973. *South India: Yesterday, Today and Tomorrow*, Mysore Villages Revisited, London: Macmillan.

Feldhaus, Anne, Aditya Malik and Heidrun Bruckner, eds. 1997. *King of Hunters, Warriors and Shepherds: Essays on Khandoba by Sontheimer, Gunter-Dietz*, New Delhi: Manohar.

Fernandes, Walter, Shanti Chetri, Satyen Lama and Sherry Joseph. 2012. *Progress: At Whose Cost? Development-Induced Displacement in West Bengal 1947–2000*, NESRC Displacement Studies Series No. 2, Guwahati: North Eastern Social Research Centre.

Fernandes, Walter, and Geeta Menon. 1987. *Tribal Women and Forest Economy: Deforestation, Exploitation and Status Change*, New Delhi: Indian Social Institute.

Fernandes, Walter, Geeta Menon and Viegas. 1988. *Forests, Environment and Tribal Economy: Deforestation, Impoverishment and Marginalization in Orissa*, New Delhi: Indian Social Institute.

Fernandes, Walter, and Enakshi Ganguly Thukral, eds. 1989. *Development, Displacement and Rehabilitation*, Delhi: Indian Social Institute.

Fernandes, Walter, and S.A. Raj. 1992. *Development, Displacement and Rehabilitation in the Tribal Areas of Orissa*, New Delhi: Indian Social Institute.

Fernandes, Walter. 1993. *The Indigenous Question: Search for an Identity*, New Delhi: Indian Social Institute.

Fernandes, Walter, and M. Asif. 1997. *Development-Induced-Displacement in Orissa 1951–1995: A Database on Its Extent and Nature*, New Delhi: Indian Social Institute.

Firth, R. 1946. *Human Types*, London: Nelson.

Furer-Haimendorf C. von. 1933. *Naked Nagas*, Calcutta: Thacker, Spink.

———. 1943. *The Chenchus: Jungle Folk of Deccan*, London: Macmillan.

Gautam, Rajesh K. 2011. *Baigas: The Hunter Gatherers of Central India*, New Delhi: Readworthy Publications.

Ghatak, Maitreya, ed. 1997. *Dust on the Road: The Activist Writings of Mahasweta Devi*, Calcutta: Seagull Books.

Ghosh, Arunabha. 1998. *Jharkhand Movement—A Study in the Politics of Regionalism*, Calcutta: Minerva Associates.

Ghosh, Dilip Kumar, and Apurba Kumar Mukhopadhyay. 2007. 'Reigning from below: A Study of Decision-Making Process in Gram Panchayats of West Bengal', State Institute of Panchayats and Rural Development, Kalyani, Nadia.

Ghose, Swapan Kanti, and Madhumay Pal, eds. 2011. *Rashtriya Santrash—Naxalbari Theke Netaigram*, Kolkata: Padatik.

Ghosh, Saumitra, Dipak Ray Chowdhury and Gopal Dasgupta. 2009. *Banadhikar Ayne-2006: Laraier Hatiyar*, Translated version of Forest Rights Act—Weapon of Struggle, Kolkata: Nagarik Mancha, Rashtriya Vana Jana Shramajivi Mancha and NESPON.

Ghurye, G.S. 1943. *Aboriginals So-Called and Their Future*, Bombay: Popular Prakashan.

Godelier, Morris, 1978. *Perspectives in Marxist Anthropology*, London: Cambridge University Press.

Guha, Abhijit, 2010. *Jami Adhigrahan Unnayan*, Kolkata: Nagarik Mancha.

Guha, Ramchandra. 1999. *Savaging the Civilised: Verrier Elwin, His Tribals and India*, New Delhi: Oxford University Press.

Guha, Ranajit. 1983. *Elementary Aspects of Peasant Insurgency in Colonial India*, New Delhi: Oxford University Press.

Guha, Sumit. 1999. *Environment and Ethnicity in India, 1200–1991*, Cambridge: Cambridge University Press.

Gupta, Ratna, ed. 1990. *Bahukaunik Drishtipate Paschimbanger Adivasi Nari*, Kolkata: Cultural Research Institute, Scheduled Caste and Tribes Welfare Department, Special Issue 33.
Gottschalk, Louis. 1958. *Understanding History: A Primer of Historical Method*, New York: Knopf.
Grigson, W.V. 1938. *The Maria Gonds of Bastar*, Oxford: Oxford University Press.
Gupta, Dipankar, ed. 1992. *Social Stratification in India*, New Delhi: Oxford University Press.
Gupta, Pabitra Kumar. 1990. *Tribal Folklore of the Sub-Himalayan North-Bengal and Other Essays*, Calcutta: Bakshilpo.
Hammond, J., and M. McCullagh. 1974. *Quantitative Techniques in Geography*, London: Longman.
Hans, Asha. 1999. *Tribal Women A Gendered Utopia: Women in the Agriculture Sector*, New Delhi: South Asian Publishers.
Hans, Asha, Amrita Patel and Minakshi Das. 2003. *Violence against Women in Orissa*, School of Women's Studies, Utkal University.
Halbar, B. G., and C. G. Hussain Khan, eds., 1991. *Relevance of Anthropology*, Jaipur: Rawat.
Hardiman, David. 1987. *The Coming of the Devi: Adivasi Assertion in Western India*, New Delhi: Oxford University Press.
Haynes, Douglas and Gyan Prakash. 1991. *Contesting Power*, New Delhi: Oxford University Press.
Hollis, B. Chenery et al. 1979. *Structural Change and Development Policy*, London: Oxford University Press.
Hunter, W.W. [1875–77] 1973. *A Statistical Account of Bengal*, vol. 3, New Delhi: D.K. Publishing House.
Hunter, W.W. [1972] 1973. *Orissa*, London: Smith Elder.
Hutton, J.H. 1921. *The Sema Nagas*, Oxford: Oxford University Press.
Iggers, George G. 1997. *Historiography in the Twentieth Century: From Scientific Objectivity to the Postmodern Challenge*, London: Wesleyan University Press.
Indian Anthropological Society. 1978. *Tribal Women in India*, Calcutta: Indian Anthropological Society.
International Labour Organisation. 1988. *The Bankura Story: Rural Women Organize for Change*, New Delhi, India: ILO.
Jain, Devaki, ed. 1975. *Indian Women*, Publication Division, Ministry of Information and Broadcasting, Government of India, New Delhi.
Jain, Devaki, Nalini Singh and Malini Chand. 1980. *Women's Quest for Power*, New Delhi: Vikas.
Jain, P.C. 1999. *Planned Development among Tribals: A Comparative Study of Bhils and Minas*, New Delhi: Rawat.

James, K.S., Arvind Pandey, Dhananjay W. Bansod and Lekha Subaiya, eds. 2010. *Population, Gender and Health in India: Methods, Process and Policies*, New Delhi: Academic Foundation.

Jana, Ashoke Kumar. 2002. *The Ethnohistory of the Koras of Bengal*, Kolkata: R.N. Bhattacharya.

Jena, Mihir, Padmini Pathi, Jagannath Dash, Kamala K. Patnaik, Klaus Seeland, eds. 2002. *Forest Tribes of Orissa: Lifestyle and Social Conditions of Selected Orissan Tribes*, vol. 1. *The Dongria Kondh*, New Delhi: D.K. Printworld.

Jewitt, Sarah. 2002. *Environment, Knowledge and Gender: Local Development in India's Jharkhand*, Farham, Surrey: Ashgate Publishing.

John, M.E. 2008. *Women's Studies in India, A Reader*, New Delhi: Penguin-India.

Kamdar, Mira. 2007. *Planet India: The Turbulent Rise of the Largest Democracy and the Future of Our World*, New York: Scribner.

Keith, Griffin. 1974. *The Political Economy of Agrarian Change*, Cambridge: Harvard University Press.

Kela, Shashank. 2012. *A Rogue and Peasant Slave: Adivasi Resistance 1800–2000*, New Delhi: Navayana.

Kelkar, G. 2009. *Adivasi Women Engaging with Climate Change*, New Delhi: UNIFEM, IFAD and the Christensen Fund.

Kelkar, G. and D. Nathan. 1991. *Gender and Tribe: Women, Land and Forests in Jharkhand*, New Delhi: Kali for Women.

Khubchandani, Lachman M. 1992. *Tribal Identity: A Language and Communication Perspective*, New Delhi: Indus Publishing.

Kishwar, Madhu and Ruth Vanita, eds. 1984. *In Search of Answers—Indian Women's Voices from Manushi*, New Delhi: Horizon India Books.

Kohli, Anju, Farida Shah and A.P. Chowdhary, eds. 1997. *Sustainable Development in Tribal and Backward Areas*, New Delhi: Indus Publishing.

Kosambi, D.D. 1975. *The Culture and Civilization of Ancient India in Historical Outline*, New Delhi: Vikas.

Krishna, S., ed. 2004. *Livelihood and Gender: Equity in Community Resource Management*, New Delhi: SAGE.

Kumar, Dharmendra, and Yemuna Sunny, eds. 2009. *Proselytisation in India: The Process of Hinduisation in Tribal Societies*, New Delhi: Aakar Books.

Kumar, Kundan, P.R. Choudhury, Soumen Sarangi et al. 2011. *A Status of Adivasis/Indigenous Peoples Land Series—2 Orissa*, New Delhi: Aakar Books in association with The Other Media.

Kumar, Nita. 1994. *Women as Subjects: South Asian Histories*, Kolkata: Stree.

Kumar, Radha. 1993. *The History of Doing: An Illustrated Account of Movements for Women's Rights and Feminism in India 1800–1990*, New Delhi: Kali for Women.

Kumar, Sunil. 2011. *Tribal and Indian Society*, New Delhi: ABD Publishers.

Mahapatra, Anadi Kumar. 1987. *Tribal Politics in West Bengal*, Calcutta: Suhrid Publication.
Mahapatra, Bhagyalaxmi. 2011. *Development of a Primitive Tribe: A Study of Didayis*, New Delhi: Concept.
Mahato, Pashupati Prasad. 2000. *Sanskritization vs Nirbakization*, Calcutta: Sujan Publications.
Majumdar, Charu. 1965. Eight Documents, 'Make the People's Democratic Revolution Successful by Fighting against Revisionism.' This is the Second Document in the Historic Eight Documents. Available at http://www.marxists.org/reference/archive/majumdar/index.htm accessed on 19 July 2010.
Majumdar, Dibyajyoti, ed. 2004. *Adivasi Samaj o Sanskriti*, Kolkata: Centre of Folk and Tribal Culture, Department of Information and Culture, Government of West Bengal.
Mamoria, C.B. 1957. *Tribal Demography in India*, Allahabad: Kitab Mahal.
Markandey, Kalpana and S. Simhadri. 2011 *Globalisation, Environment and Human Development*, Jaipur: Rawat.
Marx, Karl, 1964. *Early Writings*, translated and edited by T.B. Bottomore, New York: McGraw Hill.
Masika, Rachel, ed. 2002. *Gender, Development and Climate Change*, Oxford: Oxfam.
Mawick, Arthur. 2001. *The New Nature of History*, London: Macmillan.
McNeill, John R., Jose Augusto Padua and Mahesh Rangarajan, eds. 2010. *Environmental History: As If Nature Existed*, New Delhi: Oxford University Press.
Mehta, Lyla, ed. 2009. *Displaced by Development: Confronting Marginalisation and Gender Injustice*, New Delhi: SAGE.
Mies, Maria, and V. Bennholdt-Thomsen, C.V. Werlhof. 1988. *Women—The Last Colony*, London: Zed Books.
Mies, Maria. 1987. *Indian Women in Subsistence and Agricultural Labour*, New Delhi: Vistar.
Mies, Maria, and Vandana Shiva. 2010. *Ecofeminism*, Jaipur: Rawat.
Miri, M., ed. 1993. *Continuity and Change in Tribal Society*, Shimla: Shimla Indian Institute of Advanced Study.
Mishra, Archana. 2003. *Casting the Evil Eye: Witch Trials in Tribal India*, New Delhi: Roli.
Mishra, Asha, and Chittaranjan Kumar Paty, eds. 2010. *Tribal Movements in Jharkhand 1857–2007*, New Delhi: Concept.
Mishra, S.N., and Bhupinder Singh, eds. 1983. *Tribal Area Development*, New Delhi: Society for the Study of Regional Disparities.
Mitra, Asok. 1979. *The Status of Women: Shifts in Occupational Patterns 1961–71*, New Delhi: Abhinav.

Mitra, Manoshi. 1984. *Women and Class Struggle: A Study of Tribal Movements and Women's Participation in Bihar, India*, Geneva: International Labour Organization.
Modi, Renu, ed. 2009. *Beyond Relocation: The Imperative of Sustainable Resettlement*, New Delhi: SAGE.
Mohanty, K.K., P.C. Mohapatra, J. Samal. 1990. *Tribes of Koraput*, Bhubaneswar: Tribal and Harijan Research-cum Training Institute.
Mohapatra, P.M., and P.C. Mohapatro, eds. 1997. *Forest Management in Tribal Areas: Forest Policy and Peoples Participation*, New Delhi: Concept.
Moser, Caroline. 1993. *Gender Planning and Development: Theory, Practice and Training*, London: Routledge.
Moyo, S., and P. Yeros. 2005. *Reclaiming the Land: The Resurgence of Rural Movements in Africa, Asia and Latin America*. New York: Zed Books.
Mukhopadhyay, Lipi. 2002. *Tribal Women in Development*, New Delhi: Government of India, Publications Division.
Munshi, Indra, ed. 2012. *The Adivasi Question: Issues of Land, Forest and Livelihood*, New Delhi: Orient Blackswan with EPW.
Nagda, B.L. 1992 *Social Correlates of Fertility*, Udaipur: Himanshu Publications.
Nanda, B.K. 1994. *Contours of Continuity and Change: The Story of the Bonda Highlanders*, New Delhi: SAGE.
Nanjunda, D.C., ed. 2011. *Contemporary Anthropology*, New Delhi: Discovering Publishing House.
Narayan, S., ed. 1992. *Jharkhand Movement: Origin and Evolution*, New Delhi: Inter India Publications.
Nathan, Dev, and Virginius Xaxa, eds. 2012. *Social Exclusion and Adverse Inclusion: Development and Deprivation of Adivasis in India*, New Delhi: Oxford University Press.
Nathan, Dev, and Govind Kelkar, eds. 1997. *From Tribe to Caste*, Shimla: Indian Institute of Advanced Study.
———.1991. *Gender and Tribe*, London: Zed Press.
Nayak, Birendra. 2000. *Voices of Gopalpur*, published from Berhampur with Prafulla Samantara.
Nayak, Ramesh C., and Joseph M. Kujur. 2007. *State Aggression and Tribal Resistance: A Case of the Police Firing at Kalinga Nagar*, Delhi: Indian Social Institute.
Nelson, Cary, and Larry Grossberg, eds.1988. *Marxism and the Interpretation of Culture*, Urbana, Il: University of Illinois Press.
Nussbaum, Martha C. and Jonathan Glover. 1995. *Women, Culture, and Development: A Study of Human Capabilities*, Oxford: Clarendon Press.
O'Malley, L.S.S. [1910] 1984. *Bengal Districts Gazetteers Santhal Parganas*, New Delhi: Logos Press.
Padel, Felix. 2009. *Sacrificing People: Invasions of a Tribal Landscape*, New Delhi: Orient Blackswan.

Padel, Felix, and Samarendra Das. 2010. *Out of This Earth: East India Adivasis and the Aluminium Cartel*, New Delhi: Orient Blackswan.
Padhi, Soubhagya Ranjan. 2011. *The Gadaba Tribe of Orissa: A Study in its Socio-Economic Transformation*, Delhi: Abhijeet Publications.
Pal, Samir, ed. 1997. *Assignment: Giving Voice to the Unheard*, New Delhi: National Foundation for India.
Panda, G. 2004. *Bonda Banabasinka Vivaha Pratha Parab*, Koraput: District Council of Culture.
Pandey, Balaji. 1998. 'Depriving the Underprivileged for Development', Bhubaneswar, Orissa: Institute for Socio-Economic Development.
Pandey, Shivkumar. 2006. *Bhagoria Ki Baat*, New Delhi: Medha Books.
Pankaj, Ashok K. 2012. *Right to Work and Rural India: Working of the Mahatma Gandhi National Rural Employment Guarantee Scheme (MGNREGS)*, New Delhi: SAGE.
Pathy, Jagannath. 1987. *Anthropology of Development: Demystifications and Relevance*, New Delhi: Gian Publishing.
Pati, Sikta. 2012. *Industrialization and Displacement: An Economic Impact*, New Delhi: Concept.
Patnaik, N., B. Chowdhury, P. S. Das Patnaik. 1984. 'The Bondos and Their Response to Development', Bhubaneswar: Government of Orissa, Tribal and Harijan Research and Training Institute.
Pattnaik, N. 1972. *Tribes and Their Development: A Study of Two Tribal Development Blocks in Orissa*, Hyderabad: National Institute of Community Development.
Paul, Suma, and Anil Bhuimali. 2011. *Forest Resources and the Poor*, Delhi: Abhijeet Publications.
Pradhan, Manoj, and Council of Professional Social Workers. 1994. 'State of Orissa's Environment: A Citizens' Report', Bhubaneswar.
Prasad, Archana. 2003. *Against Ecological Romanticism: Verrier Elwin and the Making of an Anti-Modern Tribal Identity*, New Delhi: Three Essays Collective.
Prasad, Sushama Sahay. 1988. *Tribal Woman Labourers: Aspects of Economic and Physical Exploitation*, Delhi: Gian Publishing House.
Radhakrishna, R., and Alakh N. Sharma, eds. 1998. *Empowering Rural Labour in India: Market, State and Mobilisation*, New Delhi: Institute for Human Development.
Rajan, Rajeswari Sunder. 1993. *Real and Imagined Women: Gender, Culture and Post-Colonialism*, London and New York: Routledge.
Ranjani K. Murthy, ed. 2001. *Building Women's Capabilities: Interventions in Gender Transformation*, New Delhi: SAGE.
Rao, Nitya. 2008. *Good Women Do Not Inherit Land: Politics of Land and Gender in India*, Delhi: Social Science Press and Orient Blackswan.
Rao, Varavara. 2010. *Captive Imagination: Letters from Prison*, New Delhi: Penguin-Viking.

Rao, Vijayedra, and Michael Walton, eds. 2004. *Culture and Public Action*, Palo Alto, Ca: Stanford University Press.

Rath, B. 2005. *Vulnerable Tribal Livelihood and Shifting Cultivation: The Situation in Orissa with a Case Study in the Bhuyan-Juang Pirh of Keonjhar District*, Bhubaneswar: Vasundhara.

Rath, Govinda Chandra, ed. 2006. *Tribal Development in India: The Contemporary Debate*, New Delhi: SAGE.

Rath, Navaneeta, Mitali Chinara, Namita Mohanty and Aliva Mohanty, eds. 2012. *Social Exclusion and Gender: Some Reflections*, New Delhi: Abhijit Publications.

Rathgeber, Eva M. 1989. *WID, WAD, GAD: Trends in Research and Practice*, Ottawa: International Development Research Centre.

Razavi, Shahrashoub, and Carol Miller. 1995. *From WID to GAD: Conceptual Shifts in the Women and Development Discourse*, Geneva: United Nations Research Institute for Social Development.

Ray, S.N. 1982. *Migrant Women Workers*, Ranchi: Bihar Tribal Welfare Research Institute.

Ray, Shashibhushan. 1926. *Santal Pargana, Past and Present*, Deoghar.

Rekha. 2015. *Gender, Space and Creative Imagination: The Poetics and Politics of Women's Writing in India*, New Delhi: Primus Books.

Ritchie, Donald A., ed. 2011. *The Oxford Handbook of Oral History*, Oxford: Oxford University Press.

Rivers, H.H. 1973. *The Todas*, London: Macmillan.

Roy, J.K., and B.C. Roy. 1982. *Hunger and Physique: A Study of the Juang Population of Orissa*, Kolkata: Government of India, Anthropological Survey of India.

Roy, S.C. [1912] 1995. *The Mundas and Their Country*, Ranchi: Catholic Press.

——— [1915] 1984. *The Oraons of Chhotonagpur: Their History, Economic Life and Social Organization*, Ranchi.

——— [1928] 1985. *Oraon Religion and Customs*, Delhi: Gyan.

Saberwal, V., M. Rangarajan, and A. Kothari, eds. 2000. *People, Parks and Wildlife: Towards Coexistence*, New Delhi: Orient Longman.

Sachchidananda. 1968. *The Tribal Village in Bihar: A Study in Unity and Extension*, Delhi: Munshiram Manoharlal.

Samaddar, R., ed. 1997. *Reflection on Partition in the East*, Delhi: Vikas.

Sangari, Kumkum, and Sudesh Vaid, eds. 1989. *Recasting Women: Essays in Indian Colonial History*, Delhi: Kali for Women.

Sarin, Madhu. 1998. *Who Is Gaining? Who Is Losing: Gender and Equity Concerns in Joint Forest Management*, New Delhi: Society for Promotion of Wasteland Development.

Sarkar, Amitabha. 1993. *Toto: Society and Change (A Sub-Himalayan Tribe of West Bengal)*, Kolkata: Firma KLM.

Sarkar, Chanchal. 1998. 'Tilting against Odds: Bankura's Rural Women Organised for Empowerment', New Delhi: CWDS.

Sarkar, Goutam K. 1995. *Agriculture and Rural Transformation in India*, New Delhi: Oxford University Press.
Sarker, Lakshmindra Kumar. 1991. *Puruliar Daini Birodhi Andolon*, Kolkata: Sachayan Prakashani.
Sarkar, Sumit. 1997. *Writing Social History*, New Delhi: Oxford University Press.
Sathe, Makarand, ed. 2007. *Vijay Tendulkar Omnibus*, Delhi: Amar Kumar Publishers.
Satnam. 2010. *Jangalnama: Travels in a Maoist Guerrilla Zone*, translated from the Punjabi by Vishav Bharti, New Delhi: Penguin Books.
Satyanarayana, E. 2010. *The Plays of Mahasweta Devi, A Critical Study*, New Delhi: Prestige.
Savara, M., and C.R. Sridhar. 1994. *Report on a Survey of Sexual Behaviour Patterns and Attitudes amongst Men and Women in Maharashtra*, Mumbai: Shakti.
Schenken-Sandbergen, L., ed. 1995. *Women and Seasonal Labour Migration*, New Delhi: SAGE.
Sen, Ilina, ed. 1990. *A Space within the Struggle—Women's Participation in People's Movements*, Kali for Women.
Sen, Padmaja, ed. 2003. *Changing Tribal Life: A Socio-Philosophical Perspective*, New Delhi: Concept.
Sen, Suchibrata. 2003. *Purba Bharater Adibasi Astitver Sankat*, Kolkata: Dey's Publishing.
Sengupta, Nirmal, ed. 1982. *Fourth World Dynamics: Jharkhand*, Delhi: Authors Guild Publications.
Shah, Alpa. 2010. *In the Shadow of the State, Indigenous Politics, Environmentalism, and Insurgency in Jharkhand*, New Delhi: Oxford University Press.
Shah, Mihir, D. Banerji, P.S. Vijay Shankar and P. Ambasta. 1998. *India's Drylands: Tribal Societies and Development through Environmental Regeneration*, New Delhi: Oxford University Press.
Shashi, S.S. 1990. *Nehru and the Tribals*, New Delhi: Concept.
Sherin M. Raj, ed. 2000. *International Perspective on Gender and Democratisation*, New York: Macmillan.
Sherman, Carol. 1993. *The People's Story: A Report on the Social Impact of the Australian-Financed Piparwar Coal Mine, Bihar, India*, Sydney: AID/WATCH.
Shiva, Vandana. 2001. *The Violence of the Green Revolution: Agriculture, Ecology and Politics in the South*, Goa: Other India Press.
———. 1988. *Staying Alive: Women, Ecology and Survival in India*, New Delhi: Kali for Women.
———, ed. 1994. *Close to Home; Women Reconnect Ecology, Health and Development Worldwide*, Philadelphia, PA, New Society Publishers.

Shiva, Vandana, and Afasar H. Jafri. 1998. *Stronger than Steel: People's Movement against Globalisation and the Gopalpur Steel Plant*, Delhi: Research Foundation for Science, Technology and Ecology.
Shukla, V.N. 2004. *The Constitution of India*, Lucknow: Eastern Law Company.
Singh, A.K., and M.K. Jabbi, ed. 1995. *Tribals in India: Development, Deprivation, Discontent*, New Delhi: Har Anand.
Singh, B. 1984. *The Saora Highlander: Leadership and Development*, New Delhi: Somaiya.
Singh, J.P., N.N. Vyas and R.S. Mann, eds. 1988. *Tribal Women and Development*, Udaipur: MLV Tribal Research and Training Institute, Tribal Area Development Department, Rajasthan.
Singh, K.S. 1983. *Birsa Munda and His Movement: A Study of Millenarian Movement in Chhotonagpur 1874–1901*, London: Oxford University Press.
———. 1982. *Tribal Movements in India*, vols 1, 2, New Delhi: Manohar.
———. ed. 1972. *The Tribal Situation in India*, Shimla: Indian Institute of Advanced Study.
Singh, R., ed.1991. *Managing the Village Commons*, Bhopal: Indian Institute of Forest Management.
Sinha, Chandan. 2013. *Kindling of an Insurrection: Notes from Jungle Mahals*, New Delhi: Routledge.
Sinha, Shashank Shekhar. 2005. *Restless Mothers and Turbulent Daughters: Situating Tribes in Gender Studies*, Kolkata: Stree.
Singha Roy, Debal K., ed. 2010. *Dissenting Voices and Transformative Actions: Social Movements in a Globalizing World*, New Delhi: Manohar.
———. 2004. *Peasant Movements in Post-Colonial India—Dynamics of Mobilization and Identity*, New Delhi: SAGE.
———. 1995. *Women, New Technology and Development: Changing Nature of Gender Relations in Rural India*, New Delhi: Manohar.
———. 1992. *Women in Peasant Movement: Tebhaga, Naxalite and After*, New Delhi: Manohar.
Skaria, Ajay. 1999. *Hybrid Histories: Forests, Frontiers and Wildness in Western India*, New Delhi: Oxford University Press.
Smith, L. 1999. *Decolonizing Methodologies: Research and Indigenous Peoples*, London: Zed Books.
Spivak, Gayatri Chakravorty. 1997. *Mahasweta Devi: Breast Stories*, Calcutta: Seagull Books.
——— 1987. *In Other Worlds: Essays in Cultural Politics*, New York: Methuen.
Srinivas, M.N, A.M. Shah and E.A. Ramaswamy, eds. 2002. *The Fieldworker and the Field: Problems and Challenges in Sociological Investigation*, New Delhi: Oxford University Press.
Srivastava, Anup. 2011. *The Criminal Tribes of India*, New Delhi: Mohit Books International.

Thakur, Devendra. 1994. *Tribal life in India*, 10 vols. *Tribal Women*, vol. 16, New Delhi: Deep and Deep.
Thompson, Paul Richard. 2000. *The Voice of the Past: Oral History*, Oxford: Oxford University Press.
Tinker, Irene, ed. 1970. *Persistent Inequalities: Women and World Development*, New York: Oxford University Press.
Tirkey, Agapit. 2002. *Jharkhand Movement: A Study of its Dynamics*, Delhi: All India Coordinating Forum of the Adivasis/Indigenous People.
Troisi, J., ed. 1979. *The Santhals*, vol. 1, New Delhi: Indian Social Institute.
Troisi, J. 1979. *Tribal Religion: Religious Beliefs and Practices among the Santals*, New Delhi: Manohar.
Update Series 18, 2010. 'Adivasi in India' (March), Kolkata: Update Publications.
Vansina, Jan, Selma Leydesdorff, Elizabeth Tonkin. 2009. *Oral Tradition: A Study in Historical Methodology*, translated from the French by H.M. Wright, Piscataway, Nj: Transaction Publishers.
Venkateswaran S. 1992. *Living on the Edge: Women, Environment and Development*, New Delhi: Friedrich Ebert Stiftung.
Verma, R.K. and Gopal Verma. 1988. *Methodology and Techniques of Research*, New Delhi: Anmol.
Viegas, Philip. 1991. *Encroached and Enslaved: Alienation of Tribal Lands and its Dynamics*, New Delhi: Indian Social Institute.
Vidyarthi, L.P. 1977. *The Tribal Culture of India*, Delhi: Concept.
Vir, Dharam and Kamlesh Mahajan. 1996. *Contemporary Indian Women: Collected Works*, Delhi: New Academic Publishing Co.
Waugh, Patricia. 1984. *Metafiction: The Theory and Practice of Self-Conscious Fiction*, New York: Methuen.
Weiner, M. 1978. *Sons of the Soil*, Princeton: Princeton University Press.
World Bank. 1991. *Gender and Poverty in India*, Washington, DC: The World Bank, available at http://www.worldbank.org accessed on 18 February 2010.
———. 1995. *The World Bank and Gender in India*, New Delhi: The World Bank.
Zedong, Mao. 2009. *Collected Writings of Chairman Mao: Volume 3—On Policy, Practice and Contradiction*, edited by Shawn Conners, El Paso, North Tx: El Paso Norte Press.
———. 1965. *Selected Works*, vol. 3, Beijing: Foreign Languages Press.
———. 1954–56. *Selected Works*, vols. 1 and 2, Delhi: People's Publishing House.

Index

adivasi, xx, xxvii, xxviii, xxxii, xxxvii, 4, 51, 201. *See also* government policies; land; women
    adivasi children. *See* education; health
    democracy, xii, 12, 242
    as indigenous, xix, xlii, 16, 37–38, 96, 130, 135, 141, 259–51
    marginalization, xxxix, 22, 31, 159, 163, 201–203, 251, 255, 258, 260
    vs tribal, xix, 22
    violence against, 156. *See also* violence
adivasi occupations
    animal husbandry, xvii, 52, 166, 173, 182
    grazing, xvii-xviii, 57, 116
    handicrafts, 50, 52, 55, 178
    horticulture, 164, 174, 178
    household industry, 91, 94, 182
    hunting and gathering, 11, 72–73, 149
    livestock, 36, 145, 164
    pastoralists, 12, 50, 171
    nomadic, 72, 146–47, 184, 215
    silviculture, 115, 117
adivasi women
    autonomy, xviii, xxiv, 1–2, 28, 35, 114, 202, 231. *See also* patriarchy

bride price, xxv, 165, 170, 176, 184, 209
consciousness, xxxiv, 174
contraception, 212. *See also* sexuality
empowerment, xxix, 193–94
female economy, 28, 30, 90
as 'fourth world', 31, 250, 254
health, 221–23, 260. *See also* health
livelihoods, 34, 38, 72, 120. *See also* agriculture; Forest Rights Act 2006
Mahasweta Devi, 72, 74, 214, 238–40
K.S. Singh, iii, 9, 19, 72
agency, of subaltern, xxiii, xli, 34, 220, 242, 262
agriculture, xviii, 30, 50, 90, 114, 162, 166, 114, 177. *See also* land
    constraints, 164–65
    harvesting, 53, 54, 71, 92–93, 99, 119, 137, 164, 183
    middlemen, 59, 102, 59, 136, 234–35
    patta, 34, 55, 77, 79, 143, 192
    sharecropper, 53–54, 71, 136
    tea plantation, 52, 56, 58, 185, 208, 220
    as settled, 2, 12, 30, 113, 162, 173, 182

Index

slash and burn agriculture
  slash and burn, xviii, 2, 23, 30, 50, 52, 80, 96, 148–50, 162–69, 171–75, 179, 182–87, 261
  Kondh, 175, 178
  Koras, 54–55
  Koya, 171–73
  Santhals, 53–54
  women labour, 73, 90–93, 113, 117, 186, 251
anthropology, xiii, xxii, xxvi, 7, 12, 13, 78, 207

Bengali literature, xiv, xxiii, xxxvi, 235–36, 39, 262. *See also* class
Bengali cinema, 240–42
British rule, consequences, 5, 8, 38, 121, 158. *See also* legislations

capitalism, xvii, 4, 6, 8, 9, 17, 40, 44, 239, 250
caste, xxiii, xxv, xxxiii, xxxiv, 7, 10–11, 15, 128, 236
  dalits, 56, 88, 159, 196, 230, 236, 256. *See also* scheduled castes
  dominant caste, xxxiii, xl, 13, 30, 232
  G.S. Ghurye, 5, 7
  D.D. Kosambi, 6–7
  Kshatriya, 15, 53
  OBCs, 89, 223
Census, 1991, 2001, 181
  missing tribes, 88, 203–04, 235
  1941, 16
Christianity, 9, 98, 127–28, 219. *See also* witch hunt
Christian missionaries, xxiii, 3, 9, 218
class, xii, xxiii–xxxvi, xxxix, 24, 50, 96, 214, 237–38, 242, 262

colonialism, xx, xxx, 13–14, 40–41, 128, 257. *See also* industrialization
committee reports, 9, 12, 132, 158, 223
corporations, xvii, 101, 160. *See also* displacement, xvii
  Balimela Hydro Electric Project, 169
  Bharat Aluminium Company (BALCO), 33, 186
  Gandharman Iron Ore, 185, 186
  Koel Karo Hydro Electric Power Project, xli
  National Aluminium Company Ltd. (NALCO), 34–35, 38, 160–62, 182
  POSCO, xli, 20, 191, 195, 252–55
  SEZ, 252
  Tata Iron and Steel Company (TISCO), xv, 121, 131, 194–95
  Upper Indravati Power Project, 35, 38, 160
  Upper Kolab Project, 30, 38, 160, 182
  Utkal Alumina International Limited (UAIL), 35, 189–90
  Vedanta, xv, xli, 191, 204, 256–57
culture
  assimilation, xxxiii, xxxiv, 73, 128, 131, 231, 257
  genocide, xxxiii, xxxiv, xxxv, xxxvii, 201
  of silence, 202, 205–06, 243
  tribal, xxii, xxxii, xxxvii, xxxviii, 5, 10, 29, 173, 177, 202

Dandakaranya, 169, 171, 173, 187–88, 192–93
deforestation, xv, 29, 30, 67, 73, 75, 119, 136, 147, 175, 185, 216, 228

denotified tribes, 74–78. *See also* tribes
development, programmes, xvii, xxviii, 21, 29, 31, 36, 49, 132, 157, 226, 228
   GAD, 28, 114
   rural, 32, 193
   WED, 114, 115–18. *See also* ecofeminism
diku, xxiv, 133–34
displacement, 32, 36–37, 40, 63, 129, 160. *See also* protest
   Arundhati Roy, xxviii, xxx, 201
   coal mining, 69–70, 121, 131
   dams and, 38–39, 134, 135, 160, 169, 191
   development and, 31, 125, 196
   eviction, 250, 255–56, 261
   Felix, Padel, xix, xxxvii, 38
   M. Areeparampil, 130
   Walter Fernandes, 29–30, 189,
dormitory/dhumkuria/ghotul. *See* sexuality

ecofeminism, 21–22, 114–15, 117, 150, 251
   Vandana Shiva, xxxi, 115, 117
economy
   forest, xvii, 29, 47, 49, 115, 124, 150, 198, 222
   global market, xv, xxxi, 94
   market economy, xxxi, 50, 94, 96, 203, 227
   weekly market/haat, 52, 75, 105, 167, 171, 173
education, xxv, 210, 226, 232. *See also* government policies
   adult education, 52, 54, 68, 182
   of daughters, 23, 107–10, 228
   hostels, absence, 89
   illiteracy, 99–100, 202
employment, xxv, xxxvii, 6, 30, 35, 50, 127, 165, 221, 233

ecological crisis, xxxi, 5–6, 21, 40, 129, 151. *See also* corporations; government policies
Verrier Elwin, 4–5, 8–9, 27

festivals, xxxviii, 64, 107
forest, 78. *See also* land
   management, xxxiv, 115–18
   resource, 68, 73, 80, 115, 118, 186, 255–56
   wildlife, 32, 72, 119
Forest Rights Act, 2006, 80–81, 89, 204, 254

Gandhi/Gandhian, xxxix, 5, 74–75
gender, xii, xiii, xvi, 17, 22, 31, 125, 145
globalization, xvi–xvii, xxv, 5–6, 19, 32, 156
   liberalization, 19, 50–51, 189
   monetization, 50, 216
government policies/organizations
   Annapurna Yojana, 62, 177
   Antyodaya Anna Yojana, 229–30
   Backward Regions Grant Fund Programme, 119
   Below Poverty Level (BPL), 55, 58, 62, 65, 79, 81–82, 177, 184
   Bokaro Steel Plant, 122, 132
   Bonda Development Agency (BDA), 168, 174
   Common Property Resources (CPRs), 29, 34, 162
   Dandakaranya Development Authority (DDA), 187–88, 199
   Demarcated Protected Forest/Reserve Forests, 186

Index

Didayi Development Agency (DDA), 169
District Rural Development Agency, 145, 170
Dongria Kondh Development Agency (DKDA), 177
Five-Year Plans, 32, 153
Forest Protection Committees (FPC), 68, 78, 118, 151
Integrated Child Development Services (ICDS), 89, 225, 229
Integrated Rural Development Programme (IRDP), 50, 145
Jawahar Rozgar Yojana (JRY), 50, 145, 166
Joint Forest Management (JFM), 68, 78–79, 117–18, 188
Juang Development Agency (JDA), 186
Large-size Adivasi Multipurpose Co-operative Societies (LAMPS), 51, 67, 73, 220
Mahila Samriddhi Yojana, 50
Mid-Day Meal, 24, 74, 81, 179, 224–25, 229
Memorandum of Understandings (MoUs), xxxiv, 142. *See also* corporations
NABARD, 61
National Family Health Survey (NFHS), 23, 158, 221. *See also* health
National Human Rights Commission, 65
National Mineral Policy, xvii
National Rural Employment Guarantee Scheme (NREGS), 58, 62, 183
Panchayati Raj, xl, 170, 223

Paschimanchal Development Board, 23
Planning Commission, 32, 234
Prime Minister's Rozgar Yojana, 50
Primitive Tribal Groups (PTGs), 11, 77, 79, 140, 146, 148–49, 169–70, 174, 179, 204
Public Distribution System (PDS), 62, 184, 229–30
Rajiv Gandhi Grameen Vidyutikaran Yojana, 75, 179
Resettlement and Rehabilitation (R&R), xxix, 32, 40, 261
Rourkela Steel Plant, 38, 160
Uranium Corporation of India Ltd. (UCIL), 134

health, 23, 26, 137, 139, 217, 221–25, 240, 260
 centres, 24–25, 81, 89, 175, 206, 219, 225, 229
Hinduism, 8–9, 107, 177, 184
Hinduization/Sanksritization, xxiii, 7, 9, 128, 142, 173, 183, 202
Hindutva, 20
hunger, xxx, xxxi, 73, 86, 89, 175, 202, 216, 256, 258
 Right to Food, 229
 starvation, 22–25, 59, 177, 190, 222, 226

identity, adivasi, xxviii, 4, 14–16, 25, 29, 141, 146, 169, 242, 255, 261
industrialization, 128, 204, 233. *See also* corporation; government policy
 CNTA Act, 132–33
 Jharkhand, 120–21, 123–24
 labour, 69, 136, 156

industrialization (*cont.*)
   land alienation 182. *See also* land
   rejas, 97–106, 132, 204, 233

labour, xxxvi, 29, 56, 71, 02, 103, 123
   child, 82, 110, 185
   division of, 27, 97–98, 117, 151, 227, 251, 262
   Dev Nathan, 24, 37, 96, 115, 117
   rejas. *See* industrialization
land, 151
   alienation, 125, 131, 134, 140, 142, 158, 159, 182, 233, 261
   Bina Agrawal, xv, 114
   inheritance, 140–42, 186
   Madhu Kishwar, 138
   Nitya Rao, 141
   ownership, 113, 139, 143–44, 203
   usufructory right, 113, 138–39, 216
language, xxiv, 230–32
   Oriya, 168, 177, 180, 184
   scripts, xxxiv, 174, 231, 234
legislations
   Armed Forces Special Powers Act (AFSPA), xxvii
   Bidi and Cigarette Act, 1966, 100
   Chotanagpur Tenancy Act (CNTA), 1908, 132, 144
   Coal Bearing Areas Acquisition and Development (CBA) Act 1957, 133
   Contract Labour (Regulation and Abolition) Act, 1970, 100
   Criminal Tribes Act, 72, 77
   Damodar Valley Corporation (DVC) Act, 1948, 133
   Denotified and Nomadic Tribes Act, 72
   Fifth Scheduled Areas, 9
   Forest Rights Act, 2006 (FRA), 75, 80–81, 89, 133, 158, 172, 204, 254–55
   Forest Conservation Act, 256, 261
   Forest Preservation Act, 76
   Habitual Offender's Act, 72
   Inter-State Migrant (Regulation of Employment and Conditions of Service) Act, 1979, 126
   Land Acquisition (Mines) Act, 1885, 133
   Minimum Wage Act, 1948, 54, 65, 100
   Panchayats (Extension to the Scheduled Areas) Act, 35, 133, 158
   Prevention of Terrorism Act, 2002 (POTA), 21
   Right to Fair Compensation and Transparency in Land Acquisition, Rehabilitation and Resettlement Act, (LARR), 2013, 133
   Right to Information Act (RTI), 136
   Santhal Pargana Tenancy Act, 1949 (SPTA), 132
   Special Economic Zones, xvii, 252
   Terrorist and Disruptive Activities (Prevention) Act (TADA), 21

Maoist, xxx, 65, 119, 172, 191–92, 196
Salwa Judum, xviii, 21, 191
Sendra, 21

Index

matriarchy/matriliny xv, 26–27, 46, 51, 79–80, 179
migration, 37, 39, 77, 126–28, 165, 233. *See also* displacement
movements, unrest, xx xxix, xxx, 18, 20, 124, 159, 199, 240

Non-Governmental Organizations (NGOs), 76, 120, 220, 234
    Action for Welfare and Awakening of Rural Environment (AWARE), 192
    Adivasi Women's Organization, 192
    Amlasole Birsa Munda Village Development Committee, 24
    Birbhum Adivasi Gaonta (BAG), 64, 66
    Centre for Science and Environment, 129–30
    Centre for Women's Development Studies, 67
    Chasi Mulia Adivasi Sangha (CMAS), 159, 196
    Grameen Mahila Shramik Unnayan Samiti, 67
    Mahila Mandali, 193–94
    Mahila Samitis, 67, 69, 181
    Malkangiri Adivasi Sangha (MAS), 159
    Nari Bikash Sangha, 67–69
    Nari Ijjat Bachao Committee, 5, 253
    Manjhi Pargana Baisi, 64
    Self-Help Groups (SHGs), 119, 140, 170, 179, 181
    Society for Participatory Action and Reflection (SPAR), 140
    Tribal Cooperative Marketing Development Federation of India (TRIFED), 89–90

Non-Timber Forest Products (NTFPs), 23, 79–80, 82, 95, 116, 175
minor forest produce (MFP), vii, 41, 52, 55, 72–74, 80, 136, 145, 150, 251
    babui grass, 68, 74, 77
    fire wood/fuel wood, 61, 79–80, 93, 147
    kendu, 73, 76
    mahua, 5, 64, 68, 73, 117, 137, 147, 149–50, 211
    sal, 55, 64, 67, 73–74, 76, 116–17, 119–20, 137, 150, 173, 185, 189
    tendu leaves, 67, 120

Panchayati Raj, xl, 169–70, 181, 223
    gram panchayats, 64, 74–75, 82, 178–79, 183, 190, 228
    gram sabha, xl, 35, 80, 118, 140, 204, 254–55
    sarpanch, ix, xl, 169
patriarchy, xiv, xvi–xvii, xli, 150, 202, 214, 219, 250, 259
patrilineal/patrilocal, 2, 80, 93, 113, 137, 139–40, 148, 163, 170–71, 174
polyandry, 239
polygyny, 15, 124, 171
primitive tribal groups (PTGs), 11, 74, 77, 79, 140, 146, 149, 170–74, 179, 204, 227, 263
prostitution, 30, 36, 96 108, 128, 133, 185. *See also* sexuality

rituals
    animal sacrifice, 184
    human sacrifice, 176
    jani shikar, 116
    tattoo, 178

scheduled castes, 15, 203, 262
    Dhangar, xxxii

scheduled castes (*cont.*)
  Dombo, 11
  Mahato, 74, 77
  Namasudra, 53
  Paniya, 3
  Rajbansis, 15, 53
  Sadan/Sadani, 232
scheduled tribes (ST). *See* adivasis; tribes
sexuality, 207–208. *See* also prostitution
  dormitory, xv, xxiv, 127–28, 167, 174, 177, 209–210
  marriage, 170, 181
  with outsiders, xxi
subaltern, xvi, xviii, xxxv, 10, 18, 25, 205, 214, 240, 242

trafficking, xxxvi, 19, 59–60, 233, 235. *See also* industrialization
  agents, 59, 97, 101–02, 150, 234–35
  arkattis/arkatia, xxxvi, 102
  sardar/sardarni, 101–03, 108–09
  brick kilns xxxvi, 66, 97–110, 124, 126–27, 136, 212
tribal revolts, xli
  Bastar, 19
  Chipko, xv, 22, 33
  Gond and Kolam, 19
  Gorkhaland, 15
  Jharkhand, 69
  Koya, 18
  Lalgarh, 25, 253
  Maoist, 119, 200
  Munda Ulghulan, xxix
  Narmada Banchao Andolan, xv
  Sardar Sarovar Dam, xvii
  Naxalites, 239
  Rampa rebellion, 18
  Santhal Hul, xxix, xxxi, 18–19
  Sardari, 18
  Tebhaga, 20, 53
  Telangana, 20

tribes. *See also* agriculture; displacement; land
  Baiga, 27, 31, 90, 149–50, 211
  Bhil, xv, xxxiii, 3, 131, 207
  Bhumij, 16, 51, 91
  Bhutia, xv, 33, 51–52
  Bhuyan, 184–85, 204
  Birhor, xviii, xxiv, 51, 72, 89, 91, 109, 146–48, 211, 215
  Bodo, 3, 179, 227, 231
  Bonda, 11, 163, 166–68, 172–74, 187
  Didayi, 11, 169–72, 187
  Dongria Kondh, xv, 174–78, 187, 201, 209, 257
  Gadaba, 11, 163, 173, 179, 181–84, 203
  Gond, xxxi, 3, 19, 27, 88, 91, 163, 203
  Gorkha, 15, 226–27
  Ho, xxiv, xxvi, 91, 123, 136–40, 143
  Jhoria, 11, 190
  Juang, 184–86
  Kharia, 27, 56, 73–74, 91, 136, 156, 204, 218, 231–32
  Kol, 19, 237–38
  Kora, 54–55, 91
  Koya, 18, 171
  Lepcha, 51
  Lodha, 52, 72, 76–79
  Lohra, 97, 106
  Munda, 81–82, 132, 136, 140, 156, 215, 225–26, 232
  Naga, 19, 27
  Oraon, 53, 106, 115–18, 126, 132, 136, 140, 205, 215, 225
  Pahari/Paharia, xxxvii, 3, 91, 148, 195
  Paraja, 11, 163, 173, 179, 182, 203
  Parenga, 11, 203
  Rabha, 51, 79–81
  Sabar, xxxii, 24–25, 72, 74–79, 226

Index

Santhal, 118, 120–24, 208–09, 215, 219, 225, 230–32, 236–37, 241–42, 261
Saora, xxxii, 3, 157, 163, 176, 180–81, 185–87, 204
Totos, 16, 52, 204, 226–28

violence, 22, 202
  alcoholism, 93, 165, 215
  Chuni Kotal, 77–78
  domestic, xi, 93, 165
  sexual, 19, 95. *See also* sexuality
  state, xxviii–xxx, 33. *See also* corporations; displacement

witch hunt, 113, 206
  ojhas, 107, 206, 215, 217–18, 220–21
  Poonam Toppo, 221
  property, 216
  sacred grove, 183, 218
  shamanins, 176
  Vijay Tendulkar, 213–14
  women targets, 214–19
witches, 215–17, 220–21. *See also* Christianity

World Bank, 40, 165
writers on tribes
  Arjun Appadurai, 24
  Crispin Bates, xix, 8, 14
  Simone de Beauvoir, xvi, 97
  André Béteille, 8
  Partha Chatterjee, 12
  Soma Chaudhuri, 214
  Susan Devalle, 13
  Verier Elwin, 4–5, 8–9
  C. von Fürer-Haimendorf, 27
  W.V. Grigson, 27
  Ranajit Guha, 19
  G.S. Ghurye, 5, 7
  David Hardiman, 16
  J.H. Hutton, 27
  Govind Kelkar, 115
  D.D. Kosambi, 6, 11
  Gail Omvedt, 16
  Jagannath Pathy, 13
  Archana Prasad, 6
  Baidyanath Saraswati, 8
  Mihir Shah, 12
  L.P. Vidyarthi, 50
  Myron Weiner, xix

About the Author

Debasree De is Assistant Professor, Department of History, Maharaja Srischandra College, University of Calcutta. She has a PhD in history from Jadavpur University. She has many contributions in journals and in edited books. Her special interests are Tribal Studies, Gender Studies, Environmental History, Ancient Indian History and Indology.